To the Memory of Jean Houchins Cecil,
whose professional contributions to the fields of school counseling
and counselor education are beyond measure.
Her influence continues through those of us
whose personal and professional lives she touched.

and to
Don Adams and J. D. and Chris Henderson,
whose unwavering support helped us turn this idea into a book.

PREFACE

The first edition of this book, entitled *Handbook of School Counseling*, emerged from conversations between two counselor educators. Along with other school counselor educators around the country, we recognized a need for instructional materials reflective of the transformations that have taken place in the school counseling profession. The second edition is updated and retitled to reflect recent developments in the field. In addition to the National Standards for School Counseling Programs developed by the American School Counselors Association (ASCA), school counseling specialty standards articulated by the Council for Accreditation of Counseling and Related Educational Programs (CACREP), and the expanded view of school counselors' roles emerging from recent reform efforts, the ASCA National Model for School Counseling Programs has informed the revised content and structure of this text.

The "Three Cs" model of school counseling (counseling, coordination, and consultation) has been updated and expanded over the past decade to include leadership, advocacy, and collaboration as primary school counselor roles. The addition of these roles, both in practice and in training, provides the school counselor opportunities to firmly establish links between the school counseling program and the total educational enterprise, thereby operationalizing the concept of school counselors working collaboratively with other educational professionals to maximize the academic, career, and personal/social development of all students.

Our goal has been to provide a book focused on teaching school counseling students how to develop, implement, manage, and evaluate a comprehensive developmental school counseling program that contributes to the mission of the school in meaningful and productive ways. To be successful in this task, we have used the specialty area content for school counselor preparation articulated by CACREP and the National Standards for School Counseling Programs adopted by ASCA and integrated them with the ASCA National Model.

Coverage

Developing an Effective and Accountable School Counseling Program provides counselor educators with a text that emphasizes the school counselor's role in education, with particular emphasis on placing counselor interventions in the school context.

The text covers the following areas of emphasis:

- *Foundations of school counseling.* Chapters 1–3 and 12 are designed to increase students' understanding of the school environment and the school counselor's place in the total school program. Emphasis is placed on the development of the school counseling profession, the factors that promote or inhibit learning, and the skills and competencies necessary to be an effective school counselor. As well, the school counselor's role as an educational leader, advocate, and change agent in promoting the school success of all students is emphasized. A new chapter, 12, brings focused attention to the legal and ethical issues with which school counselors are confronted.

- *Contextual dimensions of school counseling.* Chapters 4–6 are designed to increase students' understanding of program models and their components and school counselor accountability. Emphasis is placed on developmentally appropriate counselor skills and interventions in the context of the four program delivery components: guidance curriculum, individual planning, responsive services, and system support. New chapters describing developmental transitions and accountability have been added to this section.
- *Standards-based school counseling programs.* Chapters 7–11 include studies in specific approaches used by school counselors to achieve program goals and objectives in elementary, middle, and secondary schools. Chapters provide concrete grade-level examples of how sample programs are organized around implementation of the National Standards for School Counseling Programs (ASCA) and local needs. Each of the four service delivery components is described. New to this edition is the separation of the topic of responsive services into two chapters describing direct methods and indirect methods of intervention.

Format

Information is provided in an easy-to-follow format with a logical structure from which to teach. The following sections are included in each chapter:

- *Case.* Real-world case studies introduce the major topics in each chapter. Real problems are posed that can be addressed by students after mastering the material covered in each chapter.
- *Chapter introduction.* Each chapter begins with a list of objectives keyed to the important concepts.
- *Margin notes.* Throughout the text, brief notes and questions challenge students to think critically about the material being presented. Also, active learning strategies are incorporated to challenge students to identify, discuss, reflect on, and apply the concepts they are studying.
- *Text boxes.* Concrete examples from real-life school counseling programs predominate.
- *Portfolio components.* At the end of each chapter, students are encouraged to complete one or more of the suggested activities for their professional school counselor portfolios. These activities can help students identify not only individual areas of strength but also challenges to their development as they progress through the text.

Features

Developing an Effective and Accountable School Counseling Program offers the following special features:

- Provides a contemporary, integrated view of school counseling in a well-recognized organizational framework.
- Describes a practical, logical sequence for program development, implementation, and evaluation.
- Integrates real-life examples, thereby conceptualizing learning to the school environment.
- Uses active learning strategies throughout each chapter to develop competence and efficacy.
- Encourages reflection and planning for professional growth and development.

In addition, relevant documents and forms that students may find useful as they plan, design, implement, and evaluate school counseling programs at all developmental levels are provided in the appendixes.

Ancillary Products

The Instructor's Manual contains test questions and suggestions for additional classroom activities. Objectives, key concepts, and a brief outline for each chapter are included.

A slide presentation accompanies each chapter, and the Companion Website includes updated resources for each chapter.

ACKNOWLEDGMENTS

We wish to acknowledge the foundational work of Norman Gysbers and Patricia Henderson, who have provided an organizational structure for school counseling programs that is both practical and manageable. This program model is the one adopted, in some form, most frequently by those state departments of education that have adopted a program model. In large measure, it supports the ASCA National Model for School Counseling Programs. Additionally, the work of those committed professionals who contributed to the development of the ASCA national standards and the model program has moved the profession forward immeasurably. Our colleagues from around the country, who have gathered whenever possible to share ideas and discuss needs and trends in the profession, have been a major inspiration for this project.

The students who give us feedback both before and after graduation about what they need from us to be better prepared to enter the profession continue to influence our thinking about school counselor preparation. Andrea Owens and Lisa Adams, doctoral students at Auburn University, have created ancillary products that enhance faculty and student use of the book.

Finally, no project of this magnitude is accomplished by the author alone. Publisher Kevin Davis at Merrill/Prentice Hall has been patient, encouraging, and instructive throughout the development of this book. Our thanks and appreciation go to him and the entire team at Merrill for their efforts.

We would also like to thank the following reviewers for their suggestions and insight: Sandy Magnuson, University of Northern Colorado; James L. Moore III, Ohio State University; Sally Murphy, George Mason University; Martin Ritchie, University of Toledo; and Thomas Russ, University of Wisconsin, River Falls.

Discover the Companion Website Accompanying This Book

The Prentice Hall Companion Website: A Virtual Learning Environment

Technology is a constantly growing and changing aspect of our field that is creating a need for content and resources. To address this emerging need, Prentice Hall has developed an online learning environment for students and professors alike—Companion Websites—to support our textbooks.

In creating a Companion Website, our goal is to build on and enhance what the textbook already offers. For this reason, the content for each user-friendly website is organized by chapter and provides the professor and student with a variety of meaningful resources.

Common Companion Website features for students include:

- **Chapter Objectives**—Outline key concepts from the text.
- **Interactive Self-quizzes**—Complete with hints and automatic grading that provide immediate feedback for students. After students submit their answers for the interactive self-quizzes, the Companion Website **Results Reporter** computes a percentage grade, provides a graphic representation of how many questions were answered correctly and incorrectly, and gives a question-by-question analysis of the quiz. Students are given the option to send their quiz to up to four email addresses (professor, teaching assistant, study partner, etc.).
- **Web Destinations**—Links to www sites that relate to chapter content.

To take advantage of the many available resources, please visit the *Developing an Effective and Accountable School Counseling Program* Companion Website at

www.prenhall.com/cobia

RESEARCH NAVIGATOR:
RESEARCH MADE SIMPLE!

www.ResearchNavigator.com

Merrill Education is pleased to introduce Research Navigator—a one-stop research solution for students that simplifies and streamlines the entire research process. At www.researchnavigator.com, students will find extensive resources to enhance their understanding of the research process so they can effectively complete research assignments. In addition, Research Navigator has three exclusive databases of credible and reliable source content to help students focus their research efforts and begin the research process.

How Will Research Navigator Enhance Your Course?

- Extensive content helps students understand the research process, including writing, Internet research, and citing sources.
- Step-by-step tutorial guides students through the entire research process from selecting a topic to revising a rough draft.
- Research Writing in the Disciplines section details the differences in research across disciplines.
- Three exclusive databases—EBSCO's ContentSelect Academic Journal Database, The New York Times Search by Subject Archive, and "Best of the Web" Link Library—allow students to easily find journal articles and sources.

What's the Cost?

A subscription to Research Navigator is $7.50 but is available at no additional cost when ordered in conjunction with this textbook. To obtain free passcodes for your students, simply contact your local Merrill/Prentice Hall sales representative, and your representative will send you the Evaluating Online Resource Guide, which contains the code to access Research Navigator as well as tips on how to use Research Navigator and how to evaluate research. To preview the value of this Website to your students, please go to www.educatorlearningcenter.com and use the Login Name "Research" and the password "Demo."

BRIEF CONTENTS

CONTENTS

NOTE: Every effort has been made to provide accurate and current Internet information in this book. However, the Internet and information on it are constantly changing, so it is inevitable that some of the Internet addresses listed in this textbook will change.

DEVELOPING AN EFFECTIVE
AND ACCOUNTABLE
SCHOOL COUNSELING PROGRAM

CHAPTER 1

The Profession of
School Counseling

UNDERSTANDING THE PROFESSION: THE EXPERIENCE OF MARK

Mark, a counseling student, has completed most of his required academic work and is ready to begin his 600-hour internship, split between a secondary school and an elementary school. Mark knows from his experience that the local community has some racial strife and an economic underclass, and that a large percentage of students go from high school directly into the workforce. Mark assumes, as he has been taught in graduate school, that the counseling program will be designed to address these needs as well as those of economically advantaged, college-bound, academically proficient students. Mark's view of school counseling is influenced by the philosophy that school counselors bear some degree of responsibility for the academic, career, and personal/social development of all students.

During the second week of the internship, Mark expresses confusion during his group supervision seminar and asks for assistance from his peers and university supervisor. Specifically, he found that the counselors in his particular secondary school placement spend most of their time working with college-bound students in individual sessions, registering or withdrawing students, and preparing transcripts and letters of reference for college applications. These counselors and this particular counseling program emphasize preparing students to make vocational choices, with a

great deal of attention to those who are preparing to enter colleges or universities. In the elementary school placement, greater emphasis is placed on classroom guidance aimed at developing academic, career, and personal/social competence in which all students participate. Additionally, there are numerous special programs for students with particular needs, such as those who have recently experienced a family loss. Mark asks, "Are all secondary counselors so burdened with administration and paperwork that they can only spend their counseling time with a relatively small percentage of the school population? If the counselors are not going to address student needs such as developing an appreciation for diversity or career planning for non-college-bound students, who will?"

Mark is frustrated because what he had been taught in graduate school did not seem to apply in the real world. He is also concerned about the large number of students who are not receiving guidance and counseling services, particularly those in traditionally underserved populations. Additionally, he is confused about the difference in philosophy and practice evidenced by elementary and secondary counselors within the same district. Mark's university supervisor determines that a review of the history of the counseling profession and a discussion of school counselors' ethical responsibilities to those they serve is in order.

What are the elements of a profession? A profession typically has an agreed on set of preparation standards and qualifications one must have to occupy the role of "professional" in a given field. These standards are based on an established literature that provides both theoretical and empirical support for the profession's existence. Additionally a profession governs itself, usually by establishing minimum standards of care or practice to which members of the profession subscribe. Often these standards are articulated in ethical guidelines. Finally, there is consensus about the role, identity, and functions performed by a person who enters the profession (VanZandt, 1990).

All these conditions are true for the profession of school counseling. The American School Counselor Association (ASCA) has adopted a role statement that describes the role of a school counselor (see Appendix A). Once you graduate and assume the role of professional school counselor, you will be expected to address all students' academic, personal/social, and career development needs through a comprehensive school counseling program that promotes and enhances student achievement (ASCA, 2004a). You will be called on to provide assistance to students who are experiencing life transitions related to growth, family, or life circumstances outside the student's control and specific problems related to learning and behavior. You have had, or will have, a number of courses designed to assist you in working with students at all stages of development. In this book, we focus on the special skills and knowledge you will need to work effectively as a counselor in a school setting, managing a comprehensive, developmental school counseling program. To fully understand the profession, and some of the reasons for widely divergent practices, we believe it is important to place the current status of school counseling in a broader historical context.

After reading and discussing this chapter, you should be able to

- Identify the significant historical events that led to the current status of the school counseling profession.
- Describe the differences between philosophies of school counseling based on a services-oriented versus a comprehensive developmental approach.
- Explain the role of a school counselor in today's schools.
- Explain the ethical responsibilities of the school counselor toward students, parents, colleagues, community, profession, and self.

LEARNING FROM THE PAST

Mark might be able to reconcile the differences between his two different experiences of school counseling by considering the major historical events that influenced the development of school counseling as a profession. How could our professional history have led to two such different philosophies of school counseling? If we go back 100 years or so, we find "guidance" curriculum components delivered in the United States by teachers to help young people become moral, productive citizens (Baker & Gerler, 2004). The need for this component emerged during the Industrial Revolution with the large-scale migration of families from agricultural communities to northeastern cities in search of better occupational opportunities (Cecil & Cobia, 1990). Previously, children reared in farming communities expected to become farmers themselves and may have had limited access to formal education. Consequently, little attention was given to occupational planning. As these children relocated to cities and enrolled in public schools, school personnel quickly became aware of the need to provide them information about possible occupations and teach them the skills necessary to make decisions about their futures.

Some people instrumental in school counseling history responded to these needs. At the California School of Mechanical Arts in San Francisco in 1895, George Merrill provided experiences for students to explore occupations.

Counseling, job placement, and follow-up services were also included (Schmidt, 2003). In 1907, Jesse B. Davis, a high school principal in Grand Rapids, Michigan, set aside one session of English class each week for guidance. Believing that individuals could only make responsible choices about their future if they had information about themselves and about the vocations they were considering, Frank Parsons organized the Vocational Bureau of Boston in 1909 to make career information available to out-of-school youth (Baker & Gerler, 2004). Davis and Parsons have been identified as the fathers of school guidance (Aubrey, 1982). In 1913, the National Vocational Guidance Association (NVGA) was founded and in 1915 began to publish a bulletin that later became the current *Journal of Counseling and Development* (Gladding, 2004). This bulletin was the beginning of a professional literature devoted to what we have come to call counseling. Adding momentum to the guidance movement was the passage of the Smith-Hughes Act of 1917 that provided funding for vocational education in public schools.

> The long-standing assumption that guidance was a function of teaching and could only be provided effectively by classroom teachers was based in this early history of the guidance movement.

Another significant influence on the development of school counseling was the emphasis on testing and measurement. During both World Wars I and II the armed forces developed and used instruments designed to measure individual personality traits, skills, and aptitudes (Myrick, 1997). These instruments were used to test and place inductees in jobs for which they demonstrated the most ability and to ensure the best use of all available human resources. Instruments developed, especially in the areas of career interest and aptitude, were based on the trait and factor models introduced by Parsons and further developed by E. G. Williamson during the 1930s (Gladding, 2004). Guidance personnel embraced the use of tests, believing that an emphasis on precision and science legitimized their programs (Baker & Gerler, 2004).

In his development of a directive counseling approach, Williamson (1950) outlined six steps to counseling students that may still influence school counselors in the 21st century. He explained that helping students should proceed through

1. Analysis: gathering information about the person and the person's environment
2. Synthesis: selecting the relevant information, summarizing and organizing it to understand the person's strengths and weaknesses
3. Diagnosis: developing a rationale to explain the problem
4. Prognosis: predicting outcomes based on the actions the person chooses
5. Treatment: using various counseling approaches and techniques in the counseling relationship
6. Follow-up: evaluating the effectiveness of the counseling relationship and of the person's plan of action

After World War II, society was rapidly changing and traditional values were being challenged. The need for mental health services was recognized, and there was a corresponding need for people who could provide such services. Training programs for counselors and counseling psychologists experienced rapid growth. Keep in mind that the principal theoretical influences on counseling up to this point had been trait and factor approaches and Freudian

Initial, wide-scale entry of school counselors into secondary schools was to identify academically talented youth and help them get into colleges and universities. How do you think this event influenced the philosophy of school counseling in the secondary school where Mark is placed?

analysis. Because such approaches were not helpful to all persons seeking assistance, Carl Rogers had articulated a person-centered versus counselor-centered approach to counseling in 1942 (Gladding, 2004). Thus, a more humanistic theoretical perspective influenced the preparation programs for counselors and counseling psychologists that emerged during the 1940s, 1950s, and 1960s. After the publication of Rogers's first book, the term *guidance* was replaced by an emphasis on counseling, of which guidance may be a part (Gladding, 2004).

In 1957, the Union of Soviet Socialist Republics (USSR) launched Sputnik, the first artificial satellite. American citizens were shocked that the USSR had developed this technology and launched into space before the United States. In response, Congress passed the National Defense Education Act in 1958 (NDEA). Part of this bill provided funding to put in every high school counselors who were specially trained to identify and encourage talented youth to attend college. Special emphasis was placed on those students who showed promise in math and science, for they were perceived as our future technological saviors. Schmidt (2003) noted the following changes after NDEA:

- Full-time counselors increased 126 percent (from 12,000 to 27,180) and student-to-counselor ratio dropped from 1:960 to 1:530.
- State guidance consultants increased to 257.
- The government funded more than 400 counseling institutes that trained more than 13,000 counselors.
- Local school districts' spending on guidance and counseling services increased from $5.6 million to over $127 million. (p. 13)

With limited preparation, persons will naturally assume responsibilities for which they feel prepared. For school counselors trained during the early years, this often meant vocational guidance, college placement, and quasi-administrative tasks such as scheduling, registration, records maintenance, and testing.

As noted above, the NDEA provided funds to colleges and universities to develop programs to train school counselors. Counselor preparation varied widely and was directed toward secondary school personnel. The preparation programs often required as few as five additional courses for teachers holding master's degrees in any field of education to gain certification in school guidance and counseling. The early counselor preparation programs were quite experimental, for there was no research or professional consensus about what kind or how much preparation was necessary to be a qualified or effective school counselor. A common thread was that all school counselors came from the teaching ranks, continuing the perspective that preparation for teaching was the foundation for guidance.

A major step in the evolution of school counseling as a profession distinct from teaching was the establishment of the American School Counselor Association (ASCA) in 1958 as a division of what was then called the American Personnel and Guidance Association, now the American Counseling Association (ACA) (Myrick, 1997). With nationally recognized leadership in school counseling, a commission was created to study the role and function of school counselors. As chair of the committee, Gilbert Wrenn (1962) submitted a written report in 1962 entitled *The Counselor in a Changing World*. This report identified the goals of the school counseling profession. The goals centered on the personal development of students, and the commission recommended that counselors add the identification of the developmental needs of students to their emphasis on vocational guidance and testing. Further, the report suggested that counselors use various interventions such as individual and group counseling to help meet those needs. The timing of this report was quite remarkable in that the federal government extended the NDEA in 1965 to provide funds for training elementary school counselors. The report submitted by Wrenn on behalf of the commission provided a valuable resource for persons who were preparing counselors with NDEA funds in intensive summer institutes and greatly influenced contemporary models of counselor preparation and practice. From the early 1960s to the present, school counselor preparation and practice have changed dramatically. The emphasis on human growth and development suggested by Wrenn and his colleagues has continued to gain momentum and is now widely accepted as the foundation for the profession. The publication in 1988 of Gysber's and Henderson's *Developing and Managing Your School Guidance Program* provided counselor educators and school counselors a coherent framework for a systematic approach to program planning and management.

The 1990s might be characterized as the decade during which the need for multicultural awareness and competence gained prominence. Numerous publications focused on the need for counselors to be better prepared to meet the needs of a diverse society, and the Association for Multicultural Counseling and Development (AMCD) developed Multicultural Counseling Standards focusing on attitudes and beliefs, knowledge, and skills necessary for the practice of culturally competent counseling (Sue, Arredondo, & McDavis, 1992). These competencies established the baseline for culturally competent practice.

The preparation of school counselors has received professional consensus, as evidenced by the establishment of the Council for Accreditation of Counseling and Related Educational Programs (CACREP) as an affiliate organization of ACA (Gladding, 2004). CACREP refined the national standards proposed in the early 1970s by the Association for Counselor Education and Supervision (ACES). National standards for the accreditation of school counseling programs, as well as other counseling specialties, was an important step in having counseling recognized as a distinct profession. Instead of adding five courses to an existing master's level teaching certificate, persons enrolled in CACREP accredited school counseling programs were engaged in studies requiring a minimum of 48 semester hours or 76 quarter hours including extensive supervised clinical experiences through practicum and internship placements in school settings.

Further defining the goals, objectives, and responsibilities of school counselors, ASCA developed *National Standards for School Counseling Programs* (Campbell & Dahir, 1997). The standards clearly articulate expected student outcomes in academic, career, and personal/social development for those students who have participated in a comprehensive developmental program of school guidance and counseling (see Appendix B). At about the same time, the Education Trust (2003a) received funding from the DeWitt Wallace Reader's Digest fund to initiate an effort to transform school counselor preparation, emphasizing ". . . teaching future counselors specific skills in advocacy, leadership, teaming, collaboration, counseling, consultation, and use of data. These efforts are focused on preparing school counselors to use these skills to effect systemic change that removes barriers that impede student achievement" (www2.edtrust.org/edtrust/transforming+school+counseling/rationale.htm). This work led to the establishment of the National Center for Transforming School Counseling, a collaborative effort between the Education Trust and MetLife (Education Trust, 2003b). The center is a nationwide network of organizations, state departments of education, school counselor professional associations, institutions of higher education, and school districts working together to place school counselors at the heart of the effort to educate all students to the highest levels (Education Trust, 2003b).

In 2003, ASCA published *The ASCA National Model: A Framework for School Counseling Programs* (see Table 1.1). The purpose of this model was to create a single vision and voice for school counseling programs. The model was developed by ASCA using the best and most important concepts represented in state, district, and local models (ASCA, 2003a). *The ASCA National Model* serves as a framework for the development of a school counseling program that incorporates both the *National Standards for School Counseling Programs* (Campbell & Dahir, 1997) as well as the particular needs of the local school community.

This brief historical sketch of the development of the school counseling profession helps identify the various ways that this job has been approached (see Table 1.2). Today some efforts are being made to identify the best practices undertaken by school counselors. For example, researchers at the University of Massachusetts–Amherst have established the Center for School Counseling Outcome Research, which produces research briefs summarizing aspects of implementing school counseling programs. Those monographs can be found on this Web site: http://www.umass.edu/school counseling/Research_Monographs.htm. Additionally after some research summits attended by school counselor educators and school counselors, the National School Counseling Research Center has been established to develop and direct research in this area. The vibrant profession of school counseling continues to grow.

A number of significant changes have occurred in the history of credentialing school counselors, too. Persons aspiring to be school counselors are governed by the requirements for certification or licensure by their state department of education (SDE). To practice as school counselors, persons must meet the minimum qualifications established by their respective SDE. All states require graduate training to be certified as a school counselor. Unfortunately, SDE regulations have not always kept pace with the meaningful changes in the profession at large. As a case in point, the state where Mark is working certified teachers with a master's degree in any field of education who had 2 years of teaching experience with only five additional courses until as recently as 1994 and currently requires only about half the hours of supervised field experiences necessary for CACREP accredited programs. A few states still require teaching experience as a prerequisite for school counselor certification, even though research has not supported the assumption that teaching experience translates into counselor competence and establishes that former teachers, as well as nonteachers, have adjustments to make as they take on new professional roles in schools (Baker & Gerler, 2004). Although Mark does not have teaching experience, he is attending a 78-quarter-hour program with preparation in human growth and development, group

TABLE 1.1 ASCA National Model: Framework for a School Counseling Program

Elements			
Foundation	Delivery System	Management System	Accountability
• Beliefs and Philosophy • Mission Statement • ASCA National Standards	• School Guidance Curriculum • Individual Student Planning • Responsive Services • System Support	• Agreements • Advisory Council • Use of Data • Use of Time • Calendars	• Results Reports • School Counselor Performance Standards • Program Audit
Themes			
Leadership	Advocacy	Teaming and Collaboration	Systemic Change

Source: Reprinted by permission of the American School Counselor Association (ASCA, 2005).

counseling, career counseling, social and cultural implications for counseling, appraisal, helping relationships, research and evaluation, and professional orientation. In addition, he took special coursework related to the work of a school counselor and will spend approximately 1 year in the schools for supervised practicum and internship prior to his graduation. He feels confident in his ability to perform the duties described in the ASCA role statement previously mentioned and is determined to find employment in a school system that embraces a contemporary vision of school counseling.

In addition to state certification or licensure as a school counselor, two types of national certification have emerged in recent years. The National Board of Certified Counselors (NBCC) offers the Nationally Certified School Counselor credential to persons who qualify (Snow & Jackson, 2004). Additionally, the National Board for Professional Teaching Standards (NBPTS) adopted standards for professional school counselors that lead to the Early Childhood through Young Adulthood school counseling certificate. Both of these national credentials attest to counselors' commitment to achieving the highest qualifications available to them and, in some states, result in a substantial increase in salary for those attaining the NBPTS credentials (Snow & Jackson, 2004).

> How might this historical account help Mark understand the frame of reference of those counselors with whom he currently works, both elementary and secondary? Based on this information, how might Mark reconsider his view of the counselors?

WORKING IN TODAY'S SCHOOLS

Now that we have a historical context for understanding the development of school counseling (see Table 1.2), let us turn our attention to the current status of the profession. The school counselor is one professional among many working in today's schools to promote the academic success of all students. What do we mean by academic success? The educational outcomes of American education have been much debated in both public and private sectors (Dahir, Sheldon, & Valiga, 1998). Reform efforts sparked by these debates have led to the development of national standards across academic disciplines and, most recently, in school counseling. The standards (Campbell & Dahir, 1997) advocate a shift from the service/activity approach practiced by the counselors in Mark's school to a programmatic approach

TABLE 1.2   Important Historical Influences on the Development of the School Counseling Profession

Date	Historical Influence
1907	First classroom guidance lessons were delivered.
1908	Vocational Bureau was established in Boston.
1913	National Vocational Guidance Association was established.
1915	Forerunner of *Journal of Counseling and Development* was published.
1917	Smith-Hughes Act funded vocational education.
1930s and 40s	Numerous assessment tools were developed to measure personality, skills, and aptitudes.
1942	*Counseling and Psychotherapy* was published by Carl Rogers.
1957	Sputnik was launched by USSR.
1958	National Defense Education Act (NDEA) was passed.
1958	American School Counselor Association (ASCA) was established.
1962	*Counselor in a Changing World* was published by Gilbert Wrenn.
1965	NDEA provided funds for training elementary counselors.
1970s	Declining enrollments in schools resulted in reduction in school counselors.
1981	Council for Accreditation of Counseling and Related Educational Programs was created.
1985	American Personnel and Guidance Association was renamed to become American Association of Counseling and Development.
1988	*Developing and Managing Your School Guidance Program* was published by Gysbers and Henderson.
1992	American Association of Counseling and Development was renamed American Counseling Association.
1997	ASCA published *National Standards for School Counseling Programs*
1997	The Transforming School Counseling Initiative was introduced by the Education Trust.
2003	Education Trust and MetLife established the National Center for Transforming School Counseling (NCTSC).
2003	*The ASCA National Model: A Framework for School Counseling Programs* was published.
2004	ASCA Ethical Standards for School Counselors were revised.

that is "comprehensive, developmental and measures program effectiveness and the achievement of attitudes, skills and knowledge by students" (Dahir, Sheldon, & Valiga, 1998, p. 3). Recently, a definition of school counseling has been proposed as part of the transformation of school counseling initiative that further clarifies the school counselor's role in promoting academic success (Education Trust, 2003c).

School counseling is a profession that focuses on the relations and interactions between students and their school environment with the expressed purpose of reducing the effect of environmental and institutional barriers that impede student academic success. The profession fosters conditions that ensure educational equity, access, and academic success for all students K–12. To accomplish this function, the trained school counselor must be an assertive advocate creating opportunities for all students to nurture dreams of high aspirations. They assist students in their academic, social, emotional and personal development, and help them to define the best pathways to successfully achieve their dreams.

Serving as leaders, as well as effective team members, school counselors work with teachers, administrators and other school personnel to make sure that each student succeeds. As consultants, they can empower families to act on behalf of their children by helping parents/guardians identify student needs and shared interests, as well as access available resources.

The function necessarily requires focused attention to students for whom schools have been the least successful—poor students and students of color. A concentration is required on issues, strategies and interventions that will assist in closing the achievement gap between these students and their more advantaged peers. Measurable success resulting from this effort can be documented by increased numbers of these students, as well as other students, completing school academically prepared to choose from a wide range of substantial post-secondary options, including college.

With the *ASCA National Model* as a framework, school counselors implement programs that are central to the academic mission of the school, are accessible to all students, include the knowledge and skills all students need, are comprehensive in design, and are delivered systematically to all students (ASCA, 2004b). The foundation for such a program includes guiding principles or beliefs held by all stakeholders involved in program development and implementation, a mission statement that describes the program's purpose and goals, and the incorporation of the *National Standards* (ASCA, 2001a).

> Work with your classmates to develop a set of guiding principles detailing your beliefs about students, families, teachers, and the educational process. Once you have achieved consensus in your group, develop a brief philosophy statement that addresses the ability of all students to achieve; every student's developmental needs; the advocacy role of counselor; persons to be involved in program planning, delivery, and evaluation; data-driven decision making; and ethical practices.

WHAT DO SCHOOL COUNSELORS DO?

A number of experts in school counseling describe the practices of school counselors. Schmidt (1999) discusses counseling, consulting, coordinating, and appraising as the essential services provided by school counselors. Myrick (1997) adds peer facilitator programs and projects to the school counselor intervention list. Gysbers and Henderson (2000) describe the elements of a comprehensive program as the guidance curriculum (large group guidance), individual planning (advising and assessing), responsive services (counseling, consulting, and referring), and system support (managing, outreach, and public relations). Finally, Baker and Gerler (2004) include advocacy and accountability as counselor responsibilities. The work of these authors helps us understand the variety of ways school counselors make sense of their professional responsibilities, and many of the important elements of their work have been incorporated into the *ASCA National Model*.

Mark's understanding of the activities of counselors can be further enhanced by considering the four elements of the *ASCA National Model* (2003a) (see Table 1.1).

Building on the foundation described previously, school counselors deliver their programs through four delivery system components: School Guidance Curriculum, Individual Student Planning, Responsive Services, and System Support. School counselors act as managers for their programs, complementing the delivery system with management strategies that ensure the goals of the program are met. Finally, school counselors are accountable for the results of their programs and interventions. They collect and use data to ensure that programs are implemented, effective, and changed when needed. The following sections of this book will expand the definitions and applications of the four elements of the ASCA *National Model*.

As Mark's colleagues in group supervision hear his confusion about the differences between his understanding of school counseling and the practices of his supervisors at the high school, his peers who are placed in community agency, mental health, and other specialty area settings express their own confusion about the differences between school counseling and their own practice settings. Some clarification of these differences might be achieved by reviewing the standards for preparation established by CACREP (see Table 1.3). All of the counselors-in-training in Mark's program take foundation coursework that includes skills and knowledge in the areas necessary for effective practice regardless of work setting. Students who specialize in school counseling take additional coursework to develop competence in the areas identified in Table 1.3 as the foundations, contextual dimension, knowledge and skills, and clinical instruction specific to the work of counselors in school settings.

> Compare the CACREP specialty standards for school counselors with those of the other counseling specialties. What conclusions may be drawn about the different ways that counselors work in their respective work settings based on these comparisons?

HOW DO SCHOOL COUNSELORS UNDERSTAND THEIR RESPONSIBILITIES?

Another way for Mark to explore the profession's stance on the practice of school counseling is to examine the ethical standards that guide the professional school counselor. The ASCA (2004c) ethical standards (see Appendix C) are organized around the responsibilities a professional school counselor has to students, parents and guardians, colleagues and professional associates, the school and community, self, and the profession. This organization identifies the variety of people to whom counselors are accountable. The discussion of these responsibilities will be expanded in Chapter 12 of this book.

Responsibilities to Students

The professional school counselor's first responsibility is to his or her student counselees. Each of these students has rights, including to be treated with respect; to have access and opportunity to participate in a comprehensive program that promotes optimal development; to be fully informed about the purposes, goals, techniques, and rules of procedure at the beginning of a counseling relationship; and to have a reasonable expectation of confidentiality. Confidentiality implies an assurance to the client that what is communicated in a counseling relationship will not be repeated except in those limited circumstances noted in the disclosure statement. A counselor actively protects the privacy of a counselee's communications

TABLE 1.3   Specialty Standards for School Counselors

Foundations	1. history, philosophy, and current trends in school counseling and educational systems;
	2. relationship of the school counseling program to the academic and student services program in the school;
	3. role, function, and professional identity of the school counselor in relation to the roles of other professional and support personnel in the school;
	4. strategies of leadership designed to enhance the learning environment of schools;
	5. knowledge of the school setting, environment, and pre-K–12 curriculum;
	6. current issues, policies, laws, and legislation relevant to school counseling;
	7. the role of racial, ethnic, and cultural heritage, nationality, socioeconomic status, family structure, age, gender, sexual orientation, religious and spiritual beliefs, occupation, physical and mental status, and equity issues in school counseling;
	8. knowledge and understanding of community, environmental, and institutional opportunities that enhance, as well as barriers that impede student academic, career, and personal/social success and overall development;
	9. knowledge and application of current and emerging technology in education and school counseling to assist students, families, and educators in using resources that promote informed academic, career, and personal/social choices; and
	10. ethical and legal considerations related specifically to the practice of school counseling (e.g., the *ACA Code of Ethics* and the *ASCA Ethical Standards for School Counselors*).
Contextual Dimensions	1. advocacy for all students and for effective school counseling programs;
	2. coordination, collaboration, referral, and team-building efforts with teachers, parents, support personnel, and community resources to promote program objectives and facilitate successful student development and achievement of all students;
	3. integration of the school counseling program into the total school curriculum by systematically providing information and skills training to assist pre-K–12 students in maximizing their academic, career, and personal/social development;
	4. promotion of the use of counseling and guidance activities and programs by the total school community to enhance a positive school climate;
	5. methods of planning for and presenting school counseling-related educational programs to administrators, teachers, parents, and the community;
	6. methods of planning, developing, implementing, monitoring, and evaluating comprehensive developmental counseling programs; and
	7. knowledge of prevention and crisis intervention strategies.
Knowledge and Skills	1. Program Development, Implementation, and Evaluation
	a. use, management, analysis, and presentation of data from school-based information (e.g., standardized testing, grades, enrollment, attendance, retention, placement), surveys, interviews, focus groups, and needs assessments to improve student outcomes;
	b. design, implementation, monitoring, and evaluation of comprehensive developmental school counseling programs (e.g., the *ASCA National Standards for School Counseling Programs*) including an awareness of various systems that affect students, school, and home;
	c. implementation and evaluation of specific strategies that meet program goals and objectives;

(Continued)

TABLE 1.3   (Continued)

---

       d. identification of student academic, career, and personal/social competencies and the implementation of processes and activities to assist students in achieving these competencies;

       e. preparation of an action plan and school counseling calendar that reflect appropriate time commitments and priorities in a comprehensive developmental school counseling program;

       f. strategies for seeking and securing alternative funding for program expansion; and

       g. use of technology in the design, implementation, monitoring, and evaluation of a comprehensive school counseling program.

  2. Counseling and Guidance

       a. individual and small-group counseling approaches that promote school success, through academic, career, and personal/social development for all;

       b. individual, group, and classroom guidance approaches systematically designed to assist all students with academic, career, and personal/social development;

       c. approaches to peer facilitation, including peer helper, peer tutor, and peer mediation programs;

       d. issues that may affect the development and functioning of students (e.g., abuse, violence, eating disorders, attention deficit hyperactivity disorder, childhood depression, and suicide)

       e. developmental approaches to assist all students and parents at points of educational transition (e.g., home to elementary school, elementary to middle to high school, high school to postsecondary education and career options);

       f. constructive partnerships with parents, guardians, families, and communities in order to promote each student's academic, career, and personal/social success;

       g. systems theories and relationships among and between community systems, family systems, and school systems, and how they interact to influence the students and affect each system; and

       h. approaches to recognizing and assisting children and adolescents who may use alcohol or other drugs or who may reside in a home where substance abuse occurs.

  3. Consultation

       a. strategies to promote, develop, and enhance effective teamwork within the school and larger community;

       b. theories, models, and processes of consultation and change with teachers, administrators, other school personnel, parents, community groups, agencies, and students as appropriate;

       c. strategies and methods of working with parents, guardians, families, and communities to empower them to act on behalf of their children; and

       d. knowledge and skills in conducting programs that are designed to enhance students' academic, social, emotional, career, and other developmental needs.

| Clinical Instruction | Internship of 600 hours in an approved school setting with 240 hours in direct service. |

Source: Reprinted by permission of the Council for Accreditation of Counseling and Related Educational Programs (CACREP, 2001).

and is guided by federal and state laws, written policies, applicable ethical standards, and policies that impact the services provided to students and to confidentiality.

Counselees are provided information, preferably in writing, that explains the limits of confidentiality, privileged communication, legal constraints, and the possible necessity for consulting with other professionals. This document (following) is called a professional disclosure statement and is provided as an example of the types of information to which all student counselees are entitled before they agree to participate in counseling. Although student clients are entitled to confidentiality, there are circumstances under which a counselor discloses information to prevent clear and imminent danger to the counselee or to others. Counselors discuss information when legal requirements dictate that the confidential communication be revealed.

The professional school counselor also works with all students to develop a long-range plan including career and academic goals. Within the context of the school counseling program, the counselor provides opportunities for the systematic review and revision of such plans. If students need individual or group counseling services, counselors provide these services in a way that is consistent with standard

Riverside/Middle School

School Counseling Program Disclosure Statement

We have developed this statement to tell you about the counseling program at Riverside and about our role in your educational development. We hope that after reading this statement you will have an understanding of the ways we provide assistance to students in achieving their full academic potential. If you ever have questions about what you read here, please ask us so that we might provide answers.

Counseling Approaches and Background

Mr. I. M. Harris, M.Ed., School Counselor. This is Mr. Harris's fifth year as a school counselor. His approach is based on helping students identify those issues and emotions in their lives that may interfere with their ability to learn. He uses a variety of methods to help identify these barriers, and then helps students, teachers, and families develop plans to address the issues so that students are free to pursue their academic goals.

Ms. H. R. Patterson, M.Ed., School Counselor. Ms. Patterson has been a school counselor for 12 years. Her approach is based on helping students identify the negative thoughts they are having that may lead to distress and interfere with their ability to learn. She uses methods that help students identify these thoughts, and then helps students, teachers, and families develop plans to change the thoughts so that students are free to pursue their academic goals.

Appointments

Counselors are assigned to work with students and teachers in grade-level teams. You can make an appointment with your assigned counselor, or, if he or she is available, you may walk in without waiting for service. If you need to see a counselor right away and your assigned counselor is not available, the other counselor will be happy to assist you. Counselors are also available for after-school appointments on the second and fourth Wednesday of each month until 7:00 P.M

Confidentiality

The information shared between a student and a counselor is confidential. Confidential means that, except under specified circumstances, what you tell your counselor will not be shared with others. The exceptions, or conditions under which your counselor may share information about you with someone else, are listed below:

- If you ask your counselor to tell someone else
- If your counselor believes that you are in some danger from others or that you present a danger to others or to yourself
- If a judge orders your counselor to tell others
- If you report behavior in violation of school policy that your counselor is required to tell the school administration (identified in your student handbook)
- If your counselor needs to consult with someone else to provide better service (with your permission)

Benefits

You may experience increased understanding of the issue(s) that brought you to counseling and you may feel better because you have talked things over with someone who will try to help you resolve your concerns. If you achieve the goals that you and your counselor set together, you may feel confident and successful about your accomplishments.

Risks

Entering into a counseling relationship may create some anxiety for you. You may be challenged to think about yourself in ways that are not comfortable.

practice (e.g., screening for groups). Counselors who become aware that students need services beyond those available in the school make referrals, informing both counselee and parents/guardians of the identified concerns. Interventions with students who may be a danger to themselves or others are focused on minimizing the threat. Counselors take care not to enter into relationships with students or other school personnel that might negatively affect student-counselor relationships.

School counselors maintain records, separate from the student's educational records, to help him or her effectively render services. These records are purged at routine intervals, with the exception of those that may be needed in court, such as those documenting actions taken in cases of abuse, violence or other threats of harm, and harassment. Counselors are responsible for securing any records or private student information that may be maintained electronically.

At times, the counselor will need to conduct evaluations or assessments and to interpret the results to students, parents, and teachers. The counselor uses only those instruments within the scope of his or her practice, monitors the use of results to ensure that tests are not being misused, and seeks additional training for administering assessments, electronic or traditional paper and pencil, with which he or she is unfamiliar.

Professional school counselors ensure that computer applications suit the individual needs of a counselee. They explain the benefits and limitations of computer programs to counselees. Counselors determine that counselees understand how to use the computer program and provide follow-up counseling assistance. Counselors ensure that underrepresented groups have equal access to computer technology and are not subjected to information that is discriminatory. Counselors who communicate with counselees via a computer follow ACA Ethical Standards for Internet Online Counseling (http://www.counseling.org). Further, counselors advocate for all students, particularly the historically underserved, to have access to technology.

Peer Helper Programs

School counselors are responsible for anyone who participates in peer helper programs that are under their direction. Counselors protect the welfare of all the students who are involved at all times. The National Association of Peer Helpers Web site includes more specific guidelines for developing and implementing peer helper programs (http://www.peerprograms.org).

Responsibilities to Parents

A professional school counselor respects the rights and responsibilities of parents for their children. A counselor tries to build a collaborative relationship with parents to enhance the development and welfare of the counselee. Counselors work with sensitivity to the cultural and social diversity among families and adhere to laws and local guidelines when helping parents. Parents are provided with an explanation of the role of the professional school counselor that emphasizes the confidential nature of counseling. Counselors provide accurate, comprehensive, and relevant information in a manner consistent with all ethical guidelines and make reasonable efforts to honor the requests of parents and guardians for information while protecting the counselee.

Responsibilities to Colleagues and Professional Associates

The boundaries and levels of the counselor's professional role are well established and maintained in working with faculty, staff, and administration. Colleagues are viewed as competent professionals and are treated with respect, courtesy, and fairness. As stated previously, a counselor educates other professionals about confidentiality. If information necessary for assisting the counselee is provided, the counselor ensures that it is accurate, objective, concise, and meaningful. After the parent and student consent, professional school counselors may inform other mental health professionals if one of their counselees is also receiving services in the school.

Responsibilities to the School and Community

School counselors defend an educational program from anything that might interfere with the best interest of the students. Accordingly, counselors honor the confidentiality between themselves and their counselees but report to appropriate officials situations that may be disruptive or damaging. Recent legislation in some states aimed at limiting school violence creates strict reporting criteria for threats. School counselors must monitor their state and district policies regarding these procedures.

The scope of a school counselor's duties is clearly articulated in this section of the ethical standards. Counselors help in developing (1) appropriate curricular and environmental conditions, (2) developmentally correct, standards-based educational procedures and programs, and (3) a system of evaluation for school counseling programs, services, and personnel. The results of the program evaluation guide the planning process for the school counseling program. Additionally, in the best interest of counselees, the professional school counselor collaborates with others in the community without expectations of reimbursement.

Responsibilities to Self

Counselors practice within the limits of personal competence and take responsibility for their actions. Counselors monitor themselves and diligently protect counselees from harm. Counselors maintain professional competence and up-to-date knowledge, recognizing the lifelong process of professional growth. Counselors also recognize ways their own personal values and beliefs affect the counseling process and use this awareness as well as their understanding of diverse cultural backgrounds when working with counselees.

Responsibilities to the Profession

Professional school counselors accept these ethical policies and procedures as well as relevant statutes, conducting themselves in ways that advance individuals, ethical practice, and the profession. Clear distinction is made between actions and statements made as a private individual and those made as a representative of the school counseling profession. The school counselor does not use the professional position for unjustified personal gains, unfair advantage, sexual favors, or unearned goods or services. School counselors conduct and report research appropriately, always ensuring the privacy of any participants. Finally counselors are affiliated with professional associations and make contributions to the development of the profession.

In the preamble of ASCA code of ethics the following assumptions are listed as the foundations for the responsibilities discussed in the standards:

1. Each person has the right to respect and dignity as a human being and access to a comprehensive school counseling program that advocates for all students without prejudice as to person, character, belief or practice, regardless of age, color, disability, ethnic group, gender, race, religion, sexual orientation, marital status or socioeconomic status.

2. Each person has the right to receive information and support needed to move toward self-direction and self-development, particularly those who have been traditionally underserved.

Sidebar (left margin):

If Mark's supervisors were certified under the minimum requirements previously described, what professional development activities might they pursue to update their knowledge and skills? Working in small groups, discuss your potential professional development goals for your time in school counselor training. Project 5 years into the future and identify professional development goals you may be working toward.

Secure a copy of the statute mandating the reporting of child abuse in your home state. In the larger group, discuss the similarities and differences among the statutes. Based on reporting procedures described, develop a reporting system or protocol that might be used in your school counseling program to ensure that all requirements for reporting suspicions of child abuse are met.

3. Each person has the right to understand how his or her educational choices affect future opportunities.
4. Each person has the right to privacy and thereby the right to expect the counselor-counselee relationship to comply with all laws, policies, and ethical standards pertaining to confidentiality. (ASCA, 2004c, p. 1)

School counselors are confronted with many situations that require difficult decisions. Counselors who remember the rights cited above and who study the definitions of ethical behavior provided in the standards will be better prepared to resolve those situations using their careful judgment to preserve the best interest of the student.

SUMMARY

After a review of the history, philosophy, definitions, preparation, and standards of the school counseling profession, Mark will have gained a broader perspective on the many influences that go into the development of a school counselor's philosophy. Examining the current context for counseling in schools should help him understand the role of a school counselor as he enters the profession. Hopefully this experience will also emphasize for him the need to update his knowledge and skill throughout his career. An understanding of the ethical guidelines that govern the practice of school counselors should lead to greater awareness of his responsibilities to students, parents, colleagues, community, self, and profession.

More than any other counseling specialty, school counselors have opportunities to serve an array of clients in a variety of ways. Schools are a microcosm of society with the strengths and challenges of the larger world affecting each school. As they encounter these multiple demands, school counselors who are informed about the history, definitions, and standards of the school counseling profession continually strive to improve their practice.

PORTFOLIO COMPONENTS

1. Prepare a reflection statement by describing your motivation for seeking entry into the school counseling profession. Include a summary of your interpersonal and intrapersonal strengths that will help you become a competent school counselor. Also, identify any limiting factors and describe how you will compensate for or overcome them.
2. Reflect on and identify your beliefs about the purposes of education. Describe the role you wish to play in assisting your future clients achieve these purposes, as well as their own individual goals.
3. Review the ASCA role statement (see Appendix A) and identify any aspects that are different from your previous perceptions of a school counselor's role. Reflecting on these differences, speculate about how you came to hold these beliefs. How might your awareness of these preconceptions influence your training experiences?

The School Counselor: Promoting Academic Excellence for All Students

UNDERSTANDING SCHOOLS AND STUDENTS

Ms. Angelica Lopez has been a counselor at Warm Springs Middle School for 10 years. She has worked tirelessly to integrate the school counseling program into all parts of the school with all school personnel involved. Ms. Lopez recognizes the need for careful organization and focused management. She coordinates the many activities that are ongoing in Warm Spring's counseling program and collaborates with many groups to accomplish her goals. Generally her days are spent counseling students and working with teachers, parents, and administrators to support a school setting in which students can thrive. Throughout the school year Ms. Lopez monitors the progress and outcome of the activities and makes modifications as necessary. Overall, she and her colleagues are pleased with the implementation of the counseling program, ongoing evaluations, and resulting improvements. Warm Springs Middle School has become a valuable part of the community and a place where students have many opportunities to excel.

Her achievements have been noticed. The counseling liaison at the State Department of Education has asked Ms. Lopez to develop some materials that promote the importance of a school counseling program in the academic success of all students. The impetus for this request emerged from the state's continuing efforts to explain the priorities of the federal act titled *No Child Left Behind*. Ms. Lopez has accepted the challenge, realizing that she will need to begin with a look at the many factors that affect school practices and the success of students.

Ms. Lopez had no experience in schools before she accepted this position. She remembers her preparation and the knowledge base that guides her practice as a school counselor. Ms. Lopez has studied human development and counseling theories. She has had many experiences in which she's seen the helpfulness of those ways of understanding human beings. She has also studied extensively children's mental health and risky behavioral patterns. As a school counselor she uses information from those fields daily. She recognizes also that children exist within multiple systems, such as family, community, peers, and school. She has learned the limitations of program planning and implementation efforts that focus only on the individual student and ignore the impact of the other factors that touch a person's life. She appreciates a more global view of understanding the person and the school. Therefore, with her we will consider the many influences on the education of young people, school counseling programs, and strategies and resources to support school success.

A professor in a human development course introduced Bronfenbrenner's (1993) ecological model to Ms. Lopez. He theorized that understanding a person requires knowing the contextual or environmental situation in which the person exists. One of those dimensions includes the environment closest to the person—the family, schools, neighborhoods, and communities in which the individual lives. A more distant but nonetheless influential component is the macro system or the contexts such as education, religion, government, business, and media that affect a person's everyday existence. Global contexts extend to politics, global events, culture and environment, or other world and national events that have an impact on one's life. That impact varies by the amount of direct involvement of the person. The tragic events associated with terrorist attacks of September 11, 2001, provide an example of global contexts that affected those in New York City differently than those in China. Bronfenbrenner emphasizes the interrelatedness of all these levels and the interaction of the person and the environment as critical understanding of the complexity of the world. Frequently Ms. Lopez uses his idea of embedded systems to think about the many layers that influence a person and an institution. She knows that several groups help shape the education of young people and remembers her struggles to grasp the intricacies of the American educational enterprise.

After reading and discussing this chapter, you should be able to

- Describe the structure and governing of the education system in the United States.
- Explain school reform efforts.
- Discuss resiliency and strengths-based explanations of students.
- Identify educational strategies and community resources that promote success.

THE EDUCATIONAL ENTERPRISE

The American School Counselor Association (2004a) role statement on professional school counseling contains these words:

> Professional school counselors serve a vital role in maximizing student achievement. Incorporating leadership, advocacy and collaboration, professional school counselors promote equity and access to opportunities and rigorous educational experiences for all students. Professional school counselors support a safe learning environment and work to safeguard the human rights of all members of the school community. Collaborating with other stakeholders to promote student achievement, professional school counselors address the needs of all students through prevention and intervention programs. . . . (ASCA, 2004a)

Those statements substantiate the belief that a school counseling program is an essential part of the learning environment of schools. School counseling programs contribute to school effectiveness and increase students' ability to concentrate, study, and learn. Students who attend schools that have counseling programs earn higher grades, report fewer classroom disruptions, and show improved peer behavior (Lapan, Gysbers, & Sun, 1997; American Counseling Association [ACA], 2000). Gerler, Kinney, and Anderson (1985) also report that underachieving students who receive counseling improve in classroom behavior and in mathematics and language arts grades. To accomplish their goals, professional school counselors plan and implement comprehensive school counseling programs that serve as vital parts of a school setting. Being familiar with the many facets of the entire educational enterprise allows counselors a deeper understanding of ways to work effectively within schools as well as in other settings that may affect the policies and procedures of educating young people. School counselors need to understand the purposes of schooling, the responsibilities of different governing bodies that influence school policies, and the roles of all the people related to schools.

Goals of Schooling

Some basic assumptions have guided education in the United States across the years. These assumptions were stated in 1918 by the National Education Association Commission on the Reorganization of Secondary Education when it recommended that secondary education should "develop in each individual the knowledge, interests, ideals, habits and powers whereby he will find his place and use that place to shape both himself and society toward ever nobler ends" (as cited in Ballantine, 2001, p. 136).

This statement reflects the purposes of education related to intellectual, economic, political, and social purposes. Schooling is ultimately designed to help students increase their cognitive knowledge and skills, an intellectual goal. Education also provides students with the credentials they need to practice their careers, which in turn advances the nation's economic growth through a skilled labor pool. Goldberg (2000) identifies those skills that the business community asks for in employees: to be motivated, creative, well educated, constant learners, excellent communicators, and able to work in groups. Schools also help develop responsible citizens by attention to patriotism, law and order, leadership building, and knowledge of the governmental systems within the nation. Those topics indicate the political functions of the educational enterprise. Schools provide places in which cultural ideals are transmitted. Schools are optimally places where one can "come to terms with the diversity of voices within . . . an educative task for society, for the individual and for the school. It is what growing up means in a multicultural society and in a multicultural world . . . the appropriation of multiple voices—in dignity and without coercion . . ." (Erickson, 2001, p. 54). Although these general intellectual, economic, political, and social purposes serve as guideposts, different ways of translating the goals into operating principles occur at both the state and the local level. Recognizing the roles of state and local agencies will provide Ms. Lopez more ways of incorporating those influences into her school's goals for a school counseling program.

School Structures

FEDERAL

In the United States schools are supported and controlled by federal, state, and local governments. The primary responsibility to educate young people rests with the state and local authorities, but the federal government also has considerable influence on public education, particularly as we consider the Bill of Rights. The fundamental individual rights enjoyed in America are identified in the first 10 amendments of the U.S. Constitution as well as the Fourteenth

Amendment. Webb, Metha, and Jordan (2003) review those with relevance to education, which include the following:

The *First Amendment* states these personal freedoms:

> Congress shall make no law respecting an establishment of religion, or prohibiting the free exercise thereof; or abridging the freedom of speech or of the press; or the right of the people peaceably to assemble, and to petition the Government for a redress of grievances.

This amendment has been the focus of disputes related to school practices on what might be considered promotion or inhibition of religion, to curriculum content, and to concerns about public funds used to support nonpublic schools.

The *Fourth Amendment* grants people the right to be "secure in their persons, houses, papers, and effects, against unreasonable searches and seizures, shall not be violated and no warrants shall issue, but upon probably cause." The implications of this regulation in schools affect confidentiality of records as well as interrogations and searches, among other things.

The *Fifth Amendment* guarantees due process of law. It states that no person shall be "compelled in any criminal case to be a witness against himself, nor be deprived of life, liberty, or property, without due process of law; nor shall private property be taken for public use, without just compensation." In the *Eighth Amendment* protection against "cruel and unusual punishments" has been used to challenge the practice of corporal punishment in schools. Finally the *Fourteenth Amendment* asserts that states must guarantee the same rights to its citizens as secured by the Constitution. It states:

> No State shall make or enforce any law which shall abridge the privileges or immunities of citizens of the United States; nor shall any State deprive any person of life, liberty, or property, without due process of law; nor deny to any person within its jurisdiction the equal protection of the laws.

In addition to this framework of personal rights, the federal government provides other guidelines. Some include financial support and others are mandated imperatives to state school agencies. Additionally, the federal government provides a large portion of the funds for programs and services for special populations such as students with disabilities and youth who are educationally disadvantaged. For example, Public Law 94-142, now known as the Individuals with Disabilities Act (IDEA), affects every school and the ways children with disabilities are educated. Another federal mandate was issued with Title IX of the 1972 Education Amendments Act that was designed to assure gender equity in schools. The Elementary and Secondary Education Act (ESEA) includes Title I, an act that designates funds to enable children from low-socioeconomic level schools to meet performance standards. The funds allocated from Title I may be used for children from preschool through high school. It is the largest federal education program with a budget of $8.6 billion in fiscal year 2001 (Ubben, Hughes, & Norris, 2004). The reauthorization of the ESEA included the No Child Left Behind act, a national program with the goal of raising academic achievement. More information on that federal law appears in the school reform section of this chapter.

STATE

As noted earlier, the primary responsibility for public education rests with the state. Each state constitution has a reference to education that outlines who makes what decisions related to schooling in the state and how those decisions occur. A clause common in all state constitutions refers to the obligation of each state to maintain a free system of public schools open to all students in the state (Pipho, 2000a). States have other common elements. A K–12 grade structure exists in all states. All states have similar standards for licensing teachers (Webb, Metha, & Jordan, 2003), and national standards for teaching excellence are available for some subject areas. In the fall of 2001 about one out of every four persons in the United States participated in formal education as a student or an employee (U.S. Department of Education, 2002), a fact that highlights the enormous effort of educating students. American education includes 50 state educational agencies, approximately 15,000 school districts, and around 94,000 schools (National Center for Education Statistics, 2003).

Governors, state legislators, and state and local boards of education set educational policies. Funds for elementary and secondary education often make up the largest item in state and local government budgets, with the majority of the money coming from state and local taxes. A recent multiyear study of school governance resulted in the following possible model for schools:

- The state creates a context for schools and districts to excel;
- The district creates an environment that allows schools to focus on teaching and learning; and
- The school creates an environment focused on teaching and learning and is held accountable for the results. (Pipho, 2000b, pp. 341–342)

At the state level the administration of schools generally includes a state board of education (SBE) that makes policy, a state department of education (SDE) that serves as an administrative agency, and a chief state school officer who is the executive officer of the state board as well as an administrator of the state department. Chief state school officers supervise the state education system. Those officers direct the state education agency in supporting the public schools. State education agencies (SEA) supervise all the educational institutions as well as the certification procedures for school personnel.

Ziebarth (2004) summarized the different models of state education governance. In the majority of the states the governor appoints the SBE. The chief state school officer may be elected, appointed by the governor, or named by the SBE. Other configurations of state governance exist with details available from the Education Commission of the States (www.ecs.org) and from the National Association of State Boards of Education (www.nasbe.org).

State boards of education oversee state standards and district policies, especially those that depend on state funds. These boards determine minimum standards for teacher licensing, graduation, the length of the school day, and the number of school days in a year. SBEs may also establish policies, provide

> Check the Web sites noted in the text to determine whether the state and local school board members in your area are elected or appointed. Discuss the advantages and disadvantages of each selection method.

technical assistance, monitor schools, and provide others with information about schools (Webb et al., 2003).

Gysbers, Lapan, and Jones (2000) surveyed state school boards to determine the nature, structure, and content of policies for counseling programs across the country. In their analysis of 24 state school board association policies, they concluded that those policies are outdated and are not written to recognize counseling as an integral school program. They provide a sample policy statement from the Missouri School Board that can serve as a template for rewriting less inclusive policies.

LOCAL

Local districts often provide the greatest amount of funding for education. According to the National Education Association (2002), average local funding was 47.6%, state funding was 45.8%, and federal funding was 6.6%. Besides the significant contribution to financing, local districts have oversight into the provision of education. Local school boards oversee the operation of the school system within which an individual school exists. Some of the duties of those boards include hiring, determining salaries and contracts, and providing transportation, budgets, and building facilities. Often the board delegates the administration and teaching aspects of its duties to the superintendent and devotes its attention to policy concerns, much like a board of directors of a corporation. Ms. Lopez recognizes the importance of keeping the local school board aware of the effectiveness of school counseling and of the part school counseling plays in effective schools. She grabs opportunities to publicize her program outcomes. In preparing for board meetings she uses guidelines prepared by ASCA and available to members on the Web site. She has board members, parents, and other interested parties respond more positively when she illustrates her points by using data to show the ways students have been affected. You can find more specific ideas for working with a board of education at www.schoolcounselor.org.

Henderson and Gysbers (1998) explain the different ways a counseling program may be placed in the organization of the school district. The placements reflect the district's concept of the mission of counseling. According to Henderson and Gysbers, if the counseling program is perceived to be student centered and based on a developmental perspective, it will be placed with the instructional components. If the program is perceived as student centered with priority given to responsive services, the counseling program may be placed within the student services part of the structure. Finally if the school counseling program is centered on operations and reactive to the demands of administrators and teachers, it may be aligned with the administrative part of the structure. Gysbers and colleagues (2000) maintain that local school boards should revise policies for counseling programs to provide a sound organizational structure for counseling programs. Those policies would allow counselors to work closely with teachers and parents within the framework of a comprehensive counseling program focused on critical aspects of student development. Adelman and Taylor (1998) also urge school boards to revisit all policies that similarly fragment and therefore reduce the impact of programs and services.

The local school board may be unaware of the resolution related to guidance that has been approved by the National School Boards Association. It provides support for school counselors by encouraging local boards to support comprehensive counseling programs across grade levels and to ensure that the school counselors in those programs are professionally trained (National School Boards Association, 1986). An illustration of these and other influences on the process of education appears in Figure 2.1.

People

SYSTEM ADMINISTRATION

Superintendents manage school systems. They serve as conduits among schools, the school board, and the community. They operate as the chief executive officer of a school system, supported by a staff of specialists in curriculum and instruction, business services, personnel services, and special services. They report to the school board and are responsible for the operation of all the schools in the district. Their leadership guides the implementation of the

FIGURE 2.1 Influences on the Process of Education

Federal Government and Agencies	*EXAMPLES:* *Bill of Rights*	*IDEA*	*Title IX*	*No Child Left Behind*
	State Government and Agencies	*EXAMPLES:* *Licensing Personnel*	*School Term*	*Technical Help*
		Local School Board	*EXAMPLES:* *Budget Facilities*	*Hiring, Transportation*
			Central Office	*EXAMPLES:* *Management*
				School

district goals with the ultimate responsibility for the integrity of education resting with their office.

School Administration

The smallest but most critical unit in a school district is the individual school. The principal is the designated leader of the school and the person charged with the primary responsibility for its success or failure. Principals use leadership, management, and planning skills as they support teachers, manage the budget, oversee school personnel, work with students, and interact with the public along with other day-to-day responsibilities. The level of the school, the types of students who attend, the size and location of the school, and the district all interact in affecting the way a principal carries out that role. Ballantine (2001) summarizes the following as behaviors of effective leadership of principals in schools that have raised student achievement:

- Leaders are concerned with instruction.
- They convey their views about instruction.
- They take responsibility for instruction-related decisions.
- They coordinate the instructional program.
- They emphasize learning as well as academic standards.

McEvoy and Welker (2000) summarized the elements common in effective schools. Those characteristics include students' sense of efficacy in learning, a safe environment in which to learn, a shared mission among the school staff, effective administrators, and high expectations for all students. Principals influence most of those essentials.

From this short explanation of school structures and administration, you can see how many groups of people make decisions related to the practices involved in educating young people. Some of the frustrations of educators can be directly related to the policies and procedures in which they have had no input. Lambert (2003) has addressed ways for school personnel to develop what she calls leadership capacity. Her model provides a blueprint for principals, teachers and other school personnel, parents, and students to build collaborative relationships with shared responsibility among themselves and with other decision-making bodies in order to sustain high student achievement.

Her review of the governing and financing of schools as well as the different responsibilities at the federal, state, and local level leads Ms. Lopez to a renewed appreciation for the investment in children all these efforts represent. She knows she can find many ways to support her building leader and other school personnel in the practices that support an effective and caring school environment. She also knows that her work on the document for the state department of education needs to be addressed to a broad audience interested in children learning. She has also refreshed her desire to model collaboration and support as important aspects of building strong, mutually respectful relationships.

SCHOOL PERSONNEL

Principals are only one part of a school staff. Other positions include specialists and services workers such as office workers, media specialists, school psychologists, special education teachers, maintenance personnel, paraprofessionals, food service workers, bus drivers, and nurses. All school personnel affect the education of children, and all should be involved in creating environments that allow young people to be active learners, respected participants, and caring citizens. Ms. Lopez recognizes that any of the Warm Springs staff are valuable resources for the students and their families. For example, office workers are often the first people to greet parents when they visit the school. If the main office is staffed with warm and caring persons, parents or guardians who may otherwise view schools as inhospitable (e.g., parents who did not consider their own school experiences to be successful) may come to experience schools as warm and inviting environments. Other noncertificated personnel may form positive, lasting bonds with students who have few such relationships with adults. These significant adult figures have the opportunity to exert positive influence on the school behaviors of the youths with whom they become involved.

Teachers stand in the center of the work of schools. They work in many ways to share their knowledge and skills, create and use learning environments, and control the teaching process so that pupils can learn. Sometimes they have more contact with students than parents do. Their commitment, energy, and expectations play crucial parts in the academic accomplishments of their students. They teach children how to learn, how to hope, and how to be members of society. The behaviors and attitudes they demonstrate in their classrooms affect many areas of the student's development. A teacher is expected to be an instructional leader, a classroom manager, and a caring person. According to the U.S. Department of Education (2000), effective teachers set and communicate high standards, explain and demonstrate what is expected, assign meaningful homework, and help students with study skills.

Ms. Lopez recognizes the interactive relationships that exist at all levels of schooling. She knows that different school counseling initiatives require working at different levels. Her program concern may need to be addressed by a policy group at the state or local level. A consortium of five groups concerned with school counseling—National Association for College Admission Counseling, American Counseling Association, The Education Trust, American School Counselor Association, and Sallie Mae Foundation (2000)—suggests the policies listed in Figure 2.2. She decides to review some of these policies to determine whether some guidelines at Warm Springs Middle School or in that school district may need revision.

Finally, knowing the roles of the many people involved in the educational enterprise allows Ms. Lopez to access the information and resources she may need to assist all of those within the scope of her program. She will continue to lobby for professional development to support teachers and to provide them pertinent resources she gathers at their request. Her recognition of the formal roles and structures involved in education will help her with program planning and

FIGURE 2.2   School Counseling Program Policies per the National Association for College Admission Counseling

The Role of School Counseling in Preparing Students for the 21st Century

Policies that Foster Effective School Counseling Programs

School Counseling Program and School Counselors are not interchangeable terms. Although the school counselor is a vital part of a school counseling program, the individual is not the program. A school counseling program has a curriculum, goals, objectives, and outcomes just as other educational programs do. School administrators, classroom teachers, students, parents, and the community at-large all have important roles in the delivery of successful school counseling programs that will reap benefits for students. We recommend:

At the national level—

- The federal government identify and disseminate information about effective models for school counseling programs and for high quality school counselor preparation and professional development.

- The federal government support research on school counseling programs, including studies on programs and practices that increase school success for all students. Information on school counseling should be collected as part of the core data elements at the National Center for Education Statistics.

- The federal government fund initiatives that support school counseling, including professional development (both pre-service and in-service), student services, and capacity building.

At the state level—

- States develop standards for school counseling programs that are aligned with the state's vision

for student success, including academic standards, graduation requirements, postsecondary options, and personal, social attributes.

- States ensure that school districts have the resources to implement school counseling programs that meet the state standards.

- States require that school counselors meet certification requirements that include completion of an approved graduate program.

- States recognize only school counselor preparation programs that provide the knowledge and skills needed for new professionals to implement the state standards.

At the local level—

- Students have access to counseling programs that are part of the education program of the school system.

- Students have access to counseling programs that are approved by the school board and, at a minimum, should feature measurable results, access to students, parental involvement, highly qualified, professional staff, and strong administrative support.

- Students have access to counseling programs that have adequate fiscal, human and technological resources to implement the school counseling program.

change initiatives as well as with her daily activities. She also knows that she must be aware of the more informal aspects of schooling.

School Atmosphere

Most states have compiled a formal curriculum that guides the focus of instruction for the school district in that state. That curriculum provides a broad outline of the learning content, outcomes, and standards for students in topic areas such as language arts, mathematics, science, history, and so forth. A more informal, yet ever present aspect of schooling consists of the hidden curriculum.

Hidden curriculum refers to the unintended effects of schooling. Apple (1988) identifies three areas of the hidden curriculum. One involves the social messages presented in textbooks and other curriculum material. Another area includes the norms and values that are expressed in the regulations, rituals, structure, and interactions in the school. These allow students ways to cope with power, praise, reward, criticism, and authority (Apple, 1980); to move through social and physical spaces (Bowers, 1984); and to learn the value of competition, obedience, use of time, and seriousness of purpose (Webb et al., 2003; Anyon, 1995). The third area of the hidden curriculum is the information that is excluded from the formal curriculum, either on purpose or unintentionally. Ballantine (2001) considers the rules, routines, and regulations of the hidden curriculum. She cites Snyder, who explains that these are the "implicit demands (as opposed to the explicit obligations of the 'visible curriculum') that are found in every learning institution and which students have to find out and respond to in order to survive within it" (p. 6) (Ballantine, 2001, p. 225). Table 2.1 contains an example from Ballantine of the comparison of the actual curriculum to the hidden curriculum.

Ripley, Erford, Dahir, and Eschbach (2003) acknowledge that district and school policies also have some bearing on this implicit curriculum. Rules related to attendance, discipline, tardiness, suspension, makeup work, and other

TABLE 2.1 Actual Curriculum and Hidden Curriculum

Actual Curriculum	Hidden Curriculum
Teacher: Name	*Teacher:* What should I call the teacher?
Texts: Name	*Texts:* Do we have to read them?
Topics: Listed	*Topics:* What is the teacher going to cover? What is the teacher interested in?
Requirements: Readings Projects Exams	*Requirements:* What do I really have to do to get by? Will it help if I speak up in class? Will the teacher grade easy or hard? What should I study?
Bibliography	*Bibliography:* Am I supposed to use this?

Source: From *The Sociology of Education: A Systematic Analysis,* 5th edition (p. 225), by J. H. Ballantine, 2001, Upper Saddle River, NJ: Merrill/Prentice Hall. Copyright 2001 by Pearson Education, Inc. Adapted with permission.

policies about school activities incorporate embedded messages that make up the hidden curriculum.

Adults can use the power of the hidden curriculum by becoming more conscious of it, examining the assumptions within the materials and practices used, and finding ways to take advantage of these opportunities for learning (Apple, 1988; Webb et al., 2003). For example, Wren (1999) provided a list that could help administrators and other school personnel to examine symbolic aspects of a school's hidden curriculum. Warm Springs Middle School has a committee in place to review and adopt textbooks. Ms. Lopez has decided that she wants to use the process they have in place to review the supplemental materials she has been using in the guidance curriculum. She will create a checklist to use as she plans for classroom presentations. She will also work on a method to review the other material in the counseling office.

School Culture/Climate

Any organization has its own particular culture composed of the characteristics that distinguish it and the social interactions within it. Schein (1990) defines an organizational culture as

> a pattern of basic assumptions, invented, discovered or developed by a group as it learns to cope with its problems of external adaptation and internal integration, that has worked well enough to be considered valid and therefore, to be taught to new members as the correct way to perceive, think, and feel in relationship to those problems. (p. 111)

He explains that the observable behavior, shared values, and organizational assumptions are the three levels of culture.

School culture incorporates the school district and state policies, resources, local community, occupational systems, and professional environment (Talbert & McLaughlin, 1999). Student involvement, teacher factors, community support, educational leadership, and the curricular focus determine school culture (McWhirter, McWhirter, McWhirter, & McWhirter, 2004). School culture in effective schools includes collaboration, open communication, and continuous improvement (Tang, 2004), and as Rooney (2005) explains, culture is the context for everything that happens in a school.

The term *school climate* also incorporates many factors within a school. It has been defined as "how people feel about the qualities of a school and the people in that school" (Kaplan & Geoffroy, 1990, p. 8). Dorsey (2000) says four relationships are involved: that of a student to him- or herself; of a student to peers; of a student to parents and community, and of a student to school personnel. The ASCA definition also focuses on the interrelationships: "collective personality of a school or enterprise, the atmosphere as characterized by the social and professional interactions of the individuals in the school" (ASCA, 2003b). Hernandez and Seem (2004) define school climate as the related factors of attitude, feeling, and behavior of individuals in a school.

School climate helps determine the interactions that occur within schools (McEvoy & Welker, 2000). Belonging to a group may help children feel more connected to school, thus helping build a learning community. School climate has been credited with predicting school adjustment in urban, minority, and low-income children (Esposito, 1999); teacher satisfaction and sense of efficacy (Taylor & Tashakkori, 1995); counselor self-efficacy (Sutton & Fall, 1995); antisocial behavior (McEvoy & Welker, 2000); and school disorder (Welsh, 2000). Gottfredson (1988) discusses how a positive climate can reduce delinquency, and Hernandez and Seem (2004) help school counselors determine how to affect school climate.

Ubben, Hughes, and Norris (2004) identify four characteristics of effective school climate:

1. Clear, firm, and high teacher and administrator expectations;
2. Consistent rules and consequences that directly relate to infractions;
3. A decided and well-implemented emphasis on the self-esteem of all students;
4. Public and private acknowledgement and rewarding of positive behavior.

The presentation module *Taking Your School's Temperature* (ASCA, 2003b) contains a more extensive list of positive and negative signs of school climate.

Ms. Lopez's study of the dimensions of the atmosphere within the school provides her with essential information. She has helped the people with whom she works create a positive school climate by teaching them about Purkey's invitational learning (Purkey & Schmidt, 1990; 1996; Purkey & Novak, 1996; Purkey & Strahan, 2002). Purkey offers a blueprint for counselors, teachers, principals, supervisors, superintendents, and others to create physical and psychological environments that encourage development that he refers to as invitational learning. The goal of invitational learning is to build an optimally inviting environment for each person in the school. To accomplish this counselors and educators learn invitational behaviors and assist students in relating to the school. Students can then develop a sense of control over their lives, invest in their futures, and cope with school expectations. The method, according to Purkey (Purkey & Novak, 1996; Purkey & Schmidt, 1996), is a system of beliefs and a guide to professional practices. The process is based on four elements that interact and lead to inviting relationships:

- *Respect*. This element refers to an appreciation of each person and every culture; the beliefs that people are able, valuable, responsible, capable of self-direction, and deserve to be treated accordingly.
- *Trust*. The foundation of this aspect includes the belief in the interdependence of humans; a high priority on human welfare; and the idea that education should be a collaborative, cooperative activity in which the process is as valuable as the product.
- *Optimism*. The notion denoted by this variable is that people have untapped potential in all areas, displayed by a confidence in and perseverance with people.
- *Intentionality*. The potential of human beings is best realized by places, policies, programs, and processes designed to affirm human worth and to invite development and by people who are deliberately inviting with themselves and with others.

In the interconnectedness of schools, everything and everyone contributes to creating an environment that invites all to reach their potential. This includes arranging the following five factors:

- *Places*. Structuring an attractive and efficient physical environment that is functional, clean, warm, and accessible creates a setting for inviting behavior. This relates to building a school climate in physical ways (Esposito, 1999; Welsh, 2000; Bulach & Lunenberg, 1995; Freiberg, 1998).
- *Policies*. School personnel can influence regulations, plans, rules, and mandates that encourage student responsibility and participation. Inviting schools write inviting policies related to admission, enrollment, attendance, promotion, grading, discipline, and inclusion.
- *Programs*. Counselors help develop, monitor, and advocate for programs founded on the assumptions of invitational learning, such as peer helpers, faculty mentoring, and other collaboration efforts. For example, counselors and other school staff encourage enrichment activities, multicultural emphasis, parental involvement, community service, recognition, and cocurricular programs.
- *Processes*. Invitational learning assumes that the processes influence quality of life. School characteristics such as clarity and fairness in rules, order, and expectations are important to processes. In their work, counselors who establish norms of collegiality, professional development, mutual assistance, and ongoing discussions with other educators contribute to inviting schools. Everyone in school works to build relationships that are inclusive, integrative, and cooperative. Everyone helps build positive climates. They all work to demonstrate respect for all students and give attention to their needs.
- *People*. Invitational learning is based on valuing systems, regulations, and policies by putting people first. The interactions in schools among all the educators and between educators and students determine the success of the inviting learning community.

List all the school staff for one of the schools in which you were a student between grades kindergarten through 12. Talk about the ways each of these influenced your school day.

Ms. Lopez introduced the school staff to these ideas 4 years earlier. She has decided to be more consistent about helping with some annual training for incoming teachers and staff and to offer refresher opportunities for others. She is convinced that the attitudes of invitational learning help create environments that overcome some of the barriers to learning that students encounter. She has now looked at the ways a school system's structure and personnel affect learning. She has considered the aspects of hidden curriculum, school culture, and school climate. She will now consider some specific issues related to success in education as she considers other ways to connect school counselors to school reform measures.

School Improvement

The U.S. Department of Education (2005a) explained comprehensive school reform as a program that is "helping raise student achievement by assisting public schools across the country to implement effective, comprehensive school reforms that are based upon scientifically based research and effective practices"

(U.S. Department of Education, 2005, www.ed.gov/programs/compreform. html). Those efforts focus on reorganizing and revitalizing entire schools rather than more isolated attempts at reform. That attention to changing schools has evolved from earlier calls for action.

The report entitled *A Nation at Risk: The Imperative of Educational Reform* (National Commission on Excellence in Education, 1983) stimulated a debate about the quality of education in the United States that continues today. The publication highlighted achievement differences of students in Western Europe, the Pacific Rim countries, and the United States. The lower academic achievement of students in the United States sparked concerns that evoked reform efforts in the educational system. The comparison of student achievement in the United States with students in other countries continues.

The National Governors' Association published *Time for Results: The Governors' 1991 Report on Education* endorsing high educational standards and adequate measures to determine whether students were meeting those criteria. Consequently *Raising Standards for American Education* (National Council on Education Standards and Testing, 1992) proposed high-stakes testing as a viable measure of academic achievement and a suitable means of accountability, a notion that has been widely accepted. One other influential report, *What Work Requires of Schools: A SCANS Report for America 2000*, charged that schools did not prepare students with skills needed to succeed in holding a job. All states have now responded with educational reforms and systems of monitoring the educational progress of students.

Congress passed Public Law 107-110, an amendment to the Elementary and Secondary Act, in 2000. This federal law, also known as the No Child Left Behind Act (NCLB) of 2001, incorporated many of the recommendations made in earlier studies. The U.S. Department of Education (2001) provides a document (http://www.ed.gov/nclb/overview/intro/guide/guide.pdf) that summarizes those major provisions designed to provide stronger accountability, expanded flexibility and local control, more options for parents, and more reliance on research-based teaching methods. The specific guidelines include these stipulations, which are excerpted from the fact sheet.

- Testing: Each state will create a way to measure children's progress and achievement in reading and math in grades 3 through 8. Each child will be tested every year.
- Report Cards: Data will be published in annual report cards on school performance and on statewide progress. The reports will give parents information about the quality of their children's schools, the qualifications of teachers, and their children's progress in key subjects.
- Achievement Gap: The reports will include performance data disaggregated according to race, gender, and other criteria. The data will demonstrate not only how well students are achieving overall, but also whether states and schools are making progress in closing the achievement gap between disadvantaged students and other groups of students.
- Public School Choice: Parents with children in failing schools may transfer their child to a better-performing public or charter school.

- Supplemental Services: Federal Title I funds (approximately $500 to $1,000 per child) are available to provide supplemental educational services—including tutoring, after-school services, and summer school programs—for children in failing schools.
- Charter Schools: The law provides more opportunities for parents, educators, and interested community leaders to create new charter schools.
- Reading: Federal funding for reading increases from $300 million in FY 2001 to more than $900 in FY 2002, with strong encouragement to use scientifically proven methods of reading instruction.
- Highly Qualified Teachers: States provide a highly qualified teacher in every public school classroom by 2005.
- All students who have limited proficiency in English will be tested for reading and language arts in English after they have been in school in the United States for 3 consecutive years.

DeVoss (2004) summarizes models for school improvement. She discusses a guide developed for North Central Regional Education Laboratory that includes components and action steps for reform. Programs such as the Learning School, New Designs for Learning, and the Coalition of Essential Schools are also outlined in her article. Across several reform efforts DuFour (2004) explains his core principles of professional learning communities. The first component is the focus on student learning with strategic, timely interventions for any student who experiences difficulties. The culture of the school is one of collaboration for school improvement and removing barriers for success. The community focuses on positive results. He describes the professional learning community model as a new way of working together for educational practices, a method that requires commitment and persistence. Whatever the approach to school improvement, the atmosphere within the school building creates significant impact. Ms. Lopez knows that identifying the strengths of students and fostering those skills directly relates to sustaining any improvement.

CONTRIBUTING TO ACADEMIC SUCCESS

During a school day many things occur that increase the chances for children to learn and develop positively. Everyone in the school contributes to those possibilities, and those who act from their belief in the potential of each individual focus on strengths and wellness. Ms. Lopez has studied some ways of understanding the well-being of young people and practices that support student success.

Brazelton and Greenspan (2000) provide one explanation she finds useful. From their lifelong work with children, these physicians have identified what they consider the essential needs of children, the building blocks of emotional, social, and intellectual growth. They also discuss the implications of those needs for family life, child care, education, and systems that serve young people. Their list of irreducible needs includes:

- Ongoing nurturing relationships;
- Physical protection, safety, and regulation;

- Experiences tailored for their individual differences;
- Developmentally appropriate experiences;
- Limit setting, structure, and expectations; and
- Stable, supportive communities and cultural continuity.

The organization Child Trends (www.childtrendsdatabank.org) collects data on key indicators of children's well-being, variables that correspond to the needs identified by Brazelton and Greenspan. These descriptions of fundamental needs coincide with another way of understanding strength in children and their supportive environments, the concept of resilience. Benard (2004) summarizes this concept as the capacity all young people have for healthy development and successful living. Rak and Patterson (1996) relate the ability to youth who may be considered at risk of developing problem behaviors in their definition of resilience as

> the capacity of those who are exposed to identifiable risk factors to overcome those risks and avoid negative outcomes such as delinquency and behavior problems, psychological maladjustment, academic difficulties, and physical complications. (p. 368)

Benard (1991), Werner and Smith (2001), and Masten (2001) focus on the strength of humans and see resilience as a natural drive, the self-righting tendency toward health not limited to any ethnic, social class, or geographic boundary. Ms. Lopez finds this view of wellness helpful as she considers ways school counselors work. We will consider characteristics of the resilient individual as well as protective factors or buffers in the school, family, and community that can help adults nurture all children.

Benard (2004) suggests four categories can be used to explain the personal strengths that are the positive developmental outcomes of resilience and describes the attributes within those groupings. Her explanation coincides with the descriptions of other researchers (Rak & Patterson, 1996; Berry, Shillington, Peak, & Hohman, 2000; Canino & Spurlock, 1994). Resilient young people demonstrate social competence, problem solving, autonomy, and a sense of purpose. Social competence relates to the characteristics, skills, and attitudes needed to form positive relationships and to become attached to others. The socially competent person has a friendly nature, the ability to elicit positive responses from others, and good verbal skills. These young people can communicate their personal needs in an appropriate way, have social competence, and show empathy, compassion, altruism, and forgiveness toward others. Resilient children receive affection and support from caregivers. They are friendly. These youth have "good intellectual functioning" (Masten & Coatsworth, 1998) and are active problem solvers. They are proactive. They have abilities in planning, being flexible, using critical thinking, and developing insight. Autonomy relates to developing one's sense of self, of one's positive identity, and of power. Autonomy also involves acting independently and having a sense of control over the environment. Benard includes the concepts of internal locus of control, initiative, self-efficacy, mastery, adaptive distancing, mindfulness, and humor in this category of personal strengths. The fourth category, sense of purpose, relates to the sense that life has meaning. Young people have faith in a positive and strong future, which strongly correlates with academic success, positive self-identity, and fewer risky behaviors. Goal direction, creativity, special interest, optimism and hope, faith, and sense of meaning are attributes of this grouping. Benard (2004) suggests these assets can also be seen as developmental possibilities in all individuals. She has also compiled a summary of research from several theoretical models that support these concepts as critical life skills. As examples she has connected resilience to the basic needs described by Maslow (1954), to emotional intelligence (Goleman, 1995), to multiple intelligences (Gardner, 1993), to Erikson's developmental stages (1963), and to the SCANS report (U.S. Department of Labor, 2000).

McWhirter, McWhirter, McWhirter, and McWhirter (2004) have also summarized the positive skills of young people that increase their opportunities to succeed. McWhirter and colleagues base their approach on the assumptions that all young people have the capacity to become more mature, to have an interest in learning, and to function competently. They identify five characteristic skills for children to have a high potential for success: critical school competencies, concept of self and self-esteem, communication with others, coping ability, and control. Critical school competencies include basic academic skills in reading, writing, and mathematics as well as academic survival skills or habits that make it possible to learn. Staying with a task, following directions, and writing legibly are examples of the academic survival skills. The concept of self and self-esteem are the perceptions people have about themselves and the value they place on that self-concept. Communication with others allows students to achieve and maintain positive interpersonal relationships. The ability to cope effectively with anxiety and stress is a fourth essential skill and includes how one deals with conflicts. Finally McWhirter and colleagues discuss having decision-making skills, being able to delay gratification, and having a purpose in life as the skill of control.

Adults may increase these many individual skills by creating environments that allow caring and supportive relationships, contain high expectations, and provide opportunities for young people to participate and to contribute (Benard, 2004). Ms. Lopez concentrates on promoting those factors in her school. She knows that adults who connect with young people serve as models. Caring adults also express positive support and acceptance yet do not lower their expectations for the child's success. These adults are accessible and kind. Some schools have created deliberate ways to match each student in a school to an adult in that school, including all school personnel—cooks, bus drivers, maintenance people, and all others.

Other factors help provide nurturing schools. In a caring school the environment feels like a supportive community, small learning opportunities are created, and early intervention are available. The school staff is connected, and families and community are contributing partners to the school. Additionally, clear and positive expectations guide the activities in the school as well as challenge students. Underlying messages of competence, goals, and success abound. Adults focus on strengths. Schools are structured to support the learning environment. In this type of school students have chances to grow, make decisions, and meet the challenges of high expectations in a safe, caring environment. They have a voice in the school. They have opportunities to participate in experiential activities and with small groups. Finally the discipline process allows them to take responsibility for their actions and to atone for their misbehavior.

McWhirter and colleagues (2004) discussed factors that can be found in effective schools. One of these components is leadership behaviors that allow decisions to happen at the school site, have a clear mission, and emphasize strong instruction. A vigorous curriculum, high expectations for students, frequent checks on student progress, well-used instructional time, and continuous improvement all relate to the component on academic emphasis. Teacher and staff factors in successful schools relate to collegial relationships among the staff, collaborative planning, and low turnover. Students in these schools have a sense of belonging and feel safe at school. Students have clear goals. Adults handle discipline concerns fairly, clearly, and consistently rather than punitively. Community support is evident. Finally McWhirter and his colleagues discuss social capital, the relationship networks that surround the individual. The overlap in these descriptions from McWhirter and from Benard (2004) provides Ms. Lopez with crucial information about ways to help build an environment that will support academic success. She will continue in her efforts to manage the counseling program as a foundational in the effectiveness at Warm Springs Middle School.

SUMMARY

Ms. Lopez has reviewed the organizational structures of education in the United States. She has reminded herself of the many governing bodies and the financing of schools as well as ways she can communicate with the many people involved. The explanation on school reform helps her understand the impetus to improve schooling for all students. She has rediscovered the growing research on resilience and is appreciative of the connections with several strength-based concepts. She feels ready to create the document to help others understand how school counselors support academic excellence for all students.

Clearly, school counselors have an opportunity to identify and influence existing policies that promote unintended student learning. Additionally, Ms. Lopez and other school counselors are ideally suited to promote a positive school climate where all students feel attached, safe, respected, and competent.

PORTFOLIO COMPONENTS

1. Develop a profile of an ideal school that includes the organizational structure and school climate.
2. Reflect on your own public school experiences. What did you learn from the hidden curriculum about the value of education? Achievement? People who were or were not "valued" by society? Yourself?
3. Review the basic components of the No Child Left Behind Act. What role might you as a school counselor play in meeting the goals inherent in this act?
4. Assume that you have been asked to complete the task assigned to Ms. Lopez. Based on the reading and resources cited in this chapter, develop a brochure describing the role of a school counseling program in promoting academic success.

Promoting Systemic Change through Leadership, Advocacy, Collaboration, and Teaming

COUNSELORS UNDER CONSTRUCTION

Eric, Jill, Marcus, and Paige, graduate students in a school counseling program, are enrolled in an orientation to school counseling course. They are collaborating on a course project in which they are required to articulate the knowledge, skills, and dispositions required of an effective school counselor. The students have several goals for their initial meeting. First, they agree to set specific goals they wish to accomplish through the completion of this project. Marcus states, "In addition to developing the content Dr. Adams has asked us to compile, I would really like to know how the knowledge, skills, and dispositions we are working to acquire and demonstrate actually relate to the work of school counselors. Do you have ideas about how we might find out?" After some discussion, Jill suggests that they interview practicing school counselors to ask about the importance of the knowledge, skills, and dispositions and how they find themselves using or drawing on these during their day-to-day worklife. The students agree that this would breathe life into the project for themselves as well as the other students in class who will be hearing a report on their final project.

Second, they want to divide the work according to their primary interests. Eric will focus on knowledge. Jill and Marcus will cover leadership and systemic change, and Paige will focus on advocacy and collaboration. The group members have determined that they will need at least 8 weeks to complete their project. They will meet together every 2 weeks. This schedule will allow them ample opportunity to pursue their individual tasks as well as to regularly coordinate and check progress toward their overall goal. They recognize that even though the work begins with individual assignments, they will need to evaluate their progress as a group several times throughout the term to balance the workload and make other necessary adjustments to insure a thorough, accurate, and cohesive outcome.

Third, they want to identify resources that might help them in each of their individual tasks. Eric is going to focus on the standards articulated by the Council for Accreditation of Counseling and Related Educational Programs (CACREP). Jill and Marcus are going to review the American School Counselor Association's (ASCA, 2003a) model school counseling plan to identify the skills necessary to implement all aspects of the plan. Paige is going to review the extensive literature regarding the qualities that seem to be most important for counselors to demonstrate. Finally, the team will put their information from the research and interviews together in a presentation format that will be interesting and informative for classmates and one that with minor modifications might also be used to communicate information to other publics about the professional preparation and areas of competence of school counselors.

As described in Chapter 1, a major unifying advancement in the profession of counseling was the establishment of CACREP. This professional hallmark represented agreement across professional counseling bodies about the general areas of knowledge necessary for all counselors as well as specific knowledge required for counseling specialties (Holcomb-McCoy & Rahill, 2002). Additionally, other historical developments referenced in Chapter 1, such as the transforming school counseling initiative, led to a new, clearer vision of the competencies required to facilitate the educational development and academic achievement of all students. Prior to this initiative, the most recognizable models for school counseling focused on the "three Cs" of school counseling: counseling, consultation, and coordination. The contemporary view still includes counseling and coordination as well as leadership, advocacy, collaboration and teaming, and assessment and use of data (Education Trust, 2003d). Infused throughout the ASCA National Model (ASCA, 2003a), the skills associated with leadership, advocacy, and collaboration and teaming are emphasized as necessary ingredients of school counselors' efforts to promote systemic change.

Numerous studies of effective schools have identified common characteristics, but simply adopting those characteristics has not proven an effective strategy for those schools wishing to become effective (DeBlois, 2000). Schools that work well involve the efforts of all school personnel with planning, implementing, evaluating, and revising the institutions' programs and policies. Therefore, leading change efforts requires that leaders of such movements be able to establish relationships in the day-to-day work environment. Professional school counselors spend most of each workday developing and maintaining relationships with students, teachers, parents, administrators, and community resource persons. School counselors have unique skills, abilities, and knowledge that enable them to provide leadership in some instances and to support the emergence of leadership in others.

After reading and discussing this chapter, you should be able to

- Describe the foundation and specific areas of knowledge necessary to be an informed, effective school counselor.
- Identify the skills and styles of effective leadership.
- Explain systems and systemic change.
- Understand how to lead efforts in advocacy.
- Describe collaboration and team building.

KNOWLEDGE

The establishment of the CACREP signaled professional consensus regarding standards of preparation of counselors and includes foundation areas of knowledge common to all types of counselors as well as specific knowledge required for students in various specialties such as school counseling. The foundation areas include professional identity, social and cultural diversity, human growth and development, career development, helping relationships, group work, assessment, and research and program evaluation (CACREP, 2001). All students in CACREP accredited programs also are required to have supervised practice in their chosen work setting. Persons preparing to become school counselors also have special studies in the foundations of school counseling, contextual dimensions of school counseling (e.g., studies that prepare counselors for all aspects of program coordination), program development, implementation and evaluation, counseling and guidance, and consultation.

Eric has scheduled an interview with Dr. Thomas, a middle school counselor. Dr. Thomas has been working as a school counselor for over two decades and has been named middle school counselor of the year several times during her tenure. Eric believes she will be a good source of information for him about the relevance of the knowledge areas identified by CACREP and the actual practices of an effective school counselor. Eric asks, "How have you applied the knowledge or skills identified in the foundation areas to your own school counseling practice?" Dr. Thomas, "Studies in professional identity helped me develop a picture of the type of counselor I wanted to become. After gaining an understanding of the history and philosophy of the counseling profession, I knew I wanted to be a professionally involved, well-educated, fully credentialed, ethical practitioner. These are aspirations I have pursued throughout my career. I am a long-term member of both the American Counseling Association and the American School Counselors Association and my state and local branches. I have made numerous presentations, held offices, and served on special committees to inform others about, and advocate for, the counseling profession. I am a certified school counselor, a nationally certified counselor, and licensed by my state as a professional counselor. I am currently pursuing national certification as a school counselor. In addition to training and experience, one additional requirement for attaining most of the credentials I have mentioned is the commitment to abide by the ethical standards and best practices in my field. My studies in this foundation area helped shape the professional I have become and instilled in me the desire to engage in continuous efforts to improve my performance."

Eric asked Dr. Thomas to elaborate on the other foundation areas. "My understanding of my student clients has been greatly influenced by studies in development and diversity. My work as a school counselor is primarily aimed at helping students learn, a goal I could never achieve without an understanding of how and under what conditions learning occurs and the many factors, including social and cultural contexts, that directly and indirectly influence learning. Assessing students' personal social, academic, and career development needs and then developing appropriate interventions to meet those needs is also an important aspect of my role. Therefore, the coursework in assessment, helping relationships, groups, and career development have all been directly applicable to my practice. Finally, as an ethical professional it is essential that I continually evaluate my own effectiveness and the extent to which program goals are achieved. Even though I admit that the research and evaluation coursework was not as interesting to me as the courses that focused on student development, I have used the knowledge extensively in my school counseling practice."

"What about the specialty area coursework? How important has that been to your practice?" Eric asks. "When I was a graduate student, the emphasis in these specialty courses was on counseling, coordination, and consultation. There have been a number of important developments in the field of school counseling since I graduated," states Dr. Thomas. "Even though I did not study about

Visit http://www. cacrep.org for a full description of the content of these studies for both foundation and specialty areas.

the ASCA Model, I have read extensively about the model in the school counseling literature and have been able to work with other counselors in my school district to implement the model here. Throughout the years, I have engaged in my own studies of new developments related to program development, implementation, and evaluation. I think you and your peers have a distinct advantage in that you are studying school counseling at a time when new ideas, models, and skills are being incorporated into your training. However, school counseling is a dynamic field that changes with the needs of the students served in schools and research findings that support emerging interventions. Therefore, you will need to keep current of new and important changes and trends that affect your practice and actively seek out professional development opportunities to acquire new skills throughout your career."

Finally, Eric asks Dr. Thomas what professional changes she has seen since the completion of her own training that most influenced the direction of her school counseling practice and program. Dr. Thomas, "The addition of leader, advocate, and collaborator to the previously identified roles of counselor and consultant has been a major change and one which has helped me move from a position of relative isolation to a more integrated position within the total school program. Also, the emphasis on multicultural competence has been very important as the demographics of my own school population have changed a great deal during my tenure as a school counselor. These new emphases have led me to revise my view of the school counseling program, see it as part of a larger system. A more systemic view has resulted in the awareness that changes at the systems level may at times be more helpful to groups of students than helping students individually or in small groups."

SKILLS

Marcus and Jill are investigating the specific skills of promoting systemic change and leadership for their part of the class presentation. After considering Dr. Thomas's remarks to Eric about the importance of viewing school counseling in the context of a system, they decided to include a brief introduction to systems in their presentation to establish the context for the skills they will describe. Jill volunteers to do the research in this area. She finds that in contemporary management and leadership theories, the "professional community" is often referred to as a "system." A system refers to interactions and interdependencies of subsystems or units committed to a common goal. Scholtes (1998) identifies the following as characteristic of a system:

- A system is the whole comprised of many parts.
- A systemic unit has a purpose.
- Each part of the unit contributes to the system's purpose, but no part can achieve that purpose by itself.
- We can understand a part of a system by seeing how it fits into the system, but we cannot understand the system by identifying each part.

- Looking at the interaction between parts in a system might help us understand how the system works, but to understand why the system exists we must look outside the system.
- To understand a system we must understand its purposes, its interactions, and its interdependencies (when you take a system apart it loses its essential characteristics).
- When we look at an organization such as the school we're looking at a complex social system. (p. 21)

Jill had not previously considered the various roles and functions of school personnel as subsystems (such as counseling and guidance) interacting with other subsystems (such as instructional, extracurricular, administrative) to achieve the common goals of the larger system in which they all worked, the school. Counselors often talk about supporting the academic mission, for example, but may spend little time interacting with the teachers (instructional unit) about sharing this responsibility. Similarly, teachers frequently refer to the counselors those students who seem to have poor social skills, low self-esteem, or difficulty making relationships, but spend little time interacting with counselors about sharing responsibility for improving conditions for those students. Schools can be viewed as places with three nested systems of connected activity, including students, teachers, and parents interacting within classrooms, the school system, the home, and the world at large (Senge, Cambron-McCabe, Lucas, Smith, Dutton, & Kleiner, 2000).

Senge and colleagues recognize that viewing schools as systems necessitates a continuous exploration of the theories of everyone in the professional community. The shift from an individual, program focus to systems thinking requires practice and commitment. Jill found a model articulated by Demming (cited in Scholtes, 1998) that was helpful in making a shift from individual to systems thinking. According to this model, members of the school community need to consider their mutual purpose (mission statement); identify the beneficiaries of their services (the school and greater community); design a process or method to meet the needs of their beneficiaries; identify the policies, plans, specific needs, and the environment needed to achieve the purpose of their system; and develop a mechanism for informing those working within the system as to how the system is functioning in order to identify improvements or changes needed to meet the purposes of the system (Scholtes, 1998). Such a model requires everyone to examine his or her current, individual practices in the light of the new, systemically oriented vision.

> Within the school, what are the interacting interdependent parts, what are their purposes, and how may each affect the school's ability to achieve its purpose? If one looks outside the school to society at large to understand the purposes of schools, what might those purposes be?

> As a member of the professional school community, you have been asked to facilitate a faculty/staff discussion regarding the shared values of the school and community related to educating youth. Develop a list of open-ended questions you would use to lead such a discussion. Describe how the answers to these questions relate to the development of a mission statement for the school.

LEADERSHIP

Leadership occurs within an organization and involves both the internal and external stakeholders of the organization which, in our case, is the school (Phillips, Sears, Snow, & Jackson, 2005). Leadership involves influencing others to create a shared commitment to a common purpose (Phillips et al., 2005).

Jill and Marcus are somewhat confused about the differences between school leadership and school administration. They decide to seek clarification in an interview with Ms. Schroeder, an elementary school counselor who has agreed to be interviewed. They asked Ms. Schroeder to describe how she provides leadership in her school or system. She responds by describing her first role as the leader of an effort to increase parent involvement in the schools in her system that were considered high poverty. She was recommended for this role by Mr. Terman, the system-level program coordinator, who described Ms. Schroeder as a natural leader. Like many counselors, she viewed herself more as a support for the administrators who provide leadership and as a collaborator with teachers in their efforts to identify and respond to the needs of the student body rather than as someone who initiates change efforts. She had always assumed that the principal was the only person in the school who served in the leadership capacity. When questioned, Mr. Terman explained to Ms. Schroeder the differences between management and leadership. Lewis, Lewis, Packard, and Souflee (2001) identify these components of management:

- Planning—developing visions and strategies, setting goals, and selecting models
- Designing—structuring and coordinating the work to be done to accomplish the plans
- Developing human resources—enabling the people needed to make things work and enhancing their potential
- Supervising—monitoring and supporting the skills of personnel
- Managing finances—planning the use of resources to reach goals and control expenses
- Monitoring—tracking progress on objectives and activities
- Evaluating—comparing accomplishments with standards set at the planning stages and using the results as a base for change (pp. 10–11)

Ms. Schroeder acknowledges that her work as a school counselor involves these management activities, and she feels confident about her management abilities. Additionally, as she read more in the organizational and school literature about leadership, she began to understand what Lewis and colleagues mean when they say that what unifies these management processes is leadership. The idea of leadership being a process of social influence directed toward a goal expands the possibilities for leadership in schools. Strong leadership enables an organization to work as an integrated system, the way schools need to operate. Leadership involves moving beyond the individual's concern (managing the school counseling program, in Ms. Schroeder's case) and assuming more responsibility for the collective concerns of the organization (DeBlois, 2000).

In schools, the principal usually occupies a position of authority and is charged with managing the school, or with duties such as having buses run on time, keeping order in schools, monitoring budget and facilities, and handling other operating responsibilities. Some authors (Neuman & Simmons, 2000; Lambert, 1998; Hibert, 2000; Bemak, 2000) separate management from leadership based on the idea of shared responsibility. Neuman and Simmons

(2000) use the phrase *distributed leadership* to explain a concept of leading in which every person associated with schools—principals, students, teachers, all school staff, district personnel, parents, and community members—takes responsibility for the academic achievement of students, with particular individuals assuming leadership in areas of their competence and skill. Essentially, all who are involved adhere to shared values and adopt roles that are determined by the current tasks exhibiting what Jackson (2000) refers to as skills of "followership."

Katzenbach, Beckett, Dichter, Feigen, Gagnon, Hope, and Ling (1995) characterize people who contribute to growth and high performance in organizations as having the following attributes:

- Dedication to making things better
- Courage to challenge the status quo
- Initiative to question current definitions
- Motivation of themselves and for others
- Caring about how people are treated and are supported
- Willingness to keep attention on the process and goal rather than on self
- A sense of humor

These are the skills and attributes that led Mr. Terman to label Ms. Schroeder a "natural" leader. Further, based on these attributes, it is possible to identify others in the schools who are potential leaders. According to Rosener (1995), leadership efforts include encouraging participation, sharing power and information, enhancing other people's sense of self-worth, and energizing followers. Ms. Schroeder explains to Jill and Marcus that her transition efforts were successful because she provided leadership in the following ways:

1. Helped all participants develop the shared vision of the school community's values by including staff and community in a dialogue that permitted them to reflect on their values, listen to the values of others, and merge the personal and community values into a shared vision statement.
2. Organized, focused, and maintained direction in the conversations about student learning.
3. Interpreted and protected school community values such as parent involvement while ensuring a focus and commitment to learning.
4. Worked with everyone to carry out decisions.

Further, Ms. Schroeder described specific leadership behaviors that helped her accomplish these four objectives (Lambert, 1998):

- Asking questions that challenged underlying assumptions.
- Remaining silent so that other voices were heard.
- Promoting conversations.
- Generating a range of possibilities and avoiding simplistic answers.
- Focusing on the shared values.

Identify a person you have observed providing leadership to a group of others committed to a common goal. Was this person the official leader or did the person emerge as a leader as the work continued? Make a list of the skills and behaviors you observed this leader use that seemed to be effective in moving the work forward.

Based on the attributes and skills discussed so far, as well as your own experiences as a follower or leader, work in a group to develop an inventory of leadership qualities. Rate yourself on the inventory and identify your strengths as well as skills and qualities you need to develop to be an effective leader.

- Using data to inform decisions.
- Turning concerns into questions.
- Publicizing strategies in a way that models, demonstrates, and teaches others to use them. (p. 27)

A professional community, such as a school, provides a place in which adults contribute to the decision making, have a stated and shared sense of purpose, work together, and accept joint responsibility for the outcomes of their work (Lambert, 1998). To meet the challenges faced by their school system, Ms. Schroeder focused on building such a community. According to Newmann and Wehlage (1995), the most successful schools were those that used restructuring tools to help them function as professional communities. That is, they found a way to channel staff and student efforts toward a clear, commonly shared purpose for student learning; they created opportunities for teachers to collaborate and help one another achieve the purpose; and teachers in these schools took collective—not just individual—responsibility for student learning. Schools with strong professional communities were better able to offer authentic pedagogy and were more effective in promoting student achievement (p. 3).

PROMOTING SYSTEMIC CHANGE

One of the constants in any organization or system is that the system will either change or stagnate (Lewis et al., 2001; Scholtes, 1998). The challenge for the school community is to determine how that change will occur. Lewis and colleagues (2001) explain three methods of organizational change. One method involves leaders as change agents who guide as well as empower their staff. The second method is change that is initiated and driven by the staff, such as the initiative led by Ms. Schroeder.

Jill and Marcus discuss the merit of these first two methods. Although Ms. Schroeder is clearly both a manager and a leader, this will not always be the case. Principals, for example, will evidence many different styles of leadership and may or may not be leaders of change or systems thinkers. Some may be excellent managers and strong leaders in some situations but not in all situations. In such cases, the skills of the counselor or others in the school may lead to the building of a professional community. Under this organizational change method, counselors and other leaders may facilitate systemic change by focusing on student learning, making appropriate suggestions about quality, posing stimulating questions, volunteering to take responsibility for tasks, and giving constructive feedback.

Finally, Lewis and colleagues (2001) discuss a third method of change in which a person outside the organization leads the change process. School systems often hire experts to consult with school personnel to affect change in particular areas such as curriculum revision, program development or evaluation,

TABLE 3.1 Approaches to Organizational Change

Critical Intervention Variables	Administrative Change	Outside Consultation	Staff-Initiated Organizational Change
Change agent/ action system	Administrators with officially prescribed authority to initiate change	Outside consultant retained by agency administration to facilitate change	Employees with no prescribed authority or responsibility to initiate change
Primary sources of legitimacy	Legislative order, formal roles and authority, policy	Contract with administration	Professional ethics and values, employee or professional associations
Primary sources of power	Formal authority, control over resources and information	Expertise (knowledge and skill regarding change processes)	Other workers, knowledge of the problem, professional expertise
Common tactics	Directives, fiduciary control, personnel changes, visionary leadership, restructuring, consensus building through staff participation	Data feedback and problem solving, team building, strategic planning, employee empowerment, Total Quality Management (TQM), reengineering, analysis of processes	Participation on agency committees, fact finding, building internal support through education and persuasion
Major constraints and sources of resistance	Subordinate inertia stemming from fear or skepticism, entrenched interests, scarce resources, lack of external support, limited control of implementation	Limited time involvement, lack of administrative support, employee distrust of outsider, employees' prior negative experiences with consultants	Superiors' disagreement, insufficient time or energy, uncertain legitimacy, fear of reprisal and disapproval, job insecurity

Source: From *Management of Human Service Programs* by J. Lewis, M. Lewis, T. Packard, and F. Souflee, 2001, Belmont, CA: Wadsworth/Thomson. Copyright 2001 by Wadsworth/Thomson. Adapted with permission.

increased sensitivity to diversity, and so forth. The differences and similarities in these methods are depicted in Table 3.1.

Senge and colleagues (2000) discuss other methods to compel change, such as rational empirical arguments and coercion. They have identified the following keys to successful change in schools:

1. Change is only sustainable if it involves learning.
2. Change starts small and grows.
3. Significant change initiatives raise two questions about strategy and purpose: "Where are we going?" and "What are we here for?"
4. Successful change takes place through multiple layers of leadership.
5. Challenges are a natural part of organizational change.

Read the original article to see how an elementary counselor used this approach systemically to transform a school culture.

Ms. Schroeder: "In the change initiative that I led, the participants decided to follow a problem-solving approach described by Littrell and Peterson (2001)." The approach follows four basic steps, including defining the problem(s); investigating attempted solutions; setting minimal, concrete, and reachable goals; and implementing a plan to produce change. Ms. Schroeder and her team were able to agree on the desired outcomes, and perhaps most importantly were able to discontinue the use of solutions that were not effective and replace them with new solutions that had greater potential for success. "I encourage you both to develop your expertise in problem solving and to expand the traditional view of this approach from individually based counseling interventions to include the model's application in facilitating systemically based changes," said Ms. Schroeder.

ADVOCACY

Paige had not considered the school counselor's role as an advocate prior to her enrollment in this class. In the course of her research into this role, she discovered that literally millions of people in society lack the opportunity to participate fully in establishing those rules and policies that affect their lives (D'Andrea & Daniels, 1999). As D'Andrea and Daniels (1999) note, young people are often disempowered by the policies and practices in the institutions that purport to serve them. The primary role of school counselors as advocates is to create opportunities for all students to define, nurture, and accomplish high aspirations (House & Martin, 1998). House and Martin (1998) suggest that school counselors work as change agents and advocates for the elimination of systemic barriers that impede academic success for all students.

Advocates in schools work to reduce institutional barriers that lead to achievement gaps between poor and minority youth and their more advantaged peers. According to House and Martin (1998), school counselors have a broader view of the academic achievements and failures in their schools than perhaps any other single professional, because they routinely receive information from multiple sources about student successes and failures, test scores, course-taking patterns, and student placements. Although the activities described here are in the context of advocating for a systemwide change initiative, school counselors are in a position to identify issues such as these at the building level and to advocate for needed change.

The social advocacy position is based on the belief that individual or collective action must be taken to improve conditions for the benefit of an individual or group (House & Martin, 1998). Therefore, school counselors who believe that all students can achieve at high levels work to create conditions that promote achievement and reduce systemic barriers that do not. Sears (1999) states that school counselors accomplish these goals by using data to help the whole school look at student outcomes; using data to effect change; advocating for student experiences to broaden career awareness; and placing students in challenging courses. House and Martin (1998) suggest that school counselors do the following to become successful advocates who empower students to achieve at the highest level:

- Actively work to remove barriers to learning.
- Teach students how to help themselves (e.g., organizational skills, study skills, test-taking skills).
- Teach students and their families to successfully manage the bureaucracy of the system (teach parents how to enroll their children in academic courses that will lead to college).
- Teach students how to access support systems for academic success.
- Use local, regional, and national data to promote system change.
- Collaborate with all school personnel to promote change.
- Offer staff development training for school personnel promoting high expectations for all students.
- Challenge the existence of low-level and unchallenging courses.
- Highlight information that negates the myths about who can and cannot achieve in rigorous courses.
- Organize community activities to promote a supportive structure for high standards for all students.
- Help parents and community organize efforts to work with local schools to institute higher standards.
- Work as a resource broker within the community to identify available resources to help all students achieve.

During her interview with Mrs. Smith, a secondary school counselor with approximately 10 years of experience at Washington High School, Paige learns about the four different types of advocacy practiced by this veteran counselor. First, student advocacy involves standing for the needs of students and their families, even when others in the school or system take a different position. Basically, Jackson (2005) defines this type of advocacy as any intervention undertaken on behalf of a student. As an example, Mrs. Smith states, "This morning I attended an administrative hearing for a student who has excessive absences. The student's family circumstance requires that she frequently stay at home to care for an elderly relative while parents are working at seasonal jobs. The student keeps up with her work and is passing all of her classes. My advocacy task was to lobby for an exception to the standing policy that students must repeat classes in which they are absent more than 10 times per term."

Second, Mrs. Smith routinely practices program advocacy by demonstrating accountability for program success through publication of a quarterly newsletter, dissemination of program brochures, and maintenance of a school counseling program Web site for students and parents. Additionally, at the conclusion of every 9-week grading period, the counselors generate accountability reports detailing how many students, parents, and teachers have been served and the interventions they received. These reports are shared with building-level and central office administrators as well as board of education members. Through educational advocacy, the counselors at Washington High School work within the overall educational system to promote effective school programs. Finally, through political advocacy Mrs. Smith and colleagues participate in efforts to influence the decisions that have an impact on schools, school counseling programs, and students' opportunities to participate in effective educational programs (Jackson, 2005).

Mrs. Smith continues, "In this school grade-level and subject-area teams have been established to more effectively advocate for all students. The counselors for each team have agreed to serve as the data managers, systematically reviewing and reporting to the team all basic information on the students for whom they are responsible." The counselors review the collected data to detect patterns of possible inequities that extend beyond a particular grade level to the entire school experience of groups of students. Systematic, regular reviews of data, as well as serving on grade-level teams where more anecdotal data are also plentiful, are integral to the success of change initiatives at Washington High School and may lead to any of the four types of advocacy described.

Paige asked Mrs. Smith to elaborate on the challenges associated with advocacy. Surprisingly, Mrs. Smith indicated that sometimes the person for whom one is advocating may be suspicious and resist the advocate's efforts (Bailey, Getch, & Chen-Hayes, 2003). Mrs. Smith related that she is sometimes viewed as an adversary rather than an advocate by her colleagues and that this perception of others leaves her feeling isolated and alone (Baker & Gerler, 2004). To combat fatigue and burn out, Mrs. Smith recommends that new school counselors take time to get to know the system, how change is usually accomplished, and the key players in facilitating change. Additionally, she recommends a strong commitment to and practice of collaboration as a way to engage others in the advocacy process.

> Share with the class a time when you have worked together with someone else to achieve a common goal. Read on to discover the defining characteristics of collaboration and then describe how the circumstance you recalled either was or was not a collaborative process.

COLLABORATION AND TEAMING

When the Washington High staff decided to incorporate teaming as a strategy to identify student needs, it was necessary to create an environment in which people felt encouraged to work together rather than to continue to work as separate, individual entities. Friend and Cook (2000) define collaboration as a "style for direct interaction between at least two coequal parties voluntarily engaged in shared decision making as they work toward a common goal" (p. 6). O'Looney (1996) discusses the informal process or spirit of collaboration as sharing goals, values, ideas of fairness, and the experience of joint activity. Abramson and Rosenthal (1995) propose stages of collaboration that require key tasks. At the formation stage, collaborators establish a common mission, a shared view of tasks, and clear operating ground rules. At the implementation stage, collaborators deal with communication difficulties, group dynamics, and interpersonal problems that interfere with completing the work. At the maintenance stage, more issues or tensions may arise about power, leadership, goals, strategies, and follow-through. Paige asked Mrs. Smith to describe some of the ways she collaborates to improve the educational experience of students at Washington High. "Largely, I share information with the people who can use that information to make a difference. For example, if I discover that there are disproportionately fewer female students enrolled in upper-level math classes, I take that information to the math team and work with them to generate creative solutions for the problem. I may take other types of information, such as the large number of students who are new mothers in our school, to agencies in the community who can bring resources needed by these students into the school. Additionally, I may work with these agencies to coordinate services for the identified students." These types of tasks as well as working with parents, administrators, and other support personnel to meet mutually agreed upon goals are typical of collaborative activities performed by school counselors (Baker & Gerler, 2004).

The terms *collaboration, consultation,* and *teamwork* are often used interchangeably and do, in fact, share some common characteristics. Dettmer, Dyck, and Thurston (1996) state that in schools, all three approaches involve

- Addressing problems within the school context.
- Engaging in interactive processes.
- Using specialized content for the purpose of achieving goals.
- Sharing resources.
- Serving as catalyst for change or improvements.

Paige goes back to her exploration of collaboration as a distinct process and finds that Friend and Cook (2000) identify some of the defining characteristics of collaboration:

- Collaboration is voluntary.
- Collaboration requires equal value and equal power in decision making of all participants (parity).
- Collaboration is based on mutual goals.
- Collaboration depends on shared responsibility of participants.
- Collaborators share resources.
- Collaborators share accountability for outcomes.

During prior efforts to make systemic changes at Washington High School, each person worked on different parts of a puzzle without any sense of how the pieces were supposed to fit together to lead to better educational outcomes for students. Mrs. Smith told Paige that to begin their efforts at teaming, the faculty and staff decided to get together in a daylong retreat. The retreat took place off school grounds, and everyone was asked to bring their favorite picnic dish to contribute to lunch and invited to dress casually. The goal of the retreat was to establish an inviting atmosphere in which team members might get to know each other beyond the impressions associated with their individual roles at the school.

At the retreat, participants were asked to divide themselves into four groups, each facilitated by a school counselor, to take an inventory of the activities in which they were currently engaged that directly related to the school mission. During this process, the participants discovered that there was a great deal of similarity, overlap, and sometimes redundancy reflected in their individual efforts. They spontaneously, and voluntarily, began to identify ways to share their tasks, resources, and responsibility for the achievement of their goals. One outcome of the activity was that the employees affirmed their desire to establish more formal opportunities for collaboration through teaming. An evaluation of the retreat indicated that the individual participants felt less isolated and more connected with each other than they had prior to their day together. In fact, they requested that Dr. Pickens, their principal, arrange for a similar planning retreat during the next professional development day to establish formal structures and procedures for grade-level and subject-matter teams.

The commitment to continue talking and working together provided the necessary momentum to build their teams. The counselors for each grade were recruited to help the team development effort. They began by asking a local counselor educator to lead some professional development sessions for them to refresh their knowledge about groups and to teach them more about team building. Those sessions included definitions and characteristics of effective teams, as well as leadership functions and team development patterns. After their study and practice of these concepts, the counselors agreed they had the skills and knowledge to help the teams organize and structure themselves.

Johnson and Johnson (1997) define a team as a group of people whose interactions are focused on accomplishing a shared goal. The team "is more than the sum of its parts" (p. 508). To function effectively teams incorporate the following components. First, the members commit to developing and maintaining constructive relationships among themselves. Furthermore, helpful teams have established goals, roles, and ways of functioning. All individuals know the focus of the group, responsibilities of each member, and how the team will go about accomplishing their task. A final component of effective teams is continual work on improving relationships and its work (Basham, Appleton, & Lambarth, 1998; Correa, Jones, Thomas, & Morsink, 2005).

Henderson and Gysbers (1998) identify the advantages of teams. They recognize that when all members help in an effort, the level of support for the work and for each other increases. A team provides a forum for its members to be challenged to take risks, to be creative, and to contribute. Another advantage noted by these authors is the team accepting responsibility for its work.

Developing productive teams requires attention to fostering

- The team members' trust, dependence on each other, and mutual respect.
- Problems-solving skills, conflict resolution, and building relationships.
- Accountability for accomplishing the task and for influencing the work process.
- Encouragement and help in promoting everyone's efforts to achieve.

The counselors learned that a group becomes a team as members move into sharing goals and commitment. As counselors, they have led many student groups, focusing on the growth of the individual members. As team facilitators, they help the group focus on the mutually defined tasks. The counselors brought their understanding of group dynamics, relationship patterns, personality characteristics, and the educational process to the team-building process. Besides their knowledge about the different focus of small groups and team building, the counselors needed to investigate the phases of becoming a working group. They studied a team-building model described by Kormanski (1999). Based on group

TABLE 3.2 The Work and Outcome of Each Stage of Team Development

Team Stage	Member Behavior	General Theme	Task Outcome	Relationship Outcome	Facilitator Behavior
Beginning	Cautious Observing	Awareness	Commitment	Acceptance	Linking Modeling
Transition	Resistant Exploring Careful	Conflict to cooperation	Clarification Involvement	Belonging Support	Modeling Challenging differences
Working	Participating Dealing with issues Listening, understanding other points of view	Productivity	Achievement	Pride	Focus on work, solutions, negotiations Collaboration
Ending	Learning put in perspective Discussion of lessons learned	Separation	Recognition	Satisfaction	Summarizing

Source: From *The Team: Explorations in Group Process,* by C. Koramski, 1999, Denver, CO: Love Publishing. Copyright 1999 by Love Publishing. Adapted with permission. "Engaging Preservice School Counselors and Principals in Dialogue and Collaboration," by M. F. Shoffner and R. D. Williamson, 2000, *Counselor Education and Supervision, 40(2),* pp. 128–140. Copyright 2000 by American Counselor Association. Adapted with permission.

development theory, this model emphasizes the work and outcome of each stage of team development. Table 3.2 summarizes those components.

Mrs. Smith described to Paige what she might expect as teams develop. "In the beginning members become oriented to the team concept. They learn what behaviors are acceptable to the group and transition from an individual to a member status. The members may exhibit testing behavior and may depend on the leader to provide structure. Members will attempt to identify tasks, parameters, and methods of accomplishing the goal as well as decisions about what information is needed and how it will be used. During this early stage members may be reluctant to participate. As facilitators of the team-building process at Washington High, the counselors helped each grade-level group in this early stage begin to identify its philosophy and rules. Counselors led the teams in determining their commonly held assumptions about teaching and learning as well as their areas of disagreement."

Paige also knows that the developing team will need to discuss good team communication strategies, the steps they would use to reach their goals, and how they would go about making decisions. Team leaders also need to lead a discussion on confidentiality about sensitive matters and on loyalty to the team and its work. Early work on these basic concepts will prepare the team members for building their competence and accomplishing their work to improve the educational climate of the school for the students in each grade level—each team's overarching goal.

During the transition stage members look for more clarification and explore the trustworthiness of other members and of the process itself. This will hopefully lead to a better sense of the team's direction. Mrs. Smith indicated that an initial challenge was helping team members learn to listen and understand each person. Counselors may use their mediation skills to help resolve any defensiveness that could sabotage the team's effectiveness. As members demonstrate a respectful regard for each other, they will move to a greater sense of belonging and purpose, setting the stage for an acceptance of the team, team norms, their own roles, and each other. At this point team boundaries are well established and easier to maintain and more work is accomplished. Counselors would expect more open communication and cooperation among team members.

The working group will move into effective problem solving in an interdependent way. During this productive phase of the team, the counselors' facilitating job will become less difficult as they help the group focus on the work, solutions, and negotiations necessary for agreements. Members will be participating more fully and openly about dealing with issues as they emerge. During the working stage the team members will listen carefully to each other and understand other viewpoints. Mrs. Smith shared with Paige that this was her favorite stage of team development, paralleling her favorite stage of development in counseling groups.

Mrs. Smith described what happened as the end of the school year approached, "We, the counselors, helped team members summarize their progress and discuss future collaborations. Team members were encouraged to discuss the lessons they learned and to reflect on the perspectives they gained. The team also reviewed outcomes they accomplished as well as identified goals for the next year."

Johnson and Johnson (1997) provide more specifics for structuring and nurturing teams:

> These graduate students recognize that along with knowledge and skills, certain counselor qualities or dispositions are necessary to implement the new roles for which they are preparing. Divide into three groups representing the content covered by Eric, Marcus and Jill, and Paige. Identify the counselor characteristics and values that you believe would enhance one's ability to use the knowledge and function effectively as leaders, agents of change, collaborators, and team members. Combine your lists and construct an inventory of these qualities.

1. Encourage the team to define their compelling purpose and their goals specific to their team.
2. Have frequent and regular meetings for opportunities to interact personally and to promote each other's success.
3. Pay particular attention to the first meeting.
4. Establish clear rules of conduct at the outset especially some pertaining to attendance, discussion topics, confidentiality, confrontation, and contributions.
5. Measure the progress of the team toward its goals.
6. Show progress.
7. Expose the team to new facts and information.
8. Provide training to contribute to the work on the task and to team skills.
9. Celebrate team and member success.
10. Ensure frequent team-processing sessions. (pp. 521–523)

Paige left her meeting with Mrs. Smith feeling excited about the roles of advocacy, collaboration, and teaming. She believes these roles and their associated skills will be exciting to learn about and rewarding to practice. Eric, Jill, Marcus, and Paige have put together a presentation they believe will be informative to their classmates. They are also pleased to be able to include real-life examples provided by the counselors they interviewed of the ways the knowledge and skills focused on in their preparation program will be used.

SUMMARY

In this chapter, we have described leadership, systems thinking and change, and processes that lead to systemic change (e.g., advocacy, collaboration, teaming). School counselors possess the most important leaderships skills—the ability to establish relationships and create conditions where collaboration is possible. Collaboration is an essential process for promoting systemic change. School-based teams, such as grade-level teams, are examples of collaborative efforts where the team members are all working toward a common, agreed-upon purpose. Finally, advocacy was discussed as a process for achieving desired systemic change on behalf of specific groups of students who encounter institutional barriers to academic success.

PORTFOLIO COMPONENTS

1. Based on the outcome of the inventory of leadership qualities you completed earlier, identify specific learning activities in which you will practice to develop the skills and behaviors you currently do not display. Include a description of the method of evaluation you will use to determine whether these activities have been successful.
2. In no more than one page, describe a team-building activity you might use if asked to facilitate an initial team meeting such as the one Mrs. Smith was asked to chair.
3. Take the inventory of counselor qualities constructed by you and your classmates. Of those needed to enact the roles described in this chapter, which do you possess and how might they increase your effectiveness? Which do you lack? How might the absence of these qualities hinder your effectiveness? How might you develop some of the qualities, attributes, or values you lack?

Comprehensive School Counseling Programs: Planning, Implementation, Evaluation

MS. WEST IMPLEMENTS THE ASCA MODEL

Ms. Martha West recently accepted a school counseling position to work in a suburban school system in the Southeast. The school to which she was assigned, Kingston Court Elementary School (KCES), serves approximately 900 students in grades 3 through 5. The staff includes 40 classroom teachers, 5 teachers of students with special needs, 3 administrators, 2 counselors, a nurse, an attendance officer, a sheriff's deputy, a registrar, an attendance clerk, 3 secretaries, 5 cafeteria workers, 4 custodial staff, and 9 bus drivers. The school counselor Ms. West replaced retired with 12 years of service at KCES. Her colleague, Ms. Nancy Jones, has been at KCES for 10 years. When Ms. West interviewed with the principal of KCES, she was told that the school counselors are currently involved in conflict-resolution programs and in prevention programs aimed at reducing school violence and preventing substance abuse. They are also in charge of the crisis response and student assistance teams. However, the system in which KCES is located has made a commitment to implement a model school counseling program based on *The ASCA National Model* (2003a).

Ms. Jones oriented Ms. West to her new position. Each grade level includes 12 sections and is divided into two teams of six teachers each, their students, and students' parents. Ms. Jones is responsible for all of the teams in grade 3 and one of the teams in grade 4. Ms. West is responsible for the other grade 4 team and all of grade 5 teams. Ms. Jones emphasized that the counselors had traditionally executed the following tasks: scheduling all parent conferences, chairing meetings related to serving low-achieving students and students with special education needs, calling the parents of students with excessive

absences, gathering homework assignments and instructional materials for students who are absent due to illness, providing individual counseling services for members of their teams, and determining the appropriate academic placement for new students.

Ms. West asked to see the school counseling programs' mission statement and program goals, the role statement for the school counselor, data from the most recent needs assessment, and a copy of the most recent program evaluation. Ms. West was informed that counselors at KCES had traditionally responded to individual student needs as they arose. Further, KCES had no "formal" role statement for the school counselor, nor was there needs assessment data available. The recently retired counselor had intended to write up their program goals, but simply had not found the time to do so before she retired. Ms. Jones states, "There are a lot of needs in this school that go unmet. When I came here 10 years ago, I was enthusiastic about adding preventive activities, but the program and counselor were both well established and well liked. I basically stepped into an existing role that eventually came to fit. I am pleased by the commitment our system has recently made to revise the school counseling program, but am also uncertain about how to proceed."

Ms. West left the school after her orientation feeling excited and challenged. She had imagined that her first school counseling job would be in a well-established developmental comprehensive program with specific goals and objectives articulated. Instead, she found a loosely organized set of services aimed primarily at remediation. The prospect of being an integral part of changing such a program was both thrilling and daunting.

The challenge of creating or revising a comprehensive school counseling program might begin by asking, "What constitutes an effective school counseling program?" Borders and Drury (1992) reviewed existing counseling models and found that effective school counseling models were

1. Independent education programs; comprehensive, purposeful, sequential, and guided, in part, by outcomes.
2. Integral to the primary educational mission of schools; that is, they support, facilitate, and encourage classroom instruction and student achievement.
3. Established with developmental theory and research in mind.
4. Designed to serve all students in an unbiased way.

In 2001, ASCA's Governing Board decided to bring together leaders in the field of school counseling to create a national school counseling program model that would include characteristics such as those identified by Borders and Drury and would also build upon the national standards for school counseling programs published by ASCA in 1997 (ASCA, 2003a). The purpose of the model is to provide a framework for counselors to promote academic achievement, career planning, and personal social development through a comprehensive, systematically delivered program. The counselors at KCES will use the national model as a template in their program revision efforts.

After reading and discussing this chapter, you should be able to

- Identify the essential elements of planning and implementing a successful school counseling program.
- Explain the importance of a strong infrastructure to the development of a comprehensive, developmental school counseling program.
- Identify appropriate methods to collect and use local data from a variety of sources to design, implement, and evaluate a comprehensive, developmental school counseling program.
- Describe the process of formulating program goals and objectives.
- Explain how program goals and objectives are evaluated.

Two models of school counseling that served as precursors to the development of the ASCA Model are Norman Gysbers and Patricia Henderson's (2000) Comprehensive Guidance Program Model, and Robert Myrick's (1997) "practical approach" to Developmental Guidance and Counseling. We will briefly discuss both of these models so that you may see how they contributed to the development of the ASCA Model.

THE COMPREHENSIVE GUIDANCE PROGRAM MODEL

The testing, refinement, and implementation of the Comprehensive Guidance Program Model, also known as the Missouri model, started in 1971 under the direction of Norm Gysbers and his associates at the University of Missouri—Columbia. Gysbers and Henderson (2000) describe an organizational schema with well-defined procedures and systems. Life career development is the base of the model, and the three domains of self-knowledge and interpersonal skills; life roles, settings, and events, and life career planning are emphasized. Those are defined as follows:

- Self-knowledge and interpersonal skills. Students develop awareness and acceptance of themselves and others, incorporate personal skills for health maintenance, assume responsibility for their decisions, develop and maintain effective relationships, and engage with others.
- Life roles, settings, and events. Students develop and incorporate practices that lead to effective learning, responsible daily living, and a purpose in life; they recognize the interactive effects of various life roles.
- Life career planning. Students understand and use a decision-making process in determining their life goals.

The Comprehensive Guidance Program Model offers three elements and four components. The elements include the content of the program, the organizational framework, and resources. The content includes student competencies. The framework has three structural components (definition, assumptions, and rationale) and four program components (guidance curriculum, individual planning, responsive services, and system support). The resource element incorporates the human, financial, and political requirements for implementing the program. A counseling program, according to this model, has components that incorporate activities and roles and responsibilities of all involved in the counseling program. Some examples are listed and defined below:

- Guidance curriculum: classroom activities, schoolwide activities
- Individual planning: appraisal, advisement, placement follow-up
- Responsive services: consultation, personal counseling, crisis counseling, referral
- System support: research and development, professional development, staff/community public relations, community outreach, program management

In conclusion, this model presents a complete framework that can easily be adapted for each school. It has comprehensive lists of procedures and a recommended process for change. It may be considered a template from which to start a discussion of a site- or system-specific model.

DEVELOPMENTAL GUIDANCE AND COUNSELING

Robert D. Myrick's (Myrick, 1997; Gonzalez & Myrick, 2000) program also includes procedures and specific recommendations. Myrick suggests six basic counselor interventions for a counseling program: individual counseling (4 to

6 cases); small-group counseling (4 to 6 groups, seen twice a week); large-group guidance (2 to 4 classrooms, once or twice a week); peer facilitator training (1 to 2 hours a week); consultation with teachers and parents (1 hour a day); and coordination of guidance activities.

This model also includes a process for including teachers specifically in the counseling curriculum. The teacher advisor program (TAP) is based on the assumption that each student needs a friendly adult in the school (Gonzales & Myrick, 2000). This adult knows and cares about the student in a personal way, helping the student advisee with problems of developing and with maximizing the school experience. The program is designed so that every student in the school belongs to a small group of 15 to 25 peers that meets regularly. Teachers hold these meetings in a homeroom or home base and help students explore their personal interests, goals, and concerns. Teachers thus help deliver the counseling curriculum in these small groups.

To accomplish this, teachers receive training in leading group discussions and in planning guidance units. School counselors not only help teachers in developing the units, but also serve as members of a curriculum team. Counselors may help establish guidance objectives and provide activities that teachers may select or discard according to their needs. This design allows teachers to be more directly involved in the personal development of their students.

Myrick also emphasizes peer helping programs as an intervention. Students who participate in peer programs as helpers and as helpees may gain in productive behavior, attitudes toward school, self-esteem, and report card grades (Campbell, 2000). Other members of the school community also benefit from peer helping programs. Professional school counselors train and coordinate the peer facilitator programs and projects. The focus for peer helper training is in interpersonal and communication skills. According to Campbell systemic training is the most critical variable in the effectiveness of peer programs. Other training needs are determined by the specific skills needed in individual projects, which evolve from the needs of the schools. After the needs are assessed, the projects can be developed to address them. Examples of peer helper projects involve students serving as buddies for newcomers, mediators of disputes, presenters of college preparation seminars, and academic supporters (Campbell, 2000).

Myrick (1997) also provides a reminder for counselors about four approaches to working that need to be incorporated into a developmental program: crisis, remedial, preventive, and developmental. Crisis interventions are inevitable in the counseling office. Counselors may respond to crises by acting as mediators, as listeners, as calm centers, and in other ways to lessen the intensity during the critical time. The remedial approach focuses on identifiable problems with a suggested or applied remedy emphasizing learning or relearning skills that have not developed as expected. Another way to approach problems is attempting to prevent them from happening. These preventive interventions are focused on lessening the possibilities of such problem behaviors as delinquency, absenteeism, substance abuse, and others. Finally, through the developmental

---

Search the Web for information related to peer helper/facilitator programs currently used in schools. Locate the National Association of Peer Programs Web site and review information about training peer helpers at various grade levels.

approach counselors identify competencies students need to have to be successful and then provide opportunities for those skills to develop.

THE ASCA NATIONAL MODEL

A comprehensive school counseling program is preventive, developmental, an integral part of the total educational program, and systematically delivered to all students by a credentialed school counselor; it is conducted in collaboration with key partners, monitors student progress, is driven by data, seeks improvement, and shares successes with stakeholders (ASCA, 2003a). Inclusive of these characteristics, the ASCA Model consists of four interrelated components. First is the foundation, which requires an examination of the beliefs on which a program is built, articulation of a clear mission statement, and specified student outcomes derived from the ASCA national standards in each of three developmental domains: academic development, career development, and personal social development. Second is the delivery system, which provides for the systematic delivery of services to all students through four program elements: the guidance curriculum, individual student planning, responsive services, and systems support. Third is a system for managing the program that includes agreements with administrators about what counselors are expected to accomplish each year, an advisory council to review and make recommendations about the program, data to support each program activity, action plans, and annual calendars. Fourth is accountability in the form of results reports, program audits, and counselor evaluation (ASCA, 2003a). Infused throughout these four interrelated components, one will find the counselor competencies described in Chapter 3: leadership, advocacy, collaboration and teaming, and change agency. School counselors are clearly the program leaders, but successful implementation of the model is predicated upon collaboration with all of the constituent groups who have an interest in students' academic success.

Currently, the school counseling program at KCES consists of services delivered on demand and bears little resemblance to the ASCA model program (ASCA, 2003a). To revise the current program into one that is comprehensive and developmental, Ms. West needs to step away from her confusion and take a broader view. That is, she must be able to see how the school counseling program fits into the larger system (KCES). VanZandt and Hayslip (1994) define a system as "a structure whose orderly whole comprises integral parts (subsystems) that function together to accomplish a specific mission" (p. 15). Each school typically has a unique mission statement to guide the development and evaluation of school-related programs. Take a moment to examine the mission statement for KCES. KCES, in this instance, is the "orderly whole" of which the counseling program is an "integral part." This means that the counseling program exists to contribute to, or facilitate the mission of, KCES and is only successful to the extent that it does so. The mission that drives the school's educational enterprise also drives the school counseling program.

Kingston Court Elementary School Mission Statement
The mission of Kingston Court Elementary is to provide a safe, respectful environment where all students have equal access to the human and technological resources needed for academic success. Further, Kingston Court Elementary promotes the development of skills needed to become productive citizens, lifelong learners, and responsible members of a diverse community.

PLANNING FOR CHANGE

Building any type of program requires determining and describing what is to be achieved as well as what is necessary to produce the desired results, and then checking to see if what was planned has been accomplished. Therefore, planning a comprehensive developmental program involves a number of steps and many people. The planning must take place in the broader system or context in which it is to be implemented and must include careful consideration of local, regional, and national initiatives to reform or improve education. Additionally, all of the school constituents served by the program must be invested in its development and success. The program planners must be able to project into the future and identify what students should be able to do as a result of participating in a school counseling program (Dahir, Sheldon, & Valiga, 1998). Dahir and colleagues articulate a five-phase process of program development: discussion, awareness, design, implementation, and evaluation. In their book, *Vision Into Action* (1998), they develop each phase fully and include planning forms and suggested activities to help school counselors plan and implement programs. Ms. West and Ms. Jones will follow this planning model to achieve their program revision goals. However, before we move into a discussion of what happens at each stage, a brief discussion of the process of change is necessary.

Ms. West and Ms. Jones will probably experience more difficulty revising a well-established, if incomplete, program than they would if hired to create a program for a new school. Peter Senge (1999) states that most change initiatives fail. Why do counselors and other educators fail to implement change processes such as those described in Chapter 3? New initiatives often do not produce the desired results. Additionally, many change initiatives are imposed on educators from powerful external sources (e.g., governors, state education leaders, federal committees) and overlook the need to gain the commitment of all constituent groups necessary for long-term, systemic change. Educators who have been working for 10 to 20 years have seen many change initiatives intended to "fix" the broken educational system in America. Based on their experiences, some educators may have developed a cynical attitude regarding such reforms and are reluctant to encourage other efforts, even those initiated locally.

The school counselor and his or her constituents must be aware that change is ongoing and that every program must grow and change to make a viable contribution to the school's mission (Dahir et al., 1998). To provide leadership for this change, the school counselor must understand the tensions between growth processes, those that enable an organization to change, and limiting processes, those that tend to impede or stop growth (Senge, 1999). Effective programs are carefully conceptualized, planned, implemented, and evaluated. Ms. West will be guided by her ethical understanding (see Appendix C, Standard D1g) that the school counselor "assists in developing (1) curricular and environmental conditions appropriate for the school and community, (2) educational procedures and programs to meet students' developmental needs and (3) a systematic evaluation process for comprehensive, developmental, standards-based school counseling programs, services and personnel. The counselor is guided by the findings of the evaluation data in planning programs and services" (ASCA, 2004c).

Even though the central and school administrations express the desire to revise school counseling programs in this system, Ms. West is entering a well-established system as a new employee at Kingston Court Elementary School. Currently, she is discouraged by the state of the counseling program and overwhelmed by the challenge ahead of her. She needs to recognize that the responsibility for a comprehensive program is not hers alone. She is part of an educational team, of which all members have as their common goal to promote the academic success of students. A basic principle when initiating change is that the rationale for change must be clearly communicated to all those who are involved. People affected in the change process should be involved in designing the changes, thus encouraging their support. Consequently, the counselor's first step is to form a leadership team to review and discuss the current program and to provide direction regarding its revision and implementation. The leadership team should be diverse and represent the total school community. Faculty and student representation should include persons from all grade levels; parent and community members should represent all geographical areas and socioeconomic levels; all social, cultural, and ethnic groups should be represented; and the business community should be represented (Blum, 1998). Ms. Jones should be an integral part of the team, providing valuable information about past efforts, key constituents, and community insights.

> What steps could Ms. West take to ensure that Ms. Jones feels included and does not feel personally or professionally diminished by the change initiatives Ms. West wishes to facilitate?

> Who do you believe should be represented on Ms. West's leadership team? What process would you use for selection—nominations, volunteers, or invitations? What are the advantages and disadvantages of each type of selection?

Developing the Foundation

Program planning begins with Dahir and colleagues' (1998) first phase of program development, discussion, the purpose of which is to reach consensus about the purpose of and vision for the school counseling program. The leadership group has two early tasks. Following the suggestions of Blum (1998), the group begins by specifying its purpose, terms of membership, and criteria for appointment to the group, and by adopting an operating procedure with regard to meetings, agendas, and selection of officers. An action plan with time lines for completing the necessary tasks helps the team accomplish its purpose (Basham, Appleton, & Dykeman, 2000). Drawing on her skill as a group facilitator, Ms. West continually encourages the interactions of the group members that are aimed at accomplishing their goals.

At this stage, Ms. West and Ms. Jones need to identify the potential limiting processes that could impede the work of the team as well as the strengths of the group that will help contribute to success. Some of the common reasons for resistance to a team are previous negative experiences, the activity being perceived as a waste of time, and not accepting the team's purpose (Basham et al., 2000). One of the most frequently cited barriers to change is the time required to plan. How do persons who are extremely busy "doing" incorporate time for "visualizing" into their workdays? Integrating initiatives, scheduling time for focus and concentration, building capabilities for eliminating busywork, and saying "no" to nonessential demands are some ways to respond to the barrier of insufficient time (Senge, 1999). Another potential limiting factor in the

With your classmates, develop a list of 10 questions Ms. West and Ms. Jones might use to facilitate the articulation of beliefs and philosophy. Use your discussion as a basis for developing a list of the beliefs that will guide the development of the KCES counseling program.

discussion phase is relevance. Team members may ask, "How does what we are doing here relate to me and my role in the education and development of students at KCES?" Spending time within the leadership group discussing these barriers and how they compare to the potential positive outcomes of program planning will hopefully lead to greater commitment to the team goals.

Once decisions about how the team is to operate have been determined, the group can begin to identify their individual and collective beliefs about school counseling and student achievement. Ms. West and Ms. Jones have developed a list of key questions about student achievement, learning, the diverse needs of learners, the relationships of the school counseling program to learning and student development, and the role of parents and the community in education. They believe these questions will help guide the discussions such that consensus about the beliefs and philosophy underpinning the new program will develop. Following the articulation of beliefs, philosophy and mission statements consistent with the mission of the school will be drafted.

The philosophy is a set of guiding principles that inform school counselors as they implement a program (ASCA, 2003a). The philosophy should include statements about what the leadership team at KCES believes about students and their relationship to the school counseling program, what the comprehensive program should include, and what the KCES counselors will do. The mission statement gives the program focus, describing the program's purpose. Blum (1998) suggests that the mission statement contain a clear rationale for including counseling as an integral part of the instructional program, be reflective of the entire school community, and specify goals and objectives for the counseling and guidance program. Therefore the mission statement will include who is being targeted, what is to be accomplished, and what are the expected outcomes as well as the significance of this mission. The mission statement is an expression of the shared values of the faculty and staff and provides the direction needed to develop goals that are consistent with the school's mission. Lewis and colleagues (2001) state that a good mission statement is current, relevant, and useful and answers the questions: Who are we? What basic needs do we address? What do we do? What makes us unique? What is our niche? Because people who have participated in the formulation of goals are much more likely to feel accountable for the achievement of those goals, the committee believes the first step to success is to develop a mission statement on which most can agree (see following).

Sample Mission Statement

The entire school community of Washington County is committed to providing a high-quality, challenging, and culturally appropriate curriculum for all students in a safe and respectful school environment. We intend that all graduates be prepared to exercise a wide variety of postsecondary options and take full advantage of opportunities ranging from immediate entry into the workforce to admission to the college or university of their choice and to persist in their chosen educational and vocational placements. Additionally, we fully expect our graduates to demonstrate the skills necessary for successful relationships with peers, family, and a culturally diverse community.

Next, the leadership team needs to reach a mutual understanding of what needs to be done to achieve the vision articulated. This can be accomplished through activities identified by Dahir and colleagues (1998) as phase two of the planning process, awareness. Creating awareness generally involves multiple steps to develop a full understanding of the students, their families, and the social and economic conditions they face. Steps include reviewing existing documents and standards related to school counseling programs as well as examining local data about the community, the school, and the students. The questions that guide the team in this step are: Who are our students? What are their needs? What are the best means of meeting these needs? At this stage the leadership group develops a thorough description of the student body, the school setting, and the community in which it exists.

Information gleaned from student files such as patterns of student placements, academic successes and failures, and course taking, as well as the number and types of discipline referrals will aid in understanding the students' needs. Other important information includes

- Rates of absenteeism for students who may be considered at risk for academic failure.
- Dropout rates for those schools attended by KCES graduates.
- Numbers of children receiving free and reduced-price lunches.
- Standardized test scores for students at KCES.
- Follow-up studies of graduates and dropouts.

In addition to existing documents, other local data may prove helpful in identifying the needs of students at Kingston Court Elementary School. Community demographics provide useful information. Specifically the following local data may be used to identify needs and strengths within the school community:

- Unemployment in the community
- Estimated numbers of children living in poverty
- Juvenile crime rates
- The rate of births to teenagers
- Approximate number of foster families
- Divorce rates in the community
- Racial and ethnic composition of the community
- Major sites of employment for KCES' parents

These data need to be reviewed with some regularity as the needs of the school community change in response to employment opportunities, population shifts, and other environmental conditions. Based on the careful and complete review of available information, a report detailing the specific needs of the school community is generated. Careful attention is given to school and community demographic data. These data will be used throughout as a checkpoint to ensure that all plans are inclusive and culturally relevant.

A comprehensive needs assessment strategy forms the foundation for program design and makes it possible to set priorities, establish program goals and objectives, select activities, and schedule the counselor's time (Blum, 1998).

> Using the list of beliefs you and your classmates developed and the five questions proposed by Lewis and colleagues, work as a group to develop a program philosophy and then create a mission statement for the new KCES program.

Working in small groups, develop a one-page survey instrument suitable for fourth graders to identify types of small groups they feel would be beneficial and in which they would like to participate during the coming academic year. How would the local data already reviewed inform decisions about the types of groups you include on the selection list? How would consideration of the student competencies identified in the National Standards for School Counseling Programs (ASCA, 2000) influence these decisions?

According to Anderson and Reiter (1995), the guiding question for this assessment is: How are students different as a result of the school counseling program? Therefore, the leadership team might begin by examining existing documents such as school policy and procedure manuals; local, state, and national standards for school counseling programs; and other materials that would help determine the areas to be included in their plan. The ASCA National Standards for School Counseling Programs (Dahir et al., 1998; Appendix B) specifies student competencies in academic, career, and personal/social development across all grade levels. The leadership team will examine the current program to ascertain the extent to which these competencies are being realized for KCES students. ASCA (2003a) describes a procedure called the curriculum crosswalk to help with this task. Using the 122 competencies listed in the National Standards, counselors and the leadership team may compare the competencies with the goals of their current curriculum to determine which competencies are currently being met, in what grades, and by whom; to identify the competencies not currently being met but which need to be incorporated as the program is revised; and to add to the list of competencies those needs unique to KCES that were identified through the review of school and community data and comprehensive needs assessments.

Much of the data compiled to facilitate awareness also serves to address one of the principal limitations to change, the question of relevance. Establishing the school counseling program as integral to achieving the overall KCES mission and identifying and using data such as those described above can be influential in demonstrating the relevance of a school counseling program to all persons on the leadership team and to others who will be affected by the school counseling program.

DESIGNING THE KCES PROGRAM

Assuming the leadership team has gathered and analyzed the various types of data described in the awareness phase, they are ready to consider the program design, phase three of the planning process. As stated previously, the ASCA National Model is the one chosen by KCES as the template for their revised program. During the design phase, the leadership team will integrate its vision with the needs of the school to create a responsive and effective counseling program, including the services and activities one might incorporate into the program to support the competencies prioritized by the leadership team (Dahir et al., 1998). The ASCA National Standards and competencies are translated into goals and objectives for students at each grade level.

The school counselors must identify through what strategies or activities the competency will be addressed. Individual and group counseling, classroom guidance activities, peer mediation programs, special events, consultation, and peer facilitation programs are but a few of the mechanisms in the counselor's repertoire for addressing the competencies in academic, career, and personal/social domains. Information from school counseling outcome research helps to determine strategies that have a higher likelihood of success. For instance, interventions on career planning have received positive outcomes with students who have a range of exceptionalities such as being gifted or learning disabled. Instructing parents in ways to help students with career decisions has also been tested positively. Group interventions, particularly at the elementary level, have also received strong empirical support (Whiston & Sexton, 1998).

The ASCA Model (2003a) includes a four-part delivery system: school guidance curriculum, individual student planning, responsive services, and system support. Through the school guidance curriculum, all students participate in curriculum activities that promote academic achievement, career development, and personal social growth. This part of the total program is well planned and systematically delivered to students at all grade levels. Examples of strategies used to deliver the curriculum are classroom instruction, small-group discussion, parent groups or presentations, and assemblies. Individual student planning involves those strategies and activities used to help students and their families establish and work toward their educational and career goals. Responsive services refer to those student needs that are immediate and require more specialized intervention than is provided through the guidance curriculum or individual planning. Individual or group counseling, consultation, crisis counseling, peer facilitation, or referrals are interventions often used to meet these student needs. System support involves the management activities necessary to maintain and enhance the school counseling program such as professional development, consultation and collaboration with teachers, and program management. Each of these four vehicles for delivery of services will be discussed in greater detail in later chapters.

> Download a copy of the ASCA National Model District Readiness Survey from the Center for School Counseling Outcome Research at http:// www.umass.edu/ schoolcounseling/ and discuss with your colleagues how such an instrument might be used by the leadership team at KCES to facilitate the transition. Read the related article by Carey, Harrity, and Dimmitt (2005) to see how the instrument was developed.

IMPLEMENTING THE PROGRAM

Once the leadership team is satisfied with the program design, implementation can begin. The ASCA Model (2003a) includes a management system to describe who will do what, when, and how (Dahir et al., 1998). To complete the implementation plan, the leadership team may proceed by setting and prioritizing goals, assigning responsibilities, and scheduling services. Eventually an annual plan of goals, objectives, and services will be created. Based on the previously identified needs, the leadership team will set priorities that influence the scheduling of activities. That prioritization may occur according to the level of intervention at which the need will be based—crisis, remediation, prevention, and/or developmental. The planning group will also consider time-management concerns, the scope and immediacy of the needs, and the school instructional program. Dahir and colleagues propose that one also consider carefully the implementation time line to complement the existing school calendar.

With the priorities agreed upon, the leadership team turns to specifying the content and form of the goals. That specification determines the services and activities identified for accomplishing each goal. As different activities are identified the team needs to recognize the different learning styles and needs of the student population. Therefore, strategies should include a variety of possible activities for accomplishing the goal. Providing activities for auditory, visual, and kinesthetic learners is an inclusive way to approach this task. Next, the team attempts to establish who will be responsible for addressing each goal. Finally, a schedule is designed for the implementation of the program.

Accountability

Even though accountability and evaluation are discussed as the fifth and final phase of program development, in actuality accountability measures must be considered from the very beginning. Ethical standards (see Appendix C, Standard D1g) state that evaluation is a component of the school counselor's responsibility to the school and to the community. The evaluation guides in planning programs and services (ASCA, 2004d). The purpose of the evaluation is to determine the extent to which program goals are being met and provide information that will lead to program improvement. Goals that are not clearly articulated in measurable, observable terms are difficult to monitor. However, if the program design incorporates student competencies, evaluation will be a fairly straightforward activity.

Various types and forms of evaluation strategies are used to assess the counseling program; to determine the effects of the program on students, teachers, and parents; to monitor the use of time; and to provide evidence of the value of the counseling program. In other words, evaluation helps determine effectiveness, efficiency, and worth. Just as with the other parts of the counseling program, this assessment needs to be integrated into the total school program. Questions to be answered through the evaluation include "What have our students achieved?" and "What did we do to help our students achieve?" Blum (1998) lists the following steps for the evaluation process:

- Assess the needs of students, parents, and teachers each year.
- Identify program goals and student competencies.
- Design the program to achieve the goals and learning objectives.
- Implement the program.
- Measure ongoing activities and assess progress toward goals.
- Maintain, modify, or discard program strategies and activities based on the results of these evaluation activities.

The accountability system described in the ASCA Model (2003a) consists of several parts. First, results reports are produced to describe how students are different as a result of participating in the school counseling program. Such reports include information about the school counseling program and its activities. For these reports, counselors collect short, intermediate, and long-term data to measure immediate results of a program activity as well as longer term results. The data collected for these reports assist counselors in identifying those program activities that lead to the achievement of stated goals and those that do not.

Thus, counselors and the leadership team are able to make corrections and use measurable outcomes to demonstrate program efficacy. Second, school counselors' performance is evaluated based on the basic standards of practice expected of those implementing a comprehensive program (ASCA, 2003a). Many states have in place a performance-based assessment for all certificated personnel. These evaluations should be based on the basic standards of practice and should also include self-assessment measures or procedures. Third, the system for accountability includes a program audit designed to facilitate a continuous process of evaluation and improvement. The program audit leads to improvement that is evident in improvements in results.

SUMMARY

Effective school counseling programs are comprehensive, purposeful, and focused on student competencies. These programs support the school mission, are designed to help all students, and are based on developmental theory. Professional school counselors lead program development by recognizing growth processes as well as limiting processes and by working with others in a five-phase process of discussion, awareness, design, implementation, and evaluation.

ASCA has developed a four-part program that may serve as a model for schools that are committed to and wish to implement a comprehensive developmental school counseling program. The ASCA Model program is built on a solid foundation and includes systems for delivery, management, and accountability. The ASCA Model incorporates the best thinking and practices in school counseling, such as those previously articulated by Gysbers and Henderson, Myrick, and many others about whom you read in Chapter 1. To fully implement such a model, counselors use the skills described in Chapter 3.

PORTFOLIO COMPONENTS

1. Reflect on an experience when you participated in an effort to effect change in an organization or system. How did you react emotionally? How did you react behaviorally? Did your response lead to facilitation or blocking of change efforts? How might you use this experience to identify skills and behaviors you need to develop to become an agent of change? What are those skills?
2. Taking the themes identified in Chapter 3 (advocacy, leadership, collaboration, systemic change) describe ways that the presence or absence of each theme may either facilitate or block progress with the type of planning described in this chapter.
3. For a hypothetical school in which you are the counselor, develop a graphic representation of the model program you would implement. Include the ASCA Model elements and references or symbols that represent the specific beliefs and the mission of a program in which you would hope to work.

Data-Driven School Counseling Programs: Management and Accountability

USING DATA FOR CONTINUOUS IMPROVEMENT

Ms. West and Mrs. Jones, along with the KCES leadership team, recognize that the full implementation of the program they have outlined may take 3 or more years. They have agreed that one of their most important objectives is to establish a data-driven program with clear methods for demonstrating both program and counselor effectiveness. The work of the leadership team over the next few months will focus on these efforts. To maximize their ability to be helpful in establishing the management and accountability systems for the program, the team members determine that they need more education about the types of data used, management of the data, and the types of results for which they are aiming. Ms. West agrees to identify someone with expertise in evaluation and assessment to provide the necessary training. She turns to her former program evaluation professor, Dr. Shannon, who agrees to assist the team.

Dr. Shannon established the following objectives for his consultation with the group based on the needs described by Ms. West. First, team members will be able to articulate the need for a data-driven school counseling program. Since they have already gathered data about the characteristics of the student population and community (see previous chapter), Dr. Shannon will provide information that should help the team recognize additional types of data that when collected and disaggregated will lead to the identification of students who are not fully participating in the learning community. Next, the team will be able to distinguish between different types of results reports and describe the data used to compile the reports. Finally, the team will be able to use results from an annual program audit to continually plan for program improvement.

The emphasis on accountability—demonstrating what counselors do to make an observable difference in the academic success of students—is one of the most important professional discussions taking place today (Gysbers, 2004). However, the importance of demonstrating counselor and or program efficacy is not a new concept. Gysbers points out that the emphasis on accountability for school counselors was expressed as early as the 1920s and has continued throughout the life of the profession. Demands for accountability can be met through programs that are data-driven and results based (Lapan, 2001). School counselors have access through schools' computerized databases to information typically available in students' cumulative records. These databases make it much easier to monitor students' progress today than in the past when most records were only available in individual hard copy folders stored in locked file cabinets.

Results-based school counseling programs are systematically planned based on identified student needs or competencies and are evaluated on the basis of whether the desired results are achieved. The ASCA (2003a) model provides a framework through which school counselors may demonstrate program effectiveness. The well-articulated competencies expected of students in three developmental domains suggest the "results" to be achieved by all students. Additional program objectives are developed to address the needs of students who may be at risk for academic failure or who may experience educational inequities.

After reading and discussing this chapter, you should be able to

- Identify data sources that might be used to identify students who are at risk for academic failure.
- Use data to plan interventions for students who are at risk for academic failure.
- Collect and use data to determine how students change as a result of participating in the school counseling program.
- Describe how to conduct a program audit.
- Participate in an annual school counselor performance evaluation process.

USE OF DATA

Visit the U.S. Department of Education Web page http://www.ed.gov/index.jhtml and read about evidence-based practices in education. Discuss with your classmates how the information you read relates to leading and managing data-driven school counseling programs.

Dr. Shannon opens his first session with the leadership team by providing an opportunity for attendees to ask questions about what they hope to learn from him. One member of the leadership team asks how changing their current program from one that responds to needs as they arise to one that is data-driven will result in improvements. Dr. Shannon responds to the question by referring to the accountability system described by ASCA (2003a). Data may be used to demonstrate that the school counseling program objectives are being achieved; to monitor student progress; to identify areas where change is needed and create the impetus for that change; to engage all concerned parties in decision making based on data rather than speculation or intuition; to challenge the status quo; to uncover and expose access and equity issues; to direct resources where they are most needed; and to support proposals for program expansion (i.e., grants). This approach to research is typically described as an "action" orientation and differs from the traditional purpose of extending knowledge, although that certainly may be accomplished as well (Stringer, 2004). Action research involves gathering data related to a specific problem, examining the data, and reflecting on the effectiveness of current practices and behaviors, and, based on new understandings, changing current practices and behaviors to those more likely to result in change. Additionally, measuring the impact of interventions and programs to provide evidence of their effectiveness is an important part of accountability.

A second question for Dr. Shannon concerns the types of data that the leadership team might be asked to consider. Most of the members describe themselves as competent in their own work and life circumstances, but somewhat uncertain about analyzing and using data. They envision large computer programs, statistical manipulations, and reams of paper with difficult-to-interpret results. Dr. Shannon assures team members that the data involved are those that school counselors have been prepared to collect, analyze, and interpret. The role of the team is to consider the student needs identified through the analysis of data, help establish program goals, and identify resources needed to meet goals. The types of data with which they will be working include achievement-related data used to monitor student progress, data related to standards and competency, and program evaluation data (ASCA, 2003a). They will look at data that is disaggregated or separated by some type of category. They will want to amass longitudinal data to look at trends across time. Additionally, they need to cross-tabulate some data to see how groups compare across selected criteria. The team decides to schedule additional meetings during which they will focus of the various types of data.

> The ethical standards from ASCA (2004c) state that school counselors are responsible both to the school and to the community in determining and promoting the counselor's role and function in meeting the needs of those served (see Appendix C, Standard D1d). Thus identifying student needs and using that information to design a counseling program is an ethical imperative.

Monitoring Student Progress

Student progress can be measured through achievement data such as standardized and specialty test results, grade point averages, promotion and retention rates, and subject-area proficiency (e.g., reading on, above, or below grade level) (ASCA, 2003a). Other achievement-related data include enrollment patterns in challenging courses, discipline referrals, attendance patterns and rates, parental involvement in school, involvement in extracurricular activities, rates of use of controlled substances, and rates of suspension or expulsion from school. A question arises from the leadership team. "Once we collect these various types of data, what do we do with the information?" Ms. West responds, "The first thing we want to do is look over the data in aggregate form to see what patterns emerge. For example, we will identify our overall rates of absenteeism; the percentage of students in our school who are reading at, above, or below grade level; the percentage of students who were suspended both in and out of school; and so forth. Then we will examine these results more closely to see which students are most likely to be absent, reading below grade level, spending time out of class due to discipline problems, et cetera. We identify students who are disproportionately represented in these categories by disaggregating the data we have collected. That is, we examine the data by groups of those demographic variables that the professional literature suggests are most likely to experience gaps in achievement."

The Achievement Gap

Although numerous initiatives have been directed at reforming public education to ensure that no child is left behind, the 21st century began with gaps in student achievement by income, race, ethnicity, gender, and disability (Johnson, 2002; Grant & Sleeter, 2001). Explanations for the gaps along these dimensions are varied. Some students (e.g., students with disabilities) may experience low expectations or the assumption of educators that they cannot learn (Danielson, 2002). Aronson (2004) cautions that students (e.g., students of

The National Education Association (NEA) has prepared a multi-themed guide to help educators learn about the differences in student achievement and ways to improve academic success. That guide, *C.A.R.E.: Strategies for Closing the Achievement Gaps* is available electronically and can be used for planning programs focusing on eliminating bias in the school community (National Education Association, 2005).

With your classmates, discuss the school counselor's role in demonstrating high expectations for students.

color) may be negatively affected by the threat associated with stereotyping. He contends that in an evaluative situation a member of a group that has a negative reputation (e.g., being less intelligent) adds stress not experienced by groups of students who are not threatened by stereotyping. That additional stress may threaten students' sense of competence, feeling of belonging, and trust in people necessary for optimal intellectual performance and motivation (Aronson & Steele, 2005).

Adelman and Taylor (2006) advise that not all barriers to learning can be explained by considering either environmental causes (e.g., poverty) or factors in the person (e.g., disability). They propose a transactional model for understanding the complex causes of learning difficulties that consider the person, the environment, and the interaction of the person and the environment. For example, the student of color (personal variable) does not experience negative consequences of stereotyping because of his or her race. The negative consequences are from the interaction of his or her race and the dominant views of society held toward his or her racial or ethnic group. Therefore, one cannot understand the barriers to learning encountered by black or Latino youth without considering the attitudes, policies, and practices in the school (environmental variable) that have a negative impact on these students. Regardless of the reasons for inequities, the consequences of low achievement are far reaching. For example, Mortenson (2000) describes some of the barriers that limit students' access to postsecondary education opportunities (see Figure 5.1). The lifelong implications of limited access to education are further detailed in Figure 5.2 (U.S. Census Bureau, 2004).

All people connected to school must be aware of factors that reduce the quality of education and must strive to create environments of equity and promise for all. Dimmitt (2003) completed a study of academic failure in a high school that could serve as a template for collecting information related to academic success and failure in any school. Dimmitt encourages expanded conversations about the impact of race, gender, and socioeconomic status on academic achievement in all schools. Data, disaggregated by demographic and performance variables, are intended to help educators identify policies and practices in the school or system that negatively affect equity (Stone & Dahir, 2004). As she begins a discussion of these factors, Ms. West emphasizes that the school counselors' role is to challenge the beliefs associated with these factors that limit students' options and design interventions, challenge policies, and advocate for changes that will lead to increased options and opportunities. Data will allow the counselors to determine what is really happening at KCES, as compared to what most believe is happening. Consider the pervasive belief that socioeconomic status and color determine a student's ability to learn (Stone & Dahir, 2004). KCES has consistently proclaimed a commitment to high expectations and equity for all students. A review of retention rates, disciplinary referrals and action, and course placements by race and socioeconomic status will provide the school counselors, faculty, and

FIGURE 5.1 Barriers to Postsecondary Education

Academic Course-taking in high school Study skills Commitment	***Cultural*** Aspirations Language
Financial Type of financial aid Amount of aid	***Functioning*** Learning disabilities Behavioral disorders Health-related disabilities
Geographic Place bound Cultural divides	***Institutional*** Admissions criteria Academic and social environment
Information Technology Computer/Internet access and use	***K–12 Education Reforms*** High-stakes testing
Parents Troubled families Uninformed parents Preoccupied parents	***Social*** Community values Peer pressures

Source: From "Postsecondary Education Opportunity," by T. Mortenson, 2000, *The Mortenson Research Seminar on Public Policy Analysis of Opportunity for Postsecondary Education, 92,* p. 11. Reprinted with permission.

FIGURE 5.2 Earnings Outlook by Educational Attainment

Mean Earnings for Persons 18 Years and Older, 2003								
Less than 9th Grade	HS Dropout	HS Graduate	Some College	Associate's Degree	Bachelor's Degree	Master's Degree	Doctoral Degree	Professional Degree
$18,978	$18,622	$27,915	$29,533	$35,958	$51,207	$62,512	$88,471	$115,212

Source: U.S. Census Bureau, Current Population Survey, 2004 Annual Social and Economic Supplement.

administration with information about the extent to which their expressed ideals are being realized.

Gender

In promising news the National Center for Educational Statistics (Bae, Choy, Geddes, Sable, & Snyder, 2005), reports that females are now doing as well as or better than males on many indicators of achievement and educational attainment. According to this recent report, the gaps that once existed between male and female students in math and science have either been eliminated or significantly reduced. Some fields of study still attract fewer females, but there have been substantial changes in the past 30 years. Robinson and Howard-Hamilton (2000) have suggested that girls' school performance exceeds boys' in speaking, reading, and counting in the early grades, but by the time they graduate from high school, females perform more poorly than males in mathematics and science. Although this circumstance still exists, the latest figures indicate that the differences are marginal (Conlin, 2003). According to recent reports, by the time they reach eighth grade, girls are more likely to say they like or that they are competent in science or math than boys (Bae et al., 2005).

Unfortunately, there is less reason for optimism about boys' school performance. They are one and one-half years behind girls in reading and writing (U.S. Department of Education, 2000). Boys earn 70% of low grades (Ds and Fs), are 90% of discipline referrals, and represent 80% of dropouts. Some proposed explanations for gender differences in achievement include race, biology, sociology, self-esteem, and attitudes toward certain topics (Brusselmans-Dehairs, Hencry, Beller, & Gafni, 1997). The International Association for the Evaluation of Educational Achievement conducted a cross-national comparative study in many areas and concluded that the "gender differences in ability and achievement are mainly due to societal and cultural influences and not to biological causes" (cited in Brusselmans-Dehairs et al., 1997, p. 19). Others refer to the structural and functional differences in the brain and the failure of schools to recognize and fulfill these gender-specific needs (Gurian & Stevens, 2004). Whatever the underlying causes, it seems prudent for the school counselors to examine performance data on male students separately from female to identify the unique needs of both groups.

Race/Ethnicity

The National Assessment of Educational Progress (NAEP) compiles achievement data for school students across the nation. Scores in geography, mathematics, reading, science, and history are presented with breakdowns for various groups within the student population. Too often data demonstrate the significant gaps in achievement found across ethnic groups (http://nces.ed.gov/nationsreportcard/naepdata/). Consider the following comparisons:

- Nationally 11% of all students were retained for at least one grade. However, the numbers across ethnicities varied with 9.3% of white students, 18% of Native American students, 13.2% of Latino students, and 17.5% of African American students being retained (Children's Defense Fund, 2005a).
- In 2003, of the 8% of 16- to 19-year-olds who had dropped out of school, 17% were Latinos compared with 6% of white teens and 10% of African American and 10% of American Indian teens (Annie E. Casey Foundation, 2005).

- White students had higher scores in reading and mathematics than black and Latino students at every grade level (NCES, 2005a).
- Children of color and low-income students are more likely to be taught by less experienced teachers, to be in high poverty schools, to be in larger classes, and to have out-of-field teachers (Aronson, 2004).
- Black, Latino, and Native American youths with disabilities have 67% more likelihood than white children to be removed from school on grounds of dangerousness (Children's Defense Fund, 2005b).

Understanding whether such disparities exist at KCES and the upper-level schools attended by its graduating fifth graders will provide the leadership team and other KCES constituents with a clear picture of imbalances that need to be addressed.

Income

Rothstein (2004) proposes that economic class background relates to student achievement everywhere. Socioeconomic status correlates with school achievement and completion more than any other variable (Conger, Conger, & Elder, 1997; Lee & Burkam, 2002). Poverty is not a "cause" of underachievement, teen pregnancy, risk of dropping out, and other problems, but there is a significant relationship (Adelman & Taylor, 2006). Children who are from poor families typically have fewer opportunities to develop the readiness skills for learning than their more financially advantaged peers. Additionally, these children are more likely to live in declining, violent neighborhoods where additional stressors affect their adjustment to school.

Currently over 17 million children between the ages of 6 and 17 (38% of our young people) live in low-income families (National Center for Children Living in Poverty, 2005). The greater proportion of Latino (62%) and black (60%) children face those economic problems than white (26%). Approximately 20% of all elementary children have problems reading. However, 60% to 70% of those children from poor families and those with limited English skills experience reading difficulties (Ademlan & Taylor, 2006). Further, parents from low-income homes are less likely to be involved in schools by volunteering, serving on committees, or attending school events (Child Trends, 2003). To determine what change initiatives need to be introduced at KCES, Ms. West and colleagues need to understand what relationships exist between their students' socioeconomic status and their performance.

Children with Disabilities

Other children who have barriers to success are those who have difficulty performing everyday activities, such as communicating, moving, or taking care of themselves, or who have learning difficulties. These difficulties include specific learning disabilities, speech or language impairments, mental retardation, serious emotional disturbance, hearing impairments, orthopedic impairments, other health impairments, visual impairments, autism, and multiple disabilities. The numbers of students served in programs for the disabled is increasing slowly (U.S. Department of Education, 2004). During the 1991–92 school year, 11.6% of students were served in these programs compared with 13.4% in 2001–02. Some of the rise may be attributed to the increase in numbers of children identified as learning disabled. By the late 1990s, approximately 50% of students identified as needing special education services were labeled as learning disabled (LD) (Adelman & Taylor, 2006). Lyon (2002) reports that reading and behavior problems led to a substantial number of referrals leading to LD classifications (cited in Adelman & Taylor, 2006).

Statistical data maintained by the National Center for Educational Statistics (2005b) is disaggregated to provide more information about students classified as learning disabled. Males were classified as having one of these disabilities at almost twice the rate of females (11% of males vs. 6% of females) (NCES, 2005b). Males represented 67% of all children classified as having one of these three categories of disability in 2000, and they made up a larger percentage than females classified as having an emotional disturbance (78%), a specific learning disability (67%), or mental retardation (58%). Variations among those labeled LD also exist by race/ethnicity. While black children represented 17% of public school students in 2000, they made up 22% of all children classified as LD. Black and American Indian children were both overrepresented in this disabled population. In comparison, only 8% each of all white and Hispanic children and 3% of all Asian/Pacific Islander children enrolled in public schools were classified as disabled. Black public school students were also disproportionately represented in each of the three disability categories: they made up 33% of mentally retarded children, 27% of children with an emotional disturbance, and 18% of children with a specific disability. There is little disagreement among professionals that students referred for special services need assistance. However, there is much debate about the nature of their problems and whether the LD classification is a mislabeling of other learning or behavioral difficulties (Adelman & Taylor, 2006). Ms. West and Mrs. Jones are involved in the interactive team established at KCES to address the needs of students who demonstrate difficulties in learning. They are most eager to review their placement patterns along gender and race/ethnicity variables in order to identify groups of students who may be overrepresented in special education.

The leadership team now has a better idea of how performance data examined across demographic variables may be used to identify students who experience limited access and opportunity to educational advantages. As well, these data may enlighten the entire school community about existing policies and practices that maintain these inequities. Once the barriers to learning have been identified, the team is in a better position to develop goals and strategies to assist the affected students in capitalizing on their strengths and overcoming barriers to achievement. The overall goal is to develop an action plan designed to systematically reduce the achievement gap at KCE until it is eliminated. Dr. Shannon offers to assist the team in using one of their data-related discoveries to develop an action plan. Fifth grade boys at KCES are referred for an average of three disciplinary infractions per semester. The average rate for all fifth grade students combined is one referral per semester. For all boys in all grades, the average number of referrals per semester is one. The result of these referrals for fifth grade boys is out-of-class time spent in the administrative offices, in-school suspension, alternative school programs, or suspension. Out-of-class time increases the likelihood that fifth grade boys will fall behind their peers who are not missing class. A review of performance data for fifth grade boys who have received three or more discipline referrals in a single semester reveals that they are performing below grade level in reading and math. Based on these data, the team develops an action plan to reduce the number of discipline referrals and improve reading and math performance for selected students (see Figure 5.3).

Standards and Competency-Related Data

The second type of data the team considers is that related to standards and competencies. The KCES team has already made a commitment to implement the ASCA National Model, so they have already identified goals for each student in their program in academic, personal/social, and career development domains.

FIGURE 5.3 Action Plan for Closing the Achievement Gap

Action Plan for Fifth Grade Boys							
Expected Outcomes	**Developmental Domain**	**ASCA Student Competency**	**Program Activities**	**Number of Students**	**Evaluation Method**	**Start/ End**	**Coun- selor**
Decrease average number of discipline referrals to one or fewer per semester.	Personal/ Social A and B	A1: Acquire self-knowledge B1: Self-knowledge application	Group Counseling: Self-management and conflict resolution	15*	Comparison of discipline records for group participants**	1/06– 3/15	West
Increase grade earned in math and language arts by at least one letter grade per grading session (two per semester).	Academic A and B	A2: Acquire skills for improving learning B1: Improve learning	Peer Tutoring: Math and Language Arts		Comparison of grades for tutees**		Jones

*Perception data; **Results data

Divide into small groups of three or four and agree upon a state in which you all might like to practice school counseling upon your graduation. Review state documents such as those described above and compare these to the national model competencies. Identify those that overlap and those that are unique to each set of standards. Create a table of your findings to share with other groups.

Additionally, the ASCA Model includes specific student competencies that related to each of the national standards (goals). However, the ASCA national standards are not the only ones KCES students are expected to master. State documents such as state education rules and regulations, state guidelines for school counseling programs, state board of education policies, academic content standards, and state accreditation standards also specify core skills and competencies expected of students in each state (ASCA, 2003a). In addition to state standards, there may be other pertinent standards to which a school system has committed. For example, the National Career Development Guidelines (America's Career Resource Network, 2005) offer goals in three different domains that are designed to help students acquire the personal, educational, and career skills they need to be successful after completion of high school. As you can see, these three domains correspond to the developmental framework of the ASCA Model.

The exercise you and your classmates have been asked to complete will also be completed by members of the KCES leadership team. ASCA refers to this as one of the activities performed as part of a curriculum crosswalk (ASCA, 2003a). The purpose of the crosswalk is to identify all of the competencies expected of students in the three specified domains; identify at what grade levels these competencies will be addressed; and specify the program activities the school counselor, teachers, or other school personnel will use to implement the identified strategies. Most of the programming associated with the crosswalk will be delivered through the guidance curriculum and individual planning components of the school counseling program. More information about these two delivery systems may be found in Chapters 7 and 8 of this book.

Each competency or set of related competencies are measurable. Let us take another example from the KCES data. The team discovered that students in grades 3 through 5 turned in their assigned homework at a rate of 70%. They wish to increase the average rate of homework satisfactorily completed and turned in to 90%. They believe that the ASCA competency to be addressed is A:B26 understanding the relationship between classroom performance and success in school (ASCA, 2003a). The action plan for achieving this goal will be developed by Ms. West and Mrs. Jones. Competency-related data measure the students' mastery of the competencies specified in the school counseling program. Ms. West and Mrs. Jones will know whether the intervention described in the action plan you developed was successful if 90% of students satisfactorily complete and turn in homework assignments.

Using Figure 5.3 for an example, develop an action plan for helping all students master this competency.

Program Evaluation

School counselors must be able to demonstrate that the work they do has a direct impact on student achievement. To do this, ASCA (2003a) advocates a multipronged approach to program evaluation that involves three types of data: process, perception, and results. These data are used to measure program effectiveness, to ensure that programs are implemented and that every student is served, and to improve services and programs (Brott, 2005). The first type of data, process, involves keeping track of what the counselor does, for whom, and when. In Figure 5.3, we can see that the counselors delivered or coordinated group counseling and peer tutoring services for 15 students between January 6 and March 15. Other examples of process data might include such things as:

- Conducted eight study skills groups, five sessions each, that included a total of 64 students
- Delivered classroom guidance on conflict resolution to 1,000 students in grades 3 through 5
- Met with 200 high school students and 300 parents to review and revise 4-year plans during the first semester

The second type, perception data, refers to knowledge gained, attitudes or beliefs held, and competencies achieved (ASCA, 2003a). Pre–post measures, skill demonstrations, and evaluation forms are typical types of measures of perception data. For example, KCES fifth grade students are expected to use a decision-making and problem-solving model. They are taught such a model and provided an opportunity for supervised practice during classroom guidance sessions in the fall term of the fifth grade. To determine whether the competency has been mastered, all fifth grade students will be provided a typical "case" in which they are asked to demonstrate the application of the model to make a decision about how to spend their designated study time during the week before standardized tests are administered. This evaluative activity will take place approximately one month prior to the administration of the district-mandated achievement tests.

> Use this example to design a brief case and an instrument that will allow you to determine whether fifth grade students have mastered this competency.

The third type of data, results, assesses the ways that students are different as a result of participating in the school counseling program (ASCA, 2003a). Results data come from many sources and may include such things as attendance improvements, decreases in discipline referrals for a specific issue (e.g., tardiness), increased numbers of students of color enrolled in higher level courses, improved graduation rates, and lower dropout rates.

The three types of data described may be used to document the immediate, intermediate, and long-term impact of the school counseling program (ASCA, 2003a). Immediate data refer to the evaluation of the impact of interventions or activities on participants (Brott, 2005). For example, Ms. West has identified a group of fourth grade students who are at risk for failing science because they consistently receive grades of zero for failure to complete homework assignments. She plans to conduct a six-session small group with the specific goal of completing and turning in homework assignments. She will collect pre- and post-data to identify changes in the studying-related knowledge, attitudes, and skills of fourth grade students who participate in the group. These data represent what the students know, believe, and can do immediately after the group compared with what they knew, believed, and did before participating in the group.

Further, Ms. West will assess students' ability to apply acquired knowledge and skills by following up after the next grading period. Specifically, Ms. West will ask the fourth grade science teachers to share with her the homework grades for students who participated in the group. These data, intermediate, will provide Ms. West information about the percentage of students who are completing and turning in homework assignments over a short period of time.

Long-range data collected annually include but are not limited to attendance, graduation and suspension rates, parent participation in planned activities, improved performance on grades, and increases in scores on standardized tests. Additionally, data collected for immediate and intermediate use may be compiled and used to determine impact over time (Brott, 2005). Long-range data provide specific information school counselors and the leadership team can use to identify program priorities, problems that need attention, and areas where improvements are evident. Let's consider an example of long-range data collected for 2004 for students at KCES (see Table 5.1). The data in this table provide the KCES leadership team with a baseline for identifying problem areas in student performance. By converting the raw numbers to percentages, the students who are disproportionately represented among those experiencing academic difficulty will be easily identified. This information is then used to establish program goals and develop an action plan to achieve the goals. The same data will be collected and

> With one or two classmates, choose one of the performance indicators, convert the numbers to percentages according to race/ethnicity, and identify a specific group of students you wish to target for improvements in the selected performance area. Using the action plan in Figure 5.3 as an example, develop a plan to respond to this concern.

TABLE 5.1   Long-Range Results Data Collection Form: KCES Student Progress Data 2004

		African American	White	Latino	Total
Number of Students		**309**	**518**	**16**	**843**
Retained in 2004	M	62	26	5	93
	F	10	5	2	17
Promoted in 2004	M	77	187	4	268
	F	150	300	5	455
Below Grade Level: Reading	M	196	100	8	304
	F	48	48	4	100
Below Grade Level: Math	M	88	60	4	152
	F	30	16	4	50
Absent more than 15%	M	50	40	10	100
	F	7	9	6	22
Discipline Referrals (2+ per grading period)	M	50	22	8	80
	F				9
Suspension Rates (1 or more per term)	M	10	2		12
	F				

analyzed in 2006, 2007, and 2008 to identify changes in student performance that result from program initiatives.

REPORTING AND PRESENTING DATA

School counselors are expected to report their results to the stakeholders in order to advocate for the school counseling program. Results data are key to establishing the effectiveness of one's program (ASCA, 2003a). According to ASCA (2003a) results data document

- That the program was carried out as planned.
- That each student was served.
- That developmentally appropriate interventions were used.
- The process, perception, and results data.
- The program's immediate, intermediate, and long-range impact.
- The program's effectiveness.
- The program's successes.
- The program's improvements.
- The need for system-level change when needed.

ASCA (2003a) also suggests that results reports include information for each counselor that includes the grade levels served, content areas of lessons delivered and the curriculum or materials used, the numbers of students receiving lessons (process data), results of pre–post tests documenting knowledge gained (perception data), longer term results of the intervention such as the impact of behavior or achievement (results data), and the implications of the results for the school counseling program.

Additionally, results from an annual program audit performed by the school counselors determine the extent to which they have implemented the ASCA National Model (2003a) by program element. The program audit results are part of an ongoing data collection process leading to program improvement. The program audit developed by ASCA leads to the identification of major strengths of the program, areas where improvement is needed, and the establishment of short- and long-term goals.

SCHOOL COUNSELOR PERFORMANCE EVALUATION

The performance of all personnel involved in delivering the school counseling program is also evaluated annually. All states have a requirement for the performance evaluation of educational personnel. Some states evaluate counselors in the same way that teachers are evaluated (ASCA, 2003a). However, others have evaluation instruments that more specifically assess the school counselor's performance in the light of his or her responsibilities. To be helpful in planning for improvement, instruments used to evaluate school counselors need to include specific standards or competencies the counselors are expected to demonstrate. Examples include one's ability to plan, deliver, and evaluate a

Visit the Alabama State Department of Education Web site and view the multifaceted evaluation system for school counselors. http://www.alabamapepe.com/specialty.htm#

school counseling program; competence in each of the delivery systems; ability to work effectively with constituents; and demonstration of key skills in counseling, consultation, leadership, and advocacy. Counselors are expected to use the results of performance evaluations as data to help them identify strengths and areas for improvement. Professional development goals are a natural outgrowth of an annual performance evaluation.

SUMMARY

The accountability movement in education has led to renewed focus on the need for school counselors to provide evidence that their interventions and programs have an impact on the academic achievement of students. Additionally, documentation of gaps in achievement for specific groups of students has all educators renewing their commitment to alleviating inequities in education. To eliminate these gaps in achievement, school counselors, along with their other colleagues in education, are using data to identify needs, set goals, and implement interventions for which there is evidence of effectiveness.

School counselors use computerized student databases to disaggregate data related to achievement, attendance, discipline, and so forth to develop action plans that are designed to close the gap. Additionally, such data are used to uncover inequities in opportunity and placement that are maintained by existing policies. Once identified, counselors advocate for system level change to ensure that policies are fair and equitable for all students.

Additionally, counselors collect, analyze, and use three different types of data to support and inform their efforts. Process, perception, and results data document the number and types of services delivered; the numbers of students, parents, and professional consultees who receive services; the impact of the services provided; and the ways that students change as a result of participation in the program. School counselors conduct annual program audits to determine the extent to which programs have been implemented and to identify strengths and weaknesses to be addressed in future plans. Finally, school counselors undergo an annual performance evaluation to identify their strengths and weaknesses with respect to the responsibilities of their jobs.

PORTFOLIO COMPONENTS

1. Reflect on your own experiences in junior and senior high school. Were you or any of your friends or acquaintances in one of the groups of students at risk for gaps in achievement discussed in this chapter? If so, how were your experiences or those that you observed among your peers consistent with or different from the descriptions you read here? How did the policies or practices at your school either maintain or eliminate barriers for students at risk for the gap?

2. As you read this chapter, what thoughts and feelings did you have about your role in discovering and addressing inequities in education? What are some of

your concerns/weaknesses? How might you prepare yourself to overcome these barriers? What are some strengths you bring to these issues?

3. Based on the information in this chapter, develop a list of interview questions you might ask a potential employer that would help you understand what particular students may be most advantaged/disadvantaged in their school and system.

C H A P T E R 6

Facilitating Academic Transitions

PROMOTING DEVELOPMENT: KINDERGARTEN THROUGH GRADUATION

As a result of their year-end program audit, the school counselors in Brewster County determined that they needed to improve their programming designed to facilitate smooth transitions for students as they progress through their academic careers. Additionally, they wish to use their student progress data to identify specific students who are at increased risk for academic, career, or personal social difficulties due to failure to successfully transition from one level to another. The counselors decide to meet in grade-level teams over the next few months to accomplish the following goals.

- Elementary counselors, Ms. Sara and Mr. Goldberg, will identify the transitions common to children as they begin their academic careers, progress through elementary school, and move into the middle school. Based on these issues, they will identify the relevant student outcomes already included in the systemwide school counseling program and add outcome statements for any issues that are not currently being addressed. Finally, they will specify the "who, what, and when" of activities related to achieving the specified outcomes.

- Middle school counselors, Ms. Hernandez, Mr. Al-Mabuk, and Ms. Clark, will identify the

academic transitions most closely associated with middle schools. They will identify the relevant student outcomes already included in the systemwide school counseling program and add outcome statements for any issues that are not currently being addressed. Strategies and interventions to meet the unique needs of these students will be articulated and placed on the annual program calendar.

- High school counselors, Ms. Moriarty, Mr. Coopersmith, Mr. Brown, Ms. Beim, Ms. Moore, and Ms. Lindsey, will accomplish each of the tasks proposed by the other two groups for the high school counseling program. Additionally, these counselors will be concerned with the student outcomes associated with successful transition out of the secondary school.

Finally, the counselors agree that they need to work across grade levels to identify the groups of students who seem to have difficulty making transitions. To that end, they schedule an additional systemwide meeting to discuss the problems they consistently see among the groups of students who do not demonstrate the expected outcomes associated with successful transitions. Based on these descriptions, they will consider responsive services options at each grade level for specified students.

During their academic careers, students experience predictable physical, cognitive, and personal/social changes. School counselors incorporate their knowledge about these changes and the likely needs of students experiencing them into their programs. Specifically, they plan programs that will help students transition smoothly from one grade level and life stage to the next. The consensus among professionals in school counseling is that the challenges and tasks students experience may be categorized as personal/social, career, and academic development.

After reading and discussing this chapter, you should be able to

- Identify the developmental issues and student competencies associated with transitions from home to elementary school, elementary to middle school, middle school to high school, and high school to a variety of postsecondary options.
- State the issues and competencies as student and program outcomes and articulate when and how related program activities will be implemented at each grade level.
- Identify students for whom the "typical" academic transitions may be experienced as "atypical" challenges.
- Identify at least three strategies to determine whether program objectives and student outcomes related to facilitating academic transitions have been met.

CHILD AND ADOLESCENT DEVELOPMENT

Developmental theory influences all parts of a comprehensive school counseling program. Counselors use their thorough understanding of life stages and contexts to shape the span and sequence of their program activities to facilitate personal/social, career, and academic development. Specifically, the concepts of psychosocial development (Erikson, 1963), cognitive development (Piaget, 1954), interpersonal perspective taking (Selman, 1980), career development (Super, 1994), and moral development (Kohlberg, 1969) map a predictable sequence of growth in those areas. Quintana (1998) describes four levels of children's understanding ethnicity and race. Other theorists such as Fowler (1981) on spiritual development, Gilligan (1982) on moral development, and Helms (1994) on ethnic-identity development help explain the ways circumstances affect behavior. Bronfenbrenner (1979) suggests that the context in which a youngster exists both has an impact on the child and is changed by the young person, and Vygotsky (1978) focuses on ways to use a person's social interactions as teaching zones. Bowlby (1988) discusses children, their attachment to adults, and the implications for their development. Havighurst (1972) outlines the tasks to be mastered at different ages. The theories give a framework for describing children and adolescents and for explaining their behaviors (Tharinger & Lambert, 1999). These works also provide school counselors with the vocabulary, concepts, and research to support the school counseling program's process (Paisley, 2001).

Although many of these theorists concentrate on understanding the intrapersonal components of development, the interaction between the person's environment and the person's development cannot be underestimated. Listing all the possible variables that influence a child's maturation would be a demanding task. The most essential thing to remember is that the person's level and type of development will influence their response to needs, tasks, and situational stressors. Figure 6.1 includes only a few of those potentially significant interaction factors.

According to Tharinger and Lambert (1999) the integration of development theories generates six general principles of the developing child. The children are

FIGURE 6.1 Developmental Interactions

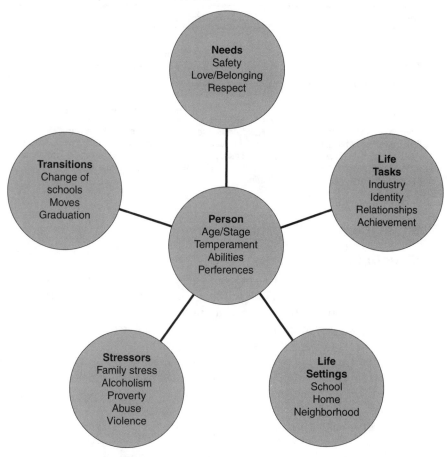

active agents in their own development. The interaction between the child and the environment is complicated and reciprocal. Development includes qualitative changes, which relate to new phenomena such as racial identity, as well as quantitative changes, which incorporates the amount or degree of behavior such as becoming more efficient or consistent. These authors discuss later development being dependent on previous changes. They examine the assumption that early competence results in success in subsequent tasks. The fifth principle addresses the effects of factors of vulnerability and of protection on development. Finally the authors propose that responding to developmental changes presents an optimistic process, particularly if those responses are planned for times of transition.

At each level, our school counselors will review the developmental tasks of their students as a foundation for their programmatic plan for the transitions all of those young people will encounter. The counselors will concentrate their efforts on assisting young people to reach the target behaviors rather than the problem behaviors listed in Table 6.1.

TABLE 6.1 Potential Outcomes of Developmental Interactions

Target Behaviors	Problem Behaviors
Social competence	Teen pregnancy
Problem solving	Substance abuse
Autonomy	Violent/delinquent behaviors
Having a purpose in life	Eating disorders
Finding meaning in life	Risky sexual behavior
Habits of wellness	Self-harming behavior

Source: From *Counseling Children and Adolescents*, 3rd edition, by A. Vernon, 2004, Denver, CO: Love Publishing. Copyright 2004 by Love Publishing. Adapted with permission; and *At-Risk Youth: A Comprehensive Response,* 3rd edition, by J. J. McWhirter, B. T. McWhirter, E. H. McWhirter, and R.J. McWhirter, 2004, Belmont, CA: Brooks-Cole. Adapted with permission from Wadsworth Publishing.

ELEMENTARY SCHOOL COUNSELING

Developmental Tasks

Elementary school counseling programs are integrally linked with the developmental tasks of early and middle childhood. Specifically, children from 6 to 11 years old are learning the physical skills needed to play ordinary games. They are developing wholesome attitudes toward self and others; learning to read, write, and calculate; developing concepts necessary for everyday living; developing an understanding of right and wrong; achieving independence; and developing attitudes toward social groups and institutions (Havighurst, 1953, cited in Muro & Kottman, 1995). They can think more logically and therefore have improved their problem-solving abilities even though abstractions or expanded possibilities are still beyond their range (Vernon, 2004). They learn by questioning, exploring, and participating in guided practice (Gauvain, 2001).

Children in middle childhood begin to see themselves more complexly and have a multidimensional view of themselves (Vernon, 2004). They are moving toward an internal locus of control (Vernon & Al-Mabuk, 1995). According to Herr, Cramer, and Niles (2004), elementary age children are generalists willing to interact with an extended range of stimuli. They have not yet become as bound by social realities, stereotypes, and other constrictions that may distort someone older. Their ideas about life and their position in the world are being formed and are easily influenced by information about their competence and their options, as well as by stereotyping.

Good relationships with peers and being accepted in a group lead to a sense of competence. These associations also broaden their view of the world and their interaction skills. They learn to cooperate and to compromise. They take on roles as leaders and followers and begin to understand the viewpoints of other people. They also encounter more complex emotions such as guilt, shame, and pride and begin to realize that a person can experience more than one emotion at a time. Their reactions to events change as they age. Baker and Gerler (2004) consider this the age to help children develop attitudes and positive habits, expand their horizons, and access relevant general information. A developmentally based elementary school counseling program helps students acquire the skills and attitudes that are necessary for success in school and in life.

Additionally, the need for early identification and intervention for at-risk youth has received considerable attention in the education literature. Researchers have identified specific behavioral, situational, and attitudinal precursors to such risk factors as substance abuse, school dropout, and aggressive and violent behavior toward self or others. These precursors are often manifested during the elementary years. For example, McWhirter, McWhirter, McWhirter, and McWhirter (2004) state that students who fail to complete high school express a dislike for school and the perception that school is irrelevant to their needs; exhibit poor grades and low academic achievement; live in poverty; and feel that they do not belong in school. All four of these factors are linked to self-esteem and self-concept, a major focus of elementary school counseling programs. The seeds of hope, motivation for success, perception of self, and the behaviors that will lead to identity and commitment can be found in these early years. A school environment that pays attention to a child developing a positive attitude, making informed decisions, and knowing about one's self and about a larger world influences life success for students (Herr, Cramer, & Niles, 2004). Effectively implemented elementary school counseling programs facilitate optimal development for students and result in the identification of those students who experience barriers to their normal, healthy development.

> Consider the information you have just read about development in the elementary school years. Discuss with your peers the implications for a successful transition to middle school. Which of the developmental tasks identified seem most important to academic and social success at the next level?

Developmental Stressors

Beginning school, referred to by Broderick and Blewitt (2003) as a new frontier, is accompanied by a set of developmental transitions for children. Children spend considerable time away from their parents or other primary caretakers, navigate a new social system and peer structure, and learn a new set of rules and expectations. They are confronted with social, physical, and intellectual challenges as they attempt to make friends, play physical games, and develop skills and master academic competencies. According to Cole and Cole (1996) as children begin school they also start comparing themselves to other children. They become more critical of themselves, feel less competent, and may experience a lower sense of self-worth, a concept that develops around 8 years (Harter, 1996). They must also learn to cope with peer pressure, rejection, and approval, and conform to social standards. What happens during the transition into school may be critical to their future success. Rathus (2006) emphasizes the particular importance of this for children of low-income families who may be unable to provide the material and the emotional supports for school adjustments.

The new situations children encounter as they move through elementary school may lead to anxiety about their abilities in school performance or making friends (Vernon, 2004). They may worry about grades, failing a test, not being liked by their teachers, their appearance, and their health (Vernon, 2004). Socially, they may be concerned about things like being different from others, losing friends, being picked on, or being lonely. The desire to be perfect

> Reflecting on what you already know about the influences of socioeconomic status along with the developmental stressors discussed here, work with your classmates to identify some of the potentially negative outcomes in the three areas of development with which school counselors are concerned for elementary students. What types of disaggregated school data might you examine to test your hypotheses?

and frustration as they strive to become more independent also create stress for this age group (Porter, 1999). Other concerns may arise from situational problems such as living in poverty, growing up in an abusive home, living with an alcoholic parent, or adjusting to a divorce or remarriage. Such difficulties may add to the challenges of succeeding in elementary school. Ms. Sara and Mr. Goldberg recognize that the initial focus for transitional programming needs to be on these and other related issues in the academic and personal/social domains of student development.

Programming for Developmental Transitions

Ms. Sara and Mr. Goldberg want to identify the curricular offerings already in place to assist students with some of these challenges. Their first step is to conduct a curriculum crosswalk and to review their scope and sequence chart (Alabama State Department of Education, 2003) (Appendix D) of student competencies associated with each of their program standards to identify those that are necessary for successful transitions into and throughout the elementary school (Table 6.2). Once the competencies are specified, the ASCA developmental crosswalking tool may be used as a matrix to identify at what grade level the competencies will be addressed. Their second activity is to review the annual program activities (see Annual and Monthly Calendar) to determine whether the identified competencies are adequately addressed at the appropriate grade level. Finally, they determine what strategies will be used to identify students who fail to successfully meet the developmental challenges of elementary school and evaluate the effectiveness of the interventions currently in place for these groups of students. Based on the outcomes of these review procedures the elementary school counseling program may be revised.

> Review the student competencies in Table 6.2 and develop an annual calendar of classroom guidance topics that addresses them. Compare your ideas to those of Ms. Sara and Mr. Goldberg in their Annual and Monthly Calendar.

A review of the annual program calendar reveals that the program adequately covers these transition-related competencies for all students through the classroom guidance curriculum. However, when Ms. Sara and Mr. Goldberg reviewed disaggregated systemwide data they discovered some indicators that the transitional needs of specific children were not being met. For example, they found that children of color were disproportionately represented among students retained in kindergarten. Therefore, they believe that the transition from home to school has not been successful for these students. They are not developing the skills they need to read, write, and calculate. These academic deficits may also result in a lack of efficacy in their ability to succeed in school and a failure to bond with the school as an institution where they feel safe and successful. Additionally, they will be separated from the peers with whom they began this new experience of schooling and may doubt their ability to form new friendships. To frame their interventions for this group of students, the counselors have identified research into school readiness (Ramey & Ramey, 1999; Meisels, 1999; Kagan & Neuman, 1998).

> Discuss how the counselors might assess whether these strategies have been successful in reducing the retention rates about which they are concerned. What types of data need to be collected? In addition to collaboration and the peer program introduced by the counselors, what other interventions might be necessary? Hint: Think systemically.

The National Association for the Education of Young Children (NAEYC) (2002) endorses the position that it is the responsibility of the schools to be ready for all children and to provide whatever services are needed to help them. Ms. Sara and Mr. Goldberg are concerned that the needs of the

TABLE 6.2 Transition-Related Competencies for Elementary School Students

Grade Levels	Academic	Career	Personal/Social
K–2	• Know when and how to ask for help • Take responsibility for actions • Apply skills necessary for academic success • Understand relationships between classroom performance and school success	• Learn about traditional and nontraditional occupations • Develop awareness of abilities, skills, interests, motivations • Use time and task management skills • Understand the relationship between academic success and career success • Learn to use conflict management skill with peers and adults	• Develop positive attitudes toward self • Understand change is part of growth • Identify and express feelings • Distinguish between appropriate and inappropriate behavior • Understand the need for self-control and how to practice it • Recognize that everyone has rights and responsibilities • Recognize, respect, and appreciate individual differences • Recognize, respect, and appreciate cultural diversity • Use effective communication skills • Learn to make and keep friends • Understand consequences of decisions • Identify alternative solutions for problems • Learn about dangers of substance use and abuse • Learn techniques for managing stress and conflict
3–5	• Articulate feelings of competence and confidence as learner • Accept mistakes as essential to learning • Demonstrate how persistence and effort affect learning • Work competently alone and cooperatively with others • Share knowledge	• Work and interact cooperatively in teams • Learn to make decisions • Learn to set goals	• Demonstrate cooperative behavior in groups • Identify personal strengths and assets • Respect alternate points of view • Use decision-making and problem-solving models • Demonstrate persistence and perseverance in acquiring knowledge and skills

(Continued)

TABLE 6.2 (Continued)

Grade Levels	Academic	Career	Personal/Social
	• Become a self-directed and independent learner • Demonstrate the ability to balance school, studies, family life, and leisure activities • Understand how academic achievement enhances future opportunities		• Demonstrate ability to set boundaries • Learn to cope with peer pressure

Source: From *Comprehensive Counseling and Guidance Model for Alabama Public Schools,* by Alabama State Department of Education, 2003, Montgomery, AL: Author. Reprinted with permission.

Annual and Monthly Calendar: Elementary School

	Guidance Curriculum	Individual Planning	Responsive Services	System Support
August	Orientation to program (K–5); Respect for individual differences (K–5)	Referrals for peer tutoring program; Advisement; Placement and follow-up (student support team)	Small groups: Making friends; Academic concerns	School board presentation; Calendar distribution; Tutoring program training
September	Career awareness (K–5)	Referrals for peer tutoring program; Advisement; Placement and follow-up (student support team)	Small groups: Family concerns; academic concerns; school-related concerns; Peer tutors: Study skills in subject area	Leadership team meeting; Program management; Lesson planning; Peer tutor coordination; Grade-level team meetings
October	Work habits and study skills (K–5)	Referrals for peer tutoring program; Advisement; Placement and follow-up (student support team)	Small groups: Academic concerns; school-related concerns; relationship concerns Peer tutors: Time management strategies in subject area	Leadership team meeting; Program management; Lesson planning; Peer tutor coordination; Grade-level team meetings
November	Goal setting (K–5)	Referrals for peer tutoring program; Advisement; Placement and	Groups: Stress reduction; grief/loss; academic and school concerns	State counselor conference; Leadership team meeting; Program

	Guidance Curriculum	Individual Planning	Responsive Services	System Support
		follow-up (student support team)	Peer tutors: subject area skill development	management; Lesson planning; Peer tutor coordination; Grade-level team meetings
December	Skills for academic success (K–5);	Referrals for peer tutoring program; Advisement; Placement and follow-up (student support team)	Groups: Substance abuse; bullying; academic and school concerns Peer tutors: Planning for the holidays	Leadership team meeting; Program management; Lesson planning; Peer tutor coordination; Grade-level team meetings
January	Understanding self and others (K–5)	Referrals for peer tutoring program; Advisement; Placement and follow-up (student support team)	Small groups: Making friends; academic concerns	Leadership team meeting; Program management; Lesson planning; Peer tutor coordination; Grade-level team meetings
February	Career information (K–5); Schoolwide career fair	Referrals for peer tutoring program; Advisement; Placement and follow-up (student support team)	Small groups; Family concerns; academic concerns; school-related concerns Peer tutors: Study skills in subject area	Local staff development training; Leadership team meeting; Program management; Lesson planning; Peer tutor coordination; Grade-level team meetings
March	Test-taking skills (K–5)	Referrals for peer tutoring program; Advisement; Placement and follow-up (student support team); Test preparation	Small groups: Academic concerns; school-related concerns; relationship concerns Peer tutors: Time management strategies in subject area	Leadership team meeting; Program management; Lesson planning; Peer tutor coordination; Grade-level team meetings; Counseling conference
April	Stress busters (K–5)	Referrals for peer tutoring program; Advisement; Placement and follow-up (student support team)	Groups: Stress reduction; grief/loss; academic and school concerns Peer tutors: subject area skill development	Leadership team meeting; Program management; Lesson planning; Peer tutor coordination; Grade-level team meetings

	Guidance Curriculum	Individual Planning	Responsive Services	System Support
May	Safety survival skills (K–5)	Test interpretations; Advisement; Placement and follow-up (student support team), Middle school registration (5)	Groups: Substance abuse; bullying; academic and school concerns Peer tutors: Planning for the summer holiday	Leadership team meeting; Program management; Lesson planning; Peer tutor coordination; IEP meetings
June	Transitions (K–5)	Referrals for peer tutoring program; Advisement; Placement and follow-up (student support team)	Follow-up and evaluation activities for group and tutoring program participants	Leadership team meeting; Program management; Lesson planning; Peer tutor coordination; Grade-level team meetings

Review ASCA recommendations regarding allocations of time spent on each of the program delivery methods for this grade level. In what ways might the developmental tasks associated with this age group have influenced the recommendation?

children who are being retained have not been accurately identified by the school. Their reading of NAEYC's position statement reminded them that meaningful connections with each child's home, culture, and community are critical to successful school transition. Consequently, they intend to use their collaborative skills to work with teachers, community leaders, parents, and other members of the school team to provide more home visits and other types of opportunities for connections. They will also implement a new type of responsive services by initiating a buddy system that will match fifth graders with targeted kindergarten students in order to build an internal support for the youngsters.

Ms. Sara and Mr. Goldberg will continue their studies and supplement their response plan to ease the transition into kindergarten for all students. For example, Akos (2004) recommends these resources for school counselors to help the family, school, and community support a positive transition for a kindergarten student: *The Transition to Kindergarten* (Pianta & Cox, 1999), *Entering Kindergarten* (U.S. Department of Education, 2001), and *Even Start: Facilitating the Transition into Kindergarten* (Riedinger, 1997).

Review the annual calendar developed by Ms. Sara and Mr. Goldberg. Identify the program activities you think they included to address the developmental deficiencies of the students who do not achieve the transition-related competencies identified in Table 6.2.

The elementary school years are ones during which the children develop competencies essential not only to school success but also to success in life. Academic and nonacademic self-concept, physical or athletic competence, social competence, and behavioral conduct are domains of self-concept that develop during this time frame (Broderick & Blewitt, 2003). Effective elementary school counseling programs include strategies to identify students who are not achieving the necessary foundational competencies in each of these areas to respond optimally to academic transitions across the educational lifespan. Once identified, appropriate interventions are proposed, implemented, and evaluated for targeted students. The interventions that Ms. Sara and Mr. Goldberg have planned for kindergarteners are examples of that type of response.

MIDDLE SCHOOL COUNSELING

Developmental Tasks

Middle school counseling programs focus on the key developmental tasks of sixth-, seventh-, and eighth-grade students. Vernon (2004) provides an overview of the development of the middle school adolescent. Children in early adolescence (ages 11–14) experience rapid physical changes. Changes in the body associated with puberty begin. Those changes are followed by the appearance of secondary sex characteristics and generally a growth spurt. The variations in physical maturation of children in this age group may result in self-consciousness and anxiety. Both genders may become clumsy and awkward because of the disproportion of their hands and feet to their bodies. A common desire among early adolescents to be like everyone else may prove to be another source of anxiety. Likewise the physical and hormonal changes in their bodies may result in adolescents' confusion.

The cognitive shift from concrete thinking to formal operational thought starts during early adolescence. This gradual change allows adolescents to think more abstractly, reason more logically, and predict consequences. They develop the abilities to identify inconsistencies, think about the future and various possibilities, and imagine a logical sequence of events. They have a broader world than elementary children. As with physical changes, there are great variations in adolescents' cognitive development. Adults should take care not to overestimate the maturity of adolescents' thought processes.

The task of self-definition or identity formation begins in early adolescence, often leading students to push for autonomy in spite of their immaturity and lack of experience. These contrasts may lead to an increased vulnerability and dependence. Adults may be faced with a young person who both does and does not want their companionship and guidance. Those and other contradictions may accompany early adolescence. Students want to be both distinctive from and part of their crowd. Although they wish to be the center of attention, they may be self-conscious and feel awkward when they find themselves in such a position. They may also be egocentric, seeing themselves as more important than others and assuming that no one shares their experiences. An emotional rollercoaster of moodiness, emotional outbursts, and troublesome emotions may accompany this age. Peer relationships may be pleasurable sources of support or they may be negative and stressful. This overview of development hardly captures the energy with which most middle school students embrace life. Middle school students are curious about themselves, excited about the future, and eager to investigate the world. School counseling programs at this level need to include activities to develop the knowledge and skills necessary for exploring and planning students' life opportunities as they move to a more specialized schooling that is found in senior high school.

As children move from elementary to middle school they also ease, or sometimes leap, into early adolescence, a time of intense physical change and sometimes volatile emotional reactions (Vernon, 2004). These differences may be understood as stepping from less to more complexity. Schools mirror that

Identify other differences in the elementary and middle school settings that may be challenging for students.

position as students leave the familiarity of an elementary school they have known for 6 years to the more compartmentalized middle (sixth to ninth grades) or junior high (seventh to ninth grades) school. Children in middle schools find larger buildings, teams of teachers, more complicated scheduling, and different sets of peers. The confusion and anxiety typical of those changes make this transition an important event.

Developmental Stressors

As students enter middle school, grades often drop (Berk, 2004) as well as self-esteem and motivation (Alspaugh, 1998). Chung, Elias, and Schneider (1998), Rudolph, Lambert, Clark, and Kurlakowsky (2001), and Tobbell (2003) report a drop in self-esteem and increased psychological distress as young people move into middle school. According to Wigfield and Eccles (1994) students in junior high rate their learning experiences less favorably than their earlier schooling. Those pupils also state their teachers care less about them, grade harder, stress competition, and are less friendly. Anderman and Midgley (1997) equate this with young people feeling less academically competent at this age. Vernon (2004) states that depression, anger, and mood swings may be common and notes that adolescents worry too much about how they look, how they act and whether they belong, and their sexuality. They are striving for independence and often resist authority. However most do not become dependent on drugs, fail in school, or engage in violent, sexually promiscuous, or other destructive behaviors.

Identify the middle school students most likely to have control over their lives and those that have less control. Discuss with your classmates the potential problems that students with less control might experience. How might these problems impede successful transition through and out of middle school?

Those adolescents who have more control over their lives handle the transition better (Rudolph et al., 2001). In fact Akos (2002) discovered that the students he questioned found positive aspects in moving to a middle school. The young people in the sixth grade encouraged researchers to tell fifth graders that "middle school is fun and there are nice teachers" (p. 344). Akos and Galassi (2004) asked students, parents, and teachers about the things to look forward to in the transition. Students were excited about choosing classes, making new friends, and having lockers. Parents and teachers added participating in sports as an attraction of middle school. Having more freedom, changing class, and their friends were the most positive parts of being in a middle school for students. Our counselors want their school to support those optimistic views.

Akos (2004) acknowledges that predicting who may struggle with transitions proves difficult. Some suggest that females, low achievers, and urban, minority students may be more challenged than others. Others note that young people with added stresses such as family disruption, parental unemployment, or learned helplessness at the same time as the transition into middle school are at significantly greater risk for emotional problems (Rudolph et al., 2001). We suggest counselors consider the signs of a sharp drop in achievement, increased behavioral difficulties, or more absences to assess someone who may be struggling. Alerting teachers and parents to these troubling signs and the need for quick responses will improve the chances of reversing the downward spiral. The middle school counselors had already prepared a *Care Tips* collection for teachers and administrators. The small booklet provides warning signs for mental distress, reminders of developmental issues, some situational responses to difficult classroom behavior, and other helpful notions for the adults in the school. They will add a brief section to highlight behaviors that may indicate a young person needs extra support with the transition. They will also request some time in a staff meeting to introduce and to review those ideas. The counselors will also share their ideas with their colleagues at the school that welcomes their eighth graders—Brewster High School.

List your recommendations for a table of contents for a care tips publication for teachers.

Programming for Developmental Transitions

Ms. Hernandez, Mr. Al-Mabuk, and Ms. Clark review the ASCA (2003a) standards to identify areas they need to include in their program to promote middle school adjustment. They know that schools can help ease transitions with bridge programs that occur during the summer between middle and high school. The programs expose students to the culture of the new school, teach academic success skills, and help students learn about navigating the new school environment (Rathus, 2006). They recognize that all transition efforts require support from several sources, an awareness of the expectations of the new situation, and skills to meet those demands (Baker & Gerler, 2004). Similar to the study conducted by Akos and Galassi (2004), the counselors decided to ask students, parents, and teachers about the most worrisome aspects of moving to and from middle school. As with the previous study (Akos & Galassi, 2004), these counselors' survey results pinpointed the amount of homework and getting lost in the school building as significant student and parent concerns. Teachers reported concerns about the young people fitting in and making friends. These sources of information have led the counselors to the set of student outcomes to include in their program shown in Table 6.3.

The team of middle school counselors will address these competencies by teaching study skills and time management at all three grade levels in their school. As with other components of the guidance curriculum, they will identify resources for the teams of teachers to integrate into their subject-area lessons that will deepen the understanding and use of those academic skills. The counselors will ask teachers to report homework completion before and after the study skills lessons as a way to check on the effectiveness of this expanded guidance curriculum.

Review the annual planning calendar and identify those activities you believe address the transition into middle school and set the stage for moving on to high school. With your classmates, identify other topics or activities that might be helpful to all students who are preparing to go on to high school. When and how would you introduce these activities into the existing program?

They will also continue their focus on planning for the future with all the activities previously undertaken. They will emphasize decision-making and problem-solving aspects of those activities after reviewing a longitudinal study on the progress of students who had received a 2-year concentration in those skills (Elias, Gara, Schuyler, Brandon-Muller, & Sayette 1991). They realize that as middle school counselors they help welcome sixth graders to the middle school environment and prepare eighth graders for high school so they need to work closely with both the other school levels at their district. They are going to begin that collaboration earlier and try to expand the transition-enhancing activities beyond their big event orientation day.

As they have completed the merging of student competencies and their calendar of activities, the middle school counselors reviewed some informative research. Osterman (2000) notes the positive relationship between a young person's need for belonging and being accepted by peers and academic success, as

TABLE 6.3 Transition-Related Competencies for Middle School Students

Grade	Academic	Career	Personal/Social
6	• Identify attitudes and behaviors that lead to successful learning • Use knowledge of learning styles to influence school performance	• Understand the importance of planning • Develop a positive attitude toward work and learning • Learn how to work on a team • Learn how to use conflict management skills with peers and adults	• Learn goal-setting process • Recognize personal boundaries, rights, and privacy needs • Demonstrate cooperative behavior in groups • Apply conflict-resolution skills • Know when peer pressure is influencing a decision
7	• Apply time management skills • Understand how school success and academic achievement enhance future opportunities	• Develop skills to locate, evaluate, and interpret career information • Acquire employability skills such as working on a team, problem solving, and organizational skills • Identify personal skills, preferences, interests, and abilities and relate them to career choices • Use research, information resources, and the Internet to obtain career planning information	• Identify personal values, attitudes, and beliefs • Use a decision-making and problem-solving model to make safe and healthy choices • Understand consequences of decision and choices • Identify long- and short-term goals • Identify resource people in the school and community and know how to seek their help
8	• Demonstrate the ability to work independently as well as cooperatively • Develop and implement a plan of study for maximum achievement • Apply their knowledge of aptitudes and interests to goal setting	• Develop an awareness of personal abilities, skills, interests, and motivations • Apply decision-making skills to career planning and course selection • Demonstrate awareness of education and training needed to achieve career goals	• Identify long- and short-term goals • Recognize, accept, respect, and appreciate individual, ethnic, cultural, and family differences • Learn techniques for managing stress and conflict

Source: From *Developmental School Counseling Programs: From Theory to Practice,* by P. O. Paisely and G. T. Hubbard, 1994, Alexandria, VA: American Counseling Association. Copyright 1994 by American Counseling Associated. Adapted with permission.

well as for feeling connected to school, class work, and teachers. According to Osterman (2000), schools could improve those connections by holding small group activities, team building, cooperative learning, and other means to create smaller and more intimate learning communities. The counselors have reviewed their strategies to determine whether they have attended to those suggestions. For example, the peer tutoring and coaching programs should help build networks of peers who can provide accurate information and accessible help.

They have also read about the Crabapple Middle School (McElroy, 2000) transition program, the School Transition Environment Project (Felner et al., 1993), and the responsive practices of teacher teams, advisory groups, remedial instruction, and other transition strategies (MacIver & Epstein, 1991). They will discuss a schoolwide study of structures and practices that support middle school children being connected to their school with the leadership team in an effort to improve what exists and to create more possibilities. Concurrently they will again survey students to determine their perceptions and will use these data both in planning and as a baseline for evaluating the effects of any initiatives that evolve.

Review ASCA recommendations regarding allocations of time spent on each of the program delivery methods for this grade level. In what ways might the developmental tasks associated with this age group have influenced the recommendation?

Annual Monthly Calendar: Middle School

CALENDAR	Teaching	Planning	Responding	Supporting
August	Introductions (6–8); Decision-making model (8)	Referrals for grade-level peer helpers; advising; follow-up	Small groups: problem solving (7); transitions (6); academics (8)	Parent orientation; calendar finalized; new teacher training
September	Knowing Me (6–8)	Referrals for tutoring program; advising; student services team	Individual counseling; small groups as above	Community resources updates; coordination & program mgmt.
October	Working Together (6–8); Making Choices (6–8)	Referrals for service learning; advising; student services team	Individual counseling; small groups on relationships (6–8)	Community resources updates; leadership team; coordination & program mgmt.
November	Working Together (6–8); Making Choices (6–8)	Referrals for service learning; advising; student services team	Individual counseling; small groups on school-related concerns (6–8)	Community resources updates; leadership team; coordination & program mgmt.
December	What's a Career? (6) Career Awareness (7–8)	Referrals for service learning; advising; student services	Individual counseling; small groups on school-related team concerns (6–8)	Community resources updates; leadership team; project coordination & program mgmt.
January	What's a Career? (6) Career Awareness (7–8)	Placements for service learning; advising; student services team	Individual counseling; small groups on academic concerns (6–8); study skills (6–7)	Community resources updates; leadership team; project coordination & program mgmt.

CALENDAR	Teaching	Planning	Responding	Supporting
February	My Possibilities (6) My Working Self (7–8)	Placements for service learning; advising; student services team	Individual counseling; small groups on academic concerns (6–8); study skills	Community resources updates; leadership team; coordination & program mgmt.
March	My Possibilities (6) My Working Self (7–8)	Placements for service learning; advising; student services team	Individual counseling; small groups on academic concerns (6–8); stress mgmt.	Community resources updates; leadership team; coordination & program mgmt.
April	Entering High School (8) Careers and Me (6–7)	Service learning site wrap-ups; registration activities; advising; student services team	Individual counseling; small groups on stress mgmt. (6–8)	Community resources updates; leadership team; project coordination & program mgmt.
May	Putting it Together— Middle School Matters (6–8) Schoolwide Project Presentation	Registration activities; advising; student services team	Individual counseling; small groups— transitions (8)	Community resources updates; leadership team; coordination & program mgmt.

HIGH SCHOOL COUNSELING

Developmental Tasks

Secondary school programs typically serve students in grades 9 through 12. This grade placement coincides with the developmental period of adolescence identified by Erikson (1963) as a time of transition from childhood to adulthood. Steinberg (1996) describes the key markers of adolescence. Physically, adolescents experience the rapid changes associated with puberty during which time they become capable of sexual reproduction. Their growth spurt diminishes, usually around the age of 15 for females and 17 for males. Sexual urges are strong and may cause stress for the young people and for their parents (Vernon, 2004). Their cognitive development continues, resulting in more advanced, complex, and flexible abilities. Their abstract reasoning abilities allow them to hypothesize, think about the future, and move from either-or conceptualizing. Vernon suggests they will still be inconsistent in thinking and may see alternatives but still make inappropriate choices due to lack of experience or self-understanding.

Emotionally, adolescents move toward greater autonomy from parents and establish unique and separate identities. They are searching for who they are and who they are not (Vernon, 2004). They try on roles and responsibilities, discuss, observe adults and friends, speculate about possibilities, dream, question, experiment, and explore. They may need time away from others to contemplate and clarify their values and direction in life (Vernon, 2004). Their interpersonal interests shift from relationships with parents to peers. They develop the skills and capacities for achieving intimacy. Socially, they prepare for adult roles in society with regard to work, families, and citizenship. Steinberg (1996) points out that these developmental markers do not emerge for each adolescent at the same chronological time, nor do individual adolescents demonstrate them simultaneously. Some students mature earlier than others and some achieve maturity in one or more areas of development before others. The tasks of adolescence are challenging for the adolescent and for the adults in their lives. School counseling programs need to be particularly responsive to the developmental demands faced by secondary students. A summary of developmental tasks related to the life stages of school-aged young people can be found in Table 6.4.

Students, parents, and most communities view high schools as high stakes environments. Teenagers may be concerned with getting enough out of high school to prepare them for life (Kaplan, 2000), and they may be confused about career choice and whether they will be able to make enough money to live. They may be both anxious and excited about the transitions involved in moving through the last part of their K–12 education (Vernon, 2004). High school presents a last step into the adult world of work roles, relationships, and autonomy. Super, Savickas, and Super (1996) maintain that adolescents have four major tasks. They must be concerned about their future, increase control over their lives, convince themselves to succeed in school and at work, and develop

TABLE 6.4   Developmental Tasks and Life Stages

Early school age	Gender identification
	Early moral development
	Theory of self
	Peer play
Middle childhood	Friendship
	Concrete operations
	Learning skills
	Self-evaluation
	Team play
Early adolescence	Physical maturation
	Formal operations
	Emotional development
	Belonging to peer group
	Sexual relationship
Later adolescence	Autonomy
	Gender identity
	Internalized morality
	Career choice

Source: From *Development Through Life: A Psychosocial Approach,* 8th edition (p. 46), by B.M. Newman and P. R. Newman, 2003, Belmont, CA: Thomson. Copyright 2003 by Thomson. Adapted with permission.

their work habits and attitudes. Some adolescents find their lives stressful and do not think they can cope with their problems (Vernon, 2004). They may be lonely and ambivalent or apprehensive about their future.

Developmental Stressors

The curriculum selected in secondary schools prepares students for their postsecondary and work options, often with no flexibility to move from one specialized educational track to another. Unfortunately these high school tracks may exacerbate the educational inequalities of earlier school years (Berk, 2004) and limit postsecondary options for different groups of young people. Wahl and Blackhurst (2000) reviewed educational aspirations of adolescents and concluded the following: (1) students from lower socioeconomic backgrounds may not have the information they need or the skills to use what is available; (2) aspirations of Native Americans and Latinos are the lowest and least stable; (3) students of color with college ambitions need parental support; (4) students of color often lack realistic information about college. These authors have specific recommendations for counselors:

- Begin career exploration in early elementary school;
- Help middle school students achieve a realistic understanding of postsecondary opportunities, the need for training in those options, and the ways to prepare for them;
- Assist high school students in exploring a broad range of postsecondary options.

As they have talked to some of the high school students about their struggles in school, the counselors have heard about young people feeling "disconnected" from their parents. Steinberg, Brown, and Dornbusch (1996) reported their investigation of 20,000 African American, Asian American, Latino American, and European American students from California and Wisconsin. Forty percent of those young people said their parents never went to school functions. One-third said their parents had no idea how they were doing in school, and only one-third said they had conversations daily with their parents. Parents said they would like to be involved but were too busy. Parents considered education the school's job rather than theirs, and over half said they did not know their children's friends or where they went after school. The book *Beyond the Classroom* (Steinberg, 1996) contains a full discussion of this project. The counselors want to determine if the impressions they have formed about disconnected relationships between students and parents is supported by more evidence. Therefore they will develop a survey for all the students and their parents or guardians. Depending on their findings, they may need to design an intervention to help bridge this gap between adults and teenagers.

What questions would you ask on the survey? What possibilities do you see for designing interventions?

What types of problems might adolescents who do not demonstrate the proficiencies described here take with them into adulthood? What are the lifelong implications of these problems?

Students who succeed have learned self-control, can manage stress, and have both problem-solving and decision-making skills. Those students have proficient communication skills, can resist peer pressure, and are assertive in protecting their personal rights. The lack of any of those abilities will increase the likelihood of problems with the major transitions from adolescent to adult roles. Tables 6.5 and 6.6 contain a summary of student competencies related to those issues.

Programming for Developmental Transitions

The six members of the G.W. Brewster High School counseling team conducted a curriculum crosswalk and reviewed their scope and sequence chart (Alabama State Department of Education, 2003) (Appendix D) of student competencies associated with each of their program standards (ASCA, 2003a) 2 years ago. They used the ASCA developmental crosswalking tool as a matrix to identify at what grade level the specified competencies would be addressed and revised their annual program activities (see Annual and Monthly Calendar) accordingly. Additionally, they began to collect and have now twice reviewed disaggregated school data to examine course taking patterns, drop out rates, expulsion/

TABLE 6.5 Transitional Competencies for Ninth- and Tenth-Grade Students

Career	Academic	Personal/Social
Select coursework related to career interests	Apply effective study skills necessary to secondary school success	Gain self-awareness
Understand how the changing world impacts employment	Set educational and postsecondary goals	Learn coping skills for managing life events
Understand equity and access in career choice	Demonstrate dependability, productivity, and initiative	Make healthy choices
Analyze skills and interests	Gain test-taking skills	Resolve conflicts

Source: From *Developmental School Counseling Programs: From Theory to Practice*, by P. O. Paisely and G. T. Hubbard, 1994, Alexandria, VA: American Counseling Association. Copyright 1994 by American Counseling Assoicated. Adapted with permission.

TABLE 6.6 Transitional Competencies for Eleventh- and Twelfth-Grade Students

Career	Academic	Personal/Social
Assess and modify educational plans to support career goals	Set educational and postsecondary goals, identify options consistent with goals	Develop an action plan to set and achieve personal goals
Learn how to write a resume, interview, and other job entry skills	Share knowledge	Make healthy choices
Use skills in internship, mentoring, shadowing, and other experiences	Demonstrate the ability to balance school, studies, and other activities	Learn coping skills for managing stress and resolving conflicts

Source: From *Developmental School Counseling Programs: From Theory to Practice*, by P. O. Paisely and G. T. Hubbard, 1994, Alexandria, VA: American Counseling Association. Copyright 1994 by American Counseling Associated. Adapted with permission.

suspension rates, attendance, postsecondary patterns, parent participation, and involvement in extracurricular activities by relevant demographic variables. Based on the outcomes of these review procedures, the high school counseling program was revised from what was previously a reactionary, discrete services model to a comprehensive developmental school counseling program. The program priority during the first year focused on students who were not reaching their highest potential. The success of their programmatic efforts is measured by the increase in students entering four- and two-year colleges. Their priority for the coming year is to identify and increase programming for the transitional issues faced by the entire student body. The counselors want to help ninth and tenth graders adjust to high school and understand the relationship of the decisions they make to their futures. The counselors wish to assist the older students prepare for life after high school. They also have the largest proportion of transfer students in the district and want to investigate ways to support these students as they transition into a new school.

Akos (2004) recommends an organizational approach to plan for transitional programming. He identifies three categories of concerns reported by students—academic, procedural, and social. The students question their ability to cope with class work, homework, strict teachers, and the greater academic pressure. They need information about how to navigate the school building, schedules, and rules. They want to keep their friends, make new ones, and deal with difficulties such as bullies and older students. Anticipating these worries and responding to them can guide counselor activities related to transitions. The counselors at Brewster High are going to develop a bridge program for the summer between middle school and high school. The time in that program will be used to introduce students to the school building, rules, and campus culture. The program will also address academic skills.

Discuss the advantages and disadvantages of planning for transitions (1) as a special event(s) and (2) as a year-long process.

Next they consider what can be done for students moving into their school during the school year rather than at the beginning of the term. Wilson (1993) summarizes a support approach for transfer students that can guide the efforts of this counseling team:

- Attend to basic needs of the students such as selection of courses, and provide information about the building, class and bus schedule, policies about dress, absences, and other "survival" clues;
- Investigate the students' interests and goals;
- Offer a new-student support group (or academic or personal support).

Review ASCA recommendations regarding allocations of time spent on each of the program delivery methods for this grade level. In what ways might the developmental tasks associated with this age group have influenced the recommendation?

As they consider their calender the counselors know that spring activities will involve advising for registration of both high school students and eighth graders. As recommended by Akos (2004) they will work with teachers to review and strengthen students' decision-making processes prior to those activities. They will also hold presentations at the middle and high school, revise the parent brochure on courses and academic tracks, hold some transition groups, and build their coping skills curriculum. They will also coordinate school tours by parent volunteers and current students. In the fall they will focus on helping with adjustments to the new school year. Also they will provide some small groups modeled after one designed for young people with disabilities and their transition to postsecondary options (Milsom, Akos, & Thompson, 2004). The following calendar is a result of their planning.

Annual Calendar for Brewster High School Counseling Department

	Guidance Curriculum	Individual Planning	Responsive Services	System Support	Special Events
August	Orientation (all); Future Perfect	Grade-specific teacher advisement; placement and follow/up (f/u)	Individual counseling; small groups; academic success	Teacher advisor training; peer mediation training; leadership	
September	Careers and Me	Grade specific teacher advisement; placement and f/u	Individual counseling; small groups; academic success	Teacher advisor training; peer mediation training; leadership	Deadline for Oct. SAT; Senior Parents Meeting
October	Planning for the future (goal setting)	College apps; placement & f/u; teacher advisement	Individual counseling; small group—goals & decisions	Leadership team; peer mediation coordination; program mgmt.	Register for PSAT; College Fair; ACT & SAT testing dates; Service academy applications due
November	Skills for School (study skills, test taking skills)	College apps; placement & f/u; teacher advisor; support teams	Individual counseling; small groups—goals & decisions; athletes	Leadership team; peer mediation coordination; program mgmt.	SAT; Deadline for Dec. test dates; School/community involvement days
December	Skills for School	Teacher advisor; placement & f/u; support teams	Individual counseling; small groups—dating relationships; athletes	Leadership team; peer mediation coordination; program mgmt.	Financial Aid Forms available; ACT; Deadline for Jan. tests
January	R-E-S-P-E-C-T	Teacher advisor; placement & f/u; support teams	Individual counseling; small groups—families	Leadership team; peer mediation coordination; program mgmt	Financial Aid Night; Feb. ACT deadline
February	Deconstructing Stereotypes	Teacher advisor; placement & f/u; support teams	Small groups—body image; individual counseling	Leadership team; peer mediation coordination; program mgmt.	ACT, Register for March SAT; Career Fair
March	Getting Along	Teacher advisor; placement & f/u;	Small groups—body image;	Leadership team; peer mediation	Register for April ACT & May SAT;

	Guidance Curriculum	Individual Planning	Responsive Services	System Support	Special Events
		support teams	individual counseling	coordination; program mgmt.	SAT; Register for next year's courses
April	Healthy Choices	Teacher advisor; placement & f/u; support teams	Small groups—grief-loss; individual counseling	Leadership team; peer mediation coordination; program mgmt.	Register for June SAT; Junior Parent Night (college admissions panel)
May	Healthy Choices	Teacher advisor; placement & f/u; support teams	Small groups—grief-loss; individual counseling	Leadership team; peer mediation coordination; program mgmt.	Parents Breakfast; AP Testing
June	Transitions	Teacher advisor; placement & f/u; support teams	Individual counseling	Leadership team; peer mediation coordination; program mgmt.	ACT; Visit colleges of interest

Review the annual calendars at all three levels. Are the recommendations for dropout prevention evident? If not, what is missing and what activities might the counselors undertake to ensure that these well-substantiated prevention strategies are included in their program model across the K–12 grade levels?

The high school counseling team recognizes that the ultimate problem with school transitions occurs in high schools when too many students leave school before they graduate. Rathus (2006) cites excessive school absences and reading below grade level as two of the early, strong predictors of school dropouts. Other risk factors include having low grades, poor problem-solving skills, low self-esteem, problems with teachers, substance abuse, being older than classmates, dissatisfaction with school, marrying or becoming a parent at an early age (Christenson & Thurlow, 2004; Jimerson, Egeland, Stoufe, & Carlson, 2000). Alarmingly the majority of dropouts said no one on the school staff tried to talk them into staying in school. Fewer than 25% had seen a counselor to discuss their troubles (McWhirter et al., 2004). The counselors conclude something must change at Brewster High School.

The counselors have discovered a way to understanding people who drop out provided by Janosz, LeBlanc, Boulerice, and Tremblay (2000). The disengaged dropouts have no confidence in their academic abilities, have few aspirations, and do not value education. They are often uninvolved in school but may have high achievement scores relative to their lack of school participation. The low-achievers have weak commitments to education, poor grades, and learned little. Quiet dropouts are generally not noticed until they leave school; they may be involved in school activities, attend regularly, and are seldom behavior problems in school. Finally the maladjusted dropouts have discipline problems in schools. They have poor academic achievement, invest little in school, and have a weak commitment to the educational process.

The counselors find these ways of understanding students who drop out of school helpful ways to target behaviors and attitudes in order to design interventions for them. Thus they will plan some individual planning and responsive services activities to target achievement, commitment, and discipline for students who may be close to leaving school before they graduate. McWhirter and his colleagues (2004) suggest a comprehensive, competency-based guidance program as the most promising response to the multiple dimensions of this problem. Other common characteristics of successful dropout prevention programs (Christenson & Thurlow, 2004; Lee & Burkam, 2003; Rathus, 2006) include these components:

- Early preschool intervention such as Head Start;
- Identification and monitoring of students who have a high risk of dropping out throughout their school years;
- Small class size, individualized instruction and counseling;
- Vocational components that connect learning and community work experiences;
- Involved adults from families or community organizations;
- Positive school climate that makes students feel a part of a community;
- Clear educational goals, student accountability for their behavior, and motivational systems.

SUMMARY

Following a review of developmental tasks and possible stressors for students at each grade level, the counselors in Brewster County pinpointed the area of students' transitions on which their program needed additional focus. To choose effective activities for their schools, they reviewed theories of development, their state curriculum, the ASCA standards, and relevant research. With the integration of those studies, they have completed their plans for addressing the transitional needs of students at all levels in this school system.

PORTFOLIO COMPONENTS

1. Review your knowledge of child and adolescent development. Based on that information, prepare a summary of developmental milestones for elementary, middle, or high school students that could be used by teachers and parents to identify students who may be having transition-related difficulties.
2. Outline the components of a summer bridge program for students entering school, moving to middle school, or transitioning to high school.
3. For each of the three school levels discussed in this chapter, identify one significant transition-related problem you expect to encounter as a school counselor. Identify the developmental domain associated with the problem, the student competencies students need to master in order to demonstrate that they have met the developmental challenge, and describe at least three approaches that a school counselor might use to help the students achieve the competencies.

CHAPTER 7

Guidance Curriculum

TEAM K–12 PLANS A DEVELOPMENTAL GUIDANCE CURRICULUM

Dr. Symons oversees all the school counseling programs in a school district. He supervises the 91 counselors that work in the 54 schools in that system. To support the many needs of those professionals, he has appointed head counselors at each level; one for the elementary group, two for the middle school group, and two for the high school group. This system leadership group of counselors has spent time considering the daily activities of counselors and the delivery system of school counseling programs. Over the next few years they will review, revise, and streamline four areas of work: the guidance curriculum, individual student planning, responsive services, and system support. They have decided to begin with the guidance curriculum. They have several reasons for this action. First, many of the other school counselors have commented on the gaps and the redundancies of the current curriculum. Additionally, the state's Standard Course of Study has been released (c.f. http://www.ncpublicschools.org/curriculum/guidance/scos/programofstudy/). Finally, many new counselors have been hired because of retirements and relocations. Several of those recent hires have not been teachers and are not as familiar with curriculum planning and delivery as the veteran counselors.

Mr. Symons and the head counselors decide their existing curriculum will be turned into a standards-based guidance curriculum. The standards with which the counselors will be working are those developed by the American School Counselor Association (2001a) and their state model of counseling. In addition, a systemwide needs assessment has been conducted to determine what unique needs exist among the students. Survey data from parents, teachers, the community, and students have been collected and compared to the needs assessment done 3 years earlier. Information from all of these sources will serve as the basis for the new K–12 curriculum.

The school system includes 31 elementary schools with one counselor each, 16 middle schools with two counselors each, and 7 secondary schools with four counselors each. These counselors are working to develop a curriculum that addresses the priorities identified by leadership teams and endorsed by each individual school. Mr. Symons has developed the following agenda for the counselors' first meeting:

1. Develop a statement of purpose for the group.
2. Identify the steps necessary to achieve the purpose and develop a time line for achievement.
3. Identify the resources available to achieve the purpose.
4. Identify the potential barriers to success and plan ways to overcome them.
5. Organize for the work.

Through team-building exercises, group members learned more about each other and their experiences on similar tasks. Each of them then explained their understanding of the task they were undertaking and agreed on some ground rules to help make their meeting smooth as well as productive. As this initial meeting progressed they began feeling more like a team with a serious yet achievable mission. To celebrate their resolve and their partnership, the counselors proclaimed themselves TK–12 for "Think K–12" and began their work.

Students of all ages attend schools to learn. Most Americans agree that a good education is associated with success in life, and this country invests heavily in the learning enterprise to prepare children for a promising future. Ideally, students throughout their schooling acquire the knowledge, skills, values, and attitudes they need to become contributing members of society (Ballantine, 2001). In addition to the verbal and analytical skills and competencies essential to academic success, students learn the prevailing cultural norms and values about what behavior is acceptable and not acceptable. Students learn about careers, the requirements for a particular type of work, and ways to obtain the skills and knowledge they need for entering a particular profession. In short, what one learns during the first 13 years of schooling provides a foundation on which one builds for the rest of one's life. "The purpose of a counseling program in a school is to promote and enhance the learning process. The goal of the program is to enable all students to achieve success in school and to develop into contributing members of society" (ASCA, 1999, p. 30). School counselors develop, deliver, coordinate, and evaluate the guidance curriculum component as one of the ways to meet that goal.

The curriculum is designed to provide for the delivery of systematic, age-appropriate concepts to all students in the school (Wittmer, Thompson, & Loesch, 1997). The curriculum is sequential, with concepts at each grade level building on those learned at the previous level. Consequently, the planning of the curriculum should include people working at all developmental levels in any given school system, just as the TK–12 group. The purpose of the guidance curriculum is to promote optimal development of all students in educational, career, and personal/social domains.

After reading and discussing this chapter, you should be able to

- Define guidance curriculum.
- Identify student competencies in each of the three areas of development met through the guidance curriculum.
- Develop guidance units and lessons.
- Articulate the skills and competencies necessary for conducting classroom guidance lessons (implementing the guidance curriculum).
- Explain the different ways the guidance curriculum has been effective.

DEFINITIONS

As noted in Chapter 1, the earliest school counseling programs consisted of guidance "lessons" delivered by high school teachers to prepare young people to make vocational choices. These lessons were the forerunners of what we identify today as the guidance curriculum. As the profession of school counseling has evolved to its current status, so have the various program components for which the counselor is responsible. According to ASCA (2003a) the school guidance curriculum component of a program contains "the written instructional program that is comprehensive in scope, preventative and proactive, developmental in design, coordinated by school counselors and delivered, as appropriate, by school counselors and other educators" (p. 40). These activities, mostly classroom lessons, involve the instructional focus on the knowledge, attitudes, and skills for students' academic, career, and personal/social growth.

Currently, the guidance curriculum is intended to deliver the guidance content identified as essential to all students, K–12, in a systematic and sequential way (Gysbers & Henderson, 2000). The guidance curriculum is an intervention with the purpose of delivering a series of planned activities (Sears, 2005). According to Gysbers and Henderson, the curriculum generally includes the student competencies or outcomes to be achieved in each of three developmental domains (academic, career, and personal/social) across all grade levels. The academic domain relates to students' competencies in developing their learning potential. Career competencies refer to the ability to explore career possibilities and opportunities, to make career decisions, and to navigate the transition from school to work. The personal/social domain incorporates competencies of understanding and expressing self, looking at relationships, and understanding a person's emotions, actions, and behaviors. While acknowledging that local districts make the final determinations, those authors make recommendations about how much program time should be devoted to this component. They suggest that elementary and middle school counselors spend between 35% and 40% of their time (between 12 and 14 hours/35-hour week) and high school counselors about 20% of their time (about 7 hours/week) in this teaching role.

Counselors and/or teachers most typically deliver the guidance curriculum through planned activities in which entire classes of students participate. Classroom guidance includes age-appropriate lessons or a group of lessons on a common topic. Those units may be linked to class subjects such as history or language arts, may be integrated into the school curriculum or may connect across grade levels. Classroom guidance also involves grade-level activities such as the transition orientations described in Chapter 6. For example, in career development in a middle school, all seventh-grade math classes might participate in a six-session unit designed to explore careers in mathematics. All eighth graders in the same school might learn about careers in journalism during their regularly scheduled language arts class. The seventh and eighth graders might all learn about the variety of career opportunities in their community through a schoolwide career fair. All these activities are examples of methods for delivering that part of the guidance curriculum concerned with the career development standards.

Considering the information provided above and the case at the beginning of this chapter, work as a group to refine a project plan for preparing the K–12 curriculum. The first task is to develop a statement of purpose for Mr. Symons and his group of planners. Based on this statement, develop goals with clear outcomes, determine responsibilities for the tasks, and set time lines for achieving your purpose.

CURRICULUM DEVELOPMENT: SCOPE AND SEQUENCE

An initial structuring task for the TK–12 team is to determine how they are going to organize themselves to work most efficiently. On the surface, it seems that cooperative work groups based on level (elementary, middle, secondary)

What are the advantages of the decision to organize by domain for the planning team? What are the disadvantages?

might be the most expedient way to proceed. However, after further discussion, the group decides to work by domain (academic, career, personal/social). Consequently, there is someone representing each developmental level on each of the three subgroups for each domain. Ms. Serita Jones is the team leader for the academic subgroup; Mr. Tony Harris is team leader for the career subgroup; and Ms. Emmy Lou Rice is team leader for the personal/social subgroup. Each subgroup will meet throughout the school year to plan curriculum in their particular domain, with at least one full team meeting every 3 months.

Before they break into their subgroups for planning, the TK–12 team members agree to identify the values on which their work will be based. After a session of shared visions, they have identified priority descriptors for their work. They aim for a curriculum that is current, relevant, and responsive. Their primary concern is that their curriculum be sufficient in scope and sequence. They have also agreed that the curriculum will be standards based (Dahir, Sheldon, & Valiga, 1998; see Appendix B). They recognize the ASCA National Standards as meta-skills and meta-competencies that are comprehensive in nature. Those student competencies and indicators represent life skills that individuals apply in multiple settings such as schools, extracurricular activities, leisure, family, community, interpersonal, intrapersonal, and career contexts (Brown & Trusty, 2005). The topics therefore represent the life skills for success, the range of content, or the scope of the curriculum. These planning teams want to maintain that broad perspective as well as develop more specific grade-level competencies for the standards.

Most importantly, they will be guided by the needs identified by students, teachers, parents, and others (Goodnough, Perusse, & Erford, 2003). For example, in their recent school- and communitywide needs assessment, concern was expressed about an increase in bias-motivated incidents (vandalism and harassment) directed toward both people and property. The leadership team from each school identified the elimination of these incidents as a priority. With these guidelines in mind, the counselors believe they have identified the "scope" of the curriculum. The "sequence" will be based on general principles of cognitive, physical, socioemotional, and racial identity development from which the academic, career, and personal/social needs (and capabilities) of students at the elementary, middle, and high school levels are derived.

Basic developmental principles provide guidance for school counselors so that the classroom guidance activities at each grade level are appropriate to students' ability to learn at that age. Schoolwide activities that are part of the guidance curriculum also need to be planned according to the ranges of developmental levels in one's school. For example, a schoolwide career fair for grades 9 through 12 might include activities that encourage identification of career interests and exploration of broad career areas consistent with students' interests and abilities. For the seniors in the school, more emphasis might be placed on identifying and contacting prospective employers, preparing the résumé, gaining interviewing skills, and practicing successful work behaviors. A schoolwide career fair at the middle school might focus on the dissemination of information about careers. At the elementary level, a career fair may focus on careers in students' communities and the work their own and their classmates' parents and guardians perform.

According to Ormrod (2000), certain principles of development hold true for almost all children. Although development is somewhat orderly and predictable, it occurs at different rates for different children and is influenced by both heredity and environment. According to Pai and Adler (1997) development may proceed either continuously or discontinuously and is influenced by the developing person's social relationships and cultural environment. Culture refers to the knowledge, skills, behaviors, attitudes, and beliefs developed by a group and passed from one generation to the next (Pai & Adler, 1997). According to Pai and Adler, "The culture to which one belongs, then, becomes the root of the individual's identity because culture gives us a sense of power and confidence by giving us the basis of achieving our goals, determining what is desirable and undesirable, and developing the purpose of life" (p. 26). A curriculum that is developmentally appropriate builds on the skills and abilities students have at any given grade, provides enough challenge to lead to the acquisition of new skills and knowledge, and is flexible enough to accommodate individual differences within the student body, including those differences associated with students' cultural identities. Effective guidance curriculum builds on previous learning.

The leadership team members have refreshed their understanding of human development. They have reviewed a current needs assessment and have gathered both state and national standards. Now they will identify the student outcomes for their school district. In the educational literature, *outcomes* refer to what students should know or be able to do after they complete high school. Campbell and Dahir (1997) provide nine standards, associated student competencies, and performance indicators that represent outcomes in three areas: academic, career, and personal-social. An example is as follows:

Career Development Domain

Standard C: Students will understand the relationship among personal qualities, education, training, and the world of work.
    Competency C: 1 Acquire Knowledge to Achieve Career Goals
        C: C1.1: Understand the relationship between educational achievement and career success
        C: C1.2: Explain how work can help to achieve personal success and satisfaction

---

The team next wants to compare the ASCA National Standards (Campbell & Dahir, 1997) with other relevant national guidelines to see how well they correspond. Determining this alignment with other documents can be accomplished through a process called crosswalking (ASCA, 2003a), or comparing the language in the documents to each other. They are pleased to find that information summarized on their state curriculum Web site. Table 7.1 shows an example.

The leadership group decides the ASCA National Standards (Campbell & Dahir, 1997) represent the comprehensive approach they have deemed important to their district. Their state model is based on that work, and they will use those standards and competencies as the foundation of their district curriculum. Next they want to consider the developmental aspect of developing a curriculum—the sequence. They have discovered a developmental crosswalking tool in the ASCA *National Model Workbook* (2004d), and they debate about using that model. Also they have found another state's guidelines with the standards categorized across four groupings of grades. They decide to look at that document as one step in determining the sequence of content. That section of the Alabama Comprehensive Counseling and Guidance Framework is shown in Table 7.2.

The planning team has compared the standards to other documents and has identified grade clusters at which competencies will be addressed. They are now ready to write their learner benchmarks, what students need to know or do at each grade level (Goodnough, Perusse, & Erford, 2003). The leadership team will identify the instruction and activities to support students' achievement of these benchmarks. Goodnough, Perusse, and Erford (2003) discuss the importance of ensuring that grade-level material builds on rather than repeats previous learning. They also explain that vertical articulation refers to this sequential building of skills and competencies. Likewise horizontal articulation means the link between the content in the counseling curriculum and content in other subjects, the integration process. For example, students may investigate and compare salaries in various careers in a math class. As part of the final

TABLE 7.1   Sample from State of North Carolina's Blueprint for Elementary School Guidance Curriculum

Comprehensive School Counseling Guidance Curriculum Blueprint
A blueprint is a document illustrating the framework of the curriculum. Shown on the blueprint are the areas of instruction, the core competencies in each area, and the specific objectives for each competency. The blueprint illustrates the recommended sequence of instruction for each competency as well as a designation for each competency as Core or Supplemental. The Blueprint is intended to be used by counselors in planning the course of work for the year, preparing daily plans, and providing for appropriate interventions with students, parents, colleagues, and the community.

Blueprint for Elementary School Guidance Curriculum

Competency # Objective # 1	Competency and Objective Statements 2	Core/Supp 3	NCESAG Competency 4	SCANS 5	NCDGC Competency 6		
	Career Development						
1:	**2:**			**3:**	**4:**	**5:**	**6:**
006.	**Understand the relationship between personal qualities, education, and training, and the world of work.**						
006.01	Compare the relationship between educational achievement and career success.	core	X	x	x		
006.02	Appraise the importance of equal access to careers.	supp	X	x	x		
006.03	Use conflict management skills with peers and adults.	core	X	x	x		
006.04	Work cooperatively with others as a team member.	core	X	x	x		

Explanation of Headings

No.	Heading	Column Information
1	Competency # Objective #	The School Guidance Curriculum is integrated in all subject areas through the School Improvement Plan.
2	Area Competency Objective Statements	Statements of area titles: Academic Development, Career Development, Personal/Social Development; Competencies per area. Each competency combined with Outcome behavior
3	Core/Supplemental	Designation of the competencies and objectives as Core or Supplemental.
4	Integrated Skill Area: NCESAC	Shows links to the North Carolina Education Standards and Accountability Commission Standards (ABCs) created by the General Assembly in July 1993. Communication, Problem-Solving, Teamwork, Using Numbers and Data, Processing Information, Using Technology.
5	Integrated Skill Area: SCANS	Shows links to the Secretary's Commission on Achieving Necessary Skills (SCANS) Foundation Skills: Basic Skills, Thinking Skills, Personal Qualities Functional Skills: Resources, Interpersonal, Information Systems, Technology
6	Integrated Skill Area: NCDGC	Shows links to the National Career Development Guidelines Competencies (NCDGC) 1) Self-Knowledge, 2) Exploration, 3) Career Planning

Source: From *Elementary Blueprints* by Public Schools of North Carolina, 2005. Reprinted by permission of North Carolina Department of Public Instruction, 301 N. Wilmington Street, Raleigh, NC 27601.

TABLE 7.2   State of Alabama Guidance Curriculum Scope and Sequence Chart

Alabama Grade-Cluster Standards, Competencies, and Indicators—Guidance Curriculum Scope and Sequence

The following competencies for Alabama students at each grade-cluster level (K–2, 3–5, 6–8, 9–12) are linked directly to the nine national standards as presented in *The ASCA National Model: A Framework for School Counseling Programs*. The competencies describe the attitudes, knowledge, and skills that students should be able to demonstrate as a result of participating in an effective school counseling and guidance program.

Counselors should determine the student competencies and the corresponding indicators (listed below each competency) to be utilized in planning and developing the school guidance curriculum and the individual student planning components appropriate for specific grade-cluster levels within the school program. Guidance activities must be outcome-based and linked to the appropriate indicators.

The following chart is a tool to be used to assist counselors in planning the overall guidance curriculum. The solid dots highlight the grade-cluster level where each competency indicator is introduced. The competency indicators are intended to be cumulative; therefore, the hollow dots highlight the grade-cluster level(s) in which the competency indicator may be expanded or reinforced. Careful analysis of the scope and sequence of the local school guidance curriculum ensures that all students master all competency indicators by the end of Grade 12.

Guidance Curriculum Scope and Sequence Chart[*]

ACADEMIC DEVELOPMENT DOMAIN			K–2	3–5	6–8	9–12
Standard A: Students will acquire the attitudes, knowledge and skills that contribute to effective learning in school and across the life span.						
	Competency A:A1 Improve Academic Self-Concept					
	A:A1.1	articulate feelings of competence and confidence as learners		•	○	○
	A:A1.2	display a positive interest in learning	•	○	○	○
	A:A1.3	take pride in work and achievement	•	○	○	○
	A:A1.4	accept mistakes as essential to the learning process		•	○	○
	A:A1.5	identify attitudes and behaviors leading to successful learning			•	○
	Competency A:A2 Acquire Skills for Improving Learning					
	A:A2.1	apply time-management and task-management skills			•	○
	A:A2.2	demonstrate how effort and persistence positively affect learning		•	○	○
	A:A2.3	use communications skills to know when and how to ask for help when needed	•	○	○	○
	A:A2.4	apply knowledge and learning styles to positively influence school performance			•	○
	Competency A:A3 Achieve School Success					
	A:A3.1	take responsibility for their actions	•	○	○	○
	A:A3.2	demonstrate the ability to work independently, as well as the ability to work cooperatively with other students		•	○	○
	A:A3.3	develop a broad range of interests and abilities			•	○

The leftmost vertical label reads: I N D I C A T O R S

ACADEMIC DEVELOPMENT DOMAIN			K–2	3–5	6–8	9–12
	A:A3.4	demonstrate dependability, productivity and initiative		•	○	○
	A:A3.5	share knowledge		•	○	○
Standard B: Students will complete school with the academic preparation essential to choose from a wide range of substantial postsecondary options, including college.						
	Competency A:B1 Improve Learning					
	A:B1.1	demonstrate the motivation to achieve individual potential		•	○	○
	A:B1.2	learn and apply critical-thinking skills		•	○	○
	A:B1.3	apply the study skills necessary for academic success at each level	•	○	○	○
I	A:B1.4	seek information and support from faculty, staff, family and peers			•	○
N	A:B1.5	organize and apply academic information from a variety of sources			•	○
D	A:B1.6	use knowledge of learning styles to positively influence school performance			•	○
I	A:B1.7	become a self-directed and independent learner		•	○	○
C	**Competency A:B2 Plan to Achieve Goals**					
A	A:B2.1	establish challenging academic goals in elementary, middle/junior high and high school		•	•	•
T	A:B2.2	use assessment results in educational planning			•	○
O	A:B2.3	develop and implement annual plan of study to maximize academic ability and achievement*			•	•
R	A:B2.4	apply knowledge of aptitudes and interests to goal setting			•	○
S	A:B2.5	use problem-solving and decision-making skills to assess progress toward educational goals			•	○
	A:B2.6	understand the relationship between classroom performance and success in school	•	○	○	○
	A:B2.7	identify postsecondary options consistent with interests, achievement, aptitude and abilities			•	○
STANDARD C: Students will understand the relationship of academics to the world of work and to life at home and in the community.						
I	**Competency A:C1 Relate School to Life Experience**					
N	A:C1.1	demonstrate the ability to balance school, studies, extracurricular activities, leisure time and family life		•	○	○
D	A:C1.2	seek co-curricular and community experiences to enhance the school experience			•	○
I	A:C1.3	understand the relationship between learning and work	•	○	○	○
C	A:C1.4	demonstrate an understanding of the value of lifelong learning as essential to seeking, obtaining and maintaining life goals			•	○
A	A:C1.5	understand that school success is the preparation to make the transition from student to community member			•	○

ACADEMIC DEVELOPMENT DOMAIN		K–2	3–5	6–8	9–12
A:C1.6	understand how school success and academic achievement enhance future career and vocational opportunities		•	○	○

*Counselors for Grades 8–12 must guide students in the development and annual revision of a four-year educational/career plan and have students maintain a portfolio of study based on legislative and other graduation requirements. The selection of the educational/career plan must be approved in writing by the parents or guardians.

CARRER DEVELOPMENT DOMAIN		K–2	3–5	6–8	9–12
STANDARD A: Students will acquire the skills to investigate the world of work in relation to knowledge of self and to make informed career decisions.					
Competency C:A1 Develop Career Awareness					
C:A1.1	develop skills to locate, evaluate and interpret career information			•	○
C:A1.2	learn about the variety of traditional and nontraditional occupations	•	○	○	○
C:A1.3	develop an awareness of personal abilities, skills, interests and motivations	•	○	○	○
C:A1.4	learn how to interact and work cooperatively in teams		•	○	○
C:A1.5	learn to make decisions		•	○	○
C:A1.6	learn how to set goals		•	○	○
C:A1.7	understand the importance of planning			•	•
C:A1.8	pursue and develop competency in areas of interest			•	○
C:A1.9	develop hobbies and vocational interests	•	○	○	○
C:A1.10	balance between work and leisure time		•	○	○
Competency C:A2 Develop Employment Readiness					
C:A2.1	acquire employability skills such as working on a team and problem-solving and organizational skills			•	○
C:A2.2	apply job readiness skills to seek employment opportunities				•
C:A2.3	demonstrate knowledge about the changing workplace				•
C:A2.4	learn about the rights and responsibilities of employers and employees	•			
C:A2.5	learn to respect individual uniqueness in the workplace				•
C:A2.6	learn how to write a resume				•
C:A2.7	develop a positive attitude toward work and learning	•	○	○	○
C:A2.8	understand the importance of responsibility, dependability, punctuality, integrity and effort in the workplace			•	○
C:A2.9	utilize time- and task-management skills	•	○	○	○
STANDARD B: Students will employ strategies to achieve future career goals with success and satisfaction.					
Competency C:B1 Acquire Career Information					
C:B1.1	apply decision-making skills to career planning, course selection and career transition			•	○

(The left margin is labeled vertically: INDICATORS)

CAREER DEVELOPMENT DOMAIN			K–2	3–5	6–8	9–12
I **N** **D** **I** **C** **A** **T** **O** **R** **S**	C:B1.2	identify personal skills, interests and abilities and relate them to current career choice	•	○	○	○
	C:B1.3	demonstrate knowledge of the career-planning process			•	○
	C:B1.4	know the various ways in which occupations can be classified		•	○	○
	C:B1.5	use research and information resources to obtain career information			•	○
	C:B1.6	learn to use the Internet to access career-planning information			•	○
	C:B1.7	describe traditional and nontraditional career choices and how they relate to career choice		•	○	○
	C:B1.8	understand how changing economic and societal needs influence employment trends and future training			•	○
Competency C:B2 Identify Career Goals						
	C:B2.1	demonstrate awareness of the education and training needed to achieve career goals	•	○	○	○
	C:B2.2	assess and modify their educational plan to support career				•
	C:B2.3	use employability and job readiness skills in internship, mentoring, shadowing and/or other work experience			•	○
	C:B2.4	select course work that is related to career interests			•	○
	C:B2.5	maintain a career-planning portfolio			•	○
STANDARD C: Students will understand the relationship between personal qualities, education, training and the world of work.						
I **N** **D** **I** **C** **A** **T** **O** **R** **S**	**Competency C:C1 Acquire Knowledge to Achieve Career Goals**					
	C:C1.1	understand the relationship between educational achievement and career success	•	○	○	○
	C:C1.2	explain how work can help to achieve personal success and satisfaction		•	○	○
	C:C1.3	identify personal preferences and interests influencing career choice and success			•	○
	C:C1.4	understand that the changing workplace requires lifelong learning and acquiring new skills			•	○
	C:C1.5	describe the effect of work on lifestyle			•	○
	C:C1.6	understand the importance of equity and access in career choice		•	○	○
	C:C1.7	understand that work is an important and satisfying means of personal expression	•	○	○	○
I **N** **D** **I** **C** **A**	**Competency C:C2 Apply Skills to Achieve Career Goals**					
	C:C2.1	demonstrate how interests, abilities and achievement relate to achieving personal, social, educational and career goals		•	○	○
	C:C2.2	learn how to use conflict management skills with peers and adults	•	○	○	○
	C:C2.3	learn to work cooperatively with others as a team member		•	○	○

CAREER DEVELOPMENT DOMAIN			K–2	3–5	6–8	9–12
T **O** **R** **S**	C:C2.4	apply academic and employment readiness skills in work-based learning situations such as internships, shadowing and/or mentoring experiences			•	○

PERSONAL/SOCIAL DEVELOPMENT DOMAIN			K–2	3–5	6–8	9–12
	STANDARD A: Students will acquire the knowledge, attitudes and interpersonal skills to help them understand and respect self and others.					
	Competency PS:A1 Acquire Self-Knowledge					
I **N** **D** **I** **C** **A** **T** **O** **R** **S**	PS:A1.1	develop positive attitudes toward self as a unique and worthy person	•	○	○	○
	PS:A1.2	identify values, attitudes and beliefs	•	○	○	○
	PS:A1.3	learn the goal-setting process		•	○	○
	PS:A1.4	understand change is a part of growth	•	○	○	○
	PS:A1.5	identify and express feelings	•	○	○	○
	PS:A1.6	distinguish between appropriate and inappropriate behavior	•	○	○	○
	PS:A1.7	recognize personal boundaries, rights and privacy needs	•	○	○	○
	PS:A1.8	understand the need for self-control and how to practice it	•	○	○	○
	PS:A1.9	demonstrate cooperative behavior in groups		•	○	○
	PS:A1.10	identify personal strengths and assets		•	○	○
	PS:A1.11	identify and discuss changing personal and social roles		•	○	○
	PS:A1.12	identify and recognize changing family roles	•	○	○	○
	Competency PS:A2 Acquire Interpersonal Skills					
	PS:A2.1	recognize that everyone has rights and responsibilities	•	○	○	○
	PS:A2.2	respect alternative points of view		•	○	○
	PS:A2.3	recognize, accept, respect and appreciate individual differences	•	○	○	○
	PS:A2.4	recognize, accept and appreciate ethnic and cultural diversity	•	○	○	○
	PS:A2.5	recognize and respect differences in various family configurations	•	○	○	○
	PS:A2.6	use effective communications skills	•	○	○	○
	PS:A2.7	know that communication involves speaking, listening and nonverbal behavior	•	○	○	○
	PS:A2.8	learn how to make and keep friends	•	○	○	○
	STANDARD B: Students will make decisions, set goals and take necessary action to achieve goals.					
	Competency PS:B1 Self-knowledge Application					
	PS:B1.1	use a decision-making and problem-solving model		•	○	○
	PS:B1.2	understand consequences of decisions and choices	•	○	○	○

PERSONAL/SOCIAL DEVELOPMENT DOMAIN		K–2	3–5	6–8	9–12
I PS:B1.3	identify alternative solutions to a problem	•	○	○	○
N PS:B1.4	develop effective coping skills for dealing with problems	•	○	○	○
D PS:B1.5	demonstrate when, where and how to seek help for solving problems and making decisions	•	○	○	○
I					
C PS:B1.6	know how to apply conflict-resolution skills	•	○	○	○
A PS:B1.7	demonstrate a respect and appreciation for individual and cultural differences	•	○	○	○
T					
O PS:B1.8	know when peer pressure is influencing a decision	•	○	○	○
R PS:B1.9	identify long- and short-term goals			•	○
S PS:B1.10	identify alternative ways of achieving goals			•	○
PS:B1.11	use persistence and perseverance in acquiring knowledge and skills		•	○	○
PS:B1.12	develop an action plan to set and achieve realistic goals			•	○
STANDARD C: Students will understand safety and survival skills.					
Competency PS:C1 Acquire Personal Safety Skills					
PS:C1.1	demonstrate knowledge of personal information (telephone number, home address, emergency contact)	•	○	○	○
I PS:C1.2	learn about the relationship between rules, laws, safety and the protection of rights of the individual	•	○	○	○
N PS:C1.3	learn about the differences between appropriate and inappropriate physical contact	•	○	○	○
D					
I PS:C1.4	demonstrate the ability to set boundaries, rights and personal privacy		•	○	○
C					
A PS:C1.5	differentiate between situations requiring peer support and situations requiring adult professional help		•	○	○
T PS:C1.6	identify resource people in the school and community, and know how to seek their help	•	○	○	○
O					
R PS:C1.7	apply effective problem-solving and decision-making skills to make safe and healthy choices	•	○	○	○
S PS:C1.8	learn about the emotional and physical dangers of substance use and abuse	•	○	○	○
PS:C1.9	learn how to cope with peer pressure		•	○	○
PS:C1.10	learn techniques for managing stress and conflict	•	○	○	○
PS:C1.11	learn coping skills for managing life events			•	○

Source: From *Comprehensive Counseling and Guidance Model for Alabama Public Schools*, by Alabama State Department of Education, 2003, Montgomery, AL: Author. Reprinted with permission.

TABLE 7.3 Eighth-Grade Learner Benchmarks

Eighth-grade students will be able to

Academic Domain

- Evaluate the importance of balancing study time and extracurricular activities
- Develop a tentative 4-year education plan
- Identify and appreciate their individual learning styles, aptitudes, talents, and skills
- Participate in orientation activities and experiences to assist with the educational, social, and emotional transition to high school

Career Development

- Identify specific career interests and abilities using the results of assessment instruments
- Consider future career plans in making educational choices
- Describe their personal skills, abilities, and interests
- Use resources for career exploration and information

Personal/Social Domain

- Analyze their interests, abilities, and aptitudes as components of personal uniqueness
- Demonstrate knowledge and application of assertiveness skills
- Demonstrate a sense of control and responsibility for personal behavior
- Develop skills to cope with the changes associated with adolescence
- Practice dealing with peer pressure
- Evaluate how responsibility helps them manage their lives
- Analyze effective peer and family relationships, their importance, and how they are formed
- Analyze how conflict-resolution skills improve relationships with others

Source: From *Developmental School Counseling Programs: From Theory to Practice,* by P. O. Paisely and G. T. Hubbard, 1994, Alexandria, VA: American Counseling Association. Copyright 1994 by American Counseling Associated. Adapted with permission.

document, the planning team has created a document that identifies learner benchmarks for all domains for eighth-grade students (see Table 7.3).

Delivering Guidance Lessons

The school system has now established a comprehensive counseling curriculum with specific student outcomes linked to state and national standards. The TK–12 team will next turn to the delivery aspect of guidance curriculum. This may involve counselors teaching the content themselves, collaborating with teachers to work together on units or lessons, or consulting with classroom teachers who will provide the actual lessons. Whatever method used, counselors will be writing objectives to express what they want to achieve, designing lessons to plan how to present the content, teaching the units, and evaluating the outcomes of the lessons and units.

Units are groups of lessons arranged around a theme or topic. Units are composed of several lessons or sessions. The number of sessions varies. Any number of lessons from 4 to 10 is appropriate (Tollerud & Nejedlo, 2004). Planning

What personal skills do you have in teaching? What instructional abilities do you want to develop? Check with your classmates to build a comprehensive list.

units involves arranging instructional content into manageable parts in a logical sequence for effective presentation. As noted earlier a unit of instruction centers on a broad concept or a cluster of related concepts. The elements of a unit include the scope (the range of content), focus (what will be emphasized), and sequence (the order in which the content is arranged). The processes (activities that help the students learn) and the product (ways the students will demonstrate their new knowledge) are also identified. These considerations, as well as the age of students, will lead logically to decisions about how many lessons will be contained in each unit. A well-designed unit plan should contain the following information (Tollerud & Nejedlo, 2004; Blum 1998):

Grade level

Unit name or topic

Grade-level competencies

Rationale for the unit

Clear unit purpose

Unit objectives

Number of lessons

Detailed procedure of all age-appropriate unit activities

Coordinated and sequential lessons

Opportunities for students to apply, reflect, and evaluate their learning

Evaluation criteria and method

Clearly articulated goals provide the foundation for the unit planning process. Planning involves determining what the students will learn, through what activities (experiences), and with what materials. Planning a guidance curriculum requires considering each grade and breaking the material into segments by the year, term, unit, week, and day. These plans work best as flexible frameworks that help instructors start and maintain their lessons in the right direction rather than as scripts with no opportunities for elaboration.

Tomlinson (1999) explains levels of learning previously articulated by Hilda Taba. People can learn facts, discrete bits of information. They can develop concepts, or categories of things with common elements to help organize, retain, and use information. Humans can also understand principles, rules that govern concepts. Students develop attitudes, or degrees of commitment to ideas. Finally individuals can acquire skills, the ability to put to work the understandings gained. Many of the specific outcomes of a counseling curriculum are generic and therefore easily linked to other subjects. Skills such as listening, interacting, and forming goals are examples of generic skills in the counseling curriculum that could easily weave into many subjects. The ASCA National Standards presents a list of facts, concepts, principles, attitudes, or skills. The TK–12 team discusses each standard and labels it at its level of learning. Consequently, they are able to generate specific lists of what students should know (facts), understand (concepts and principles), and be able to do (skills). For example, to develop curriculum around a career development standard, decisions might include the following possibilities:

- Facts: appropriate definitions of careers
- Concepts: classifications of careers
- Principles: economic supply and demand for specific careers
- Attitudes: value of work to student and society
- Skills: gathering information about specific careers

Figure 7.1 illustrates this sequence for a particular topic in the development of the Washington County students.

According to Gunter, Estes, and Schwab (2003) a learning objective is "a statement of the measurable learning that is intended to take place as a result of instruction" (p. 27). Mager's (1975) three-part system for establishing objectives includes specifying the intended student behavior, the conditions under which the behavior will occur, and the criteria for an acceptable performance. Another

FIGURE 7.1   Sample Lesson Plan

Strand: Personal/Social Development (2nd Grade) Standard: The student acquires the knowledge, attitudes, and interpersonal skills to help understand and responds to self and others.				
A Topic of Study Consists of: Valuing Diversity				
Key Facts: Information about diverse groups of people	Organizing Concepts: Similarities and differences exist among all people	Guiding Principles: We live in a pluralistic society.	Associated Attitudes: Self-awareness; acceptance of self and others.	Essential Skills: Demonstrate respect for others.
Content: Student will be able to recognize and appreciate individual differences among classmates.	Process: Circle of Hands Activity. Each student draws his/her hands on a large piece of paper so that when drawn side by side the hands form a circle or square with blank space in the center. Inside his or her own hands, each student identifies and writes individual strengths or accomplishments. Throughout the year, significant events or accomplishments of individual students are added to the center opening of the drawing.		Product: Students are able to discuss the collective strengths of the group and identify goals that could be accomplished by the group, but not by the individual.	

Sources: From *The Differentiated Classroom: Responding to the Needs of All Learners,* by Carol Ann Tomlinson, 1999, Alexandria, VA: Association for Supervision and Curriculum Development. Copyright 1999 by ASCD. Reprinted by permission; and *Adventures in Guidance: How to Put Fun Into Your Guidance Program,* by T. Kottman, J. Ashby, and D. DeGraaf, 2001, Alexandria, VA: American Counseling Association. Copyright 2001 by ACA. Reprinted with permission.

approach presented by Gronlund (1995) begins with general outcomes and then clarifies those by listing a few of the sample behaviors that provide evidence that the student has learned. Here are some examples from a conflict-resolution lesson:

General objective: Students will apply problem-solving skills to peer interactions that involve conflict.

Specific examples:

1. Explains each side of the conflict.
2. States possible responses of each side.
3. Identifies potential outcomes for each response.
4. Discriminates between helpful and nonhelpful responses.
5. Demonstrates peaceful, nonviolent resolution to situation.

Learning objectives focus the lesson on specific student accomplishments in the cognitive, affective, and psychomotor-behavioral domains. Bloom, Englehart, Frost, Hill, and Krathwohl (1956) presented a way to identify educational outcomes and to classify those outcomes by categories in a hierarchical pattern. In their taxonomy they list the three domains of education: cognitive, affective, and psychomotor. Table 7.4 includes the general and more specific categories for the three domains of educational taxonomies. Cognitive objectives focus on the intellectual outcomes, facts, concepts, and principles mentioned earlier. In the

TABLE 7.4 Sample Developmental Guidance Needs

	Academic Development	Career Development	Personal/Social Development
Elementary School The formation of basic attitudes and information about self and life opportunities begin.	K–2: Students need help developing the following: Essential skills they need to be successful in school (read, write, and do basic computations); Descriptions for how they learn something, how they recall information, and how they plan to complete an assignment; Ability to identify situations in which learning is easy or hard; Ability to identify the benefits of learning. 3–5: Students need help developing the following:	Students need help developing the following: The ability to describe workers in various settings, type of work of family members, type of work children do; Ability to describe what they like to do and how they change from year to year; Awareness of differences among peers and themselves; Awareness of the skills they have. Students need help developing the following: Recognition of choices	Students need help developing the following: Self-awareness, confidence, and competence; Skills to describe relationships and the process of making and keeping friends; Positive description of attributes, and unique qualities of self and others; Responsibility for tasks at home, school, and regarding care of self and belongings. Students need help developing the following: Description of *(Continued)*

TABLE 7.4 (*Continued*)

	Academic Development	Career Development	Personal/Social Development
	Strategies that help them learn such as note taking, practicing memory skills, goal setting, and preparing for tests; An understanding of how learning occurs differently for different people and how it occurs both in and out of school; The ability to apply different skills to different school subjects and settings; The ability to describe things they learned about themselves from taking tests.	people make about work and their many other life roles; Ability to describe work of men and women, and relationship of interests and abilities to work; Ability to define "future" and describe what their lives may be like in the future.	themselves, their strengths; Recognition of the impact their actions have on others and that their choices have consequences; Understanding of how traits develop; Ability to express appreciation to others for their own unique qualities; Ability to know when change is and is not possible; Recognition and acceptance of cultural differences; Ability to identify and express feelings in an acceptable manner.
Middle School Exploring and reality testing attitudes and information about self, others, and opportunities.	6–8: Students need help developing the following: The ability to assert themselves by asking questions, both at home and at school; Plans for their own study areas, study schedule, and study style; The ability to achieve balance between school and other activities; A tentative four-year education plan and portfolio based on high school graduation requirements.	Students need help developing the following: Understanding how stereotypes and experiences influence their career choices; Ability to discuss career planning process and identify and use career resources; Projections for how some careers may be different in the future; Descriptions of their existing skills and how those relate to current workforce demands; Explanations for how needs can be met in work and leisure.	Students need help developing the following: Positive health habits; Good communication skills; Understanding peer pressure; Ability to apply problem-solving models to real-world problems; Ability to identify and use personal strengths; Understand how past choices influence present and future actions; Descriptions of unique qualities of self, positive self-concept, and understanding of one's uniqueness as well as similarities with others; Ability to deal with pressure; Understanding

	Academic Development	Career Development	Personal/Social Development
			of relationship between personal responsibility and life management.
High School Specific planning related to imminence of making the transition from school to work or college.	9–12: Students need help developing the following: Ability to identify and use community resources; Understanding of when and why 4-year plan may need to be revised; Ability to analyze test results and use to plan for improvement; Effective work habits; Understanding of relationship between student behavior and academic success; A plan for collecting postsecondary information, making contacts and plans for graduation; A plan for future education or training; The ability to evaluate and revise future goals based on performance, interest, and range of available options.	Students need help developing the following: Description of skills, abilities, interests, needs, and understanding of how those factors influence career choice; Understanding of nontraditional careers open to them; Congruence between educational plan and career goals; Assessment of ability to achieve goals and integrate learning into planning; Descriptions of skills and qualifications to obtain and keep specific jobs of interest; Strategies for coping with sexual harassment, sexual discrimination, and other potential difficulties in the workplace.	Students need help developing the following: Skills to respond to pressure; Recognition of qualities of people who are different from self and identification of own biases and stereotypes that interfere with establishing relationships; Ability to develop strategies for overcoming stereotypes and biases; Ability to generate alternatives and assess consequences before acting; Ability to direct and control feelings; Understanding of all that goes into making choices.

Source: From *The Revised Comprehensive Counseling and Guidance Model for Alabama Public Schools*, by Alabama State Department of Education, 1996, Montgomery: AL: Author. Reprinted with permission.

cognitive domain the categories are knowledge (recalling information and facts), comprehension (understanding, translating the information), application (using information to solve problems), analysis (breaking down information into parts and revealing organization), synthesis (creating a new idea, product, or solution), and evaluation (assessing something against a standard).

The affective domain describes the attitudes, feelings, and dispositions that students are expected to acquire (Krathwohl, Bloom, & Masia, 1964). Those objectives are receiving (being aware or attending to something), responding (showing some new behavior as a result of an experience), valuing (showing definite involvement or commitment), organizing (integrating a new value), and characterizing (acting consistently with the new value). The psychomotor domain involves ability and coordination objectives. Gunter, Estes, and Schwab (2003) explain that taxonomy in the psychomotor domain identifies these levels: readiness (being willing to participate), observation (watching the behavior), perception (recognizing the behavior), response (performing the behavior), and adaptation (incorporating the behavior into one's repertoire). Gronlund (1995) suggests using the domains to get ideas for objectives, to help in writing clear statements about expectations, and to provide a check on completeness. Examples of words that can be used in educational objectives can be found in Figure 7.2.

The following statement is a learning benchmark (educational objective) in the career development standards for an eighth-grade student: "The student locates community resources for exploration related to personal interest, aptitudes, and skills." At what level of the cognitive domain is that written? The following statement is a benchmark (educational objective) in the career development standards for a first-grade student: "The student recognizes all careers are acceptable to any gender." At what level of the affective domain is that written? The following statement is a benchmark (educational objective) in the career development standards for an eleventh-grade student: "The student applies job readiness skills to seek educational and employment opportunities." Which parts of the psychomotor domain might this objective include? Write a learning objective based on this career development standard: "The student employs strategies to achieve future career success and satisfaction" for a seventh-grade student using cognitive, affective, and psychomotor domains. Compare your objectives to those written by your classmates.

A learning objective contains four parts. The audience refers to the learners for whom the lesson is intended. For that reason many learning objectives begin with the phrase, "The learner will. . . ." Next the expected behavior is stated with verbs that describe the cognitive, affective, or psychomotor domain around which the lesson is constructed. For example, "The learner will use a decision-making model to explain his or her choices." The third part of a learning objective expresses when or how the intended behavior will be measured. In our example that would be something like "After reading a series of five dilemmas related to peer pressure, the learner will use a decision-making model to explain his or her choices." The fourth part contains the level of expected performance or at what level the learners need to perform the behavior for the objective to be considered met. Therefore, to complete our example "After reading a series of five dilemmas related to peer pressure, the learner will use a decision-making model to explain his or her choices for at least three of the scenarios."

Counselors may find the following questions helpful in their planning processes:

- What overarching understandings are desired? (What will students understand as a result of this unit?)
- What are the overarching "essential" questions? (What "essential" and "unit" questions will focus this unit?)
- What evidence will show that students understand?
- Given the targeted understandings, the other unit goals, and the assessment evidence identified, what knowledge and skill are needed?
- What teaching and learning experiences will equip students to demonstrate the targeted understanding? (Wiggins & McTighe, 1998)

The lesson plan outlined in Figure 7.2 provides a way for instructors to check on whether they have fully addressed these questions as they prepare to deliver a classroom lesson.

FIGURE 7.2   Educational Taxonomies

Sample of Verbs in the Cognitive Domain

Knowledge	to recall, to repeat, to recollect, to memorize, to list
Comprehension	to identify, to recognize, to select
Application	to use, to solve, to practice, to reproduce, to compare, to contrast
Analysis	to investigate, to separate, to study, to research, to describe
Synthesis	to combine, to formulate, to deduce, to unite, to assemble
Evaluation	to appraise, to judge, to assess, to assign value to, to accept

Sample of Verbs in the Affective Domain

Receiving	to take in, to listen, to encounter, to be aware
Responding	to react, to reply, to answer, to comply
Valuing	to accept, to reject, to esteem, to regard, to desire
Organization	to compare, to order, to prioritize
Characterization	to internalize, to personalize, to demonstrate

Sample of Verbs in the Psychomotor Domain

Readiness	willing, prepared, watches
Observation	attends, is interested
Perception	senses, has a feel for, is able
Response	practices, imitates, replicates
Adaptation	masters, develops, changes

Source: From *Instruction: A Models Approach,* 3rd edition, by M. A. Gunter, T. H. Estes, and J. Schwab, 1999, Boston: Allyn & Bacon. Copyright 1999 by Pearson Education. Reprinted by permission of the publisher.

IMPLEMENTING THE GUIDANCE CURRICULUM

The overarching goal of the guidance curriculum is for students to learn specific skills, behaviors, and attitudes that lead to school achievement and success in life. Learning has been defined in two ways: (1) the relatively permanent changes in behavior that occur due to experiences and (2) the relatively permanent changes in mental associations that occur as a result of experiences (Ormrod, 1999). These two definitions agree that learning is relatively permanent and is a result of experience (Ormrod, 2000). They differ in that the first definition specifies that changes associated with learning are behavioral, which implies that the changes are immediately observable. The second definition describes changes in mental associations, which may or may not result in immediate, observable behavioral change.

For example, consider the goal of teaching 18 fifth-grade students to resolve conflicts in a peaceful, nonviolent way through a series of lessons presented in their classroom by the school counselor (Personal/Social Development Standard C: Students will understand safety and survival skills). Assume that the subject has been introduced and the necessary skills both explained and demonstrated by the

FIGURE 7.3   Sample Lesson Plan Format

Lesson Plan
Topic: Class: Date:
Learner Outcomes: Lesson objectives The learner will . . .

Introduction: Engaging the learner in the topic, connecting the topic to something already known
    Identify focus:
    Create anticipation:
    Encourage learning:

Learning Activities: Teaching procedures and student activities
 	
    Counselor:
 	
    Student:

Assessment/Evaluation: Checking for understanding
Closing: Summary and extended practice
Follow-up: Independent practice and homework
Resources: Equipment, materials, other teaching aids

counselor. The counselor asks for five students to volunteer to role-play a conflict that they attempt to resolve using the skills previously introduced. If these five students successfully resolve the conflict using the new skills (or behaviors), we can assume that learning has occurred for them, but what about the other 13 students in the classroom? Are we to assume that no learning has occurred because they have not demonstrated the skills or behaviors to which they have been exposed? From a cognitive (mental association) point of view, students who have experienced the lessons related to conflict-resolution strategies may also learn the skills through their observations of the counselor and the subsequent student role play. The behaviors, however, may not be evident until such time as they need to use the skills to resolve a conflict. The key to learning, from either perspective, is experience. The challenge for instructors is to create situations that become meaningful learning experiences for a diverse student population.

Learning styles explain the differences in the process of learning. One approach classifies four basic styles of learning. The mastery style learner takes in information concretely, thinks sequentially, and considers clarity and practicality the most valuable terms of learning. The understanding style learner looks more at ideas and abstractions, and learns by questioning, reasoning, and testing. These learners want logic and the use of evidence in order to learn. The self-expressive style learner looks for images implied in learning. They use emotions to build new ideas and products and judge the learning process by its originality, aesthetics, and ability to surprise or delight. Finally the interpersonal style learner focuses on concrete information, prefers to learn socially, and evaluates learning in terms of its use in helping others. Silver, Strong, and Perini (1997) offer those explanations and propose that those styles complement a model of multiple intelligences.

Gardner's (1999) theory of multiple intelligences explains the content or products of learning. Gardner posits eight types of intelligence. Linguistic intelligence refers to the ability to use language for self-expression and for understanding others. Logical-mathematical intelligence requires comprehending causal relationships and for using numbers, quantities, and operations. Spatial intelligence involves mentally representing the world spatially. Musical intelligence refers to the ability to think musically, to hear patterns, recognize them, remember them, and possibly manipulate those patterns. Bodily-kinesthetic intelligence includes the ability to use the body to solve complex motor problems such as making something or performing some action. Interpersonal intelligence relates to how to build relationships and to solve interpersonal problems. Intrapersonal intelligence refers to an understanding of self, including personal abilities, limitations, self-control, and self-motivation. Finally naturalistic intelligence involves the ability to classify living things and to determine features of the natural world. People may have strengths and weaknesses in any of these eight categories. Instruction that touches as many of the fields as possible will facilitate multiple styles of learning through different styles of intelligence. Silver, Strong, and Perini (1997) believe that integration provides tools to meet high standards.

> Rate yourself in terms of these different types of intelligence. How might your talents in these be used to enhance your instruction? How might avoiding the areas in which you are less well developed have a negative on your instruction?

Organizing and Presenting Lessons

INTRODUCTION

The initial part of a lesson is designed to capture the attention of the audience. The presenter will communicate an overview of the topic, building a roadmap for what is to come. Additionally the presenter will connect the subject to something already known. This type of stimulus for learning may be accomplished by a series of questions, a video clip, a story, or a reading assignment for example. The introductions should set the stage for the lesson.

LEARNING ACTIVITIES

Counselors facilitate learning by using many methods of instruction (Woolfolk, 1998). Using a counselor-centered approach, they may choose to lecture and explain as a method for communicating material to the learners. Another approach to teaching is through recitation and questioning. Thought-provoking and varied questions increase the effectiveness of this teaching method, where students learn how to ask and how to explain. Counselors may also use supervised practice activities of seatwork and homework as follow-up to a lesson. These teaching practices are centered on the counselor who presents, questions, reacts, and corrects. These approaches might be used when explaining to high school juniors and their parents the process of applying to college.

Working in small discussion groups, identify classroom guidance topics and grade levels where counselor-centered strategies may be appropriate. Also discuss the cultural values and norms that may be transmitted by this approach and identify cultural groups whose values may be in conflict with those values on which this approach is based.

Student-centered practices require more active participation from the learner. Group discussions allow students to ask questions, answer each other's questions, and respond to each other's answers. Brainstorming allows students to generate lists and to evaluate and prioritize the possibilities. Simulations and role playing encourage students to explore many dimensions of a situation. Simulations involve the creation of an experience, perhaps a dilemma, problem, or crisis, within the classroom. Students may then propose, debate, and evaluate courses of action. Role playing involves a student accepting a role in a scenario and acting out that person in that situation. Brookfield (1990) provides guidelines for instructors to create and guide simulations and role plays. Computers, videodiscs, and other technology provide valuable tools for encouraging learning and problem solving. For example, computer simulations introduce simplified versions of real-life situations with which the student can interact. Problem-based learning is a strategy that promotes varied learning strategies. Other student-centered learning practices are cooperative learning groups. These groups create positive interdependence enhanced by interactions, social skills, group processing, and individual accountability (Johnson & Johnson, 2000).

Brown and Trusty (2005) suggest some other possible learning formats:

Discuss the cultural values and norms that may be transmitted by the cooperative work group approach and identify cultural contexts in which those values may be in conflict with students' values.

- Cooperative problem-solving teams where members share information and reach a solution to the dilemma.
- Cooperative jigsaw in which team members have separate responsibilities for a part of the task or problem.
- Group role plays and skits in which students either create their own scenarios or act out scripted situations.

As well as the selection of strategies, counselors choose materials and resources to use in their classes. Counselors are responsible for evaluating materials for suitability for the topic, age of students, and bias. Counselors should review all materials they plan to use with students to ensure that the standards for success in life, including work and family roles, are not based on traditional roles, stereotypes, or biases. Generally children up to grade 2 will respond to sensorimotor activities focusing on the present and need to practice behaviors to learn them. Young people from grades 3 to 7 are in the concrete operations stage of thinking and learn more from concrete activities. As they mature they can begin to understand the cause and effect sides of relationships. Adolescents in grades 8 through 12 have often reached the formal operations stage and may respond to activities of abstract, subjective reasoning, and more complex information.

In your small groups discuss the special needs that might be exhibited by a student or students for whom English is a second language. How might you respond to these needs? What about a student who has a physical disability such as a severe visual impairment?

TEACHING

Counselors lay the groundwork for learning with their thorough and thoughtful planning of units and lessons. The next step involves presenting the guidance lesson. Delivering information in a classroom allows counselors to use their teaching skills to help students master the guidance curriculum. Brown and

Trusty (2005), Sears (2005), and Tollerud and Nejedlo (2004) have compiled the following helpful ideas for presenting lessons:

1. Prepare the classroom ahead of time if possible. Always have materials and handouts ready. Arrange for needed equipment, be familiar with operating procedures or have someone who is.
2. Begin the lesson with something interesting that will capture the students' attention and interest.
3. Tell the students the basic goal and plan for the lesson in your introduction. For example, you could begin a lesson on career exploration with something like, "Today we are going to look at ways to find out what people in certain jobs do and see how those activities fit what you enjoy."
4. Communicate clearly and accurately. Display your confidence and strength by using the tempo of your words, the pitch of your voice, and a volume level that grabs the students' attention. Learn to project your voice. Be both businesslike and warm.
5. Move around the room. Movement stimulates the attention. Also if some students are inattentive, moving closer to them may help them become engaged.
6. Show your enthusiasm and energy.
7. Relax and smile. Keep the classroom atmosphere relaxed but well supervised.
8. Be flexible. If something you are doing isn't working, change it. Classes respond differently to activities so have backup learning formats.
9. Make an effort to draw all students into learning. Personalize the content and balance completing the task and adjusting as needed. Be aware of the time.
10. Use open-ended questions and discussion techniques. As students share, use comments to draw others into the discussion. Show that you value their ideas and opinions.
11. Check often for understanding. Ask for feedback several times during the lesson.
12. Use several learning formats such as individual and group activities and material for different styles of learning.
13. Use demonstrations, role plays, and homework often.
14. Pay attention to transitions, bridging one part of the lesson to the next. Make the logical connection and give clear instructions for all activities.
15. Create an environment that provides support and encouragement. Plan for ways students can succeed.
16. Restate your learning objective and review the parts of the lesson. Students may help with this summary. End the lesson by connecting the content to situations in the students' worlds. Providing ways to apply the lesson content in homework assignments strengthens the students' learning.
17. Keep problems in perspective. Learn from the things that do not go well, adapt the lesson plan and presentation. Timely, well-organized, and enjoyable lessons help prevent discipline problems.

Marzano, Pickering, and Pollock (2001) have prepared a summary of research-based strategies that support student learning. Those authors discuss these practices: having students identify similarities and differences, asking students to summarize and take notes, reinforcing effort, giving opportunities for homework and practice, providing nonlinguistic symbols, setting objectives, testing hypotheses, and using questions, cues, and advance organizers. They suggest that the beginning of a unit includes strategies for setting goals. During a unit instructors should monitor the progress being made toward the goals, introduce new knowledge and practice, and review learning and application of the learning. Finally at the end of a unit, teachers help the learners determine how well the goals have been met. Counselors who incorporate those practices into the delivery of the guidance curriculum increase their effectiveness.

Classroom Management

Well-designed and effectively presented lessons will decrease the likelihood of discipline problems in a classroom but school counselors also need to be prepared to address difficult behaviors. Most schools and classrooms have rules of conduct established with which students are familiar. Counselors also need to be familiar with these rules, apply them consistently, and if one intends to deviate from the norm, clearly explain to students the new rules. School counselors seldom have a classroom devoted only to them so they will be visiting someone else's room. Teachers will appreciate counselors who know their basic classroom procedures even as the counselor adapts those rules to personal styles and roles.

Saphier and Gower (1997) propose that capturing students' attention is a critical part of preventing misbehavior in a classroom. They suggest counselors keeping everyone alert, using encouragement, enthusiasm, appropriate humor, and drama as strategies to accomplish this. Other ideas include using a variety of inflections, stimulating their students' curiosity, using suspense, and connecting all topics with students' interests.

Providing a smooth flow to lessons, sometimes called momentum, also helps avoid problems. This can be accomplished by having sufficient materials available. Additionally counselors should be tuned in to everything that is happening. They need to be aware of what all the groups and individuals are doing, what is next in the lesson, and where transitions need to be strengthened (Saphier & Gower, 1997). They anticipate obstacles and work to prevent them. Some other strategies for managing classroom behavior suggested by Blum (1998) include establishing positive relationships with students, maintaining an awareness of special needs of students in the group, and incorporating a system for recognizing appropriate behavior. To deliver lessons effectively in a large group, counselors must be able to manage classroom behavior.

EVALUATION

Tomlinson (1999) explains that content is the substance of what a student learns (facts), understands (concepts and principles), and can do (skills) that results from a segment of study such as a lesson or unit. Activities and materials enhance the student's interaction with the content. Process involves the different ways students make sense of the content and work with it. Activities are more likely to be effective if they have a clearly defined purpose, focus students on one key understanding, and cause students to use a skill to work with the ideas. Some other instructional practices increase effectiveness. One involves instructors ensuring that students will have to understand rather than just repeat the idea. Another strategy is to help students relate new ideas to previous ones. Finally matching the student's level of readiness to the material also increases the likelihood of activities being effective. The other component of the equation is the product, the way that students show what they have come to know and are able to do.

Well-written learning objectives set the stage for checking to see what has been learned. Counselors establish their expectations during the planning stage with goals and objectives. Evaluation methods have been written into those statements. Instructors recognize different ways students can demonstrate they have mastered the topic and realize that strategies for checking students' learning should match their learning objective. At the conclusion of the lesson, the school counselor collects the data to see if the objective has been met. For example, recalling the learning objective above, "After reading a series of five dilemmas related to peer pressure, the learner will use a decision-making model to explain his or her choices for at least three of the scenarios," the counselor could collect papers students have written describing how they reached a decision to determine whether the objective has been achieved.

Discuss with your classmates how school counselors might report process, perception, and results data for the classroom guidance lessons designed to teach students to use a decision-making model when confronted with peer conflicts.

Objectives in the three domains of cognitive, affective, and psychomotor require appropriate types of evaluation processes. Gunter, Estes, and Schwab (2003) present a variety of evaluation procedures for the three domains. Ways of checking cognitive learning may involve oral questions, classroom interviews, journals, logs, and participation in activities and projects as well as tests. Simulated situations in which students demonstrate their learning may be particularly effective. Students could also create, either verbally or orally, a before and after summary of their understanding of the topic. Scoring rubrics may also be designed for evaluation purposes. Rubrics contain lists of categories and descriptions of varying evidence that is needed to see whether the target has been met.

Measuring attitudes, feelings, and beliefs—the substance of the affective domain—requires different strategies. Using pre- and post-unit questionnaires and checklists, making observations, tape recording class discussions, and monitoring the frequency of using materials such as occupational information are different ways to assess attitudes and beliefs. Psychomotor skills are presented in measurable parts with a degree of acceptable performance stated. In this domain, evaluation would be a careful record of the student's progress on those steps. Students may keep their own record in this skill development, in cognitive learning, or in the affective domain.

Some assignments may be designed to capture learning in all domains. In a career unit, for instance, building a career portfolio may require that students apply information by identifying the different categories of careers of all school

Working in small discussion groups, identify classroom guidance topics and grade levels where counselor-centered strategies may be appropriate. Also discuss the cultural values and norms that may be transmitted by this approach and identify cultural groups whose values may be in conflict with those values on which this approach is based.

personnel and presenting that in a graphic display; then presenting a rationale for one of those jobs they believe to be most important; and finally, recording an interview with one person who works in the school. Counselors and teachers can generate other ideas for projects, problem solutions, summary descriptions, writing a script, and numerous other possibilities for students and instructors to evaluate and confirm learning.

Goodnough, Perusse, and Erford (2003) emphasize that careful assessment of lessons, units, and other instructional operations helps counselors become more effective. They note that if students do not master the lesson, the instruction must be analyzed and improved. Counselors may consider these questions: Were the objectives clear? Were the expectations too high? Were the activities inappropriate? Were the assessment criteria inadequate? Counselors revise according to their understanding of the lesson deficiencies.

GUIDANCE CURRICULUM EFFECTIVENESS

In their review of the school counseling literature, Borders and Drury (1992) note that school counselors are the primary sources of content, plans, strategies, and materials for classroom delivery of the guidance curriculum. They also cite the effectiveness of this intervention on the academic achievement and school adjustment behaviors of children. As we have discussed, counselors may be primarily planners of the curriculum and they may also be the instructor that works in the classroom helping students master this content. Therefore, knowing what makes teachers effective will prepare them to use classroom time most constructively.

Cotton (n.d.) reviewed educational research to describe characteristics and practices that improve student learning. Counselors prepare students for lessons by attending to the following practices: explain objectives in simple language and continue to refer to those purposes to maintain focus, check periodically to be sure students understand the objectives, and connect the current topic to previous studies to help students recognize how the concepts or skills build on each other. Students' curiosity is aroused about the content by relating it to things that have personal relevance to them. Counselors let students know in advance the expectations such as participation and they gauge students' readiness to learn. Advance organizers, study questions, and predictions help prepare students for learning.

Besides these methods of preparing students for learning, counselors engage the students by providing clear and focused instruction. They review activities, give clear directions, emphasize key points, and check students' understanding. Lecture and demonstrations are clear. When possible, they use learning strategies and materials that are appropriate to different learning styles. Counselors provide opportunities for guided and independent practice with new concepts by giving instruction in studying, remembering, and applying what is learned.

Counselors choose problems and academic tasks that are varied, challenging, and well matched to the lesson so that success is high. Computer-assisted activities supplement and are integrated with teacher-directed learning.

Next teachers and counselors give students feedback on their learning progress. They respond to comments and assignments, acknowledge correct answers, and help students understand and correct errors. Specific feedback is related to unit or lesson goals. Outcomes are measured and disaggregated to determine whether one or more racial or ethnic groups fail, disproportionately, to master the objectives. If so, culturally competent instructors do not attribute lack of achievement to cultural or familial deprivation, but instead examine the curricular experiences to ensure relevance to all students in the class (Hollins, 1999). Based on this review, counselors and teachers revise and reteach lessons as necessary. They teach strategies for problem solving, decision making, and other study skills. They incorporate probing, redirection, and reinforcement to improve the quality of student responses.

Effective instructors create a positive classroom environment that encourages participation and promotes curiosity. They are in charge of their classrooms and they manage human relations well. Counselors who master the strategies described will be effective classroom instructors. Besides the teaching skills summarized above, Blum (1998) reminds counselors they need to expand their knowledge of the expectations and needs of teachers with whom they work. Effective counselors will consider teachers' time, schedules, and requirements as classroom guidance schedules are developed. Blum further suggests posting counseling schedules on doors to provide ongoing notification of the lessons, grade levels, and dates of the counselor's presentations.

OUTCOMES OF THE GUIDANCE CURRICULUM

McGannon, Carey, and Dimmitt (2005) investigated research on classroom guidance curriculum. Based on a number of studies that document positive outcomes, they concluded that comprehensive curriculums have a positive impact on student knowledge in the academic and social/personal domains.

Academics

Several studies have considered the impact of classroom guidance activities on academic achievement. Sink and Stroh (2003) found higher achievement scores for elementary age students who attended schools with comprehensive counseling programs. Bingman and Campbell (2003) also found positive effects on academic achievement and school success after students participated in a Student Success Skills curriculum. Those lessons focus on cognitive, social, and self-management skills. Gerler and Herndon (1993) and Lee (1993) looked at the effectiveness of a multimodal guidance unit on school success. Positive differences between the treatment and control groups were reported. Carns and

> Review the guidance curriculum outcomes reported by authors in the three domains and try to identify the types of data reported.

Carns (1991) described a study skills guidance program that resulted in increases in students' scores on the California Test of Basic Skills.

Social/Personal

Other studies have considered curriculum related to student behaviors and attitudes. The Committee for Children designed the *Second Step Violence Prevention* curriculum to improve students' behaviors. Grossman and colleagues (1997) used that unit with second and third graders. They found a decrease in physically aggressive behavior and an increase in pro-social behaviors in both playground and cafeteria settings. A study using another curriculum (*PeaceBuilders*) that focuses on reducing aggressive behavior and increasing social competence had similar findings (Flannery et al., 2003). However, *Warning Signs*, a curriculum for urban high school students resulted in no significant differences (Schaefer-Schiumo & Ginsberg, 2003). Classroom guidance improved student behaviors, attitude, and knowledge in areas of goal setting, problem solving, career exploration, and school resources (Schlossberg, Morris, & Lieberman, 2001). Likewise two studies, Henderson, Kelbey, and Engebretson (1992) and Omizo, Omizo, and D' Andrea (1992), that focused on stress reduction techniques helped improve self-concept, locus of control, and coping in students. Researchers also have reported improvements in stress symptoms (Kiselica, Baker, Thomas, & Reedy, 1994) and test anxiety (Cheek, Bradley, Reynolds, & Coy, 2002).

Some studies in guidance activities concentrated on social skills. That research found an increase in social attractiveness (Ciechalski & Schmidt, 1995), self-esteem, and self-efficacy and a decrease in anxiety and aggression (DeRosier, 2004). Kelly (1996) addressed the effect of classroom lessons on the concept of fairness, and Bruce, Shade and Cossairt (1996) found an increase in empathy and positive interactions after their guidance activities. A study on multicultural group guidance (D'Andrea & Daniels, 1995) helped third-grade students develop skills to reduce arguments that had arisen from negative cultural or ethnic prejudices. Graham and Pulvino (2000) also looked at multicultural conflict-resolution education that provided students with more positive perspectives and built skills but did not help with cultural understanding.

SUMMARY

School counselors reach students by planning and implementing a guidance curriculum. Indeed counselors have been urged to use their skills in the classroom as a parsimonious and visible way of helping students (Fall, 1994; Sears, 2005). Counselors can introduce themselves and cover a range of issues in this teaching role. Classroom teachers will gain by seeing how counselors contribute to students' knowledge, skills, and well-being and will learn ways to integrate the guidance curriculum into subject-matter content (Sears, 2005). This chapter has provided information necessary for understanding the meaning, scope, and sequence of a guidance curriculum. A review of some developmental milestones that affect student learning has also been provided. Finally, an overview of the specifics of planning, implementing, and evaluating units and lessons has been given. Further support for implementing the guidance curriculum is found in the outcome research. Applying these concepts will allow school counselors to engage the school in increasing students' competencies in academic, career, and personal/social content areas.

PORTFOLIO COMPONENTS

1. Reflect on the effective teachers you have observed and from whom you have learned. Develop a composite of these teachers reflecting your own ideal of how you would like to plan and deliver instruction, manage classroom behavior, and relate to your students. What skills or behaviors do you need to develop to meet your ideal? How will you go about developing the requisite abilities? Are there any natural styles of interaction you now use that need to be altered to meet your ideal? What are they?

2. Develop a description of your current stage of development in the following areas: personal/social, academic, career, and racial identity. How might your own stage or process of development in these areas be reflected in curriculum planning? How will you address any developmental needs arising from your consideration of these questions?

3. Develop a set of questions and interview a school counselor about the system used in his or her school to manage classroom behavior. Determine whether any adaptations during classroom guidance lessons are made, why, and how students are apprised of the differences in standards of behavior. Prepare a one-page reflective statement describing what you learned about classroom management and how you will use the information in your own practice.

CHAPTER 8

Individual Planning

PLANNING FOR THE FUTURE

Mr. Terman and the Washington County Schools (TK–12) team are meeting for the final time in May to discuss the status of the school counseling program. Mr. Terman begins the meeting, "Congratulations to everyone involved in developing our guidance curriculum. Both the system administration and school board have approved the adoption of the curriculum, and we are set to implement in August. Please submit a request for materials needed for implementation to me no later than June 1. Today I would like for us to discuss the program element we wish to review and revise during the next school year. I hope we can articulate our goals and develop our time line. Is that an agreeable agenda?" With the team's approval, the meeting continues.

Ms. Ina Lerner and Mr. Igor Grund observe that the highest priority identified in their most recent needs assessment—helping students and their families plan for the future—does not seem to be fully addressed in the approved guidance curriculum. The curriculum does include general planning information and the development of skills for success in the three developmental domains, but does not provide enough specificity to assist students and their families with the development of individual plans. Therefore, the group agrees that the individual planning program element will be the focus of their planning activities during the coming school year.

Ms. Amelia Farmer suggests that the skills and knowledge necessary to plan for one's career and educational future are acquired and/or developed during the elementary school years through participation in the classroom guidance curriculum. The elementary counselors agree that this is the case and remind the group that approximately 50% of their time will be spent in classroom guidance with only 10% or less spent in activities related to individual planning. Middle school and high school counselors will spend far less time on the guidance curriculum, approximately 20%, with 30% of their time devoted to individual planning.

Following an extended discussion, the group agreed on the following goals:

1. Review the skills and knowledge related to future career and educational planning supported by the elementary school guidance curriculum and supplement with individual planning activities (e.g., appraisal, placement) as needed.

2. Identify the relevant national standards associated with career and educational planning and determine the extent to which the standards are met in the current program.

3. Identify ways to strengthen the current individual planning program element, particularly in grades 7 through 12, paying specific attention to those groups of students most likely to encounter barriers.

4. Identify the means for delivering the program element at each grade level.

Individual planning provides students the support, skills, and knowledge they need to set goals for themselves and to systematically monitor their progress toward those goals (Gysbers & Henderson, 2000). The activities associated with individual planning are designed to be preventive. The interventions assist students in planning their futures as well as managing their personal and career development.

Career and educational planning are intertwined. The successful preparation for careers is predicated on appropriate academic preparation. As Graham (1993) points out, the needs of the American workforce in 21st-century American society dictate that all children must become academically proficient. For much of the 20th century the emphasis in U.S. schools was on increasing participation in and access to the educational enterprise. Graham reports that we have been successful in meeting both goals. Students from all settings, from all types of families, and with widely varying abilities participate at the greatest rate in our history in education. However, as a result of the changing economy and occupational opportunities students must graduate from high school with more than basic literacy skills if they are to be successful in the 21st-century workforce. Consequently, individual planning has an increased importance in today's society.

After reading and discussing this chapter, you should be able to

- Define individual planning and identify the relevant professional standards most appropriately met through this program element.
- Identify the goals most often associated with this program element at each grade level.
- Identify the counselor skills and functions associated with this program element.

INDIVIDUAL PLANNING

ASCA (2000) summarizes the professional association's position on education planning in the following: "The professional school counselor advocates for equal educational planning opportunities for all students. Decisions students make about a chosen course of study must be based upon information unique to the individual and his or her profile of skills and knowledge" (p. 1). Many of the counseling activities that support students' collection and understanding of information unique to them fall under the program function of individual planning.

The term *individual planning* refers to helping individual students establish personal goals and develop future plans (ASCA, 2003a). Appraisal, advisement, placement, and follow-up are some of the program activities in place to systematically deliver this program element. Individual student planning competencies are met through individual and group counseling with students, consultation with parents and teachers, coordination of community resources, classroom guidance focused on career education, and development and maintenance of career information centers. In these ways counselors and others assist all students in the development of career life plans consistent with their personal/social, academic, and career goals (Gysbers & Henderson, 2000). The career development portion of individual planning is designed across K–12 levels to build the skills and knowledge needed for careful choices and future plans. The following steps are one state's (Schwallie-Giddis & Kobylarz, 2000) sequence for accomplishing an integration of career and academic training.

1. Grades K–5: Students develop an awareness of self and the value of work. They are exposed to careers and to technology.
2. Grade 6: Counselors, teachers, and parents help students assess their personal aptitudes, abilities, and interests and then relate those qualities to careers. Students also learn the role of technology in work.
3. Grades 7–8: Students set career-oriented goals and develop a 4-year program of study for high school that supports their goals. Students, parents, and educators review plans each year.
4. Grades 9–12: During high school an "applied curriculum" relates academic concepts to the workplace.

FACILITATING CAREER AND EDUCATIONAL DEVELOPMENT

Counselors incorporate individual planning into a counseling program using standards from organizations, such as the ASCA National Standards for School Counseling Programs (Campbell & Dahir, 1997; see Appendix B). In addition to the ASCA standards for academic and career development, the National Career Development Guidelines (www.acrnetwork.org/ncdg/) offer counselors sets of skills and knowledge in three areas—self-knowledge, educational and occupational exploration, and career planning—across the three levels typically associated with K–12 schooling. The National Career Development Guidelines include over 200 indicators across three learning stages—knowledge, application, and reflection. An example of some information from the National Career Development Guidelines appears in Table 8.1. Additionally the Web site for America's Career Resource Network (www.acrnetwork.org) has resources to aid in the delivery of career and life planning services for students, parents, teachers, counselors, and administrators.

The National Occupational Information Coordinating Committee (NOICC, 1988) recommends that career guidance programs in schools include seven processes: classroom instruction, counseling, assessment, career information, placement, consultation, and referral. Drummond and Ryan (1995) summarize the specific responsibilities of counselors as

1. Helping teachers implement career education in classrooms.
2. Serving as a liaison between the school and the business community.
3. Helping incorporate career education concepts within the family system.
4. Facilitating students with their educational and career development planning.
5. At the high school level participating in job placement programs and follow-up studies of former students.

TABLE 8.1 National Career Development Guidelines

Understanding the Guidelines Framework

Domains and Goals

Domains, goals and indicators organize the Guidelines framework. The **three domains:** Personal Social Development (PS), Educational Achievement and Lifelong Learning (ED) and Career Management (CM) organize content that is further described by **eleven goals.** The goals define broad areas of career development competency as shown below.

Personal Social Development Domain

- GOAL PS1 Develop understanding of self to build and maintain a positive self-concept.
- GOAL PS2 Develop positive interpersonal skills including respect for diversity.
- GOAL PS3 Integrate growth and change into your career development.
- GOAL PS4 Balance personal, leisure, community, learner, family and work roles.

Educational Achievement and Lifelong Learning Domain

- GOAL ED1 Attain educational achievement and performance levels needed to reach your personal and career goals.
- GOAL ED2 Participate in ongoing, lifelong learning experiences to enhance your ability to function effectively in a diverse and changing economy.

Career Management Domain

- GOAL CM1 Create and manage a career plan that meets your career goals.
- GOAL CM2 Use a process of decision-making as one component of career development.
- GOAL CM3 Use accurate, current and unbiased career information during career planning and management.
- GOAL CM4 Master academic, occupational and general employability skills in order to obtain, create, maintain and/or advance your employment.
- GOAL CM5 Integrate changing employment trends, societal needs and economic conditions into your career plans.

Indicators and Learning Stages

The goals are detailed by more than **200 indicators** that highlight the knowledge and skills needed to achieve them. Together, the Guidelines goals and indicators can be the basis for K-Adult career development program content and evaluation.

Sample Indicator

Personal Social Development Domain	
	Develop understanding of yourself to build and maintain a positive self-concept.
GOAL PS1	
PS1.A1	Demonstrate behavior and decisions that reflect your interests, likes, and dislikes.
PS1.R1	Assess how your interests and preferences are reflected in your career goals.
PS1.K2	Identify your abilities, strengths, skills, and talents.
PS1.A2	Demonstrate use of your abilities, strengths, skills, and talents.
PS1.R2	Assess the impact of your abilities, strengths, skills, and talents on your career development.

Source: From http://www.acrnetwork.org/ncdg/ncdg_framework.aspx. Reprinted with permission of America's Career Resource Network.

Teacher and Parent Involvement

Teachers and parents contribute to career education and planning in many ways. Teachers work with school counselors in career education. They integrate career preparation when they include information about work skills in their lessons. Teachers help by creating or locating materials that help students understand and appreciate the career implications of their subject area. They can use career-oriented activities in their instruction and help students learn and demonstrate good work habits. Teachers also help students develop, clarify, and assimilate meaningful work values. They connect their content to real-life situations, helping students see the application to their lives outside school. Berns and Erickson (2001) say that teachers tie content to context when they include problem-based learning, cooperative learning, project-based instruction, and service learning. The collaborative work of teachers and counselors supports students' planning for their future.

Parents also play a part by helping their children gain and practice good work habits. Parents who emphasize positive attitudes toward work and who work toward maximum career development options and opportunities for their children aid the career development process (Drummond & Ryan, 1995). Seligman (1994) states that people—particularly parents and teachers—have great influence on the career choices of children. Herr, Cramer, and Niles (2004) list specific ways parents can help their children:

1. They can encourage their offspring to recognize personal characteristics such as interests, abilities and values.
2. They should exhibit the attitude that all people have dignity and worth, regardless of their jobs.
3. They can tell children about specific work requirements of various occupations.
4. They can discuss the significance and consequences of work values by relating their own experiences and those they have observed in others.
5. They can connect work, pay and economic living conditions.
6. They can promote their children's exploration of a wide spectrum of educational and occupational alternatives.
7. They can help their children find and use accurate informational resources about careers.
8. They can be vigilant in avoiding stereotyping occupational choices and workers.
9. They can provide chances for work at home and in the community.
10. They can give opportunities to learn and practice skills in decision making. (p. 349)

Trusty (1999) found that parents' home-based involvement in their children's career development had a significant impact on educational expectations (Trusty, 2001). He and others (Trusty, Watts, & Crawford, 1996; Trusty, Watts, & Erdman, 1997) advocate for school counselors focusing on parents helping children. This parental involvement is emphasized for four reasons. One incentive is that children and adolescents want their parents' help and parents want to help. Another support for that parental focus is promoting positive communication within the family. Counselor contact with parents also benefits the perceptions of schools as valuable resources. Finally, parents are continuing resources whereas counselors' efforts are more limited. Counselors may actively promote parental involvement by conducting study groups that focus on the parental role in children's career development. Counselors can also coordinate resources for parents and organize career activities for families (Herbert, 1986).

Choose three of the suggestions above and plan a parent-education workshop to teach and practice those skills.

Researchers have examined specific strategies to encourage parents' active involvement. Kerpelman, Shoffner, and Ross-Griffin (2002) worked with African American mothers and daughters. They concluded that teenagers have different support needs according to their personal characteristics and their personal, environmental, and developmental resources. The researchers promote using "possible selves" interventions to uncover those needs and to aid parents in assisting academic and career development. Likewise Cochran (1985) designed the Partners Program to help parents. By using a career exploration workbook, a career grid, and a planning workbook, parents interact with their children working toward an occupational plan. Others (Palmer & Cochran, 1988; Kush & Cochran, 1993) who have replicated those methods have found positive results. Amundson and Penner (1998) created a five-step, parent-involved career exploration process. In this intervention counselors invite students and parents to explore options and move to action planning. Counselors may find these three processes helpful in including parents in the individual planning processes.

Berns (2004) also offers ways to involve parents in learning such as asking parents for advice, help, and support and talking about what the career program is designed to accomplish. Giving written and oral information and listening to parents' concerns are other strategies. Counselors can increase parental involvement by using ideas, materials, and activities supplied by parents. Other hints include being authentic, recognizing diverse family structures and styles, and being familiar with community services and resources. Those approaches will help school counselors work with parents across K–12 schools. Unfortunately in a current survey by the ASCA (2005) over one-third of the parents reported inadequate contact with school counselors. With that discovery in mind, the counselors will look at how their work in career development will differ in elementary, middle, and high schools.

Individual Planning in Elementary School

Elementary-aged students are working to acquire the prerequisite skills for career and educational planning. Most appraisal activities at this grade level focus on academic achievement and interventions are also aimed at making sure all students have the academic skills they need to make the most of their opportunities. According to Blum (1998), elementary school students develop personal and career attributes, acquire an appreciation of learning and of following directions and rules, develop decision-making and goal-setting skills and the abilities to take the action necessary to achieve their purposes. They also learn about technology and the value of work and have opportunities to work in groups and on teams. Students in elementary settings relate school to work by acknowledging the relationships of good work habits, personal responsibility, and behavior and consequences in school and at work. By attaining career information they learn about careers and jobs and about workers in the community. Students increase their understanding of self by recognizing personal strengths, interests, and abilities and relating them to careers. They learn about a career portfolio and prepare a 6-year plan for their education. In K–6 schools counselors help children with career preparation by increasing children's self-awareness, promoting skills needed later in life, and presenting general information about occupations and work.

Research (Augur, Blackhurst, & Wahl, 2005) indicates that what adolescents think about occupations, like many other concepts, begins well before the teen years. In elementary schools, counselors focus on expanding children's understanding of the world of work and of themselves. Paisley and Hubbard (1994) guide counselors for program decisions in the career element by their explanation of goals and competencies that neatly align with the ASCA National Standards (2001a). Those are reprinted in Table 8.2.

Children in elementary schools learn through concrete experiences and observations. Successful educational and career development programs will incorporate concrete experiences for students as well as observational learning opportunities. Elementary students begin to learn their "self-concept systems," which are sets of their individual traits. The stage-related development of self-image as it relates to occupational aspirations has been discussed by Gottfredson (1996) as a movement that begins with children recognizing adult occupational roles and exhibiting same-sex preferences for adult activities. In the second stage children focus on what is appropriate for one's sex, recognizing that adult activities are sex-typed. Children tend to disregard careers that they perceive as appropriate for the other sex. The third stage involves children dismissing occupations they regard as low-status careers. Adults who work with elementary school children acknowledge the changes in children's understandings as they progress through these stages and help broaden their concept of possible careers.

In their responses to Washington County's most recent needs assessment, community employers indicated that prospective employees tend to seek jobs that are consistent with gender stereotypes. Gottfredson (1996) contends that as early as the age of 6 children have begun eliminating careers based on gender. Consequently, the TK–12 counselors are interested in examining their programs for activities and information about careers that may reinforce stereotypes and biases about gender and work. Seligman (1994) highlights influences on career development for counselors to consider. Family factors such parents' roles and early childhood experiences relate strongly to a person's occupational expectations. Students who are exposed to a variety of occupations and lifestyles and have access to role models with differing occupational status expand their exploration of the world of work. Boys and girls need to see a broad range of career opportunities to reduce

TABLE 8.2 Career Goals and Competencies in Grades K–5

Overall Goals

- Become aware of personal characteristics, interest, attitudes, and skills
- Develop an awareness of and respect for the diversity of the world of work
- Understand the relationship between school performance and future choices
- Develop a positive attitude toward work

Competencies

Kindergarten students will be able to

- Identify workers in the school setting
- Describe the work of family members
- Describe what they like to do

Grade 1 students will be able to

- Describe their likes and dislikes
- Identify workers in various settings
- Identify responsibilities they have at home and at school
- Identify skills they have now that they did not have previously

Grade 2 students will be able to

- Describe skills needed to complete a task at home or at school
- Distinguish which work activities in their school environment are done by specific people
- Recognize the diversity of jobs in various settings

Grade 3 students will be able to

- Define what the term *future* means
- Recognize and describe the many life roles that people have
- Demonstrate the ability to brainstorm a range of job titles

Grade 4 students will be able to

- Imagine what their lives might be like in the future
- Evaluate the importance of various familiar jobs in the community
- Describe workers in terms of work performed
- Identify personal hobbies and leisure activities

Grade 5 students will be able to

- Identify ways that familiar jobs contribute to the needs of society
- Compare their interests and skills to familiar jobs
- Compare their personal hobbies and leisure activities to jobs
- Discuss stereotypes associated with certain jobs
- Discuss what is important to them

Source: From *Developmental School Counseling Programs: From Theory to Practice* (pp. 218–219), by P.O. Paisely and G.T. Hubbard, 1994, Alexandria, VA: American Counseling Association. Copyright 1994 by American Counseling Association. Adapted with permission. No further reproduction authorized without written permission from the American Counseling Association.

gender stereotyping that may inhibit choices. Counselors need to monitor materials and assessments for any notions that may imply limitations. Counselors need to find models of both genders in familiar occupations. Those models may be provided in speakers, photographs, films, stories, field trips, and games.

The counselors also follow Blum's (1998) and Herting-Wahl and Black-hurst's (2000) recommendations about career counseling female and minority students to combat stereotyping. First, our counselors explore their own hidden biases by taking the hidden bias test described on the Tolerance.org (2005) Web site (http://www.tolerance.org/hidden_bias/index.html). Then, they examine the materials they use in classrooms and in parent and teacher training for evidence of hidden and more overt bias. They replace current materials that reflect stereotypes with those that reflect gender and equity fairness, a culturally diverse workforce, and persons working in nontraditional occupations. They will invite speakers who have nontraditional occupations and take field trips to see workers in different careers. They will include stories that have characters with nontraditional jobs and find career posters with gender and ethnically diverse pictures. Finally the counselors will launch a mentoring program for children who may be interested in nontraditional careers.

> In small groups, identify at least six ways counselors and other educators might expand elementary school students' conception of the career choices available to them. Think in terms of everyday behavior (e.g., modeling equity- and gender-fair language and behavior) as well as specific individual planning interventions (e.g., school-wide career fairs with representation of persons in nontraditional occupations).

Zunker (2006) and Herr, Cramer, and Niles (2004) have lists of career development activities appropriate for elementary school students. For example, in the area of self-knowledge students may be asked to play a game like "What's My Line" where one person takes the role of someone in a particular occupation and others guess the career. Listing things liked and disliked would also build self-awareness. Suggested occupational exploration strategies may be assigning a job title and having students research the necessary skills and tools of the career. These and many other career-related activities may be found in the career books by Zunker, by Herr, Cramer, and Niles, and by others.

Materials and activities that encourage a wide view of the world of work enhance this ongoing process of developing a work identity. However, elementary school children are also influenced by the values of their communities, especially families, and may experience expectations that are different from those expressed in school. Ms. Lerner states, "I am working with a large community of children from middle European countries. Their native countries do not have mandatory attendance laws. Their families expect them to work as soon as they are physically able, and girls in these families are often married before age 16. School attendance is not an expressed value, and these students are achieving at very low levels due to erratic attendance patterns. As the students become more 'Americanized' there are conflicts emerging in these families. How can I provide career and educational development activities that are both based in the American values of equity education and are culturally sensitive to these children and their families?" Such students may need special encouragement to consider a variety of career fields. Additionally, school personnel succeed by involving parents, relatives, and role models in emphasizing individual potential (Zunker, 2006).

Individual Planning in Middle School

Career development goals begun in elementary schools continue throughout grades 6 through 8. In middle school, students develop their personal and career attributes by increasing their appreciation of learning and expressing positive attitudes toward their studies (Blum, 1998). Students learn about and explore careers. They increase their self-direction as well as accept responsibility for their own behavior. They develop an appreciation for quality in their work and enhance their positive interpersonal and social skills leading to cooperative work skills. They grow in their ability to make good decisions and in self-confidence. In relating education and career learning, students in the middle grades acknowledge the relationship of educational achievement and career opportunities. They locate and use information when making academic and career plans, and they select courses related to their career plans.

Middle school students need appropriate and accurate information about careers and the pathway to enter them. Too many adolescents begin high school with incorrect assumptions about the significance of their academic choices on their future. School counselors can help make this connection for young people (Sciarra, 2004). Herring (1998) suggests the following priorities: decision-making skills and awareness of personal strengths and limitations; recognition of the relationship between schooling and work; economic awareness of supply and demand impacts; occupational awareness; and recognition of the role of work in society. Paisley and Hubbard (1994) further specify competencies related to these goals in Table 8.3.

Mr. Grund and the others agree that middle school is a place for exploration and identity development. The counselors realize students in middle school may be making tentative plans for their postsecondary lives. The young people will be helped by an increased recognition of their personal characteristics and of their relationship skills. The fit between their attributes and the world of work will facilitate their decision making and their learning about potential career paths. Young people this age are more capable of thinking abstractly and logically and making the connections necessary for planning. Consequently, the addition of appraisal activities designed to identify career interests followed up with activities that help students identify the relationships among these interests, future careers, and current academic choices are appropriate.

As in elementary school, counselors in middle school work to reduce the limitations created by ethnic and gender stereotypes. People of color are overrepresented in low-status occupations (Newman & Newman, 2003; Saunders, 1995). Improving students' chances of finishing school programs, boosting attitudes about work, supplying career information, enhancing their skills, and helping connect to community resources are ways counselors can assist young people of color in revising this trend (Zunker, 2006). Additionally the scope of occupations in which women are concentrated is narrow and those jobs often pay less than traditionally male-oriented careers (Kail & Cavanaugh, 2004; Reskin, 1993). Showing videotapes with women in nontraditional careers, having workshops focused on the lives of famous women, and asking successful women to talk to classes are strategies for encouraging girls to consider a wider range of occupations (Sciarra, 2004). The counselors will also be careful to include participants in their career fair who have jobs that do not support these stereotypes.

The counselors are happy with the career resources they have and the way that teachers integrate career development activities into the academic curriculum. Specifically, teachers encourage students to research and report on careers of

Working in small groups, identify ways that you might work with the parents of these children, in a culturally sensitive manner, to increase their view of opportunities available to their children.

TABLE 8.3   Career Goals and Competencies in Grades 6–8

Overall Goals

- Become aware of personal characteristics, interest, attitudes, and skills
- Develop an awareness of and respect for the diversity of the world of work
- Understand the relationship between school performance and future choices
- Develop a positive attitude toward work

Competencies

Grade 6 students will be able to

- Identify tentative work interests and skills
- List elements of decision making
- Discuss how their parents' work influences life at home
- Consider the relationship between interest and abilities
- Identify their own personal strengths and weaknesses

Grade 7 students will be able to

- Identify tentative career interests and relate them to future planning
- Recognize the connection between school performance and related career plans
- Identify resources for career exploration and information

Grade 8 students will be able to

- Identify specific career interests and abilities using the results of assessment instruments
- Consider future career plans in making educational choices
- Describe their present skills, abilities, and interests
- Use resources for career exploration and information

Source: From *Developmental School Counseling Programs: From Theory to Practice* (pp. 219–220), by P.O. Paisely and G.T. Hubbard, 1994, Alexandria, VA: American Counseling Association. Copyright 1994 by American Counseling Association. Adapted ith permission. No further reproduction authorized without written permission from the American Counseling Association.

interest to them, including everything from how one prepares to enter the profession or occupation to the benefits of employment, likely trends in the particular segment of the labor market, and what personal interests and personalities may be most satisfied in the occupation. They also integrate career and educational planning activities into the time periods immediately preceding and following the school's annual career exploration fair. Before the fair, they help students use the results of their career inventories to identify areas about which they wish to learn more, develop lists of questions students might ask career fair participants, and provide opportunities for discussion with peers about career options. After the fair, they spend time discussing students' experiences and identifying additional questions to be researched. They also help students learn about job searching, interviewing, and completing applications in anticipation of the job-shadowing experiences students have in the eighth grade. Sears-Jones (1995) presents some other ideas the middle school counselors can use. Students can spend a portion of a workday with a parent. Seventh-and eighth-grade students can visit a college campus for a day, visiting a class and admissions. Counselors can also form partnerships with businesses for information and role models for students.

Ms. Farmer points out that the career interest inventory currently used in the middle school needs to be reviewed for applicability to all of the students in the schools, and specifically for fairness. Additionally, screenings of the most recent participants in the career exploration fair reveal that women represent all of the occupations stereotypically associated with females. As mentioned earlier, Mr. Grund, who coordinates the career fair, commits to finding more diverse representatives in these areas.

Academically, students use the decision-making and goal-setting skills developed in elementary school to begin their 6-year educational plans and their career-life planning portfolios (Blum, 1998; Bushweller, 1995; Milone, 1995). The portfolio projects help students plan their education and set goals.

Drummond and Ryan (1995) and Sciarra (2004) outline the objectives of a portfolio program as follows. Students collect information about their learning styles, abilities, interests, and expectations and a record of their academic achievements and extracurricular activities. Students evaluate the information they have compiled and form their choices after learning about the decision-making process. Finally students design and create a portfolio that reflects their personal strengths and challenges, academic and vocational interests, social interests, immediate and future goals, and plans for completing their goals.

Through these planning tools, students, parents, teachers, and counselors can see whether students are using the assessment data available to them to achieve an understanding of themselves, including their interests and abilities, in order to plan effectively for their futures. At this level, the plans are flexible enough to allow students to make changes based on new information about themselves, the ever-changing world of work, and academic developments.

Again Zunker (2006) and Herr, Cramer, and Niles (2004) have lists of career development activities appropriate for middle school students. For example, in the area of self-knowledge students can complete a personality inventory or a life line. Counselors can encourage occupational exploration by developing "students' days" to visit sites to observe a person working in a career of their interest. They can also suggest students review job ads in local newspapers to check for needed skills and relate those needs to school subjects. Counselors can teach the steps in a decision-making model and present opportunities to practice the steps. A range of other possible activities can be found in the career books by Zunker and by Herr, Cramer, and Niles.

Peterson, Long, and Billups (1999) studied the effects of three types of interventions on the educational choices of eighth graders. As a result of their research, they suggest that counselors include a well-designed set of print materials, individual monitoring, and support from counselors and teachers in helping prepare middle school students for educational choices. Legum and Hoare (2004) had successful results with 9-week program for at-risk middle school students. Bergmann (1991) suggests that middle school counselors help the career development process by conducting needs assessments of the students, establishing peer groups for discussion and exploration, involving students in community service, encouraging age-appropriate social activities for at-risk students, and serving as a good role model and caring adult.

In small groups discuss and develop a list of ways that the influence of peers, predominant among middle school students, may both positively and negatively influence career and academic decisions of students. Identify ways that educators might respond to your list to increase the chances of positive outcomes for students.

Individual Planning in High School

During these final years of schooling, students have increased opportunities to make decisions that have long-term consequences for their professional and personal lives. In addition to gaining occupational information and making choices based on interests, aptitude, and attitude, high school students are also considering the kind of lifestyle and family life they wish to have in the future. These personal and social concerns influence the types of postsecondary opportunities pursued by high school graduates. Obviously the options chosen impact the person's search for identity, a critical developmental task during adolescence (Erikson, 1963). The young people, who are decisive and independent, know about occupations and demonstrate planning and decision-making skills have the characteristics of career maturity (Super, 1990; Crites & Savickas, 1996). They achieve the task of social adjustment by defining appropriate social roles and building peer relationships (Zunker, 2006).

High school students gradually move to more complex cognitive strategies. They can work with abstractions and include hypotheses in problem solving. They embrace their new power of thought, linking observations and responses, systematic processes, and extended introspection. They may theorize and analyze themselves and everything else that catches their attention. They have a heightened concern about other people's reactions to them. Their parents still exert the greatest influence on their long-range plans, but their friends greatly influence their immediate identity (Zunker, 2006).

As well as choices about their postsecondary lives, high school students continue to refine effective social and work readiness skills. Fundamental skills include regular attendance, punctuality, positive attitudes and behaviors, finishing tasks, good grooming, and good interpersonal skills (Turner & Lapan, 2005). Lapan (2004) listed a comprehensive set of skills for children and adolescents to master:

- Social competence—the ability to build and maintain positive relationships
- Diversity—the ability and flexibility for interacting with others from different cultures
- Positive work habits—sound judgment, responsibility, dependability, punctuality, attendance, life-planning, management skills, ethical practice
- Personal management skills—positive attitude about self, cleanliness, appropriate dress, verbal and nonverbal communication skills
- Entrepreneurship—leadership, creativity, desire, motivation, and openness to opportunity

Harkins (2001) promotes skill development through direct instruction and infusion into curriculum. Munson and Rubenstein (1992) acknowledge that school counselors are in an ideal position to contribute.

Ginzberg (1972) describes the stages of occupational choice in middle and high school years. He begins with the fantasy period that occurs during childhood, generally before 11, a time in which play gradually becomes more oriented toward work. That is followed by a tentative period until around the age of 17. The characteristics of this stage are more definite likes and dislikes, comparison of personal ability to aspirations, clearer perceptions of vocational styles, and the awareness of needing to make an occupational choice. The realistic period occurs after 17. This is the stage of integration of abilities, interests, and values and specifying choice. Savickas (2005) relates a theory of career construction that further explains the processes by which people interpret the meaning of work and the direction of their careers. He poses four questions that frame the dimension of career adaptability: Do I have a future? Who owns my future? What do I want to do with my future? Can I do it? Counselors may find those concerns useful in addressing career development in high schools. Again the work of Paisley and Hubbard (1994) gives more specifics in Table 8.4.

Working in small groups, identify the types of artifacts and reflections students might include in their portfolios.

Students in high school refine their educational and career goals and demonstrate achievement of them by successfully completing their educational plans and career-life planning portfolios. Drummond and Ryan (1995) suggest that career portfolios at this level include an activities log that lists school and leisure activities; educational courses completed; special talents, abilities, and skills; test profiles; work experience; career plans; and a resume.

Zunker (2006) and Herr, Cramer, and Niles (2004) have lists of career development activities appropriate for high school students. For example, in the area of self-knowledge students could discuss current and future roles as family members, workers, and citizens. Counselors can ask students to compare want ads in newspapers from varying geographical locations. They can also discuss leisure activities and the time required to participate in them. For career planning activities counselors can invite a representative from the state employment agency to describe the functions of government organizations in helping the job search process. Sampson, Peterson, Lenz, and Reardon (1992) suggest teens use these information processing skills in career decision making: identifying the problem, analyzing causes of the problem and problem components, determining possible courses of action, evaluating each course of action, and implementing a plan of action. Counselors and teachers can provide many activities for students to practice those problem-solving steps. A range of other possible activities can be found in the career books by Zunker and by Herr, Cramer, and Niles.

Lapan, Gysbers, Hughey, and Arni (1993) designed an 8-week program delivered by language arts teachers and high school counselors and aimed at high school juniors. The program included career exploration exercises and a research paper. The authors report increases in career development and academic achievement. Another model program was offered by McWhirter, Crothers, and Rasheed (2000). High school sophomores participated in a 9-week career education class. The class included experiential activities, small group experiences, guest speakers, and lectures. Students reported increased career-related self-efficacy and career decision making.

Access

Ms. Farmer expresses concern about the numbers of students of color and those with disabilities who do not hold high expectations for their futures. Local data suggest that both groups of students are overrepresented in unchallenging courses

TABLE 8.4 Career Goals and Competencies in Grades 9–12

Overall Goals

- Become aware of personal characteristics, interest, attitudes, and skills
- Develop an awareness of and respect for the diversity of the world of work
- Understand the relationship between school performance and future choices
- Develop a positive attitude toward work

Competencies

Grade 9 students will be able to

- Recognize positive work habits
- Refine their knowledge of their own skills, aptitudes, interests, and values
- Identify general career goals
- Make class selections on the basis of career goals
- Use career resources in goal setting and decision making

Grade 10 students will be able to

- Clarify the role of values in career choice
- Distinguish educational and skill requirements for areas or careers of interest
- Recognize the effects of job or career choice on other areas of life
- Begin realistic assessment of their potential in various fields

Grade 11 students will be able to

- Refine future career goals through synthesis of information concerning self, use of resources, and consultation with others
- Coordinate class selection with career goals
- Identify specific educational requirements necessary to achieve their goals
- Clarify their own values as they relate to work and leisure

Grade 12 students will be able to

- Complete requirements for transition from high school
- Make final commitments to a career plan
- Understand the potential for change in their own interests or values related to work
- Understand the potential for change within the job market
- Understand career development as a lifelong process
- Accept responsibility for their own career

Source: From *Developmental School Counseling Programs: From Theory to Practice* (p. 220), by P.O. Paisely and G.T. Hubbard, 1994, Alexandria, VA: American Counseling Association. Copyright 1994 by American Counseling Association. Adapted with permission. No further reproduction authorized without written permission from the American Counseling Association.

and select postsecondary options such as immediate entry into the workforce and military service at much higher rates than the white students in this particular district regardless of other indicators of academic success such as grades and achievement scores. The counselors turn to Blum (1998) to identify factors that they might emphasize in program development for the students of concern. Activities designed to increase self-confidence, provide role models, present accurate and specific information about options, explore cultural expectations, and encourage participation in a rigorous and varied curriculum are a few of the areas she suggests to increase the likelihood of success for these students.

Helms and Cook (1999) acknowledge the oppressive restrictions some people face in the world of work. The overwhelmingly negative barriers of institutional racism, heterosexism, and sexism persist. Yang (1991) recommends counselors explore the work-based assumptions under which they operate. Counselors should investigate the related beliefs of students, school personnel, and society in general. To increase awareness and effectiveness, counselors are open to another's reality, explore elements of acculturation, and look at implications of multiple heritages and social conditioning.

Counselors can increase their understanding of these issues by careful study. Holcomb-McCoy (2004) performed a thematic analysis of the literature in multiculturalism to develop a competency checklist for school counselors. Her descriptions and self-analysis could guide school counselors for their personal growth. Counselors need to consider student characteristics in developing programs and activities for student career and educational planning. The following authors provide resources for working with gay, lesbian, bisexual, and transgender (GLBT) students (Nauta, Saucier, & Woodard, 2001; Schneider & McCurdy-Myers, 1999); multicultural issues (Herring, 1998; Mau & Bikos, 2000); gifted and talented students (Colangelo, 1997; Perrone, 1997; Reis & Colbert, 2004; Rysiew, Shore, & Leeb, 1999); employment-bound youth (Herr, 1995); students with disabilities (Bowen & Glenn, 1998; Fox, Wandry, Pruitte, & Anderson, 1998; Kosciulek, 2003; Schwiebert, Sealander, & Bradshaw, 1998; Wadsworth, Milsom, Cocco, 2004); gender issues (Sellers, Satcher, & Comas, 1999; Trusty, Robinson, Plata, & Ng, 2000); and at-risk students (Aviles, Guerrero, Howarth, & Thomas, 1999; Ladany, Melincoff, Constantine, & Love, 1997; O'Brien, Dukstein, Jackson, Tomlinson, & Kamatuka, 1999; O'Brien et al., 2000). Those resources will allow school counselors to facilitate the unique career development needs of students.

In small groups choose one of the two groups about whom Ms. Farmer is concerned as the focus for your discussion. For your group of interest, identify at least one individual planning intervention that might be used to increase self-confidence and explore cultural expectations with the goal of expanding the range of options students believe to be available to them.

Career Information Resources

Counselors need to be familiar with career information to accomplish the tasks related to individual planning. They also need to make this material accessible to the students and adults. A career center that incorporates a wide variety of resources allows others to investigate materials related to occupational planning. Zunker (1998) suggests the following categories of information be included: occupational descriptions, occupational outlook projections, postsecondary education and training information, military information, apprenticeship and internship information, information for special populations, a resource-persons file, and financial aid information. Further, career planning resources may include career decision making, vocational assessment, job search skills, and job simulation. These materials may include print materials, audiovisual resources, videotapes, and Internet files.

Computer-assisted career guidance systems such as DISCOVER (American College Testing, 2000), System for Interactive Guidance Information (SIGI) Plus (Educational Testing Service, 1997), and Career Information Delivery System (CIDS) provide interactive informational systems. CIDS directors and sources of programs can be obtained from the Association of Computer-Based Systems for Career Information (www.acsci.org/acsci_states.asp). People who use the technology have immediate access to large databases of occupational and educational information as well as interest inventories and decision-making skills. Those systems can be purchased for career centers. When considering computerized guidance systems, counselors use the following suggestions from Baker (2000), Brown and Srebalus (1988), and McDaniels (1982):

1. Consider the characteristics of the people who will be using the system, their needs, and their limitations.
2. Determine how the system fits into the goals of the program and how the counseling staff will expect to interact with the system and its users.
3. Study the system for theory, consistency, validity and reliability, skills needed, and outcomes.
4. Investigate practical considerations such as cost, response time, its attractiveness to users, and customer service.

Many other resources on career information are located on the World Wide Web. The Web site of the U.S. Department of Labor (http://www.acinet.org/ acinet) helps link people to helpful career-related information. The U.S. Bureau of Labor Statistic (BLS) has posted the *Occupational Outlook Handbook* online at www.bls.gov/oco/. The BLS also has a section on occupational information for elementary school students. The U.S. Department of Education (www.ed.gov) includes information related to financial aid, grants, and educational software packages. Creating a career resource center helps counselors provide individual planning interventions for students who are investigating and planning for their future.

Career Counseling Outcomes

Hughes and Karp (2004) summarized studies on school-based career development and concluded that researchers have found benefits in guidance programs, career courses, academic counseling, and computer-assisted systems. Other studies also support the impact of counseling programs on student success. Spokane and Oliver (1983) and Oliver and Spokane (1988) performed two meta-analyses of 60 studies of career counseling interventions. They concluded that group- and classroom-based interventions were effective. Similarly Whiston and her colleagues (Whiston, Brecheisen, & Stephens, 2003; Whiston, Sexton, & Lasoff, 1998) considered 47 and 57 studies of interventions and reported positive effects of career counseling interventions. They also found that counselor-led interventions had more impact than self-directed work. Their order of effectiveness include individual counseling, group counseling, computer-assisted intervention, career development workshops, career class interventions, and self-directed career interventions. The results of these sets of meta-analyses indicate significant gains regardless of the type of intervention.

Lapan, Gysbers, and Sun (1997) studied the statewide guidance program in Missouri. Students in schools with more complete counseling programs were more likely to report higher grades, more satisfaction with their preparation for the future, availability of career and college information, and a more positive school climate. Similar positive results were found in a study of Utah's counseling program (Nelson & Gardner, 1998). Another summary reviews the benefits of career education. In a meta-analysis of 67 studies about career education, Evans and Burck (1992) concluded that the interventions had a positive impact on students' academic achievement and those effects are stronger if the program is integrated with math or language arts, is intensive, and is in at least its second year with the same cohort.

APPRAISAL

The review of career planning activities has led counselors to consider systemwide appraisal, another key activity associated with individual student planning.

Purposes of Assessment

Throughout the K–12 experience students use the information they gain from appraisal activities to identify their interests, their strengths, areas in which they want to improve, areas they want to explore, and things that are important to them. Counselors will use appraisal for several reasons (Baker & Gerler, 2004; Guindon, 2003; Brown & Trusty, 2005). Assessment enhances student development. Counselors will use assessment to determine counseling goals and to gauge whether those goals are being accomplished. Both objective and subjective assessments can assist in identifying a person's strengths, styles, and strategies for problem solving. A related second purpose of appraisals is to support students' development and to help them in making academic and career decisions. School counselors can measure the progress students are making with assessment data.

As described by Campbell and Dahir (1997), the Career Development, Standard C, is: Students will understand the relationship between personal qualities, education, and training and the world of work. Students will demonstrate how personal qualities relate to achieving personal, social, education, and career goals. Design a sequence of appraisal activities for the elementary, middle, and high school level that would assist students in identifying their personal qualities.

Assessment in schools has been essential in providing information on which student placements in academic programs have been made. Test scores are used for deciding if a student needs a remedial or an advanced educational opportunity, if a student will be permitted to move to the next grade or to graduate, and if a student has mastered academic content (Helms, 2004). Unfortunately the achievement and aptitude test results have also been misused and students limited according to some of those placement decisions. School counselors advocate for appropriate and fair vehicles of assessment in an effort to stop or reverse such usage.

Counselors also use appraisal techniques for diagnosis, interpersonal, and academic skills deficiencies and the need for treatment, remediation, or training (Zunker & Norris, 1998). Counselors base their recommendations for special services on data from testing, observation, and other types of assessment. Finally counselors can make more informed program decisions with assessment data. They can learn more about the characteristics (such as their interests, values, abilities, and skills) and the needs of students. Counselors can also use the data to evaluate the effectiveness of their work and program activities.

Appraisal activities are varied and each type requires a specialized set of knowledge and abilities. In a 1998 joint statement ASCA and the Association for Assessment in Counseling (AAC) published a document that identified the competencies and skills school counselors need in the areas of assessment and evaluation. That group identified nine competencies, or necessary skills and understandings. Those nine areas are the following: (1) skills in choosing assessment strategies; (2) abilities to identify, access, and evaluate commonly used instruments; (3) capacity to administer and familiarity with methods of scoring assessment instruments; (4) skills in interpreting and reporting results; (5) expertise in using results in decision making; (6) competence in producing, interpreting, and presenting statistical information about results; (7) competence in conducting and interpreting evaluations of their programs and their interventions; (8) ability to adapt and use questionnaires, surveys, and other assessments to meet local needs; and (9) knowledge for professionally responsible use of assessment and evaluation practices (http://aac.ncat.edu).

The statement suggests a definition of assessment as the gathering of information for decision making about individuals, groups, processes, or programs. As noted in the previous discussion, through appraisal activities, counselors collect and interpret data about students' achievement, aptitudes, attitudes, interests, skills, and behaviors. Loesch and Vacc (2001) admonish that the effective use of tests relates directly to the degree of responsibility counselors assume in the use of the instruments so it is imperative that school counselors hone their knowledge and skills in the area of assessment.

> Find the statement titled "Competencies in Assessment and Evaluation for School Counselors" on the AAC Web site. Check the specific skills listed under each competency and rate yourself on your proficiency in those skills. If you have not yet taken coursework related to assessment and appraisal, identify ways you might use the lists to assess your own needs as you progress through the preparation program in which you are enrolled.

Language of Appraisals

School counselors should understand and be able to explain several concepts related to assessment. The following brief explanation serves as a reminder of a portion of that field of knowledge. Counselors may need to be able to differentiate between quantitative and qualitative assessment. Counselors need to know the different kinds and properties of nominal, ordinal, interval, and ratio scales. They should be familiar with standard normal distribution, norm-referenced scores, and criterion-referenced scores. Scoring methods, sampling theory, and basic descriptive statistics should also be within the repertoire of the school counselor as well as the knowledge to evaluate the validity and reliability of the instruments. Counselors should be able to discuss stanines, percentiles, grade equivalent scores, and other scales that may be part of reporting assessment results. Many of those concepts will be used as counselors interpret test results to students, parents, and other educators.

Quantitative Assessments

Throughout the K–12 experience students use the information they gain from appraisal activities to identify their interests, their strengths, areas in which they want to improve, areas they want to explore, and things that are important to them. Counselors should be familiar with the types of standardized instruments that can help in the individual planning process. They should be able to

Locate one of the MBTI type tests on the World Wide Web and take and score it. After reading the descriptions of your "type" think about the implications of this assessment for your chosen career. Consider ways that you might use such an assessment to help high school students achieve a greater understanding of the types of work roles and environments with which they may be satisfied.

explain the purposes and limitations of intelligence tests and aptitude tests which may be used as measures of potential. They should be familiar with the different types of achievement tests that are used to assess academic progress, a big part of evaluating curriculum efforts in schools. Counselors may give personality tests to help describe traits and characteristics of an individual's personality, such as their attitudes, emotions, opinions, motivations, and interpersonal behaviors. Two examples used by school counselors are the Mooney Problem Checklist and the Myers-Briggs Type Indicator (MBTI). The MBTI may be used with high school students for career planning.

Student appraisal includes other forms of assessment. Interest and other types of career inventories may be used to help identify interests related to career areas, levels of career development, and career maturity. Interest inventories are ways for a person to self-report preferences for taking part in a variety of activities. Schmidt (1999) suggests that the data can verify choices, uncover other areas of interests, and stimulate exploration of opportunities. The Self-Directed Search (SDS), the Kuder General Interest Survey, the Kuder Occupational Interest Survey, and the Ohio Vocational Interest Survey (OVIS) are a few of the many interests inventories used in schools. Table 8.5 contains a list of some assessment instruments used by school counselors.

Qualitative Assessment Strategies

Goldman (1994) suggests that qualitative or nonstandard means of assessment contribute more to counseling than standardized tests. He supports his claim by stating that qualitative strategies are more adaptable and do not include the sometimes confusing statistical data, and that the participants are more active in the process. Guindon (2003) points out that nonstandardized measures may be more culturally sensitive because counselors can accommodate linguistic and socioeconomic differences more easily.

Some qualitative methods of gathering data include card sorts, interviews, rating scales, checklists, observations, and portfolios. Guindon (2003) and Baker and Gerler (2004) recommend Lazarus's (1976) multimodal approach as a structured approach to observational information about the child's behavior, affect, sensation, imagery, cognition, interpersonal relationships, and use of drugs and diet. Ellis (2004) outlines the steps to performing a structured observation that may help counselors who need a systematic approach. Finally portfolios provide a more comprehensive qualitative assessment. Portfolios contain a number of work samples chosen by students to highlight their best work. Trusty and Niles (2004) provide a framework for an education/career development portfolio to be collected across a student's school experience.

Interpretation of Assessment Results

Reporting and interpreting results is a significant part of the school counselor's role with appraisal. Counselors help students, parents, teachers, and other school personnel make sense of and use testing information. Counselors help translate the terms and results into meaningful language for the various interested

TABLE 8.5 Assessment Instruments for Counselors

Test Category	Test	Grade Level	Available from	Notes
Aptitude Tests	Armed Services Vocational Aptitude Battery	Primarily 12th grade	ASVAB Career Exploration Program	No fees for either the test or results
	Differential Aptitude Test	Level 1, Grades 7–9 Level 2, Grades 10–12	Psychological Corporation	Form C has two levels
	General Aptitude Test Battery	Grade 12	U.S. Employment Service	Available from the regional office
Achievement Tests	Educational Testing Service series	Various	Educational Testing Service	Both general survey and single-subject tests
	Houghton Mifflin series	Various	Houghton Mifflin	Both general survey and single-subject tests
	McGraw-Hill series	Various	McGraw-Hill	Both general survey and single-subject tests
Interest Inventories	Wide Range Interest Opinion Test	Grade 5+	Jastak	Assesses perception of ability, aspiration level and social conformity
	COPSystem Interest Inventory	Grade 6+	Educational and Industrial Testing Service	Assess interest related to occupational clusters
	Career Decision Making 2000: Harrington-O'Shea Decision Making System	Level 1, Grades 7–9 Level 2, Grades 11–12	American Guidance Service	Uses the Holland codes
	Geist Picture Interest Inventory	Students with reading problems	Western Psychological Services	For nonreaders
	Kuder Occupational Interest Survey	Form E, middle and high school Form DD, high school	McGraw-Hill	Occupational scales and scales for college majors
	Ohio Vocational Interest Survey-II	Grades 8–12	Psychological Corporation	24 general-interest scales related to people, data, things
	Self-Directed Search	Career Explorer, middle school Form R, high school	Psychological Assessment Resources	Based on Holland's theory
	Strong Interest Inventory	Age 15+	Consulting Psychologists Press	
	Wide Range Interest and Opinion Test	All grades	Guidance Associates of Delaware	For nonreaders

(Continued)

TABLE 8.5 (Continued)

Test Category	Test	Grade Level	Available from	Notes
Values	Values Inventory for Children	Grades 1–6	Sheridan Psychological Services	Children's values and their relationships
	Career Orientation Placement and Evaluation Survey	Junior high school-community college	EDITS	Results are for 7 work values on a bipolar scale
	Ohio Work Values Inventory	Grades 4–12	Publishers Test Service	Yields scores on 11 work values
	Salience Inventory	High school	Consulting Psychologists Press	Measures the importance of life roles according to Super's theory
	Values Scale	High school	Consulting Psychologists Press	A measure of intrinsic versus extrinsic life-career values
Personality Inventories	California Test of Personality	Elementary, middle, secondary, and adult levels	CTP-MacMillan-McGraw-Hill	Assesses personal worth, and family and school relations
	Minnesota Counseling Inventory	Grades 9–12	Psychological Corporation	Separate norms for boys and girls
	Myers–Briggs Type Indicator	High school	Consulting Psychologists Press	Most widely used personality measure
	Sixteen Personality Factor Questionnaire	Ages 16+	Institute for Personality and Ability Testing	Compares individual profile to samples of occupational profiles
Career Maturity Inventories	Career Awareness Inventory, Level 1	Grades 3 up	Scholastic Testing Service	Measures how much students know about careers and their choices
	Explore the World of Work	Grades 4+	CFKR Career Material	Assesses vocational interests
	Career Beliefs Inventory	Grades 8+	Consulting Psychologists Press	Designed to identify beliefs that prevent appropriate career decisions
	Career Development Inventory	Form S, middle and high school students	Consulting Psychologists Press	Measures of planning orientation and readiness for exploration, information and decision making
	Career Maturity Inventory	Grades 6–12	Psychological Assessment Resources	Measures readiness for decision making; includes Career Developer, a resource for skill development

Source: From *School Counseling: Foundations and Contemporary Issues*, 1st *edition* (pp. 113–114, 127), by D. Sciarra, © 2004. Reprinted with permission of Wadsworth, a division of Thomson Learning: www.thomsonrights.com Fax 800 730–2215.

people who can then identify their strengths and pinpoint the areas in which they need assistance. Holmgren (1996) reminds counselors to work with students until the children understand what the results mean as to grade level, percentile ranks, and norms.

Clark and Loesch (2004) identify the questions frequently asked by parents, including the reason for and types of tests, the timing of tests, and the different scores on tests. Parents also want to know how they can help their children and where they can find test preparation assistance. Many parents also ask for clarification about accommodations for children who have a disability. School counselors may want to prepare some answers to these questions and post them on the school's Web site. The chapter by Clark and Loesch would help with that document. Counselors may also be consultants in the appraisal process, helping teachers understand the meaning of test results and ways they can present that data to others. Counselors may help teachers by using sample profiles in an in-service session on test technicalities and interpretations. Administrators would be more familiar with the technical aspects but may need information from counselors about specific instruments.

Roeber (2004) provides details for reporting assessment results to help students learn, to strengthen parent's involvement, and to build public confidence. He explains reasons for and methods of reporting that can guide program planning for test interpretation. Guindon (2003) also gives general guidelines for presenting test results. She suggests pointing out that a test is only one source of information and should be considered in context with other data. Results should be given in terms of probability bands rather than absolute numbers and categories such as high, average, and below average give information without number comparisons. She recommends graphic aids to provide assistance. Counselors should use an interactive style when relaying information and be sure there are opportunities for questions and to check for understanding and reactions as each new part of information is delivered.

Managing the Testing Program

Appraisal in schools often refers to the administration of tests or assessment instruments and the management of the schoolwide testing program. In that role counselors may be responsible for coordinating test selection, ordering the tests, making arrangements for scoring, implementing the testing process, and disseminating the results. Baker and Gerler (2004) remind us that the testing program should be based on goals that define the rationale for each test, the information needed from that instrument, and how the data will be used. Counselors may also use interventions such as test anxiety reduction, cognitive therapy, visualization, and test preparation classes (Struder, 2005).

Challenges in Assessment

The direct tie of test results to school accountability systems has resulted in concerns about "high-stakes testing" where test scores are used to make major decisions about individuals, schools, and systems. Often those decisions have a

Visit the ASCA Web site (http://www.schoolcounselor.org/) and locate the ASCA Position Statement on High-Stakes Testing (ASCA, 2002a). Discuss this position with your classmates in the context of using appraisal information to help students plan for their futures.

direct impact on school funding and reputations as well as the individual's future opportunities. McDivitt (2004) defines a test as "high stakes" if it carries serious consequences for students and/or the educational community. This type of testing is a key component of the No Child Left Behind Act of 2001 that requires schools be held accountable for ensuring that all students are making average yearly progress in learning the state curriculum.

Special Education

Ms. Farmer notes that appraisal activities are also conducted when students are referred to school-based student assistance or support teams. Multiple professionals who interact with the student come together to share data gathered through testing; classroom work and behavior; observations by school personnel, parents, and community persons; and sometimes a student's self-assessment. Using all the data available to them, the members of this team develop a plan for helping the student reach his or her full academic potential.

The process that guides decisions related to providing services to students who have special needs is specified in the Individuals with Disabilities Education Act, or IDEA (Public Law 94-142) (http://www.ed.gov/about/offices/list/osers/osep/index.html). First the child is identified as potentially needing special education or related services. An evaluation of all related areas follows. The group of professionals and the child's parents then determine whether the student needs services. If the child is found eligible for special education and related services, a meeting is held in which an individual education plan (IEP) is written. An IEP includes information about current performance, annual goals that the child can reasonably accomplish, and the program that has been designed to meet that child's unique needs. After the parents consent, the services are provided and progress is measured and reported. Every year the IEP is reviewed, and the child is reevaluated every 3 years. School counselors participate in this process by being involved in the meetings to determine appropriate services and helping develop the IEP. They may also provide counseling for the students and consulting for parents. Counselors may work with the classroom and special education teachers also. Recent changes in the provisions of IDEA went into effect July 1, 2005. Those revisions are contained in P.L. 108-446 and summarized by Apling and Jones (2005). The identification and service provision process outlined above has not been altered.

Examine a school system's procedure for the special education process. In the procedure you reviewed, what is the role of the school counselor? Compare your findings with those of your classmates.

Students with disabilities receive special education services either under the IDEA federal education law or under the federal civil rights law Section 504 of the Rehabilitation Act of 1973. School counselors must understand these laws so they can collaborate on teams, consult with parents and teachers, and work with students who have disabilities to plan for their futures. IDEA provides federal money for specially designed instruction for students who need special education and related services because they have a disability. Section 504 provides no money but is a civil rights act requiring any otherwise qualified individual with a disability be included in any program receiving federal financial assistance. In school settings that requirement dictates that students with disability have access to the same services as all other students in the school. Newmeyer and Newmeyer (2004) have compiled the differences between IDEA and Section 504.

A few of those distinctions are the following:

- Settings: Section 504 applies to K–12 schools, postsecondary, and work settings, whereas IDEA applies only to K–12 schools.
- Eligibility: Section 504 does not list specific groups of eligible students but applies to "those who have a physical or mental impairment which substantially limits one or more major life activities, including caring for self, performing manual tasks, walking, seeing, hearing, speaking, breathing, learning, and working." IDEA is designed for students aged 3 to 20 who demonstrate a limited number of handicapping conditions (14 categories) that meet very specific criteria and have a significant impact on learning.
- Accommodations: Section 504 requires school districts to ensure that tests and other evaluative means are provided in a way that allows for the students' skills and is not affected by the impairment. IDEA contains provisions for all students with disabilities who qualify for special education and related services receive a Free and Appropriate Public Education (FAPE) in the least restrictive environment appropriate for each student.

Students who are eligible for services under IDEA have an individualized education program (IEP) developed by a team composed of parents, teachers, and others. The IEP contains eight parts: the child's needs, annual goals, services to meet the goals, justification for a separate learning environment, assessment plans, logistics of the services, transition plans, and evaluation. You can tell that the IEP provides the roadmap for meeting the child's educational needs. Although the law does not require that children served under Section 504 have a written IEP, some school districts follow similar procedures to ensure that the person receives the needed accommodations (Lockhart, 2003).

Counselors will include students with disabilities in individual planning activities as part of the comprehensive counseling program. Counselors will also work with teachers, parents, and students to be certain that needed resources and services are provided consistently. Durodoye, Combes, and Bryant (2004) provide an overview of individual planning activities aimed at African American students who have learning disabilities. Lockhart (2003) recommends that counselors give particular attention to providing social skills training, career counseling, and transition program planning as those are persistent needs for students with disabilities.

Therefore, standardized testing and other forms of appraisal may help accomplish several goals in schools. For the individual planning program element, appraisal activities help students gather information about themselves that they may then use to make informed decisions about their futures. For example, students who consider their results on achievement and aptitude tests have information for identifying their skills, proficiencies, and abilities as well as their academic achievement. Students who know their interests, abilities, and personality preferences have more valuable data and can associate their preferences with careers. Students create a successful educational and career experience using all this information.

Find the Web site of the federal government's Office of Special Education Programs and locate the information written to help parents understand services for children with disabilities. Then go to a school system's Web site and compare the services to the descriptions you found.

Visit the ASCA Web site (http://www.schoolcounselor.org/) and locate the ASCA Position Statement on appropriate and inappropriate roles for serving children with disabilities. Discuss this position with your classmates in the context of helping students plan for their futures.

Identify three other individual planning activities at the elementary school level that may result from a review of achievement test scores and student grades. How would these activities be modified for the middle school level? For high school?

Ms. Farmer and the other elementary counselors involved in the Washington County Schools team are meeting to review the types of appraisal activities conducted in the elementary school and to try to determine whether any changes need to be made. As part of the statewide testing initiative, the elementary students take tests that measure reading, social studies, and math achievement. Currently, the results of these tests are used to help parents, students, and teachers understand students' strengths and weaknesses in particular subject areas. The counselors' goal is to identify ways that these achievement test batteries might be more fully used to inform the development of activities in individual planning. One counselor suggests that the results be reviewed, along with student grades, to identify those who might benefit from training in study skills with the goal of increasing achievement in one or more subject areas.

Another counselor questions whether explanations of the test results to parents have been effective. The counselors have followed a procedure to help parents understand test results and implications described by Holmgren (1996), who recommends an evening presentation that includes illustrations and a profile of test results at various levels. Parents with their own child's profile can compare and question results. Some typical questions are "Does this test count very much?" "Who sees these test scores?" "What does standardized test mean?" and "What does it mean in relation to my child's grades?" The counselors have had good attendance and excellent feedback for their interpretive sessions and have used a similar procedure to help teachers understand test results. One of the counselors now wants to consider some follow-up activities to determine how the children and their parents relate the assessment results to future planning. She will also be responsible for creating a checklist for counselors to follow in preparing for sessions devoted to test interpretation.

With your classmates, create that checklist.

The counselors also identified areas where they were not assessing student progress or competence, primarily in career development. They have numerous program activities associated with career development, including a systemwide career day, field trips to local employers, job-shadowing opportunities, and classroom guidance units focused on the career development standards articulated by Campbell and Dahir for ASCA (see Appendix B). However, they have no idea about the helpfulness of these activities in terms of student development. They decide to investigate some inventories of career maturity, interests, and personality to use as tools in monitoring students' progress throughout their K–12 years. That information will help them check for the effectiveness of their activities and can also be included in the career portfolio students develop.

Finally, the counselors wish to use the assessment information available to them to ascertain whether particular groups of students (low income, racially and ethnically diverse students, and those with disabilities) are developing the skills needed to plan for their futures and to reach their fullest potential in their career and educational goals. As you will recall from Chapter 5, much evidence suggests that access does not necessarily equal opportunity. Counselors will help disaggregate or break down the school testing data by gender, ethnic group, and socioeconomic group to study whether inequities need to be addressed.

They will also examine the appropriateness of the tests for all groups. The counselors recently participated in a state workshop on the multicultural counseling competencies. Those competencies state that counselors know about potential bias in assessment instruments. Herring (1997) cites criteria for culture-free tests that relate to item relevance and meaning across cultures, comparable methods of assessment, cultural norms, and theoretical constructs across cultures.

Helms (2004) reminds us that the fair and valid use of assessment instruments becomes most problematic when the person being tested has different characteristics than those of the test developer's norm group on dimensions such as ethnicity, social class, racial socialization, and physical abilities. She explains that background factors may influence students' performance relative to the comparison group's performance and recommends that some high-stakes decisions should be on the characteristics of the students and schools that they attend rather than on national norms or comparison groups. Likewise Ellis and Raju (2004) conclude that group score differences result from the person's unique social and biological environments and "should not affect the high level of respect due to all racial, ethnic, and gender groups" (p. 111). Other authors supply guidelines for and identify issues in testing students who have limited English proficiencies (Goldsmith, 2004; Geisinger, 2004) as well as those who have disabilities (Elliott, 2004; Leinbaugh, 2004; Newmeyer & Newmeyer, 2004; Thurlow & Thompson, 2004). Lundberg and Kirk (2004) propose that we all recognize each person as one with undeveloped, unknown talents. They offer a realistic look at the value of tests as sources of limited information that can offer substance to a conversation rather than answers and support counselors' diligence in ensuring that the school testing program is based in fair and equitable practices. As well as checking tests for cultural bias, the counselors will interpret findings in culturally appropriate ways. They decide to identify and practice test interpretations among themselves not only to streamline their process but also to demonstrate their abilities at culturally appropriate results.

Reflecting on the types of data identified in Chapter 5 that are available to school counselors, how might one determine whether the academic and career goals are being met by students in groups that are most often underserved?

These and other activities designed to help all students plan for the future will aid in another area of the individual planning program function—advisement.

ADVISEMENT

Myrick (1997) identifies key areas of educational planning as recognizing available options, illustrating the need to plan ahead, learning the common terms of educational planning, learning the sequence of courses, identifying requirements and electives, developing a plan for the next school level, and registering for courses. Any advisement intervention should focus on students' increasing their career awareness, self-knowledge, and skills at making decisions. Optimally all school personnel are involved and community resources are incorporated. These informational programs designed for individual educational and career planning incorporate components for(1) students to focus on exploring and developing plans for their future, (2) parents to become familiar with educational decision making and to learn ways to help the processes with their children, and (3) school personnel to learn ways to incorporate the process into the classroom and other school programs.

In their study of practices of school counselors, Dykeman and associates (2003) identified the structure of advising interventions and listed over 20 school counselor activities in that area. A few examples are parent-student conferences, maturity assessments, resource centers, information interviewing, and portfolios.

After a careful review of patterns of postsecondary behaviors, Brown and Trusty (2005) conclude that the effective education/career planning effort will include adults' advice, student engagement, assessments, and plans. All school personnel, students, and parents typically share responsibility for advisement. The foundation for educational planning begins in kindergarten and continues throughout the school years. Much of this type of individual planning activity takes place in homogeneous groups organized by grade level, interest area, career objective, or postsecondary plans. Depending on the desired outcome, advisement may include individual or group exploration and discussion; information dissemination by counselor, teacher, or other expert; and whole school activities such as career fairs.

Brown and Trusty (2005) note that the way an adult approaches any advising activity with students depends on the individuals and the context. They propose that in most cases these suggestions will help:

- Give concrete information on current achievement and aptitude.
- Provide concrete information on postsecondary programs and careers.
- Specifically tie students' probabilities of success to their past, current, and future behavior and experiences in school.
- Help students explore a range of alternatives as well as back-up plans.

Middle and high schools in the Washington County School system have begun using a teacher-as-advisor program. In these programs, teachers are assigned a group of 15 to 20 students as advisees. In the high school programs, a teacher advisor has the same advisees throughout their high school experience, creating a base for the students as well as an adult who closely monitors their educational planning and school progress. Teachers develop strong relationships with their advisees during the 4-year period. The advisee groups meet regularly in a home-base period 3 days a week in the middle schools and 2 days a week in the high schools. Those advisement periods last about 30 minutes. During that period the group participates in a guidance lesson as well as in individual planning activities. Gonzalez and Myrick (2000) report some units offered in a Florida middle school: orientation to school, time management, self-assessment, communication, decision making, relationships, career development, and education planning. The home-base period includes time for the teacher advisor to meet individually with the student. When teachers find students need additional help, they refer the pupils to the school counselor.

Counselors may coordinate the teacher-as-advisor program, provide resources and topics for the home-base periods, and help teachers refine the skills they need to build an advising relationship with students. Schmidt (1999) states that teachers who have good communication and facilitation skills and who understand effective helping skills can provide excellent advisement to students. In the Washington County middle and high schools 80% of the teachers were involved in this program, and their commitment to it was high.

As a result of advisement, students have an opportunity to consider their own abilities and interests in conjunction with information about the labor market, postsecondary options, and current secondary school offerings. With this information and with opportunities for discussion and exploration with peers, teachers, parents, counselors, admissions counselors, and future employers, students plan for their futures. Trusty and Niles (2004) present a matrix (Figure 8.1) to guide the sequence of information and assessments across school levels.

Currently, Washington County students develop a 4-year plan at the beginning of ninth grade that includes coursework to support their future plans. They complete individualized career plans designed by the National Center for Research in Vocational Education (see Figure 8.2).

FIGURE 8.1   Career Information and Assessment across Grades

Area	Elementary	Middle	High
Academic achievement	High	High	High
Career exploration behavior	High	Moderate	Moderate
Perceptions of careers	High	High	Moderate
Self-perceptions	Moderate	High	High
Interpersonal skills	High	High	High
Perceptions of environments (barriers, opportunities)	Low	High	High
Self-awareness			
Strengths	High	High	High
Interests		High	High
Values		Moderate	High
Career awareness		Moderate	High
Decision making	Low	Moderate	High
Goal setting	Low	Moderate	High
Ability self-estimates		Moderate	High

Source: From A Practical Approach to Career Assessment in Schools (p, 433), by J. Trusty and S.G. Niles, 2004, in *Professional School Counseling: A Handbook of Theories, Programs, and Practices* (pp. 431–441), by B.T. Erford (Ed.), Austin, TX: ProEd. Copyright 2004 by ProEd. Reprinted with permission.

FIGURE 8.2 Career Planning Form

My Education and Career Plan

Name: _____ School: _____ Grade: _____

Course of Study:
- ☐ Career Prep
- ☐ College/University Prep
- ☐ College Tech Prep
- ☐ Occupational Prep

	8	9	10	11	12	Graduation Requirements	
		English I	English II	English III	English IV	4	4
		Math	Math	Math	Math	4*	4*
		Science	Biology	Science	Science	4*	4*
		Economic, Legal & Political Systems	World Studies	U.S. History	Elective	3	3
		PE or Dance	PE or Dance	Elective	Elective	1	1
		Life Mgmt. Skills	Health & Safety	Elective	Elective	1	1
		Elective	Elective	Elective	Elective		
		Elective	Elective	Elective	Elective		
		Total: 7 or 8	7 or 8	7 or 8	7 or 8	23	26

- - - 4 PERIOD DAY ONLY - - -

English	☐☐☐☐☐☐	Art
Math	☐☐☐☐☐☐	Foreign Language
Science	☐☐☐☐☐☐	Military Science
Social Studies	☐☐☐☐☐☐	Music
Physical Education	☐☐☐☐☐☐	Other

☐ = Required Courses; ■ = Elective Courses

*Four units of math must include Algebra 1; Science must include biology, environmental or Earth Science, a physical science and one additional science. Graduation course requirements shown are for the class of 2002 and later.

**Begining with the Class of 2004, students who do not complete a course of study will not receive a high school diploma.

Beyond High School

Post-Secondary Education Goals:
_____
_____
_____
_____

Possible Careers:
_____
_____
_____
_____

Student _____
Date _____
Parent _____
Date _____
Counselor _____
Date _____

Source: From My Education and Career Plan by Winston-Salen/Forsyth County Schools (n.d.), Winston Salen, NC: Author. Reprinted with permission.

Mr. Grund and Ms. Lerner propose that the planning begin in the seventh grade with a 6-year, flexible plan. They are also concerned about the evaluation of outcomes with regard to educational and career planning. Consequently, they propose that at the time the 6-year plan is developed students also begin a career portfolio that will serve as a qualitative assessment of students' development when they graduate from high school.

PLACEMENT AND FOLLOW-UP

Counselors and others who have been responsible for appraisal and advisement of students continue to assist them as they move from the school into the workforce or other postsecondary educational or vocational settings (Gysbers & Henderson, 2000). Some of the placement activities currently in place include opportunities for structured work experiences that are consistent with student interests; preparation for employment and college interviews; seminars and an informative Web page for students and parents about college admissions, financial aid, and applications; scheduled sessions with military and local employment recruiters; and student advisement sessions that reinforce these activities, as well as others related to career and educational placement.

Additionally, school personnel collect follow-up data from graduates and their employers or supervisors to assist with school counseling program evaluation and improvement. Counselors wish to learn how well students were prepared to set and achieve their postsecondary goals from the perspectives of the students themselves, their parents, and their employers or supervisors.

Schwallie-Giddis and Kobylarz (2000) include and expand on the interventions identified by Gysbers and Henderson (2000) to help students gather, analyze, synthesize, and organize information related to their futures. These interventions can be modified for different age levels. A few of those possible ways counselors can work that have not been mentioned earlier follow. Counselors can participate in outreach, an approach used to alert all students to the information and services available. Counselors can provide a range of career information resources that present current and unbiased information to students about occupations, educational programs, postsecondary training, the military, and employment opportunities. In some states, a computer-based career information delivery system includes comprehensive, accurate, and current information about occupations and education or training opportunities. For students who have barriers that may inhibit career development, school counselors recognize the problems and make appropriate referrals. Finally, counselors can maintain long-term contact with students as they move through their school years and beyond.

Counselors may also coordinate programs that incorporate volunteering and/or service learning opportunities to introduce students to the world of work. The placement component of individual planning helps link academics and the working world.

Reflect on your own school experiences and describe how your experiences in middle and high school influenced your educational and career planning both during and after high school graduation. Compare these experiences with those of your classmates. Identify the classmates who experienced the most comprehensive implementation of the individual planning program component during their middle and high school years. What were the long-term benefits to them?

TABLE 8.6 Primary Focus of Individual Planning Activities

	Appraisal	Advisement	Placement	Career
K–3	Special needs	As needed for special concerns	Special needs	Awareness of work/self; exposure to concepts
4–5	Special needs Achievement Intelligence	Educational planning; middle school curriculum	Middle school choices	Awareness of work/self, choices; exposure
6–8	Special needs Achievement Aptitude Intelligence Interests	Educational planning; high school curriculum	High school choices; work experience/service learning possibilities	Exploration of self/careers; set preliminary goals
9–12	Special needs Achievement Aptitude Intelligence Interests Personality Entrance exams	Educational planning/career planning; entry postsecondary preparations	Continuing high school choices; work experience/ service learning possibilities/postsecondary options	Continuing and deeper exploration of self/careers; set goals; implement plans

SUMMARY

We have described the program element of individual planning and offered some examples of the goals of this element at elementary, middle, and high school. A summary of the focus of the individual planning activities at different levels appears in Table 8.6. The principal focus of this chapter has been the interplay between educational and career planning, and equipping students with the skills they need to set and reach educational and career goals. Numerous factors influence students' progress in these two areas including but not limited to stage of individual development, worldview of the student and family, socioeconomic status, gender, race, ethnicity, and ability status. Additionally, we described several experts' views of ways to implement this program element.

PORTFOLIO COMPONENTS

1. Complete the hidden bias inventory at http://www.tolerance.org and write a reflection about how you will use your findings to guard against unintended bias in career and educational programming when you become a school counselor.
2. Consider your own K–12 school experiences and write a reflection about how these experiences relate to your decision to pursue a career in school

counseling. Be sure to consider the development of self-understanding in your discussion.

3. Using one of the NCDG goals and indicators, create a matrix that describes inadequate, marginal, adequate, and exemplary examples of student outcomes related to the goal for each grade level.

Responsive Services: Counselor Delivered Interventions

MEETING THE REMEDIAL NEEDS OF STUDENTS

Mr. Terman and his TK–12 counselors are meeting at the close of the school year to review their efforts over the past year to improve the individual planning component of their programs and to identify the next area of emphasis for their improvement efforts. They have worked diligently during this school year to fine-tune the individual planning program element. A thorough examination of both the new guidance curriculum and individual planning elements reveals that they are adequately addressing the developmental and preventive goals for their systemwide program. For this coming school year they will turn their attention to responsive services, the delivery system activities to meet the immediate concerns of students. The counselors agree that they will be able to spend more time in the responsive services area than they have in the past because the developmental and preventive activities delivered through the guidance curriculum and individual planning are now more efficiently meeting the typical developmental needs of students.

To facilitate their planning of responsive services the counselors reorganize themselves into grade-level teams. This organizational schema will allow counselors to focus on the interventions uniquely appropriate for students at their grade levels. Ms. Learning points out that this program area involves interventions delivered directly by the counselor (direct services) as well as interventions that counselors assist others in delivering (indirect services). Consequently, the TK–12 team decides to plan for these two types of interventions separately, beginning with direct interventions. Their goals for the summer are to

1. Examine existing needs assessment and other local data to identify the immediate concerns of students, parents, and teachers.

2. Develop a survey to be used with students at the beginning of the next school year to identify those whose personal circumstances may have changed and who may need immediate intervention.

3. Use the information collected to plan the responsive services they will provide during the coming academic year.

Gysbers and Henderson (2000) describe the responsive services program element as that part of the organizational framework through which counselors address remedial needs. Due to the many circumstances that have the potential to interfere with students' healthy development, the school has continuing needs for crisis counseling, individual and small-group counseling, diagnostic and remediation activities, and consultation and referral (Gysbers & Henderson, 2000). Responsive services prevent the escalation of problem areas and intervene to alleviate some of the immediate concerns of students (ASCA, 2003a).

This chapter will consider the responsive services delivered by school counselors to students, either individually or in a group, and crisis counseling. As we have stated repeatedly throughout this text, the school counselor's role is to facilitate optimal development. When students fail to learn or perform up to expectations, develop or display behaviors that are counterproductive to learning, or experience changes in performance and achievement, the associated causes are not always attributable to ability. More often, students experience situational, transitional, or cultural/social crises (Fairchild, 1997). For example, students may develop an illness or experience a family disruption such as divorce (situational), experience some difficulty moving from one developmental stage to the next (transitional), or be the victim of discrimination, abuse, or a crime (cultural/social). Any of these occurrences may result in changes in students' ability to fully participate in the activities associated with learning. If unattended, circumstances such as these may lead to ongoing difficulties with learning.

After reading and discussing this chapter, you should be able to

- Identify the most typical immediate and remedial concerns of students to which school counselors respond.
- Distinguish between students who may benefit from direct interventions such as individual or group counseling and those who may be more appropriately assisted through indirect methods such as consultation and/or referral.
- Describe procedures for developing and implementing counseling plans for students who need remedial assistance.
- Develop a weekly schedule that includes responsive services interventions at each of the three grade levels.

Throughout the program design process, counselors consider both what is important to do and how much can be done. Gysbers and Henderson (2000) suggest that elementary and middle school counselors spend approximately 30% to 40% of their time working with this program element, whereas high school counselors spend slightly less, 25% to 35%. In the sections that follow, we will discuss the direct counseling interventions most commonly associated with this program element: individual counseling, group counseling, and crisis counseling. In Chapter 10, we will expand this discussion to those indirect service interventions through which school counselors assist other professionals, colleagues, and parents to intervene with the students.

COUNSELING INDIVIDUALS

Davis (2005) identifies the opportunities school counselors have to work with individual students on academic, personal/social, and career concerns as their most distinctive role (c.f. Loesch & Ritchie, 2005). However, individual counseling in the school setting is different from the traditional view of therapy that occurs during a regularly scheduled, one-on-one interview in a mental health professional's office. School counselors are not *therapists*. They do not diagnose mental illness, and the intervention plans they develop are not called *treatment* plans (Davis, 2005). With those distinctions in mind, most school professionals would agree that there are times when students are distracted from their studies, unable to concentrate, make poor decisions, and behave inappropriately. Some of the circumstances or conditions leading to poor academic performance are amenable to change through short-term, personal counseling interventions led by the school counselor.

Some of the forms individual sessions may take in a school setting include unscheduled "walk-in"encounters for students who seek information, crisis intervention counseling, and counseling initiated as a response to teacher or parent referrals for situational, learning, or behavioral problems. Additionally students may seek out individual counseling for transitional, academic, career, behavioral, relationship, and/or emotional concerns. Most problems students bring to school counselors can be understood in one or more of the following categories:

1. Conflict with others. The student has difficult relationships with parents, siblings, teachers, or peers. Counseling is focused on building better ways of relating. An example of the importance of this type of counseling intervention is the helpfulness of social skills training for all school levels noted by Sexton, Whitson, Blever, and Walz (1997).

2. Conflict with self. A student needs help with making a decision by clarifying alternatives and consequences. Counselors may find choice theory (Glasser, 1998) helpful with these children.

3. Lack of information about self. The student needs to understand personal abilities, strengths, interests, or values. Such students may benefit from working with counselors using an Adlerian approach (Dinkmeyer, Pew, & Dinkmeyer, 1979) or rational-emotive-behavioral therapy (Vernon, 2002).

4. Lack of information about the environment. The student needs information about skills for school success or career education. Many of the activities school counselors arrange for individual planning will address those concerns. However some students may require the one-on-one attention of individual counseling to help them make life choices. Solution-focused brief counseling may be helpful to these students (Sklare, 2005).

5. Lack of skill. The student needs to learn a specific skill such as listening, studying, or asking for help. Many components of the guidance curriculum will focus on those skills. Once again some students may need additional practice or more-focused discussions, which could be accomplished in individual counseling or in small-group settings.

In their review of counseling outcome research, Sexton, Whiston, Bleuer, and Walz (1997) report that counseling with children and adolescents is as effective as it is with adults. They also note that we have too little information to identify which students benefit most from responsive services. The challenges for school counselors include how to identify students, how to conduct counseling, how to determine the effectiveness of counseling interventions, and how to incorporate responsive services into the counselor's day.

Identifying Students

Mr. Wang, a middle school counselor, states that many referrals for counseling in his school come from persons other than the prospective counselee. Parents, teachers, administrators, and others in the community may believe, based on their interactions and or observations, that a student might benefit from counseling. Currently, Mr. Wang receives referrals from teachers written on the back of student homework, on sticky notes attached to other materials being

Divide into small groups and develop a system for receiving and responding to requests for counseling services from students, teachers, parents, and others. Develop a referral form that would have the information needed to respond to the referral request, could be delivered to Mr. Wang in a confidential manner, and allows for a follow-up contact with the referring person. Be sure to include in your system how appointments will be scheduled, how students and teachers will be notified of the appointment, how students will get from classroom to counseling office and back to the classroom, and how missed assignments and instruction will be handled.

Working in three small groups, develop sample needs assessment surveys for elementary, middle, and high school students to identify the needs for individual and group counseling needs related to conflicts with self and others, lack of information about self and the environment, and lack of skills.

returned to his mailbox, and frequently by incidental contact in hallways or restrooms. Parents frequently call or e-mail their requests that he meet with their children, sometimes leaving brief messages at the front office with student aides. He wishes to establish a system that allows him to receive referrals that are more informative and more confidential. All of the counselors agree that such a system would be helpful, and they establish a program goal of developing a systematic procedure for receiving referrals for individual counseling.

Additionally, school counselors review local data to further identify students who are not performing well in school. Disciplinary referrals may be reviewed to identify those students who are experiencing conflicts with others in the school environment manifested through such behaviors as fighting, bullying, and verbal abusiveness. These referrals, along with a review of students who are excessively absent, may also help counselors identify students who experience conflicts with self that lead to behavioral expressions such as destruction of property or vandalism, withdrawal, and depression. Students who have insufficient information about themselves and the environment may be identified through a review of student schedule changes and student schedules that reflect course enrollment patterns that are inconsistent with results of academic and career assessments or reflect stereotypical course taking patterns (e.g., female students who opt for lower level math and science courses regardless of indicators of ability). Students who lack academic skills may be identified through achievement data such as grade reports. And school counselors may collect data directly from students through needs assessment surveys intended to determine the types of concerns with which students need assistance and the number and names of the students for whom these concerns apply.

As counselors receive referrals for responsive services, they consider whether individual counseling or some other intervention would be appropriate for the student. Ms. Pickens states, "The priorities of the program in my elementary school make it virtually impossible for me to provide long-term counseling for students. Because I have a limited amount of time available, 14 half hour slots each week for individual and 14 for group counseling, how might I decide who will be seen for individual counseling?" Loesch and Ritchie (2005) suggest the following question be used as a guide, "If I agree to provide individual counseling to this student, will I likely be able to provide sufficient counseling to ensure

Sample Needs Assessment Item

Instructions to Student: Circle "yes" for all that apply.

I would like help from my school counselor with the following:

Yes   Getting along with my friends

Yes   Understanding the changes in my family

Yes   Making better grades

Yes   Learning how to make friends

satisfactory change in the time available or would the student be better served if I referred him or her to another professional?" The following criteria (Blum, 1998) may further guide the counselor:

- The student's concern is unique.
- Other students (in groups or classroom guidance) would not benefit from interventions aimed at resolving the problem.
- Confidentiality is essential.
- Individual assessment or interpretation is needed.
- The behavior under consideration would be considered deviant by others in the same age group.
- The student may experience distress talking about the concern in groups.

Schmidt (1999) also identifies some questions school counselors might ask to determine whether individual counseling is appropriate:

1. Does the student see the problem in a way that is similar to the one making the referral?
2. Is the student motivated toward change?
3. How much control does the student have over the situation leading to the problem?
4. What is the student's level of commitment to change?

As a summary of these considerations, the following factors influence the school counselor's decision to provide individual counseling:

- Type of problem (school related, home related, other)
- Nature of problem (lack of skill, lack of information, conflict)
- Urgency of need (crisis, remedial, preventive)
- Age of student
- Willingness of student (voluntary, request by parent, teacher, etc.)
- Inner-directed or outer-directed problem (depression, aggression)

After school counselors receive the referral or request for counseling, they may seek additional information and schedule an initial interview with the student to determine the most appropriate type of service. In this initial meeting counselors assess the nature and extent of the problem based on the list above and decide, with the student, whether individual counseling might be helpful. During this assessment interview, school counselors may decide to refer a student to counseling outside the school. Serious disorders, personality problems, and other pervasive difficulties require more intensive therapy than most school counselors can provide. Some of the symptoms that may indicate a student needs longer term therapy from someone outside the school include eating disorders, intense sibling rivalry, intense preoccupation with sexual matters, extreme aggression with no apparent guilt, habitual lying or stealing, and sudden and unexplained changes in eating, sleeping, or behavior patterns. School counselors assess the frequency (how often the problem occurs), duration (how long it lasts), and intensity (how strong it is) to help them determine whether to work with the young person in school or to refer to another professional.

Drawing from a variety of sources, Baker and Gerler (2004) propose a three-stage model for referrals initiated by the school counselor. First, counselors identify and clarify the problem. This requires counselors to know their own limits of competence as well as the competencies of those to whom the referrals may be made. Matching the client's needs to the appropriate resource is an important part of the referral process. Second, goals are developed with each student/client to help the counselor determine whether a referral is necessary. Third, action strategies are implemented. If the student's goals for change are within the areas of competence of the counselor and may be reasonably accomplished in the time available, the student and counselor may decide to enter into an individual counseling relationship. If a referral is deemed most appropriate, strategies include determining where and how the referral will occur. The TK–12 counselors decide to discuss procedures for making referrals more fully when they focus on indirect interventions.

Conducting Counseling

If the counselor and student determine that it is in the student's best interest to receive individual counseling, the process of counseling begins. Selecting the approaches that may be most productive for a particular student is influenced by a number of factors. Specifically, the cognitive, social, and physical development of students largely determines the approach taken by the counselor. Table 9.1 summarizes the ways some of these factors affect a counseling application. Additionally, the student's cultural identity (e.g., worldview, language, individual vs. group orientation) is important for the counselor to know and appreciate. Vernon and Clemente (2005) describe ways to conduct multicultural assessment and provide culturally competent interventions for work with children and adolescents. Table 9.2 contains criteria for counselors to use in assessing whether they are providing equitable counseling services. Finally, the counselor must have a good grasp of the major counseling theories and their applications with school-aged youth in order to develop effective counseling plans.

An important aspect of counselors' professional identify development is acquiring knowledge about counseling theories and using theories to guide their counseling practices. Each of the TK–12 counselors expresses a preference for a particular theory or group of theories to help them understand the problems or concerns of their students and to work with their student clients more effectively. The various theoretical perspectives studied by counselors-in-training include a description of the nature of people as viewed through a particular theoretical lens; the theory of counseling which includes a discussion of how problems develop; the methods of counseling including the role of the counselor, the client, and the types of interventions used; strengths, limitations, and applications of the theory to diverse populations. Consistent with the emphasis on evidence-based interventions central to contemporary educational movements, counselors must be aware of the theories and methods that have been demonstrated to be most effective with particular concerns, problems, and types of clients. Reports of outcome research in counseling found in professional journals are a good source for school counselors to help inform decisions about goals and interventions for individual counseling.

TABLE 9.1 Development and Counseling Applications

Age	Typical Concerns	Situational Problems	Transitions	Counseling Considerations
Middle childhood (6–10)	Teacher and/or peer approval; being chosen last for a team; fear of being ridiculed; fear of losing a friend; school performance	Growing up in abusive or alcoholic home; living in poverty; adjustments to parental divorce and/or remarriage	Adjusting to school; missing parents; changes in friendships; too little or too much dependency	Help with problem-solving abilities; design interventions that are concrete, such as bibliotherapy, art, puppets, role-play, and games; talking less effective
Early adolescence (11–14)	Mood swings; relationships with friends and parents; worry about appearance; sexuality	Growing up in an abusive or alcoholic home; living in poverty; adjustments to parental divorce and/or remarriage; pregnancy; substance abuse	Overwhelming feelings; moving to middle school; planning for their future	Confusion predominates; concrete strategies for cause and effect, alternative behaviors, and long-range implications
Middle adolescence (15–18)	Complex relationships; sexual intimacy; family stress	Growing up in abusive or alcoholic home; living in poverty; adjustments to parental divorce and/or remarriage; pregnancy; substance abuse	Changes in role, relationships, routine, and assessment of self; future	Be aware of ambivalence; use activities to illustrate points; bibliotherapy, journaling, and homework helpful

Source: From *Counseling Children and Adolescents*, 3rd edition, by A. Vernon, 2004, Denver, CO: Love Publishing. Copyright 2004 by Love Publishing. Reprinted with permission.

An extensive discussion of counseling theories is beyond the scope of this text. However, the TK–12 counselors have some observations about the theories they most often refer to as they develop counseling plans. Person-centered counseling (Rogers, 1977, 1992) provides counselors with relationship skills for building rapport. Choice theory (Glasser, 1998), solution-focused brief counseling (Sklare, 2005), Adlerian counseling (Dinkmeyer et al., 1979), and rational-emotive-behavioral therapy (REBT) (Ellis, 1996; Vernon, 2002; Vernon & Clemente, 2005) are other theories used by many school counselors. Additionally Myrick (1997) has identified a problem-solving model for school counselors to use for individual counseling. His process includes deciding on the problem,

Choose one of the issues we have identified as appropriate for individual counseling services in the school. Review the literature to identify the evidence-based practices associated with that particular issue. Be prepared to exchange information with your classmates.

TABLE 9.2   Counseling Diverse Students—Criteria for Equity

Questions	Yes	No	Needs Improvement
1. Am I, as the counselor, familiar with strategies that promote equity in a multicultural society (e.g., utilizing culturally/gender relevant counseling practices, empathizing with and understanding the students' worldview)?			
2. Am I, as the counselor, familiar with and understanding of both verbal and nonverbal language patterns of different ethnic/racial groups?			
3. Do I, as the counselor, have high expectations for all students and assist students to acquire resources and opportunities necessary for success?			
4. In working with a diverse student population in counseling situations, do I, as the counselor, consider the interaction of gender differences, class differences, language differences, and cultural differences?			
5. Do I, as the counselor, provide career counseling on the basis of the students' abilities, interests, and skills rather than according to traditional roles based on gender, race, disability, or ethnicity?			
6. Do I, as the counselor, encourage students to take courses nontraditional to their gender, race, disability, or ethnicity if the student shows an interest in one of those areas (e.g., mathematics, science, computer technology for females, early childhood education for males)?			
7. Do I, as the counselor, assess my own values, attitudes, and beliefs and have the ability to refrain from imposing them upon the student?			
8. Do I, as the counselor, participate in in-service programs or special skill sessions for counselors dealing with culturally diverse students?			
9. Do I, as the counselor, meet with students outside of the office to show an interest in their needs beyond the classroom?			
10. Do I, as the counselor, use a multidimensional approach to identify the level and scope of a student's ability before recommending course selection, placement, and future schooling/career opportunities?			

Source: From *Elements of Equity: Criteria for Equitable Schools,* by J.M. Greenberg and S. Shaffer, 1991, Mid-Atlantic Equity Consortium. Available at http://www.maec.org. Reprinted with permission.

identifying what the child has tried to do to solve the problem, generating some other possible solutions, and determining the child's next step. Keys, Bemak, and Lockhart (1998) recommend short-term models such as problem-solving (Myrick, 1997) and solution-focused counseling (Murphy, 1997; Sklare, 2005).

Developing counseling plans involves several steps (Knapp & Jongsma, 2002). Six issues that need to be considered in every intervention plan are (1) problem selection or a statement of the concern or problem to be addressed in counseling; (2) problem definition or how the problem or concern presents itself in the student's life; (3) specific goals to be achieved that will resolve the problem; (4) short-term objectives that, when accomplished, are likely to result in the achievement of the goal; (5) activities or interventions to help the student achieve the short-term objectives; and (6) a method for evaluating whether the objectives and goal(s) have been achieved. The heart of the counseling plan is the goal or the goals toward which you and the student are striving. The goals and the means of achieving them will be guided by the concern of the student and the theoretical approach of the counselor. Young (2001) identifies several positive outcomes of goal setting, including the fact that goals help us stay focused on the concerns of the student. Clearly stated and understood goals help counselors evaluate whether they have the skills needed to assist the student or whether a referral would be more appropriate. Positively stated goals help students focus on success, specific goals provide a sound basis for making decisions about interventions, and measurable goals make it possible to determine whether counseling has been helpful to the student. You might notice that the format for developing individual counseling plans is quite similar to the format for developing classroom curriculum described in Chapter 7.

Many excellent resources are available to school counselors to facilitate their work with students who have specific concerns. Vernon (2002) provides counseling plans from an REBT perspective for students experiencing internal concerns such as self-doubt, external concerns such as anger and acting out, and developmental problems such as relationships with others. Gladding (2005) describes the use of creative arts interventions used to increase self-awareness and self-expression. Knapp and Jongsma (2002) offer plans that include goals, short-term objectives, and a variety of interventions designed specifically to achieve the goal and objectives for a number of school-related concerns such as career planning, tolerance training, and learning difficulties. Sori and Hecker (2003) have compiled a notebook in which interventions are described that address all three areas of development about which school counselors are concerned.

The counselors also keep personal records of their counseling sessions. They may keep administrative records that enumerate appointments and services received. Other types of administrative records include copies of correspondence, intake forms, or other routine papers. Counselors use case notes to help them remember particulars about the students and the content of their sessions. Remley and Herlihy (2001) recommend that counselors assume the notes they take will be read. The assumption that the notes will become public will help counselors be cautious about deciding what should be included. They advise documenting the purposes of providing services and the decisions and actions that have been made. Counselors can use the acronym SOAP to guide them in what to include in case notes (Baird, 2002):

- Subjective information is what the client reports.
- Objective data refers to the results of any assessments that have been given.
- Assessment includes the counselor's perceptions.
- Plans are the identification of the problem and intervention plan.

These personal notes are kept in a secure place and should not be left unattended unless locked in a drawer or cabinet. The notes should be destroyed after an agreed-upon amount of time. The notes are not included in school records. The counselors decide that they want to begin writing a procedures manual for

> Not all school counselors develop and maintain counseling plans for individual services they provide. As a class, discuss the advantages for school counselors and their student clients of developing plans with goals, definable and measurable objectives, and related interventions. What are the disadvantages of developing and following such a plan?

the counseling office and will include these guidelines for case notes and for student records in that manual.

Determining Effectiveness

School counselors need to demonstrate that the desired change to which the individual counseling sessions were directed has been achieved. You have probably already identified built-in accountability as one of the major advantages of developing and using a counseling plan for all individual counseling clients (Loesch & Ritchie, 2005). How might one determine if objectives have been met without first stating the objectives clearly? How does one decide whether interventions used have been effective in the absence of a clear, definable goal to which the interventions are linked? How will one know that the goals for personal counseling have been met in the absence of an evaluation method and stated criteria for success? A well-developed counseling plan provides information that allows counselors to answer these three important questions.

In addition to determining whether the intervention plan has been successful, there are some other ways to demonstrate accountability. Loesch and Ritchie (2005) describe the use of rating scales before and after the intervention to assess the degree or extent of change resulting from the intervention (see also Thompson, Rudolph, & Henderson, 2004). Additionally, students, parents, and teachers can identify in what ways and to what extent the student has changed since the initiation of counseling services (Loesch & Ritchie, 2005). Finally, they encourage the use of single-subject research designs to establish the outcomes of counseling.

Scheduling Sessions

Counselors have several options to build a caseload for individual counseling. They may wait for students to refer themselves. They may respond to parent and teacher referrals. They may seek recommendations from school administrators. And they may combine all these options. After their team's discussion of counseling, Ms. Pickens proposes that the counselors try a suggestion made by Myrick (1997). She is going to ask all the teachers at the grade level for which she is responsible, the principal, and the assistant principals for the names of children who might need some individual attention. For this school year she will counsel with two of those named most frequently for a 6-week period. She will also work with 12 other students identified by several adults. For the rest of her individual counseling she will assist those who have self-referred and those referred by others. Many of those situations may be short term, requiring one or two sessions only. However, she will schedule time for longer counseling relationships with up to four students during each grading period. Ms. Pickens and the other counselors agree to stagger the available individual session appointments throughout the school day to ensure that their individual clients do not miss the same class each time they have an appointment scheduled. Additionally, the counselors place in their schedules daily opportunities for appointments during times that do not conflict with class (e.g., 20 minutes before and after school).

Counseling Plan

Student: Tamikka Jones

Grade: 4th

Source of Referral: Parents

Reason for Referral: Grandmother died as a result of a violent crime. Since the funeral one month ago, Tamikka sleeps almost all of the time that she is not in school, eats less than usual, stays inside her room, and has withdrawn from activities previously enjoyed, including playing with friends and studying for school.

Goal: Tamikka will increase her waking time, the number of balanced meals she eats each week, and resume her previous level of social and school activity.

Short-term objectives:
1. Tamikka will stay awake between the time she gets home from school and her 9 P.M. bedtime.
2. Tamikka will play outside with her friends at least three afternoons each week until dinnertime.
3. Tamikka will eat a well-balanced meal at 6 P.M. each evening.
4. Tamikka will complete homework assignments between the end of dinnertime and 8 P.M. each evening.

Counseling Interventions:
1. Cognitive distraction will be used to have Tamikka think about a happy time she spent with her grandmother, replacing the thoughts about her grandmother's death. Tamikka will create a scrapbook to illustrate some of the happy memories.
2. Exercise and playing with friends will be used to help Tamikka leave the house and engage in physical activities instead of taking a nap before dinner.
3. Worksheets for rating her week with regard to meals, social activity, sleep, and completion of homework will be used to increase self-awareness of her behavior and track progress toward goals.

Evaluation: Counseling will be discontinued when Tamikka is sleeping no more than 10 hours per day, completing 90% of all homework assignments, spending at least 4 hours per week playing with friends after school, and eating at least two well-balanced meals per day.

COUNSELING IN GROUPS

All of the counselors report that they enjoy working with students in small groups and view this strategy as efficient and effective. Even though they have only 14 half-hour slots available each week, they see six to eight students at the same time and the group process allows students to learn from each other. Among the many reasons for group interventions is that they work (Brigman & Goodman, 2001). Whiston and Sexton (1998) found that outcome research in school-based group counseling demonstrated this to be an effective intervention format.

Some of the issues successfully addressed through groups in the research reviewed by Whiston and Sexton (1998) include social skills development, academic difficulties, behavioral and stress management, and family problems. Small-group counseling may be appropriate in a variety of circumstances such as when counselors want to address urgent needs, focus on a problem, or encourage student development. School counselors use the small-group format for both guidance (psychoeducational) goals and counseling (interpersonal) goals. These two types of groups differ in several ways. Psychoeducational groups have a learning orientation and may often be focused on the prevention of potential problems. The concerns around which groups are established are often identified through a needs assessment, or perhaps the counselor receives referrals around a similar issue for multiple students. Still other groups are offered routinely based on the counselor's knowledge of the developmental transitions with which students are most likely to need assistance. Group counseling plans are developed and goals are decided around the central organizing theme of the group. Table 9.3 lists some possible group themes.

Because people live and work in groups, it is reasonable to provide opportunities for students to practice new behaviors in group settings (Brigman & Goodman, 2001). When students are faced with problems, they tend to believe that they are the only ones experiencing such difficulty (Greenberg, 2003). Participating in group counseling with others who share their concerns helps students recognize that others face similar problems and that they can offer each other understanding. Students have the opportunity to interact with their peers, identify role models, and perhaps become a role model for someone else in the group. Greenberg has also identified some disadvantages associated with groups. Trust, the cornerstone of any counseling relationship, may be more difficult to establish in groups. Counselors cannot guarantee to keep all information confidential and must also acknowledge that the leader cannot control the actions or behaviors of other group members with regard to keeping group information private. Additionally, because the groups occur during the school day, student members may miss six to eight classes in order to belong. The TK–12 counselors are particularly concerned about this since their goal is to promote academic success. This is an issue the counselors need to resolve. As is the case with individual counseling, working groups into the calendar can be a challenge.

Group counseling leadership requires planning. An important early step for counselors is introducing group counseling to administrators and teachers

TABLE 9.3   Possible Small-Group Topics

Group Topics	Elementary	Middle	High School
Academic Development			
Academic competition	No	Yes	Yes
Academic failures	Yes	Yes	Yes
Attitudes about school	Yes	Yes	Yes
Learning styles	Yes	Yes	Yes
New student	Yes	Yes	Yes
Responsible school behavior	Yes	Yes	Yes
Study skills	Yes	Yes	Yes
Time management	Yes	Yes	Yes
Personal/Social Development			
Anger management	Yes	Yes	Yes
Communication skills	Yes	Yes	Yes
Conflict management	Yes	Yes	Yes
Peer pressure	Yes	Yes	Yes
Social skills	Yes	Yes	Yes
Valuing diversity	Yes	Yes	Yes
Death, grief, loss	Yes	Yes	Yes
Health problems	Yes	Yes	Yes
Pregnancies	No	Yes	Yes
Stress management	Yes	Yes	Yes
Family issues	Yes	Yes	Yes
Career Development			
Assessment	No	Yes	Yes
Decision making	Yes	Yes	Yes
Goal setting	Yes	Yes	Yes
Work habits	Yes	Yes	Yes
Educational achievement and career success	No	Yes	Yes
Working as part of a team	Yes	Yes	Yes

(Blum, 1998; Greenberg, 2003). Such an orientation includes an explanation of how group counseling supports student achievement in school. Therefore, group topics reflect the school's mission of helping students acquire the skills they need for a successful school, and life, experience (Brigman, & Goodman, 2001). Sharing the research of effectiveness provides support for including small-group work within responsive services. For example, Reeder, Douzenis, and Bergin (1997) used a small-group counseling intervention to improve racial relationships between second graders. Garrett and Crutchfield (1997) modified an idea from the Native American culture for a series of small-group sessions to help children develop positive self-images. Others have demonstrated the effectiveness of small-group work with low-performing students (Campbell & Myrick, 1990), with bereaved children (Zambelli & DeRosa, 1992), and with students who have been retained (Campbell & Bowman, 1993).

Identifying Students

The procedures already described for identifying individual counseling clients such as conducting needs assessments and responding to administrator, teacher, student, and parent referrals, as well as reviewing local achievement and performance data are also useful strategies for identifying students who might benefit from group counseling. School counselors review the available data, establish group topics, set a schedule, and advertise the groups to students, teachers, and parents. Students who are referred or inquire about the groups, as well as those identified by the counselor from other data sources, constitute the list of prospective members. Group size generally is limited to between five and eight members, depending on the age of participants (Myrick, 1997).

Conducting Counseling

Prior to the first session counselors screen students on the potential group members' list. Screening is an important ethical issue (ASCA, 2004c) intended to reduce the potential of psychological harm to a student who may not be ready for group participation. The selection of participants should involve a process during which the potential member receives information about the particular group and about a group member's role. Not all students will benefit from or be interested in group counseling. Some students may be too hostile, too suspicious, or too fragile to be included. Students who are screened but not included in the group should be given the option of an alternative experience. Once the counselor and the student have agreed that the student will participate in the group, the parents are provided information about the group and their student's interest in participating. Some school systems require that this information letter be signed and returned whereas others do not (Brigman & Goodman, 2001). It is the school counselor's duty to know and comply with the policies governing such issues.

School groups may have an open format in which members can enter and leave or a closed format in which the same members stay through the entire schedule of group sessions. In open groups, the leader generally facilitates the group process and teaches the content and skills. Activities are chosen that support the goals of the group. One example might be a group that meets after school to improve academic skills. Some students may need all the lessons (study skills, time management, test-taking strategies, relaxation skills, organizational skills). Others may need only one or two of the lessons and attend only the sessions that are pertinent.

Remember a time when you worked with a group of your peers to explore and solve a problem. Describe the aspects that were and were not beneficial. Share experiences in small groups and develop a list of commonalities in "helpful" and "not helpful" columns. How might you, in your role as group leader, emphasize the helpful aspects and minimize the impact of the negative?

Counseling or interpersonal groups may also have the prevention orientation. These groups may focus on some identified stressors, a conflict, or a problem that distracts young people from learning. The problem may be individual or a common problem. These groups typically have a closed format. The leader uses counseling skills to help the members who are experiencing some disturbance because of the identified problem (e.g., divorce of parents, move to a new school, difficulty in making friends or managing anger). In groups members identify the particular problem(s) they are each having within the context of the central issue, explore solutions, and make decisions about how they will attempt to solve the problem(s). This parallels the problem-solving approach Myrick (1997) suggests.

Additionally, group leaders work to balance group sessions by working on both maintenance and task functions. How members are working together and helping each other are the maintenance functions. Movement toward the group goal is the task function (Blum, 1998). Group leaders serve as models to demonstrate group membership and communication skills. The group leader uses counseling skills and techniques as well as the following tasks: directing the direction and flow of communication, guiding the group process, blocking harmful behavior, connecting ideas, reaching a consensus, moderating discussion, summarizing, and supporting (Thompson, Rudolph, & Henderson, 2004).

Similar to planning for individual counseling services, counselors develop plans that include goals for the overall experience and objectives to be accomplished in each group meeting (Greenberg, 2003). Brigman and Goodman (2001) describe a three-phase format for each session that includes a beginning, middle, and end. The beginning of the first session includes an ice breaker to help students get to know each other and begin to form cohesion and trust. The beginning of subsequent sessions includes a review of the previous session, a check-in with students to see how the lessons learned in group are being applied in life, a check on overall group functioning, and a preview of the current session. The middle of the session involves an activity related to the day's topic or goal. The leader provides new information and asks that students apply the new learning to their situations. Additionally, students are asked to evaluate the helpfulness of new strategies. Role-plays, storytelling, art, music, games, and bibliotherapy are examples of strategies that might be used to achieve the session objectives. The end of the session involves students discussing their thoughts and feelings during the activities, reflecting on what they learned, and committing to an attempt to apply some idea or skill from the session before the next group meeting.

Counselors also observe that the group itself moves through stages. Experts in group counseling have identified between three and five stages of group development. Brigman and Goodman (2001) articulate a three-stage model that parallels the session format. The first stage includes the initial sessions where trust develops and students become oriented to the group, the procedures, the rules, and build relationships with each other. The second stage is a productive period when insights occur and behaviors change. The skills and strategies that students learn inside the group are practiced outside the group and the students

Discuss with your classmates the skills students would need to learn in each session to meet the short-term objective. Prepare a mock report to demonstrate accountability.

Develop a one-page survey with group topics typical of middle school students' transitional crises. Include topics associated with students' potential difficulties in academic and career development. Using the same plan format provided for Tamikka's individual counseling, work in small groups to develop a group plan for Tamikka and five other students who have experienced the death of a family member in the previous 6 months.

offer each other support, feedback, and confrontation. The third stage is that during which the students consolidate their learning and reach closure. There are well-documented characteristics of each stage and you will learn much more about the stages, the predictable crises at each, and stage-related leader interventions in a course or courses focused on methods of group counseling.

Determining Effectiveness

As we stated previously, demonstrations of accountability must be considered during the initial phases of planning counseling interventions, including groups. A well-articulated group counseling plan will include the changes expected as a result of participating in the group. Review the group counseling plan for the *Motivated to Learn* group and describe the sources of accountability data built into the plan.

Scheduling Sessions

Counselors collaborate with teachers and administrators on the scheduling of groups to minimize disruption to instructional time. Logistical issues such as the number of times the group will meet and the length, setting, and frequency of the meetings are planned and communicated to teachers and prospective group members. Greenberg (2003) suggests meeting with the teachers of group members to set up the specific meeting dates and times. In schools the groups' duration may be tied to a grading period of 6 to 9 weeks. Groups in early elementary grades usually meet for 20 minutes, in fourth or fifth grades, for 30 minutes, and in middle and secondary schools, for a class period (45 to 55 minutes). Groups may meet before or after school, during lunch, or during other times of the day as alternatives to class time.

CRISIS COUNSELING

There are numerous examples of crises experienced by individual students that may require intervention from the school counselor (Cavaiola & Colford, 2006). Child abuse and neglect, threats of suicide, homicide or other violent acts, assault, and loss and bereavement are some of the more common crises experienced by students in schools. A crisis may occur through either natural disasters (e.g., harm to students, teachers, or parents by flood, wind, or fire) or personal disasters (e.g., harm to members of the school community by violence, suicide, or accidents). Whatever the cause, crises in schools and their surrounding communities require intervention. Crisis implies that the impact of the event is experienced immediately and needs an immediate response (Cavaiola & Colford, 2006). Caplan (1964; cited in Cavaiola & Colford, 2006) defined crisis as a temporary state of upset during which the individual's typical ways of responding and coping are not effective. A crisis is based on a precipitating event, is time limited, and results in confusion. During this temporary period of confusion, the affected individuals interpret the event(s) leading to the crisis. Each individual will have different views of the event and different behavioral

Motivated to Learn

Group Goals

1. Group members will increase grades in a minimum of two subjects by at least one letter grade during the two grading periods immediately following the completion of the group.
2. Group members will develop a daily study plan and adhere to the plan a minimum of 4 days per week for 4 consecutive weeks.

Short-term Objectives

Session One: Group members will develop clear, measurable academic and behavioral goals related to academic achievement (e.g., complete 90% of homework assignments).

Session Two: Group members will establish and adhere to a daily routine for completing homework assignments.

Session Three: Group members will apply study skills and habits to complete homework assignments and prepare for tests.

Session Four: Group members will express confidence in test-taking abilities.

Session Five: Group members will demonstrate success in test-taking performance.

Session Six: Group members will provide evidence of academic progress.

and emotional reactions based on those views. Some individuals who experience a crisis event will experience a return to previous functioning quickly and with brief interventions; others may experience extreme distress in response to crisis situations, exhibiting symptoms of posttraumatic stress disorder, acute stress disorder, and adjustment disorders (Cavaiola & Colford, 2006).

As crisis events result in a limitation of or inability to cope, the goal of intervention is to help people resume coping, returning a measure of control to their lives (Cavaiola & Colford, 2006). Cavaiola and Colford identify the following characteristics of effective crisis counselors:

- Tolerance for ambiguity
- Calm, neutral demeanor
- Tenacity
- Optimism
- Adventuresomeness
- Capacity for Empathy
- Flexibility
- Confidence

Applying the criteria previously discussed for determining appropriateness for individual counseling, how might school counselors interact with and respond to persons who have difficulty returning to previously effective levels of coping?

Create a chart that facilitates the assessment of how you stand regarding each of these characteristics. Identify those about which you are uncertain or lack knowledge and develop a plan for improvement. Adhere to the procedures for effective intervention planning discussed in this chapter.

Discuss with your classmates how accountability might be demonstrated with regard to the crisis intervention model presented by Cavaiola and Colford.

- Little need to rescue
- Capacity for listening
- Awareness of trauma indicators
- Openness to individual crisis reactions
- Capacity for information management (pp. 28–30)

Although crisis counseling is not an activity that can be written into the counselors' daily schedules, crisis counseling and crisis intervention may be based on a plan (Loesch & Ritchie, 2005). Unlike individual or group counseling, one cannot develop an effective plan and strategy for responding to a crisis in the midst of the crisis. There are numerous models for crisis intervention, all of which share the common goal of restoring balance and control. The LAPC model described by Cavaiola and Colford (2006) presents counselors with an intervention strategy or framework that is flexible enough to be useful in many situations and structured enough to guide school counselors' crisis intervention efforts.

There has been some disagreement in the crisis-oriented literature about the benefits of expressing negative emotions. Some believe that simply venting one's emotions has benefit, whereas others assert that the positive benefits are related to the interpretation or reinterpretation of strong emotions and the events that led to them (Echterling, Presbury, McKee, 2005). Crisis counselors need to both hear and validate the emotional experience of their clients. Further, they actively work to lower their clients' emotional distress and increase the positive, coping feelings of resolve to overcome the current crisis.

Schoolwide Crises

The definition of crisis as the perception that events are so difficult that coping resources are inadequate may be applied to communities and groups as well as to individuals (Cavaiola & Colford, 2006). There are numerous models for responding to schoolwide crises, and each school and system must design an intervention plan that meets their specific needs. One widely used approach is the three-stage crisis intervention model developed by Caplan (1964; cited in Cavaiola & Colford, 2006). Primary and secondary prevention and tertiary intervention are the three parts of this model. Obviously, a major goal of the school counseling program is preventing crises and many programs implemented by school counselors, along with other school professionals occur at the primary prevention level. As an example, let us consider the prevention of violence in schools. As part of the primary prevention efforts, programs are in place to emphasize school and student safety, suicide and substance abuse prevention, conflict resolution, stress and anger management, and respect for individual differences. These intervention activities are generally delivered to whole classes of students or to the entire student population in a school. Those aspects of the program for which school counselors are responsible are generally delivered as part of the school counseling curriculum.

Secondary prevention is aimed at minimizing the potential for harm once a crisis has occurred. For example, counselors may review discipline referrals to identify those students who fight, bully, or persistently argue with others. Although these identified students have participated in a conflict management

LAPC Model

Step One: Listen

During this phase, the counselor's goal is to communicate to clients that they are safe, heard, and in control. These three messages are communicated through a clear introduction and statement of intention; counselor actions that demonstrate the situation is under control (limiting access of the media, assuring safety, taking care of distracting details, etc.); providing opportunities for decision making over even minor issues (e.g., "Where would you like to sit?") in order for the client to begin assuming control; communicating that the client is heard by actively listening to the client.

Step Two: Assess

Throughout the listening stage, the counselor attends to the verbal and non-verbal messages communicated by the client. Assessment occurs across multiple dimensions: Behavior, Affect, Somatic, Interpersonal, Cognitive, and Spiritual (BASIC). An accurate assessment of each area of functioning is essential to the development of an effective intervention plan. In addition to the BASIC model of assessment, specific types of crises may have designated assessment protocols. For example, the expression of suicidal thoughts or homicidal intent call for additional assessment strategies.

Step Three: Plan

Problem-solving skills previously used in day-to-day life are applied to the crisis-related dilemmas. Thus, clients are empowered to assume control, discover their own resources for coping, and move forward.

Step Four: Commit

The client commits to a plan of action to regain control and follow-up procedures are established.

Sources: From Cavaiola, Alan and Josept E. Colford, *A Practical Guide to Crisis Intervention.* Copyright © 2006 by Houghton Mifflin Company. Adapted with permission; and *Crisis Intervention: Promoting Resilience and Resolution in Troubled Times,* (p. 13), by L.G. Echterling, J. Presbury, and J. E. McKee, 2005, Upper Saddle River, NJ: Prentice Hall/Merrill. Copyright © 2005, by Pearson Education, Inc. Adapted by permission.

or resolution program, some of them did not acquire the necessary skills to peacefully manage their disagreement with others. Additionally, all students in the school have participated in programs aimed at increasing respect for individual differences. Unfortunately, some students still verbally abuse or cause physical harm to others. These students might be ideal candidates for either individual or group counseling delivered through the responsive services component of the school counseling program.

Tertiary intervention requires long-term follow-up to address the needs of students and others in the school community who are unable to resume normal levels of coping following the crisis. Assume the worst for a moment and imagine that a school shooting has occurred in which several students and teachers were seriously injured. Those actually injured and those in closest physical or emotional proximity to them may develop posttraumatic stress disorder (PTSD), adjustment disorder, anxiety disorder, or depression. These are disturbances that may not be resolved with the type of short-term interventions provided (secondary prevention) by school counselors. Referrals to other mental health professionals in the community may be necessary to assist clients who require intervention at this level.

The TK–12 counselors have a crisis plan in place to respond to crisis events that have a negative impact on the school and, perhaps, community. This plan was developed collaboratively with a group of school personnel and selected community agencies such as law enforcement officials and medical personnel. The plan is updated annually, outlines specific responsibilities and who is responsible for carrying them out, is distributed to every staff member, and is evaluated periodically through mock drills (Blum, 1998). Their plan was implemented most recently when a car that did not yield to the stop sign displayed by a school bus struck and killed a 6-year-old student in the first grade. The accident was witnessed by all the elementary school children riding the bus. Because there was a crisis plan in place, the employees of the school and system knew to initiate their contact list and have all personnel return immediately to the school to review what would occur the next day when children returned to school. All school personnel knew to whom they should refer inquiries from the press. One person was responsible for calling in counselors from the other schools and community agencies to assist with small-group and individual counseling sessions for the children riding the bus and those in the deceased student's classroom. The teachers throughout the school system were responsible for telling the students in each of their classrooms what had happened, and they knew to provide factual information in developmentally appropriate language. Parents were invited to the school to participate in sessions with other adults. The children who witnessed or were affected by this traumatic event needed assistance with their concerns and perceptions about self. The parents needed assistance in addressing their concerns and fears for their children and their children's safety (Junhke, 1997).

Classroom announcements and activities were used to keep students informed; provide them an opportunity to express their feelings of sadness, fear, helplessness, and so forth; and attend to their needs for reassurance regarding their own physical safety. Outside consultants were brought in on the third day following the accident to debrief the adults who provided support and services for the children. Follow-up activities were scheduled at predetermined intervals, and the counselors provided staff development training for teachers about the behaviors students might display that would indicate a need for additional intervention.

The TK–12 counselors identify as one weakness of their plan the failure to systematically train new personnel. Each year, there are a number of changes in personnel in their schools including teachers, administrators, counselors, support personnel, and central office staff. A large systemwide training was conducted 3 years ago when their comprehensive plan went into effect, but no additional training has been conducted in the interim. Although the plan is updated, distributed, and

---

Search the World Wide Web to locate schoolwide crisis intervention plans. Review the plans to determine the role(s) school counselors typically play in such plans.

Even though crisis counseling may occur in large groups, in small groups, and with individuals, it is a decidedly different intervention than individual or small-group counseling. Working in small groups, discuss the differences between individual and small-group counseling and crisis counseling.

the names of new personnel added, the counselors believe that an annual training session prior to the opening of school would be a helpful refresher to continuing employees and a good strategy to inform and include new personnel as well. Otherwise, the counselors are confident about their ability to respond to the typical crises their students experience and to accurately assess needs and provide services, including referring those students who experience extreme psychological distress that requires longer term or specialized intervention (e.g., PTSD).

SUMMARY

In this chapter, you have read about responsive services delivered by the school counselor directly to students and the interventions typically associated with such services. Specifically, individual, group, and crisis counseling were presented. The importance of planning and demonstrating accountability were discussed in all three sections. Successful demonstrations of accountability begin with the initial planning and development of counseling plans that include clear, measurable objectives.

The discussions of individual and group counseling interventions included identification of students who may benefit from services, a description of the processes of counseling, the importance of accountability and ways to assess effectiveness, and how to schedule the interventions. Crisis counseling requires a different approach in that the identified clients are those affected by some event that results in their temporary inability to cope and cannot be "planned" in advance. However, crisis counseling or intervention does proceed in a systematic manner such as the LAPC method. A three-stage model of crisis intervention was described and applied to a specific type of school crisis, violence in the schools. The elements of a crisis plan were identified and the use of such a plan was described in the context of a particular school crisis, the death of a student.

PORTFOLIO COMPONENTS

1. Develop a counseling plan for a middle school student with the same problems as Tamikka and one for a student in high school. Discuss the differences in objectives and activities based on developmental life stage.
2. Create a sample crisis plan that is flexible enough to be implemented in a school, regardless of the disaster leading to the crisis.
3. Prepare a reflection statement describing how you might feel and respond to a crisis such as the one described in this chapter. How do you view death? How would you address the questions of first graders about death from a culturally sensitive perspective, acknowledging the importance of family beliefs and values?
4. Identify a student concern that would be considered a situational crisis. Develop a list of resources to be used by counselor, student, parent or guardian, and teacher to assist the student in remediating the difficulties associated with the crisis.

Responsive Services: Counselor-Supported Interventions

RESPONDING TO STUDENT NEEDS INDIRECTLY

The TK–12 counselors spent their time during the previous summer planning sessions fully articulating the direct services they needed to implement during the most recent academic term. This summer's planning focuses on the indirect services they implement through the responsive services program component. Mr. Terman proposes that the counselors remain in their same grade-level groups to continue the responsive services planning, and they agree with this strategy. Goals for this academic year are to identify those student concerns for which interventions are needed and that may be effectively delivered by persons other than the school counselor. They have agreed on some specific goals to be achieved before school opens in September.

1. To identify needs and plan for services, use data collected during the previous school year about students' absences, behaviors, achievements, and referrals for evaluation to receive special services.

2. To facilitate appropriate referrals, update the list of community resources available for students and families whose personal problems may interfere with their academic, career, or personal/social development.

3. To be effective consultants and collaborators, conduct a systemwide inventory of materials counselors have successfully used in consultation with teachers and parents and categorize them by highest needs problem areas.

Indirect interventions are those in which the counselor's participation includes planning, preparing, and supporting the helper who will deliver services and evaluating effectiveness of the intervention. The counselor is not involved, however, in directly delivering the services or interventions needed by the student. Indirect interventions are often delivered through responsive services because they are aimed at helping those students who need more assistance than they receive through the curriculum and individual planning activities delivered to all students. Another way of considering these interventions is that they occur at the levels of secondary prevention or tertiary intervention in the three-stage crisis intervention model described in the previous chapter. Some of the most frequently used interventions in this category include consultation with parents or guardians, teachers, other educators, or community agencies to help students and their families (ASCA, 2003c). Peer facilitation programs are often used in schools to mediate conflicts or tutor and mentor students who need responsive services. Peer facilitators are systematically trained and their work is monitored by school counselors. Finally, counselors refer to other mental health professionals students with needs that require tertiary intervention. (Students with suicidal ideation, those who evidence violent tendencies or who have been subjected to violence, and those whose families might benefit from intervention are among the types of issues school counselors are recommended to refer (ASCA, 2003c).)

After reading and discussing this chapter, you should be able to

- Identify the skills necessary to be an effective consultant.
- Describe the process of consultation.
- Describe at least two types of peer programs and the counselor's role in developing, implementing, and evaluating such programs.
- Develop a strategy for referring students to outside agencies.

CONSULTATION

The first question the TK–12 counselors wish to answer is, "Why consult instead of intervene directly through individual or group counseling?" For answers, they turn to Brigman, Mullis, Webb, and White (2005). Among other reasons, these authors suggest that

- Through consultation counselors may reach many more students.
- Consultation opportunities with members of the school community contribute to a positive climate and the development of trusting relationships with the counselor.
- Consultation empowers significant adults to intervene effectively with students by developing effective teaching and parenting strategies.
- Consultation provides an opportunity for counselors to work as student advocates.
- Consultation allows counselors to interact with others in the community who are concerned with the welfare of students.

Mr. Terman and his team of counselors agree that one of the advantages of working in schools is the opportunity to work with other adults who also work with students. School counselors who work as consultants provide a useful service when they help teachers, administrators, parents, and others find ways to solve problems. Consultation typically includes three people: the consultant (school counselor), the consultee (the person with whom they have direct contact), and the recipient (the person who benefits from the indirect assistance). Dougherty (2000) explains that the goal of consultation is to solve problems related to a situation that needs attention. School counselors who share their expertise and skills help both the consultees and the people with whom the consultees interact.

Mr. Terman's team reviewed their many opportunities to work as consultants. They listed some of their previous year's experiences that could be classified as consulting activities. Most often they worked with teachers who wanted counselors to give them ideas for working with students who were having academic difficulties. Teachers also asked for help in understanding children's behaviors and in creating positive classroom environments. The counselors helped teachers develop skills in working with parents and in including materials related to children's personal/social, academic, and career development into their curriculum. Administrators consulted with counselors about students with special needs as well as about relationships with parents and the community. Counselors also consulted with administrators on some schoolwide programs and with other counselors when they needed assistance resolving ethical dilemmas or assistance from a more experienced colleague. Parents requested help in understanding developmental and academic concerns experienced by their children. The counselors conducted one parent education group and wanted to extend this way of consulting with parents. The TK–12 counselors' examples illustrate some of the ways consultation fits into the responsive services component of a school counseling program.

Consultation can be approached in different ways. Kurpius and Fuqua (1993) listed the following four modes of consulting:

1. *Provision.* Within this mode the consultee has a specific need and works with the counselor/consultant who provides services to meet the need. One of the counselors on Mr. Terman's team had worked with a teacher who wanted to integrate some information and skills about emotional intelligence in her class. The counselor helped the teacher find some materials and then co-taught three classes with the teacher.

2. *Prescription.* Consultation in this way involves the counselor/consultant working as an expert who analyzes the situation by collecting information, defining the problem, and giving directions for remedying the difficulty. An example of this occurred last year, after three meetings of a small group for first-year teachers. The counselor who was facilitating the group wondered whether the classroom environments the teachers described could be improved and offered to observe the classes. Based on what she saw, she suggested that the teachers could improve their classrooms by responding to students more consistently. The counselor recommended that these first-year teachers practice this skill and helped them find some resources to show them examples.

3. *Collaboration.* This is a partnership mode of consultation in which the consultee and the counselor/consultant work together in defining, designing, and implementing the solution. A distraught parent had come to the counseling office one day after receiving the news that her partner was terminally ill. She did not know how to prepare her child for what the family was going to be facing. The counselor helped the parent think through the different things that needed to be done such as telling the child, determining how much information is needed, planning for emergencies, and explaining changes that would be happening at home. They then generated a list of possibilities for each of those and the advantages and disadvantages of each alternative. After that process they made a tentative plan with provisions for following up.

4. *Mediation.* This mode of consultation involves the consultant establishing a way for individuals or groups who are disagreeing to listen to each other's viewpoints and helping them come to a mutually agreeable resolution. An example of this type of consulting occurred when three teachers on a team were at odds about some of the arrangements in a classroom they shared. The counselor/consultant brought all three together and moderated their discussion until they reached an acceptable agreement.

Counselors have choices about ways to implement the consulting process. They may use an education/training consultation model to provide information (Gallessich, 1982; Lippitt & Lippitt, 1986). They may use behavioral consultation when the goal is a change in behavior (Lutzker & Martin, 1981). They may implement mental health consultation when the goal is to help solve a current problem as well as similar future problems (Meyers, Brent, Fahery, & Modafferi, 1993; Brown, Pryzwansky, & Schulte, 1998). They may also work as Adlerian consultants to help adults understand a child's behavior and to improve those patterns of behavior (Doughtery, 2000). Finally Kahn (2000) suggests a model of solution-focused consultation. According to Rosenfield and Gravois (1993), the skills necessary when using any of these approaches include

- Understanding and using information about context or culture.
- Using effective interpersonal and communication skills.
- Understanding and implementing effective problem-solving steps.
- Developing and evaluating interventions.
- Applying the skills and relationship factors in practice situations.
- Reflecting on the situation and evaluating one's own skills.
- Understanding the ways ethical codes apply to consultation practice.
- Applying ethical principles appropriately.

Caplan (1970) suggests that consultants consider four areas when determining how to approach consultation. The consultee difficulty may be a result of lack of knowledge. In this case the consultee may not have sufficient understanding of the problem or of some other factor that is relative to the case. The consultant may deal with this by supplying the information. Another problem that consultees may present is a lack of skill. In these situations the consultee understands the relevant factors in the case but does not have the skill to intervene effectively. The consultant works by helping the consultee explore the problem, what has been tried, and what other possibilities exist. They then determine the skills needed to work with the situation and explore ways to develop those skills. The difficulty of lack of confidence presents a third source of difficulty for consultees. These consultees need support and encouragement. The consultant would serve as one source as both worked to identify other support systems available. Lack of professional objectivity occurs when consultees lose professional distance in their work and thereby block the use of their skills with the person or persons with whom they work. The consultant helps consultees identify and lessen the impact of this loss of objectivity.

Systematic Facilitative Approach to Consultation

Myrick (1997) explains a how-to model that gives counselors a framework for practice. The steps of the model are as follows:

1. Identify the problem by listening carefully and helping the consultee explain the situation.

2. Clarify the situation by identifying
   a. The consultee's and the client's feelings.
   b. The specific behaviors of both.
   c. The expectations of the consultee.
   d. What has been done up to this point.
   e. Strengths of the consultee.
3. Determine the goal or outcomes by specifying them as behaviors.
4. Observe and record behaviors (when needed).
5. Develop an action plan that can be done in 2 weeks by the consultee by considering possible interventions, identifying the most appealing, and discussing how the interventions might work and when the plan will begin.
6. Implement the plan.
7. Follow up for evaluating and revision as well as discussion of the next steps.

Consultation with Teachers

Counselors may work with teachers in large groups, small groups, and individually. Possibilities for large-group meetings in which information is presented are topics such as classroom management, standardized tests, conflict-resolution skills, parent conference skills, and strategies for different types of learners. Blum (1998) recommends that successful staff development depends on responding to specific needs, having voluntary attendance, and scheduling the session according to the teachers' preferences. The topic should be relevant and the session short and well planned. Brigman and colleagues (2000) offer the following workshop model for working with teachers in groups:

1. Begin with a warm-up activity through which the personal experiences of the attendees may be linked to the workshop topic.
2. Ask for participants' ideas before telling or lecturing them about the "right" way to approach the students or issues of interest.
3. Use a method of tell (introduce content), show (demonstrate new skills), and do (provide participants an opportunity to practice new skills) to introduce new information and skills.
4. Practice and respond to the new material in small groups so that the experiences of each attendee might be adequately explored.
5. Ask participants to reflect on what they learned, re-learned, and will use with their students.
6. Evaluate to determine if the workshop objectives were met.

School counselors will also be approached by individual teachers who need help to work more effectively with students in their classrooms. Additionally, counselors routinely participate in school-based teams to which students experiencing learning and behavioral difficulties are referred. The counselor serves as an important resource for consultees in both individual and support team consultation. Typical areas of concern for which teachers request assistance are identified in Table 10.1.

Assume that your superintendent has asked you to provide training for new teachers at the end of their first semester on classroom management. Prepare a plan for the consultation activity, including a description of the training event, the goals or objectives of the training, the interventions used to achieve the goals, the resources you would use in the training, and a method of evaluating the event.

TABLE 10.1   Typical Foci of Consultation with Teachers and Administrators

Behavioral Issues	Academic Issues
Attention-seeking behaviors	Developmental delays
Conflicts with others	Health concerns
Failure to stay on task	Inability to concentrate
Failure to complete assigned tasks	Inadequate learning skills
Behavior or emotional disorder	Learning disabilities
Conflicts with authority	School attendance
Responding to peer or community influences	Lack of motivation

Source: Kampwirth, Thomas J.; *Collaborative Consultation in the Schools: Effective Practices for Students with Learning and Behavior Problems.* Copyright © 2006 Merrill/Prentice Hall. Adapted by permission of Pearson Education, Inc., Upper Saddle River, NJ.

Sometimes teachers are clear about the reasons for their call for help, and at other times they simply make an off-hand remark about needing assistance with a particular student or group. In the latter case, the counselor may be the one to actually initiate the formal consultation process. Because the amount of time teachers have free for consultation each day is quite limited, Brown, Pryzwansky, and Schulte (2001) describe an abbreviated, 15-minute model of consultation that might be helpful in some individual cases. Of primary importance in this time-limited approach is the identification and prioritization, from the teacher's perspective, of the problem. In addition, the counselor-consultant seeks to understand the teacher's hypothesis about the problem, elicits information about what interventions have already been attempted, and offers suggestions about some prospective interventions that are based on the teacher's description of and hypothesis about the problem. A brief follow-up session is conducted in person, by phone, or via e-mail to determine the outcome of the intervention. Obviously, there are numerous difficulties about which teachers seek consultation that would not be appropriately addressed through such a formulation. However, as Brown, Pryzwansky, and Schulte point out, recognizing that many teacher-counselor interactions occur in time-limited contexts (e.g., between classes), this model offers counselors a systematic way of responding immediately to requests for assistance.

> The TK–12 counselors indicate that they use this 15-minute model frequently, but have not been very systematic about documenting outcomes. Devise a way for the counselors to document these interactions and to record the outcomes of these brief consultations.

School-Based Teams

Mr. McDougal moves the group to a discussion of management of the internal referral process. Students who experience academic or behavioral difficulties and who are not in special education classes may be referred to the building-based student advisory team (also known as student assistance team, student support team, child study team, intervention assistance program, or multidisciplinary teams). Those groups examine reasons the student is not succeeding in school (Blum, 1998) and recommend interventions that may be implemented by the regular education teachers (Rathvon, 1999). Generally, membership includes a counselor, school psychologist, special education teacher, teachers from each grade level or subject area, and an administrator. Depending on the focus of the referral, outside agency representatives may also be asked to attend the meetings. Additionally, parents of referred students are invited to attend, as well as the referring teacher if he or she is not a permanent member of the team. When appropriate, the student being referred is also invited to participate.

Rathvon (1999) identifies four stages of the student assistance team process: problem definition, problem analysis, plan implementation, and plan evaluation. In stage one, the teacher's request for assistance is reviewed to ensure that all pertinent information is provided, student and parents are consulted, the problem is clarified, and baseline data is obtained. In stage two, factors contributing to the maintenance of the problem are identified, intervention strategies are evaluated and selected, and implementation procedures are planned. The intervention is implemented and progress monitored during the third stage. Finally, the effectiveness of the intervention is reviewed by comparing postintervention data with the baseline data. If the intervention is not successful, further intervention is planned and implemented. If committee members agree that efforts have been exhausted and change is unlikely, a request may be made to assess the student's eligibility for special education services. The information gathered by the team is included in the special education referral. Permission from parents is necessary to proceed with such a referral.

Two of the more positive outcomes associated with school-based teams are decreased numbers of referrals to special education and improved teacher attitudes toward diverse learners (Rathvon, 1999). However, Mr. McDougal states, "Many teachers are frustrated by the lack of innovative intervention strategies suggested by the team." This is consistent with research reported by Rathvon (1999) that teachers perceive the interventions offered them by teams as low in quality and lacking in variety. One reason for this is that many educators do not receive training in prereferral intervention strategies as part of their education, nor do team members typically receive training in effective school interventions. The TK–12 counselors discuss the nature of interventions proposed during their team meetings. Their most effective interventions are proactive, can be used with an entire class to enhance the learning of all students as well as the targeted student, are easily taught, can be implemented with regular classroom resources, and can be easily evaluated (Rathvon, 1999).

> Based on what you have learned so far, generate a list of possible interventions that would meet Rathvon's criteria. Discuss your list with your classmates.

The counselors are generally pleased with the interventions proposed in team meetings; however, they express a desire to share responsibility among team members for management of referral, review, and follow-up of all cases. They currently manage all cases and preoccupation with these activities limits the amount of time they spend in collaborative consultation with the team members. One of the counselors is familiar with the work of Shepard-Tew and Creamer (1998) who describe a case management process for the school-based, multidisciplinary team to follow. A referral is received and before a problem has been identified, a team member is randomly assigned as the case manager. A variety of forms are used to record any assessment, interventions, progress, and termination or referral status. The forms are designed to provide quick and accurate recording methods for accountability. The case manager begins an assessment by gathering information that may include discussions with teachers, parents, and significant others; a review of the school records and disciplinary records; an interview with the child; and formal testing. The case manager organizes the collected data using the prepared forms and then presents the case to the team. The team collaboratively develops an intervention plan for the child with the goal of diminishing the behaviors that were causing academic failure. The team works with home and school by initiating a plan for change in the behavior in both settings. The case manager coordinates and refers appropriate interventions to each team member for implementation. Each time the case is reviewed, a termination/referral summary form documents the interventions completed, the student's progress, and the recommendations for follow-up. The authors documented their successes in implementing this approach to integrated services to students by reporting that more than 70% of the parents, teachers, and children involved saw some improvement in behavior and academic success. The procedures are appropriate for all grade levels.

> Create a checklist that could be used to monitor the progress of the procedures discussed in this paragraph.

Mr. McDougal and the counselors agree that the format described by Shepard-Tew and Creamer (1998) would provide more structured and perhaps more productive meetings than they have led in the past. The assigning of a manager from the team membership on a rotating base for each student case results in greater sharing of responsibility for the administrative tasks of the committee or team. Mr. McDougal agrees to present their ideas to the system-level student assistance teams' coordinator. If she agrees, the counselors in each school will describe the approach during the first team meeting of the year for consideration by the other team members. Included in the proposed change will be a systematic method of collecting follow-up information about the students served by these teams, including those who are referred to outside agencies. In this instance, the counselors serve as consultant/collaborators in the team's development of interventions and as consultants to the team regarding ways to increase efficiency and productivity.

> Develop a list of the three or four problems for which you believe students will be referred to school-based student assistance teams. As a class, reach consensus on the top three. Divide into three teams and provide training for each other in intervention strategies that have empirical support for each of the three problems identified. Be sure that your interventions meet these criteria: are proactive, can be used with an entire class to enhance the learning of all students as well as the targeted child, are easily taught, can be implemented with regular classroom resources, and can be easily evaluated.

Consulting with Parents and Guardians

School counselors also need strategies for consulting with parents (Conroy & Meyer, 1994; Norwood & Atkinson, 1997). Counselors may work with parents in large groups to provide information about subjects such as transitions, orientation, college, financial aid, and the counseling program. Concerns about child rearing, developmental transitions, and school expectations may also be addressed. In a review of outcome research related to consultation, Sheridan and Welch (1996) found evidence to support this as an effective approach in schools. Parents may seek consultation in solving problems related to learning difficulties, undesirable behavior, relationships, peers, anxiety, depression, grief, family issues such as divorce or separation, illness of student or family member, career preparation, college selection, sexual responsibility, and school adjustment. The goal for the student is improved educational or psychological functioning (Brown, Pryzwansky, & Schulte, 2001). Brown and colleagues identify the goal for the parent as ". . . increased ability to facilitate the development of their children" (p. 235).

The methods and models already described in this chapter apply to parent consultation. In addition, Davis (2005) identifies four ways to be effective in consultation with parents. First, she encourages counselors to be available and accessible. Checking voice mail, e-mail, and messages taken by others daily is expected. Taking the time necessary to get a full understanding of the parent or guardian's concern is essential regardless of the method of interaction (live or electronic). Davis cautions counselors to be ethically responsible regarding the maintenance of consultee confidentiality, especially when leaving a phone message or responding to e-mail. Second, counselors should respond to inquiries as quickly as possible. Although it may be several days before a face-to-face meeting might be arranged, the counselor should acknowledge parents' requests immediately. Third, counselors are cautioned to avoid becoming overly involved in family conflicts or systems and to keep the focus on the student. Finally, counselors should follow up with parents once a plan has been established. Without additional contacts, counselors will not know the outcome of their consultation efforts, nor will the parents or guardians know whether the interventions they implement at home are having any effect on school behaviors. The follow-up provides an opportunity for the counselor to report the outcomes observed in school. For example, assume a consultation has taken place for parents who are separating and want to minimize negative effects on their child. Prior to the consultation, the student in question appeared depressed, distracted, and unable to concentrate on learning. The parents implemented the recommended interventions to reassure the child and to invite the child to express his or her concerns and emotions about the separation. Additionally, the school counselor invited the child to participate in a group with other children whose parents were in various stages of separation or divorce. The counselor maintained a check with the teachers of the child and was able to report to the parent in a follow-up phone call that classroom performance had returned to pre-separation levels. All consultation efforts need to be documented, the goals identified, and the outcomes reported.

REFERRALS

In the previous chapter, you read about the ways that school counselors may determine whether to enter into a counseling relationship with a student or students. In some instances, it is neither feasible nor advisable for a school counselor to provide counseling services. Such decisions are informed by the counselor's competence, the client's welfare, the nature of the client's complaint, and the receptivity of parents, guardians, and the students themselves to outside assistance. Recall the format for decision making previously described by Baker and Gerler (2004). Counselors first help to identify and clarify the problem, then set goals based on their understanding of the problem. Based on the nature of the goals, counselors determine how the goals might best be met. If the counselor's resources are insufficient or unlikely to achieve goal attainment, a referral is in order. Once the decision to refer has been made, the question of where to refer must be addressed.

According to Lockhart and Keys (1998), counselors need skills and knowledge about diagnostic criteria, managed care, child and family welfare systems, court system and juvenile services, residential programs, and the changing structure of accessing services. School counselors need to be familiar with these and other resources in their communities and make referrals based on the competence of the service providers (Remley & Herlihy, 2001). Competence of service providers in the community may be established through interactions with satisfied students and parents, contacts established through professional associations and conference attendance, collection of the disclosure statements of potential referral sources, and review of advertisements and Web sites. Counselors should compile a list of referral sources to provide students and parents with a range of payment schedules and attention to diversity of service providers. Baker and Gerler (2004) suggest routinely asking students and parents for an evaluation of the referral to ascertain the effectiveness and their satisfaction with their services. Most school systems have policy statements about how referrals are made and who coordinates or makes referrals in a given school. With few exceptions, referrals for counseling services are made with the understanding that any expense involved is the responsibility of the parents (Gysbers & Henderson, 2000).

Following the decision to refer and the selection of appropriate referral sources for the student, the counselor must decide how the referral will be made. Baker and Gerler (2004) identify two challenges associated with making referrals. First, the student may feel abandoned or rejected by the counselor with whom he or she has an existing relationship and in whom the student has confided. Second, the student may reject the suggestion. Successful referrals are more likely if the following conditions are met (Baker & Gerler, 2004).

> Assume you have been seeing an adolescent who you suspect has an eating disorder. Develop a list of referral sources in your community to provide to this student's parents.

- The student is ready for the referral.
- The student is treated as the counselor would like to be treated if in the same situation.
- The counselor has discussed the potential referral with the student prior to making the referral.
- The counselor explains why the referral is necessary in order to attain client's goals.
- The counselor obtains permission from the student and parent to provide helpful, timely information to the referee.
- Parents who may be resistant are persuaded of the necessity for the referral.
- The counselor carefully considers the likely support needed by each student referred regarding arranging the first meeting with the referee.
- The counselor considers cultural contexts when deciding on the referee for each student.
- Counselors continue to work as needed with the referred student in the context of what is helpful and also appropriate.

School counselors may coordinate many referrals during a given school year. In addition to assessing student and parent/guardian satisfaction with services and outcomes, counselors need to keep track of whether the student accessed the services of the referee, provide all materials and information requested by the referee, support the work of the student and referee if possible, consult with the referee if needed, and evaluate the outcomes of the service (Baker & Gerler, 2004).

As we described in Chapter 9, counselors are also the recipients of referrals. Teachers, parents, administrators, and at times community agency representatives may refer a student for counseling. School counselors are reminded to take care to protect the confidentiality of the student who has been referred. Most would agree that referrals to the school counselor are made out of concern for the student being referred. Just as you wish to assist in appropriate ways those students for whom you facilitate a referral, the person who refers students to you will want to provide ongoing assistance. School counselors need to be clear about the procedures for referring students and those for providing feedback to the referral agents.

> Review section C2 of the ethical standards located in Appendix C. Consider this information along with other relevant sections of the code and develop a procedure for receiving referrals from other adults and describe how you might follow up with their referral agents.

PEER FACILITATION

Peer helping programs are prevention programs that involve young people helping other young people with their problems or concerns (Varenhorst, 2003). The peer facilitation program options are varied; may be implemented in same- or cross-aged dyads and groups with diverse populations; and may be applied to tutoring, mediation, orientation to a new school, and peer facilitation of groups (Dollarhide & Saginak, 2003). Myrick (1997) describes four helping roles that may be useful for framing peer interventions. First, through the role of special assistant, peer facilitators provide indirect assistance to students by helping to support the work of the counselors, teachers, administrators, and other school personnel. Special assistants might develop and construct bulletin boards, monitor projects, and participate in planning educational programs and activities. Second, the peers may serve as tutors in any subject area. Advanced understanding of a subject area combined with effective helping skills increases the effectiveness of tutoring programs. Third, the special friend role involves facilitators developing relationships with peers, offering encouragement and support, reducing the effects of isolation, and conveying a sense of caring and concern. Fourth, the role of small-group leader is one in which facilitators may be trained to work with small groups of learners in the classroom to enhance academic and other types of learning opportunities. Facilitators may also lead small-group discussions for students who share a concern or circumstance, such as those new to a school.

Peer facilitation programs extend the responsive services offered through the school counseling programs in ways that benefit both the recipients and providers of the service. The recipients develop new skills, strategies, and knowledge that enhance academic, career, and personal/social development. The facilitators have an opportunity to develop skills of leadership and helping, and experience the values associated with helping others (Varenhorst, 2003). Research also shows improvements for both providers and recipients of peer facilitation services in attitude, productive behavior, self-esteem, and grades (Campbell, 2000). Program expansion also benefits the school counselor and the counseling program. Campbell reports that the self-referrals for counseling often increase in schools with active peer facilitation programs. This may be especially true for students who, without the encouragement of a peer, would not have sought out such services on their own.

The TK–12 counselors would like to implement a peer facilitation program in middle and high schools. Their goals, derived from a review of local data and developed with input from the leadership team, are to increase academic performance at the middle school and reduce conflict-related suspension of students at the high school. Consequently, they will start with two program initiatives: same and cross grade tutoring of middle school students and conflict mediation for the high school students. The tutoring program will be directed toward those middle school students who have persistent academic problems. A peer mediation program will target high school students who lack the skills to resolve conflicts and disputes (Whiston & Bouwkamp, 2005). Students will learn to identify conflicts early and to achieve resolution before the conflicts escalate into violence.

Mr. Terman asks, "What do we need to do to get these programs established?" Campbell (2000) suggests that there are four issues to consider when beginning a peer facilitators program:

Build support. The TK–12 counselors have already begun to build support by identifying specific needs of the school and the counseling program that might be addressed through peer facilitation. They are going to start small with two specific goals in mind, and they intend to implement highly structured tutoring and mediation programs with one grade level in each school. Peer facilitation programs do extend the services of the school counseling program, but the peers are not counselors. Counseling is a service provided by a specially prepared, credentialed professional (Myrick, 1997). There will be less resistance by teachers and parents to the peer programs if they understand that peer helpers are not counselors and do not serve as counselor substitutes. Myrick points out that when students are asked to do too much or to provide services (e.g., counseling) for which they are not prepared or qualified the programs are less likely to be successful.

Select facilitators. Campbell (2000) offers some guidance for selection of the types of students who make effective facilitators: those who have good study habits and whose grades will not suffer if the time they generally spend on academic activities is reduced; those who will take responsibility for making up any assignments they might miss as a result of their roles as peer facilitators; students who are consistent, trustworthy, and dependable; students who would naturally be sought out by their peers to listen to problems or concerns; and, students who are committed to the program. An application process that includes potential facilitators' reasons for wanting to participate, their perceptions about the problems most kids their age face, and a description of what uniquely qualifies them to serve as facilitators is a helpful starting point. Campbell also provides a checklist that might be used by teachers and others to recommend facilitators (see Figure 10.1).

Divide into three groups to develop an application form for fourth, and fifth-grade elementary peer facilitators, middle school facilitators, and high school facilitators.

FIGURE 10.1   Peer Facilitator Recommendation Form

Dear _____ :

_____ has expressed an interest in becoming a peer facilitator this year. Please help me evaluate his/her qualifications for this position by completing the checklist that follows. Thank you for helping to identify students qualified to help their peers through tutoring and conflict mediation.

Qualifications	Poor	Fair	Good	Excellent	Unknown
Respectful					
Friendly					
Responsible					
Grades					
Study habits					
Dependable					
Confident					
Stable					
Consistent					
Receptive to feedback					
Good judgment					
Cares about others					
Leadership potential					
Trustworthy					
Sensitive					
Polite					
Flexible					
Sense of humor					
Energy level					

Source: Adapted from K-12 Pear Helper Programs, by C. Campbell, 2000, in *Managing Your School Counseling Program: K-12 Developmental Strategies,* by J. Wittmer, Minneapolis, MN: Educational Media. Reprinted by permission.

Train facilitators. Special training in listening, helping and facilitation processes, confidentiality, and limits of competence are essential to peer training programs (Dollarhide & Saginak, 2003). There are numerous examples of training models in the literature. Varenhorst (2003) has developed a 15-session asset-building model featuring communication, assertiveness, and decision-making skills. This instructional model focuses on helping facilitators to learn the skills necessary to build helping relationships. The model uses a group discussion format as opposed to more traditional teaching models such as lecturing. Consequently, the adult trainer needs to be a skilled group facilitator; fortunately, these skills are emphasized in school counselor preparation programs. Each lesson plan involves developing a new skill that builds on those emphasized in previous lessons. The training begins with communication skills for starting conversations with people one does not know. The design of the training model and the format in which the lessons are delivered also promote the development of trust and cohesion among group members. Session format generally includes a review of homework from the previous session, summary of the last session and introduction to the current topics, one or more learning activities, a new homework assignment, the use of thought cards to guide deeper, individual reflections, and reflections on assets. Varenhorst's (2003) program is based on the developmental assets framework proposed by the Search Institute. Consequently, lessons are designed to help facilitators develop skills that build assets, reflect on the meaning of the assets in their own lives, and learn how they can help others develop assets. The assets include support, empowerment, boundaries and expectations, constructive use of time, commitment to learning, positive values, social competencies, and positive identity.

School counselors' personal and theoretical leanings are generally determinants of the model selected (Campbell, 2000). Additional considerations include the specific types of roles peers are being prepared to assume, the length of time available for training, and who will provide the training.

Identify projects. Projects should be identified that further the goals of the school counseling program. Peer helping projects should be limited to those activities for which facilitators are well-prepared. Myrick (1997) suggests starting small with projects likely to be successful. For special programs, additional specialized training may be necessary. As is the case with all programs associated with school counseling, there should be clear, well-articulated links to learning. Projects and activities require extensive monitoring and ongoing supervision from the counselor (Campbell, 2000). As well, the programs need to be evaluated in the same way that other interventions in this text are evaluated.

The National Association of Peer Programs (NAPP), formerly the National Association of Peer Helpers, is a professional association that offers support and information for those professionals interested in establishing peer programs. The association has developed training standards and a code of ethics to guide peer program leaders. The program standards outline the procedures for

---

Conduct some independent research to discover what special training the facilitators in Washington County High School's new peer mediation programs need.

Review the position statement developed by ASCA (2002b) regarding peer helping programs. Along with your peers, identify as many of the types of student issues requiring remediation that you think might be addressed through such programs. Group the issues according to the six types of peer helper services identified by ASCA.

Position Statement: Peer Helping

The Professional School Counselor And Peer Helping (Adopted 1978; Revised 1984, revised 1993, 1999, 2002)

American School Counselor Association (ASCA) Position

Peer helping programs enhance the effectiveness of school counseling programs by increasing outreach and the expansion of available services.

The Rationale

Peer Helping: A variety of interpersonal helping behaviors assumed by non-professionals who undertake a helping role with others, including one-to-one helping relationships, group leadership, discussion leadership, tutoring and all activities of an interpersonal helping or assisting nature.

Peer Helper: A person who assumes the role of a helping person with persons of approximately the same age who share related values, experiences and lifestyles.

Students often communicate their problems to their peers rather than to parents, administrators or counselors. In our society, peer influence may be the strongest single motivational force in a student's life. Peers can be selected and trained by professional counselors in communication and helping skills through a carefully planned peer helping program. It is ASCA's position that peer helping programs enhance the effectiveness of the school counseling program by increasing the outreach of the school counseling programs and raising student awareness of services. Through proper selection, training and supervision, peer helping can be a positive force within the school and community.

The Peer Helper's Role

Peer helpers provide a variety of useful and helpful services for schools:

1. One-to-one assistance: Talking with students about personal or school problems, referring to community resources or providing information about the school's counseling program.
2. Group settings: Serving as group leaders, counseling group assistants, teachers of helping skills to other students, communication skills trainers, peer helper trainers.
3. Educational functions: Tutoring in academic areas, serving as readers for nonreaders, assisting special education consultants in working with learning and behaviorally disabled students.
4. Hospitality: Welcoming and guiding new students and their parents around the school.
5. Outreach: Helping increase the services of the school counseling programs, serving as listeners or as a resource for populations that may feel uncomfortable talking with the professional school counselor, reducing crisis situations by alerting professional school counselors to problems of a serious nature.

6. Growth: Increasing their own personal growth and becoming more functional at higher levels, training to become more effective adults and possible future occupations in the helping professions.

The Professional School Counselor's Role

The professional counselor accepts responsibility for determining the needs of the school population and for implementing a peer helping program designed to meet those needs. Professional school counselors devise a selection plan for peer helpers compatible with the population to be served; coordinate an appropriate training program; schedule adequate time to work with peer helpers on a weekly basis for continued training, supervision, sharing and personal growth; construct a support system through positive, honest public relations; and continually monitor, evaluate and adjust the program and training to meet the assessed needs of the population it serves. The professional school counselor accepts responsibility for the design, completion and evaluation of the peer helping program. Results should be reported to the population served and other interested persons (i.e., school boards, etc.), including counselors.

Summary

Well-trained peer helpers can have a positive, supportive effect upon students that no one else can provide. Students can relate to and accept alternative patterns of behavior from peers who are struggling with similar feelings and problems. Peer helpers increase the services of the school counseling program in an outreach function and are an invaluable part of a comprehensive school counseling program.

Source: Reprinted by permission of the American School Counselor Association.

establishing peer programs, implementing programs, and maintaining programs. The standards are located on the NAPP Web site (http://www.peerprograms.org/publications/publications/standards/). NAPP also oversees certification for peer programs, professionals in peer programs, curriculum, and trainers. The association also publishes a quarterly publication.

SUMMARY

In this chapter you have read about interventions common to the school counseling program labeled "indirect" because although the school counselor is an active participant he/she does not deliver services directly to the person designated as the helpee. Consultation is an indirect intervention that involves at least three parties: the consultant, the consultee who will deliver the intervention, and the student to whom the intervention is directed. Consultation may occur with anyone who works directly with and has an interest in helping the designated student. However, school counselors spend much of their consultation time helping teachers and parents intervene with students. Referrals are made by the school counselor to other service providers when the remedial issue with which the student presents is not amenable to change within a brief, time-limited context or is outside the area of competence of the school counselor. School counselors should maintain referral lists appropriate for a culturally and socioeconomically diverse school population. School counselors conduct evaluation activities for both consultation and referrals in which they participate. Finally, peer facilitation programs were introduced as a means for students helping students. Such programs extend the services of the school counseling office to those who may not otherwise avail themselves of services. Research shows that both the providers and recipients of peer facilitation services benefit from participation.

PORTFOLIO COMPONENTS

1. Identify a problem or concern you have been told about by a friend or family member. Assume you had a client who expressed the same concern and you wanted to seek consultation to identify ways that you might be most helpful to this client. Describe the "ideal" consultant. What credentials, knowledge, and special skills are required to provide consultation for this concern? How would you identify and locate a person with these unique qualifications? What expectations might you have regarding the behavior of your consultant? What outcomes might you expect?
2. Continue to imagine yourself as the consultee in the scenario described above. How would you prepare yourself for the initial consultation? How would you present your questions and concerns? What information would you take with you? What would you want the consultant to know about you and your inclinations, personality, background, cultural contexts, special skills, and/or perceived weaknesses?
3. Review the literature to discover the disorders most frequently displayed during childhood and adolescence. Prepare a list of those you, in your future role as school counselor, believe you would refer to a professional outside the school. How might you continue to provide partial services to students diagnosed with one or more of the diagnoses you identified?

C H A P T E R   1 1

System Support

SYSTEM SUPPORT: THE FRAMEWORK

Mr. Terman and the TK–12 team are once again meeting to have their year-end review and planning session. They report surprising findings with regard to responsive services. Because they more fully implemented the program elements of individual planning and the guidance curriculum, the counselors across grade levels report having more time to provide responsive services than in previous years. Mr. Terman reports that he observed counselors spending more time providing individual and group counseling to students with remedial needs, as well as serving as a consultant to teachers and parents. All counselors report similar experiences, and Ms. Lerner observes that she spent less of her responsive services time slots each week in crisis counseling than she had in the past as well. They are eager to pursue planning and implementation activities related to the fourth program element, system support.

The counselors know that to continue to increase their efficiency and productivity, they must have a strong support system for their program. Their goals for the coming year are

1. To set specific goals for the management of their programs.
2. To collaborate with each other and distribute the effort for the program element so that all counselors are providing some aspect of the support, but no one is responsible for all of the support.
3. To be deliberate in the collection, analysis, and distribution of research and information that supports the comprehensive program.
4. To identify areas where their skills need to be updated and pursue professional development opportunities as needed.

To accomplish these goals, the counselors decide to meet several times during the summer in grade-level teams to complete assessment and prioritizing activities for this program component. They plan to develop an action plan with specific goals and a plan for implementation and evaluation.

System support is comprised of three types of activity: counselors' professional development; consultation, collaboration, and teaming; and management of the school counseling program (ASCA, 2003a). System support activities are those through which school counselors sustain their programs as well as enlist support from others for the school counseling program.

After reading and discussing this chapter, you should be able to explain the importance of and develop an action plan for:

- Professional development
- Consultation, collaboration, and teaming
- Program management

The counselors decided to meet in grade-level teams (K–5, 6–8, and 9–12) to create a list of the work activities currently performed by counselors that might be classified as system support. Once their inventory is complete, they will rank each of the items in order of importance and congruence with the overall goals of the school counseling program. Then, they will discuss ways that the tasks

Planning Inventory of System Support Tasks by Grade Level

Elementary	Middle	High
New student registration	Preregistration advisement	Preregistration advisement
Test coordination	Test coordination	Schedule adjustments
Test interpretation (teachers/parents)	Test interpretation (teachers/parents)	Graduations checks
Student assistance team	Student assistance team	Reference letters
Student referrals	Student referrals	Test coordination
Grade-level team	Grade-level team	Test interpretation
Liaison with outside agencies	Schedule parent	Student assistance team
Special testing arrangements	Follow up with absentees	Student referrals
Monitor progress reports	Liaison with outside agencies	Grade-level team
Record keeping	Supervise employees	Liaison with outside agencies
Disciplinary hearings	Monitor progress reports	Supervise employees
Coordinate program	Record keeping	Joint enrollment programs
Gifted education	Disciplinary hearings	Advanced diploma options
Attend state counseling conference	Attend state counseling conference	Business-Industry-Education Committee
Visit community counseling agencies	Provide in-service training	Monitor progress reports
Provide in-service training	Meet with juvenile offender program leaders	Attend state counseling conference
Program management	Program management	Provide in-service training
• Assess needs	• Assess needs	Record keeping
• Planning	• Planning	Disciplinary hearings
• Scheduling	• Scheduling	Program management
• Evaluating	• Evaluating	• Assess needs
		• Planning
		• Scheduling
		• Evaluating

might be accomplished more efficiently. The overall goal of this first phase of planning is to reduce the time each counselor spends in system support activities to no more than 15% of total time (6 hours/week) in elementary and middle schools and 20% (8 hours/week) in high schools.

In small groups, discuss these tasks and group them into the three system support categories identified by ASCA (2003a). Which categories seem to be overloaded and which seem to be underdeveloped? How might some of the tasks in the overloaded categories be accomplished through differential staffing or assignment to other professionals, paraprofessionals, or volunteers? What activities would you add at each of the grade levels? Remember, the activities retained by the counselors should account for approximately 15% of their time and be of the highest priority.

Identifying the various system support activities is, believe it or not, the easy part! Many factors will influence the decisions of the TK–12 counselors as they decide how to share their work responsibilities. Work preferences, interest, skills and abilities, personality, special knowledge, past experience, and managerial style are some of the considerations. In addition to their personal skills and traits, a discussion of some of the essential skills for effective program management may be helpful to the counselors as they attempt to divide their coordinating responsibilities in an equitable manner. They decide to take each of the three major categories included in system support and actively plan for improvement. Consistent with their experiences planning other delivery system activities, the counselors know to begin system support planning efforts with statements of desired outcomes.

PROFESSIONAL DEVELOPMENT

Professional development is defined as those activities through which school counselors update and share their knowledge (ASCA, 2003a). Specifically, school counselors attend in-service training to stay current regarding trends in education and student achievement, ensure that their knowledge and skills are sufficient to meet program goals, and renew their energies (Shelton & James, 2005). Another way school counselors stay current about developments in the profession is by belonging to professional associations. Professional associations that support the work of school counselors hold annual meetings and conferences, sponsor special interest continuing education workshops and seminars, and host Web-based independent study units. Most also publish professional journals that contain research reports and ideas for best practices in school counseling. The resources made available to members of organizations such as ASCA and ACA are of high quality and easy to access. Finally, counselors may complete graduate-level courses to enhance their knowledge and skills in important areas.

To be successful, school counselors, employees, and volunteers must know what they are expected to do and have the skills and knowledge to carry out their assigned tasks. The importance of continuous training and staff development cannot be overemphasized. Friend and Cook (2000) state that the many strategies considered essential for 21st-century schools cannot be implemented without staff development and support. Training is linked to program goals and is intended to increase job performance through skill enhancement. What skills and knowledge do professional, administrative, and volunteer staffs need to meet the established program goals? Some training may be group oriented, such as that provided to teachers in preparation for their role as advisor or to peer facilitators who will serve as tutors or mediators. Other training needs may be individually oriented such as a course in computer-based presentations for counselors to deliver the guidance curriculum or make presentations to community groups. The secretary may need a course in using data management software in order to secure information about student achievement and scheduling that counselors need for more effective educational planning. Cross training (Silver, 1995) may be provided by persons in the school system who work in other departments. Experts outside the system may also be used to provide specialized training (Friend & Cook, 2000). School counselors may provide training on issues of concern to others in their school community.

The developmental needs of children and adolescents are an integral part of school counselor preparation programs. However, for counselors who are leading or planning training activities for staff, developmental characteristics of adult learners must be considered. Friend and Cook (2000) identify the following characteristics of adult learners:

- They learn better when their knowledge and experience is validated.
- They learn better when they are involved in their learning activities.
- They learn better when they perceive that what they are going to learn will meet their objectives.

Annual personnel evaluations may require the submission of counselor-developed plans for growth or improvement. In the absence of such a requirement, counselors are encouraged to develop and maintain plans for professional improvement as part of their professional responsibility and commitment to those they serve. Shelton and James (2005) recommend that counselors develop a plan for professional improvement prior to the beginning of each school year. Similar to the counseling plans developed by counselors for their clients and consultees, these plans include long-term goals, short-term objectives, and the professional development activities in which counselors engage to achieve the goals.

The TK–12 counselors have attended several in-service sessions arranged for them by school system administrators over the past 4 years as they have systematically reviewed and revised their school counseling program. They have had training in using the countywide data management system to record, maintain, and publish process data to help them account for the ways they spend their time. They have also had a consultation with a professor from their local university to help them learn more about collecting and analyzing perception data and producing results reports. They all attended a grief and loss training with their local hospice. Based on this training, they developed materials and provided an in-service for teachers at each school to help them respond more effectively to students who have experienced a loss. They also revised the group plans previously used for the loss groups being conducted in each of the schools. As they discuss their goals for the coming year, the counselors identify two areas of need. First, they each have one or more types of student clients that might be helped through school-based individual or small-group counseling if the counselors knew more about the effective practices for such students. The elementary school counselors wish to learn more about effective strategies for children experiencing parental separation or divorce; middle school counselors wish to learn about using solution-focused methods with aggressive students; and high school counselors wish to learn more about academic motivation. Second, they want to update their knowledge and skills for responding to large-scale crises at school (see Figure 11.1 to review the goals the TK–12 team developed in this area).

FIGURE 11.1 Action Plan for System Support

TK–12 Counselors Professional Development Plan 2006–2007

Category/Expected Outcomes	Program Activities	Participants	Resources Needed	Evaluation Method	Dates
Professional Development					
Goal 1: To increase knowledge and skill in areas identified for improvement during annual performance appraisal.	Counselors will attend a minimum of one school counseling conference annually to address those individual professional development needs identified in the annual performance appraisal.	All school counselors.	Professional improvement leave approval and funding for conference, travel, accommodations, and meals.	Satisfactory evaluation in the designated area at the time of the next annual review will be the criterion for determining success.	August 2006–April 2007
Goal 2: Counselors will participate in systemwide professional development activities to meet common goals.	Counselors will participate in four crisis response training sessions.	All school counselors.		Counselors will score 90% or higher on a posttest designed to assess their understanding of the content of the training sessions and will receive satisfactory ratings on the crisis management section of the responsive services program component annual evaluation.	August 2006; January 2007; March 2007; June 2007

223

CONSULTATION AND COLLABORATION

Consultation and collaboration with professionals inside and outside of schools provide counselors additional resources for their students and ways to establish support in the community and school for programs. Counselors consult with teachers, staff, parents, and guardians to gather and receive information they need to assist students and families (ASCA, 2003a). They develop partnerships with staff, parents or guardians, and community leaders in order to promote the involvement of these key constituents in the school counseling program. Counselors work with their colleagues in the community to stay informed about the resources available to students and families outside of the school. And counselors serve on committees, boards, and advisory councils both inside and outside of the school to provide support to other programs and to generate support for the school counseling programs. The TK–12 counselors discuss some of the activities in which they are routinely engaged and identify areas for improvement.

Teaming

McFarland, Senn, and Childress (1995) state that leaders in the 21st century recognize the importance of bringing out excellence in others and being interpersonally sensitive. Leaders adopt a holistic approach and use a variety of qualities, skills, and capabilities in achieving their goals. Finally leaders master change rather than merely react to it. Counselors will recognize these attributes as dimensions of their everyday practice. Clark and Stone (2000) discuss opportunities for school counselors to exhibit advocacy and leadership in staff development, school reform, multicultural awareness, mentoring programs, and political involvement. They describe this shift as a natural alignment for counselors who have special leadership skills and opportunities. We concur and encourage school counselors to focus on identifying their unique leadership abilities when building or participating on teams.

Johnson and Johnson (1997) describe a team as a group whose interpersonal interactions are structured to accomplish established goals. Team members develop cooperative working relationships to achieve a shared objective to which they are committed. Effective teams have healthy, constructive relationships; established goals, procedures, and methods; and a focus on improvement in their relationships and in their task (Basham, Appleton, & Dykeman, 2000). Professional school counselors build teams by helping the group gain a common understanding of team effectiveness. They present the mission of the team to build commitment to the team's activities. They help create high levels of expectation for quality and personal commitment to the team process, and they make team meetings safe and enjoyable. They also match their leadership style and intervention strategies to developmental stages of the team process (Kormanski, 1999).

The TK–12 counselors want to improve community relations by including colleagues who work in outside agencies that provide counseling services for students and their families on their various teams. They begin by identifying key people at each outside agency with which they have routine contact regarding services for school-aged youth: law enforcement officials, juvenile and family courts, child protective services, mental health services, hospice, physicians, hospitals, health department, and in-patient psychiatric and drug and alcohol rehabilitation facilities for children and adolescents. Ho (2001) reports that federal agencies that document existing services to children tend to segment children and families into rigid categories, are crisis oriented, are unable to develop comprehensive solutions, focus on weaknesses and problems, and lack systems for functional communication among agencies. She suggests that many professionals in the education, health, mental health, and social services fields recognize that current social problems need to be addressed with an integration of services that connect the school, family, and community. In other words, teaming and collaboration need to occur in order to provide better services.

Community Outreach

Counselors also wish to establish more effective, efficient ways of helping students access resources from organizations that do not provide counseling services but do offer other forms of support to families such as local churches, food and clothing banks, recreational programs, and civic organizations. Additionally, community sources that provide academic support for students (e.g., volunteer tutors, learning centers, programs available through local colleges and universities) and those that provide challenging programs for advanced students will be identified. A Community Resource Directory with the contact information and the services and resources provided by each outside agency, as well as a description of their procedures and requirements for referrals, will be disseminated to all of the school counselors in the system prior to the beginning of the school year. The resource directory will be updated in May of each year by mailing each directory entry a copy of their current information and requesting that corrections be made and returned no later than June 15 of each year.

Collaboration

The counselors in the Washington County system wish to increase their contact with the persons in associated agencies beyond the development of a comprehensive referral resource directory. They believe that students are best served if the various entities involved in promoting the development of youth collaborate, share information, and develop an intervention plan that is comprehensive but does not include overlapping or redundant services. They will begin by honing their collaboration skills.

Collaboration provides a way that the school counselors and others in the community can fully access the resources of schools, communities, and homes. Taylor and Adelman (2000) explain that a group designed to link school, the families of its students, and other entities of the community may be called a collaborative. Collaborative members may share facilities such as schools, parks, and libraries. One example of such valuable partnerships teams child welfare services, juvenile justice systems, and behavioral health care with schools (see also Bemak, 2000). Luongo (2000) explains how such a partnership adds value to the educational enterprise. He notes that achieving the integration requires reorienting policy, practice, and activities to outcomes and explains evidence such as the following to indicate the reorientation:

- Shared decision making
- Budgeting and priority setting that acknowledges the shared responsibilities
- Transdisciplinary teams composed of members from all institutions
- Focus on the child and family
- Mechanisms for cross-training
- Shared goals

School counselors begin by becoming familiar with the ways these institutions work and by helping the personnel in those agencies learn about schools. Visits to the sites and participation in combined professional development provide other methods for school counselors to advance these collaborative efforts. To further facilitate the development of important partnerships, the TK–12 counselors wish to pursue staff development training in electronic collaboration methods, such as synchronous voice conferencing. Using this medium, persons would be able to meet from a location of their choosing, in real time, share documents and ideas, and move forward with plans when face-to-face meetings are not possible (Sabella, 2000).

The counselors develop goals to help them establish more connections with community agencies and business.

Goal 1: Agencies that offer supportive services for students and families will be identified, and one counselor at each grade level will be designated to develop a list of contacts and procedures for referral for each.

Goal 2: Employers in the community will be identified, and one counselor at each grade level will be designated to develop a list of contacts at each to identify possible areas of collaboration to improve supportive services provided students and families.

> In a small group, identify the sources you might use to identify the resources available in your community. What types of resources might be needed for elementary, middle, and high school levels? Develop a "script" that could be used for an initial contact with each individual or agency to introduce yourself, explain the reason for your call, and elicit the information you need to complete your resource directory.

> Follow the format used in Figure 11.1 and develop a plan for these TK–12 consultation, collaboration, and teaming goals.

PROGRAM MANAGEMENT

Coordination

Coordination is an indirect intervention that makes the delivery of other services possible. Myrick (1997) defines coordination as managing the many services offered in a comprehensive developmental program. Coordination encompasses all the functions and activities used to ensure the scheduled, delivered, and evaluated service, event, or project that is part of the school counseling program. Coordination is an organizational procedure that helps counselors attend to the meaning and purpose of the activities undertaken and to avoid duplication unless they are purposefully planning multiple interventions. Careful consideration of how one manages time, office, people, and tasks, coupled with a serious review of currently assigned nonguidance tasks for possible displacement or streamlining (Gysbers & Henderson, 2000) is intended to decrease the amount of time spent in administrative activities with the "gain" being spent on high-priority items (Silver, 1995).

Previously, the counselors each coordinated all program initiatives directly associated with the grades or students for which they were responsible. They wish to move to a model of more diversified or differential staffing (Blum, 1998). This means that each of them would assume responsibility for specific coordinating activities for the entire school. Eliminating duplication of effort should allow each of them more time to address the high-priority program items identified by their leadership team. For example, if they designate a peer facilitation coordinator, only one counselor from each school would need to attend in-service training activities related to peer facilitation programs. There are specific skills associated with coordination. The counselors agree that a review of these skills is in order.

LEADERSHIP

Pounder and Ogawa (1995) studied school leadership as an organizational quality. They wanted to link the relationship of leadership, effective organizations, and measures of school effectiveness. Their research supported the impact of school leadership on school performance; however, they overlooked the leadership of school counselors in their study. Professional school counselors are educational leaders. Their roles can be constructed within the same framework of effective CEOs that has been explained by Bennis (1995). School counselors are concerned with the program's basic purpose, the reason(s) it exists, and its general direction.

They are committed to doing the right things and have the following competencies:

- Vision. An ability to see what is needed or what is possible and to move toward it; for school counselors this involves some iteration of being an integral part of an educational enterprise that makes it possible for students to learn and thrive.
- Communication. The capacity to share their vision to gain the support of others; for school counselors this propels them to build teams and to inform students, parents, teachers, other school personnel, and the community about the school counseling program.
- Persistence, consistency, focus. The ability to maintain direction in spite of difficulties; for school counselors this means commitment to the students and attention to continual monitoring and revision of activities to provide excellent programs.
- Empowerment. The capacity to create environments that identify and use people's energies and abilities.

Counselors who provide direction and maintain commitment foster change. They also employ strategic planning to balance attention both on present, operational concerns and on future, strategic issues. This type of planning allows counselors and teams to determine and manage multiple change issues and to think and act more decisively about the program's future. Strategic thinking provides multiple solutions and a variety of perspectives, allowing a "stacking" effect with actions based on needs and resources (Kormanski, 1999). Professional school counselors use their leadership skills and effective teams to influence and propel change that leads to student success.

ORGANIZATION

Silver (1995) defines an organizing system as "a combination of appropriate tools and habits to get a job done or reach a goal" (p. 7). One of the first steps to achieving a highly organized counseling office is to clearly articulate program goals and priorities (as described in Chapter 3). Once this is done, organizers know what they are trying to achieve and commit to directing most of their energies to the goals. Second, one needs to decide how one's office and workload are going to be handled. Let's start with the office. One of the central features of an office is the workspace or desk. Most organizational specialists will tell you that a messy desk with lots of piles on it is not part of a productive work environment. How many times have you watched people go through every pile on their desk to retrieve something they are absolutely sure is there, only to find that the object of the search is not there? Even if the activity only takes 2 minutes, making the same search three times each day, five days each week adds up to 30 minutes per week. Multiply that weekly half hour by four and you can add 2 extra hours each month to your high-priority items!

Some suggestions for keeping a clear workspace include having only one open file on your desk at any given time, keeping only items used daily (planner, telephone, clock) as permanent desk fixtures, keeping items you use daily or several times each week most accessible to your workspace, and sorting or grouping together similar items or those requiring action (Silver, 1995). Setting up a daily paperwork system to routinely address active files and incoming paperwork is essential for avoiding a massive pile up. Silver suggests developing categories based on the types of papers that come your way each day. For high school counselors, that includes mountains of information related to postsecondary planning (military, colleges and universities, financial aid, scholarship opportunities, college testing information); requests for information about specific students; requests from students for appointments, references, and applications; correspondence; reading material; messages from parents and teachers; phone calls; priority items on which they are working; things to be filed; and items pending action, but not requiring immediate attention.

Color coding is one strategy used to increase accessibility of objects without having them out on your desk. For example, say you decide to use the color red to code all things related to parents. You keep parent programs and information for parents in a red binder divided by grade level; all correspondence to parents, including permission letters for group participation, is stored on a red diskette; a red folder is in your vertical file to receive requests from parents. Additionally, preprinted notes (e.g., referral forms for teachers, students, parents), computerized forms, storage bins, in and out boxes, three-ring binders, cabinets and boxes for long-term storage (e.g., bulletin board materials announcing Honors Day are used once annually), and magazine and literature storage containers may be helpful.

Filing systems, long and short term, need to be easily understood by others in your workplace. The following five-point filing system is suggested by Silver (1995):

1. Categorize existing files as active or inactive. Pull inactive files from your existing system.
2. Write out your filing system on a piece of paper and get input from others in the workplace who will be using the files.
3. Physically set up the system purging and consolidating files as you go.
4. Label drawers and prepare a file index.
5. Maintain your system by sticking to a routine. (p. 152)

Finally, the physical layout of your office needs to be conducive to the work that you do. Try to avoid working in one space and having materials/resources in another space. Think about the activities that you conduct in your workspace and lay out your office to maximize privacy, convenience, and comfort.

TIME MANAGEMENT

According to Silver (1995), time management is essential to good organization. School counselors who have already established and prioritized program goals are laying a foundation for good time management. Bliss (cited in Silver, 1995) suggests dividing goals into three priority levels. A-level priorities are important and urgent (e.g., student in crisis). B-level priorities are important but not urgent (e.g., a program that is planned for several months away). C-level priorities are urgent but not important (e.g., request for non-school-related information with a deadline of tomorrow). Program balance is achieved when the counselor spends most of his or her time on A and B priorities and very little time on C-level priorities. As Silver points out, most of us are competent handlers of A-level priorities, but do not do as well in making time for B-level priorities. To achieve one's goals, some time each day must be spent on B-level priorities.

Seven time management tools to consider are calendars, to-do lists, master lists, tickler systems, planners/organizers, computerized systems, and electronic organizers (Silver, 1995). A calendar is a basic tool that allows one to track events over time. Counselors should maintain only one calendar for both personal and professional information. The size should be adequate, but not burdensome. Important information should be photocopied in case of loss. The calendar should be accessible to you both in and out of the office. Some calendar systems include to-do lists where one can enter items to be completed on a given day. Try to list only those items that must be done today and commit to finishing the list. At the end of each day, one might prepare the next day's to-do list. Big projects are not so easily managed on a calendar or to-do list and might best be viewed on a master list or project management sheet. Many computer software manufacturers offer integrated e-mail, address book, scheduling, and

Effective Management of A-Level Priority

Jason had a motorcycle accident on the way home from school yesterday. He is hospitalized and will not return to school for at least 4 weeks. His parents called the counseling office to explore the options for keeping Jason up to date with his schoolwork. Mr. Larson and Ms. Fairley's secretary has called the program coordinator for homebound students and provided him the information needed to contact Jason's parents. Additionally, she has secured a copy of Jason's schedule from the school schedules database and has given it to the parent volunteer for the day. The parent will clean out Jason's locker and contact his teachers during each class period to get assignments for the rest of the week. During the last period of the day, the student assistant will take all materials for Jason to the front office where his parents will pick them up. The secretary will notify the counselors via e-mail of the actions she has taken on Jason's behalf. When the coordinator calls her back with more information, she will let teachers know how long Jason will be out of school and arrange to have his weekly assignments e-mailed to the teacher who will be working with him during his period of confinement. The secretary easily and efficiently handled this A-level priority because she had the authority and responsibility to do so. With teamwork, each person had a small part of their work time redirected toward solving the problem, but no one person had to carve out time during the day to carry out all of the necessary steps.

calendar programs. School counselors who use such programs on their office desktops or portable computers may consider an electronic organizer with compatible programming options so that a "portable" version of these important organizational tools may be easily accessed off-campus. Stay current of technological innovations that may help you manage your work and schedule.

A tickler system is a reminder system. For example, one might use an accordion file to keep cards to be mailed during a certain month, or notes about items to do (e.g., call speakers in October to schedule them for the January 6 postsecondary planning workshop). Or, one might develop an annual list of things that must be done each month. Organizers, both paper and electronic, can be effective time management tools as well. There is a wide range available and one can actually customize an organizer to meet specific needs.

Sabella (1996) identifies several time-saving methods for school counselors using their desktop computers. Consistent with our previous statements, computer usage is not intended to increase the amount of paperwork tasks completed by the counselor. The time saved by automating some of the more routine functions can be applied to other areas of importance. Specifically, Sabella recommends using various word processing, merging, data management, and e-mail functions to perform repetitive tasks such as generating forms and letters, managing student data, accounting for time spent on various tasks, keeping records and logs, and communicating with others.

Research and Development

The school counselors in Washington County know they have a unique role in the education of students and that their contributions are central to the academic mission of schools. They want to help everyone in the school community understand the importance of the school counseling program. They also want to determine what components of their program are working best. Accountability strategies will serve the multiple purposes of evaluating what works well and communicating the results of their evaluations to the interested public. The presentation of the material they gather and disseminate may vary by school level, but the substance will be consistent across levels. Johnson (2000) suggests a contemporary schematic for a strategic, three-phase initiative designed to use enhanced accountability practices to promote the professional identity of the school counseling program. Those phases move from agreeing about program goals and priorities, to evaluating their program, and finally to promoting the program. The counselors will use this framework as their guide.

Agreeing

The counselors have begun to accomplish the first step by affirming their commitment to the mission of the school counseling program. They have defined the mission through well-articulated goals and objectives. Additionally, they have identified through what program elements the goals may be addressed and have allocated time and resources needed to implement the program. See Figure 11.2 for goals the counselors have established regarding the development of action plans they will use during the coming year.

The counselors also have an established procedure and schedule for conducting needs assessments. The information they gather from students, parents, and teachers will be used to determine annual priorities. They decide some modifications may enhance the helpfulness of the survey they currently use. First, they want to revise the instrument to allow the participants to respond both to how important they consider the service and how well the service was provided. Lusky and Hayes (2001) provide a useful sample of such a survey that includes the counseling program's services of providing information, individual planning, counseling interventions, and consultation. The counselors will modify the language and length of the survey for the elementary and middle school levels but will focus on the same areas K–12 for consistency. The counselors may now use their revised survey as a needs assessment and as an evaluation instrument. Second, they want to expand the groups that are completing the survey and will include some of their business partners and some of the agency personnel with whom they will be working more closely.

Finally, the counselors want to understand the perceptions held by others of the school counseling program. Specifically, they wish to gauge the extent to which the students', parents', teachers', and others' perceptions agree with the articulated program. For this more open-ended process they are going to contact a professor at a local university and ask if some counselors-in-training would conduct focus groups and interviews with constituent groups to compile a

FIGURE 11.2 Action Plan for System Support

TK–12 Counselors Program Management Plan 2006–2007

Category/Expected Outcomes	Program Activities	Participants	Resources Needed	Evaluation Method	Dates
Program Management Goal 1: Counselors will identify areas of inconsistency between Washington County school counseling programs and the ASCA national model.	Conduct program audit.	All counselors.	ASCA National Model for School Counseling Programs Workbook.	Counselors establish specific, measurable program goals based on results of audit.	November 1–30, 2006
Goal 2: Action plans (see Figure 5.3) will be developed for each goal established as a result of the program audit.	Work in grade-level groups to develop action plans for established program goals.	All counselors.	Monthly meeting times in grade-level groups; ASCA National Model for School Counseling Programs Workbook; Consultant to help establish/identify appropriate outcome measures.	An action plan for each new program goal will be produced and approved by the counselors, administrators, and their respective leadership teams.	January–June 2007

summary description. Where the descriptions differ from the stated program, efforts will be made to understand the reasons and to formulate a response to them.

Evaluating

Systematic evaluations provide evidence of the work and outcomes of the school counseling program (Gysbers & Henderson, 2000). Information about what the program does to aid student success as well as how students have benefited from the activities is crucial. The counselors maintain daily time and task analysis logs so that they may regularly check to be sure that they are implementing all phases of the program and in the agreed upon balance of program elements. These daily logs are summarized weekly and monthly. Based on the monthly summaries, counselors identify program elements in which they may be over- or undercommitted and make adjustments as necessary. An additional benefit of the daily time and task analysis logs is that counselors can easily see (and share) the numbers of students they have seen individually, in small groups, and through classroom guidance. They can also keep track of those who have been assisted indirectly through teacher, parent, and administrator consultations and by referral to other resources in the school or community. And they are able to identify whether their interventions were aimed toward academic, career, or personal/social development. Therefore, these data help the counselors determine and describe what they are doing and if they are delivering the program they planned and articulated.

A second purpose of evaluation is to determine the extent to which goals are met. The counselors have identified specific competencies for students in grades K–12 in the three domains on which the program is based: academic, career, and personal/social development. Further, the counselors have identified through which program element—guidance curriculum, individual planning, responsive services, or system support—each competency is to be addressed (VanZandt & Hayslip, 2001). Results-oriented evaluation will determine whether students who participate in the program demonstrate these competencies (e.g., goals, outcomes) at a predetermined criterion level. Or stated another way, evaluation tells us how many students (criterion level) will be able to demonstrate a specific ability (competency, outcome, or goal) at either the conclusion of an intervention or some other specified time. To evaluate outcomes, one devises a method (or methods) for checking students' performance to determine if the specified number of students has achieved the desired outcome or demonstrated the specified competency. Outcome measures help counselors determine the impact of their program. Parents will be interested in information related to student assistance. Administrators will want to have comparative measures for across-the-school impact, and the school board members will be concerned with the cost effectiveness of the program. Three outcome measures that are meaningful and understandable to anyone are student grades, student attendance, and discipline referrals. Counselors can monitor these three areas for the students with whom they work for outcome results.

Ms. Pickens states, "I understand the importance of evaluation and that guidance for the evaluation is found in the stated objective. However, I am still uncertain about how to analyze the data for evidence of meaningful change once it has been collected." Some examples of accountability measures and their connection to impact that have been provided by Johnson (2000) may help Ms. Pickens answer her concerns.

- A pre- and postassessment of the effects on students' study skills habits as they participate in a classroom guidance unit on that topic.
- Evaluative feedback from parents collected from a questionnaire regarding their child's explanation and use of the study skills learned.
- Tabulation of the number of at-risk students persisting in K–12 school and beyond.
- A pre- and postassessment of the effects of participating in the peer mediation program.
- Case study documentation of "multiple failure" students who have reversed that trend in academic performance after collaborative interdisciplinary team efforts initiated by school counselors.
- An experimental group design (treatment group vs. no-treatment group) on the effects of small-group counseling of children who are experiencing divorce.
- Feedback from classroom teachers about the change in behaviors of children who receive individual and/or small-group counseling.

The data from these measures are generally analyzed to produce descriptions. Descriptive statistics are simple and straightforward and yield useful information such as means or averages, percentages, most frequent responses, range of scores for each response, and so forth. Other tests such as t-tests are used to compare differences between pre- and postintervention scores. The counselors agree that their master's level research course prepared them to conduct these types of data analysis. They will consult with others, such as counselor educators at the local university, if they wish to perform analyses for which they are unprepared.

Promoting

The counselors realize that they will be able to gradually incorporate this accountability system into their daily work. They will build a realistic time line as they expand the data they gather, interpret, and use. They do not want to delay all their strategies to build awareness of their program, however. They are studying the suggestions offered by Johnson (2000) to create a plan of action to be implemented this year. She provides samples of strategies that can be used to inform different constituent groups (students, parents, teachers, administrators, community) about the role and utility of the counseling program as it relates to student success. She offers the following suggestions for school counselors to consider as they advocate for their programs:

- Conduct presentations that outline the role, services, and outcomes of the program as they relate to the school mission.

- Develop a booklet that highlights the best practices of the school counseling program.
- Develop a brochure and/or flyer that promotes the program.
- Introduce the program and services in all grade classrooms.
- Hold "accountability conferences" with the principal to discuss the program and to provide data that documents user statistics, comparative measures of success and deficiency, needs assessments, and recommendations.
- Write a "Dear Counselor" column for the school newsletter to respond to student academic concerns.
- Sponsor informational workshops for parents on topics such as learning styles and developmental milestones.
- Offer in-service workshops to teachers in areas such as motivation and test anxiety.
- Develop a professional portfolio for school counselors.
- Create a department Web site with informational links for students and community.
- Develop and distribute a quarterly calendar of services and functions.

These strategies help people understand a school counseling program and the effects that effort has on student success. School counselors who identify the program goals and determine if and how well those goals are being met will have convincing evidence to support and sustain a school counseling program. Mr. Terman's team acknowledges that any of these strategies can be used across any school level with slight modifications in language.

Fair-Share Responsibilities

Mr. Terman asks the counselors about fair-share responsibilities and one counselor provides an example. Ms. Nu, a middle school counselor, states that her principal wants her to coordinate activities related to the maintenance of student records as part of her fair-share responsibilities. She has copies of the systemwide policy stating that the semester grades, standardized test scores, and attendance for all students will be printed on labels that records clerks will affix to the students' cumulative folders. Blum (1998) points out that such policies should also provide guidance regarding the procedures for amending or correcting a record, the content of the records, proper guidelines for maintenance and storage of records, procedures for reviewing records, and the identification of persons who have the right to access and review student records.

Aspects of records management about which Ms. Nu is unclear include who can actually handle and work with records containing confidential student information and under what circumstances records can be reviewed by or released to others. Generally, clerical personnel who work with counselors may have access to records as needed to accomplish the requirements of their employment (Remley & Herlihy, 2001). In fact, Schmidt (1999) points out that it is imperative to have clerical staff assigned tasks associated with records

> In a small working group, develop a one-page time and task analysis log that would enable counselors to keep track of their daily activities and the time spent in each, categorized by program element and developmental concern.

> Select one intervention typically used to deliver the school counseling curriculum. Identify two ways to evaluate whether the intervention you selected has been successful. How would the evidence you need to convince parents, teachers, principals, students, and school board members be different?

maintenance and management, with the school counselor making certain that the local, state, and national regulations are followed. If counselors are responsible for supervising these employees, they have a responsibility to make them aware of the importance of maintaining confidentiality of records.

Good citizenship within the school community includes participation in some activities that are not identified with school counseling. Counselors want to decrease the likelihood of these fair-share responsibilities interfering with their work with the school counseling program. The best advice we have for counselors to avoid being assigned more than their fair share of these responsibilities is to demonstrate their contributions to the school's mission through the implementation of a standards-based, data-driven, comprehensive school counseling program.

SUMMARY

In this chapter, we have provided information about the coordination activities required to manage a comprehensive developmental program. Examples of coordinating activities and the skills needed to effectively coordinate a program have also been presented. You have also read about the other activities common to the system support element of a comprehensive school counseling program. Procedures for designing a plan for promoting the school counseling program, evaluating the activities, and working within integrated teams to improve efficiency and effectiveness in service delivery to students and their families have been presented. Finally, you have been challenged to consider ways to fulfill the responsibilities of this program element within the recommended time allotment of 10% to 15%.

PORTFOLIO COMPONENTS

1. Describe a time that you participated in a team or group project that had a successful outcome. What did the leader do to promote cohesion and commitment to the team and its goals? How did members respond? Use this experience and others to develop a one-page description of how you would approach building a team to achieve one or more goals of your school counseling program.
2. Identify your managerial strengths and weaknesses as a potential program coordinator. Articulate a plan of professional development, including goals and activities, to become more competent in this area. Focus on specific strategies and skills you need to develop prior to your graduation.
3. Build a master calendar for the school year identifying the responsibilities associated with coordinating the school counseling program to be completed each month.

4. Identify an area of professional competence in which you need more knowledge and skill. Develop a goal statement that includes exactly what you wish to accomplish with regard to this area. Identify the steps you will take to meet your professional development goal. When you have completed the identified activities, write a reflection statement describing your progress toward the goal and how you feel about your accomplishment.

CHAPTER 12

Legal and Ethical Concerns in School Counseling

SYSTEMATIC APPROACH TO DECISION MAKING

The school counselors in Brevard County have quarterly meetings that usually focus on school district policies related to their work. Those sessions involve the counselors getting information about changing school district practices. However, during their breaks they often talk about difficult situations they have encountered in school days and ask each other for advice. Tomika, who has worked for 10 years at a middle school, has noticed those informal discussions often revolve around ethical dilemmas. She is stimulated by the conversations and has decided to create a forum where they can expand their deliberations and share their concerns.

Many of the other counselors in Brevard County accept her invitation to participate in a monthly meeting. After some unstructured sessions, the group decides to focus more on what seems to be the foundation of most of their concerns—legal and ethical issues. They invite a counselor educator to teach them ways to approach decision making and to review some current, relevant legal guidelines that affect school counseling. Then they agree on a schedule for conferring with each other about their dilemmas.

They find their monthly meetings have become valuable professional development opportunities. They discover that the number of difficult situations has not diminished, but their confidence and competence in addressing them has increased significantly. We will review what these counselors learned as well as some of the situations they have encountered.

The discussion of the ASCA (2004c) ethical standards (see Appendix C) in Chapter 1 highlighted school counselors' responsibilities to several different groups. Being accountable to students, parents, teachers, schools, communities, and a profession requires that counselors practice with diligence and care. Wise counselors look more closely at the guidelines provided in ethical standards and legal mandates for determining reasonable courses of action.

Ethical codes from several professional groups such as the American Counseling Association (2005), the National Board of Certified Counselors (2005), American Association for Marriage and Family Therapy (2001), and the National Association of Social Workers (1999) address some common issues such as principles about the competence of the practitioner, responsibilities to the person being counseled, confidentiality, cultural diversity, and potentially harmful relationships. In school settings all these concerns are compounded by counselors being sensitive to parents' needs and responsibilities, to schools that students attend and the other people in that setting, and to the students' rights to privacy. Protecting all those interests create many of the dilemmas faced by school counselors.

After reading and discussing this chapter, you will be able to

- Identify ethical dilemmas or issues of concern that may be commonly experienced by school counselors.

- Apply an ethical decision-making model to resolve an ethical dilemma.
- Identify specific legal issues related to working with minor clients in a school setting.
- Identify at least three ways to minimize your risk of committing ethical or legal violations in the context of school counseling relationships.

ETHICAL AND LEGAL ISSUES

Tomika's study group decides to call themselves the Questers. They spend some time with a university professor reviewing some decision-making models for their school counseling practices. First, the Questers study a foundation and structure for ethical decision making. Ethics, a branch of philosophy, concentrates on morals and morality as they relate to making decisions. Ethics has been defined as the customs, mores, standards, and accepted practices of a profession (Stone & Dahir, 2006; Fischer & Sorenson, 1996). For professional school counselors, ethical professional behavior refers to applying concepts of morality, values, and good and bad to the counseling relationship. Ethical codes are guides to help counselors make those decisions about what constitutes ethical practice in particular situations. Circumstances vary greatly, however, so the ethical codes are written as guides to be interpreted with judgment and ethical reasoning (Welfel & Lipsitz, 1983).

Another component of that reasoning comes from laws, the minimum standard that society will tolerate according to Fischer and Sorenson (1996). Laws include those from federal statutes, case law that emerges from court cases, and state and district school board policies (Fischer & Sorenson, 1996). Laws require that professionals "behave as the reasonably competent professional would" (Stone & Dahir, 2006, p. 301). That guideline creates a "standard of care" reference that is used to determine whether the actions of the professional meet that target. With a general idea of the scope of ethics and of the legal standard, the Questers consider the moral imperatives of practice.

Kitchener (1984, 1986) integrated moral and ethical perspectives to identify five moral principles on which to base ethical decision making. Those principles and definitions are as follows:

- *Autonomy:* Relates to independence—individual freedom in choices and actions. Counselors encourage people to make their own decisions and to act on their personal values. Counselors see complications in supporting autonomy when clients may not understand how their decisions will be received by others and how their choices may encroach on the rights of others. Of particular importance to school counselors is a second consideration related to the person's ability to make sound and rational decisions. Children may not be capable of making competent choices. Counselors must diligently balance children's rights of autonomy with their safety.
- *Nonmaleficence:* "Above all do no harm." This principle relates to not causing harm to others and is considered by some to be the most critical tenet of

all (Kitchener, 1984; Rosenbaum, 1982; Stadler, 1986). Forester-Miller and Rubenstein (1992) explain that the principle refers to the idea not only of not imposing harm but also of not participating in behaviors that may risk hurting others.

- *Beneficence:* Contributing to the welfare of others. This principle means to do good, to be proactive, and to prevent harm when at all possible (Forester-Miller & Rubenstein, 1992). Counselors who work in schools have many opportunities to apply this principle. They may also find that the welfare needs of their clients, parents, and school staff seem to conflict, thus evoking a dilemma.

- *Justice:* Treating others fairly. According to Stone and Dahir (2006), this implies that every person—regardless of age, sex, race, ethnicity, ability, socioeconomic status, background, religion, lifestyle, or any other variable— receives equal treatment.

- *Fidelity:* Loyalty, faithfulness, and honoring commitments. Counselors demonstrate these characteristics when they treat all people respectfully and stay connected to everyone in school (Stone & Dahir, 2006).

> With your classmates create a list of situations that would serve as examples of each of these principles. For instance, supporting the decision of a student who has demonstrated athletic ability to participate in band rather than in athletics would be an example of honoring autonomy.

These five tenets are valuable tools in analyzing, interpreting, and evaluating difficult decisions. The principles provide a framework to help counselors critically examine the difficult choices with which they are confronted.

Meara, Schmidt, and Day (1996) explain that principle ethics are the overt ethical obligations of counseling such as duty to warn and protect. Those authors continue by discussing that virtue ethics relate to people who exceed their obligations and strive toward the ideals to which their profession aspires (Nystul, 2003). Understanding and being sensitive to the impact of cultural issues on ethical decision making is central to virtue ethics. These authors (Meara, Schmidt, & Day, 1996; Nystul, 2003) emphasize the integration of principle and virtue ethics for decisions that balance ethical and legal mandates with the best interests of society.

Decision-Making Models

Many other authors have proposed models of ethical decision making that can be useful to school counselors. If you would like to study a variety of those models, you can investigate the following authors: Cottone (2001); Forester-Miller and Davis (1995); Garcia, Cartwright, Winston, and Borzuchowska (2003); Hill, Glaser, and Harden (1995); Kenyon (1999); Kitchener (1984); Meara, Schmidt, and Day (1996); Rave and Larsen (1995); Stadler (1986); Travydas (1987); Van Hoose and Kottler (1985). The Brevard County group is introduced to a synthesis of these models that has been provided by Remley and Herlihy (2005). Those steps are as follows:

1. *Identify and define the problem.* Begin the process by reflecting and gathering information. The authors suggest you take time to identify what is known or what can be verified about the situation. Determine the applicable ethical guidelines and note any relevant laws. Review the professional literature

and your code of ethics. If a legal issue is involved, consider involving an attorney. Think about the situation from several perspectives and do not leap to simplistic solutions.

2. *Consider the moral perspectives.* Review the moral principles that apply to the problem, identify the ways in which they compete with each other in this situation, and rank them in order of priority for this circumstance.

3. *Tune in to your feelings.* Think about the emotions you are experiencing as you contemplate the dilemma and your actions. How much are you being influenced by emotions such as doubt, an overwhelming sense of responsibility, or fear?

4. *Consult with colleagues or experts.* If at all possible, seek input from a colleague.

5. *Involve the client in the decision-making process.* Rather than a separate step, this should occur throughout the process. Making clients an active participant in the process allows counselors to avoid making decisions **for** them and creates the opportunity for making decisions **with** them, an empowering and culturally appropriate practice. In school settings counselors may need to perfect ways to allow that partnership to occur.

6. *Identify desired outcomes.* In ethical dilemmas rarely does a single desired outcome emerge even after this type of thoughtful process. You may be looking for a number of outcomes that you can sort out as essential or as desirable but not necessary. Brainstorming new options and consulting with colleagues about other options may generate other possibilities.

7. *Consider possible actions.* Think about actions you might take to get the desired results. You may find listing wanted results on one side of the page and facilitating actions beside each outcome beneficial. Identify the implications and consequences of each possibility for the client, for others, and for yourself.

8. *Choose and act.* After you have picked your action or series of actions, compare your choices with your ranking of moral principles. Pay attention to your emotions related to the choice. Finally gather the support and moral courage to carry out your decision.

With that outline to guide thinking in complex situations, the school counselors now review another document that contains helpful guidelines. The Ethics Committee of the American School Counselor Association (1999–2001) compiled a summary of tips to aid in ethical decision making. Those hints include the following:

- Always act in the best interest of your clients;
- Always act in good faith and without malice;
- Be aware of your personal values, attitudes, and beliefs; and
- Refer clients to another counselor if personal characteristics impede your effectiveness as a helper.

The study group wants to practice the decision-making model even before they look more closely at some of the ethical and legal issues. Their deliberations on a case can be found in Figure 12.1.

After that discussion and with their renewed understanding of moral principles, decision-making models, and four suggestions for practicing ethically, the Questers turn to legal concerns related to children's and parents' rights.

FIGURE 12.1 Ethical Decision-Making Example

1. *Identify and define the problem.* A 15-year-old girl, Judy, reports that she is sexually active and her current partner is her best friend's brother-in-law. She is worried about keeping secrets from her friend. The counselor, Mariah, is concerned about Judy's safety. Mariah knows about some incidents of violence in the best friend's family situation. The counselor also knows the man involved has been out of school for at least 4 years. The relevant ethical guidelines relate to maintaining confidentiality of the counseling relationship. A legal consideration is whether or not the age difference between the sexual partners constitutes statutory rape.

2. *Consider the moral perspectives.* The moral principles of autonomy, nonmaleficence, and beneficence are competing in this situation. The counselors are unable to rank those principles.

3. *Tune in to your feelings.* Four of the counselors have strong emotional reactions to the situation and want to move quickly to prevent further relations with the brother-in-law. After some discussion they conclude that their reactions are based on their keen sense of responsibility for the client's health and safety.

4. *Consult with colleagues or experts.* Using each other as consultants, the counselors in the study group weigh the costs of disclosing the information against the costs of keeping the confidence in such a risky situation. The counselors realize they need to find legal guidelines about reporting the situation as statutory rape. They need to know the age difference between Judy and her partner, and they need to investigate state laws and school district policies about reporting criminal activity before they can determine their legal obligations.

5. *Involve the client in the decision-making process.* The counselors in the study group hypothesize about how Judy might be included in this process. They decide if they would want to talk with her about the health concerns related to risky sexual activity, to assess what she knows about the brother-in-law's domestic situation, and to discuss with her the legalities about statutory rape. After that conversation, hopefully a plan could be formulated.

6. *Identify desired outcomes.* Mariah's desired outcomes include Judy keeping her friendship intact, Judy being safe, and Judy understanding the complications of her decisions. The study group counselors would also like to see Judy's additions to the list of desired outcomes.

7. *Consider possible actions.* During their discussion, Mariah and Judy will compile a sheet that includes wanted results on one side of the page and facilitating actions beside each of the outcomes.

8. *Choose and act.* The choices will be determined by the ongoing discussions.

Rights of Minor Clients

Jack, a member of the study group, bemoans the complications of working with minors. He says that many of the demanding situations he faces with children in the middle school revolve around balancing the needs of the child with the rights of their parents. For example, during the 10 years he has been a school counselor he has noticed that many students are experimenting with alcohol at younger ages. On a schoolwide basis he has implemented prevention programs, provided some in-service staff training, and worked in other proactive ways to respond to this trend. However, in a recent counseling session with an eighth grader who was dating a high school junior, he learned of some weekend binging on alcohol and once again he feels caught between protecting the confidence of the relationship and informing the parents of this dangerous behavior.

Legal and ethical responsibilities may collide when counseling minors (Remley & Herlihy, 2005). One problem revolves around the definition of *minor*. Glosoff and Pate (2002) explain that in most states a person is considered legally mature at the age of 18 and then has control of personal privacy rights. Children have the right to be supported by their parents and they have the right to be protected from abuse or neglect. Legally minors are not considered competent to make fully informed, voluntary decisions (Davis & Mickelson, 1994). Some states have laws that allow minors to give informed consent when there is an emergency or when they need treatment for substance abuse, sexually transmitted diseases, pregnancy, or birth control (Lawrence & Robinson Kurpius, 2000). School counselors need to study closely the variations in state laws about the rights of minors and stay informed about the statutes of the state in which they practice.

English and Kenney (2003) have gathered a state-by-state description of the legal status of minors in their book *State Minor Consent Laws: A Summary*. That book contains information about minors' rights to ask for different types of health services such as outpatient mental health services. The book also explains laws about minors' health privacy and confidentiality statutes, disclosure to parents, and other mandates affecting young people. Other valuable resources on minors' rights include the policy briefs and summaries of laws provided by the Guttmacher Institute (www.guttmacher.org/pubs), Linde's (2003) comprehensive chapter, and the article by Guillot-Miller and Partin (2003) on Web-based resources. Abbreviated information about state laws that allow a minor to consent to some types of medical treatment can be found in Table 12.1, which has been compiled by the American Bar Association (2005).

> Based on the discussion of rights of minors, list the things in Jack's situation that would argue for maintaining the privacy of the child's communication with Jack.

Rights of Parents

Most laws still favor parents' rights over their children's. Therefore, before the age of majority, privacy rights belong to parents (Remley & Herlihy, 2005). Stone (2004) discusses the dilemma this causes school counselors. The counselor may be caught between protecting the student client's right to privacy and the parent's right to know what is happening in their child's life. Noncustodial parents have rights also. Counselors will need to understand legal issues that

TABLE 12.1   Facts about Children and the Law

State Laws Allowing a Minor to Consent to Medical Treatment

State	Contraceptive services	Prenatal care	STD-HIV/AIDS services	Alcohol and/or drug treatment	Outpatient mental health services
Alabama		x	x	x	x
Alaska	x	x	x		
Arizona			x	x	
Arkansas	x	x	x		
California	x	x	x	x	x
Colorado	x		x	x	x
Connecticut			x	x	x
Delaware	x	x	x	x	
District of Columbia	x	x	x	x	x
Florida	x	x	x	x	x
Georgia	x	x	x	x	
Hawaii	x	x	x	x	
Idaho	x		x	x	
Illinois	x	x	x	x	x
Indiana			x	x	
Iowa			x	x	
Kansas		x	x	x	
Kentucky	x	x	x	x	x
Louisiana			x	x	
Maine	x		x	x	x
Maryland	x	x	x	x	x
Massachusetts		x	x	x	x
Michigan		x	x	x	x
Minnesota		x	x	x	
Mississippi	x	x	x	x	
Missouri		x	x	x	
Montana	x	x	x	x	x
Nebraska			x	x	
Nevada			x	x	
New Hampshire			x	x	
New Jersey		x	x	x	
New Mexico	x		x	x	x
New York	x	x	x	x	x
North Carolina	x	x	x	x	x
North Dakota			x	x	
Ohio			x	x	x
Oklahoma	x	x	x	x	
Oregon	x		x	x	x
Pennsylvania		x	x	x	
Rhode Island			x	x	
South Carolina					
South Dakota			x	x	

(Continued)

TABLE 12.2 (Continued)

State Laws Allowing a Minor to Consent to Medical Treatment

State	Contraceptive services	Prenatal care	STD-HIV/AIDS services	Alcohol and/or drug treatment	Outpatient mental health services
Tennessee	x	x	x	x	x
Texas		x	x	x	x
Utah		x	x		
Vermont			x	x	
Virginia	x	x	x	x	x
Washington			x	x	x
West Virginia			x	x	
Wisconsin			x	x	
Wyoming	x		x		

Source: From Table 1: "State Laws Allowing a Minor to Consent to Medical Treatment," published in *Facts About Children and the Law,* by the American Bar Association Division for Media Relations & Public Affairs, published online at http://www.abanet.org/media/factbooks/childlaw.pdf. Copyright (c) 1997 by the American Bar Association. Reprinted with permission.

affect noncustodial parents and their rights to information about their child. In the court case *Page v. Rotterdam-Mohonasen Central School District* (1981) the court determined that school districts have a duty to act in the best educational interest of their students and that means giving educational information to both parents (cited in Fischer & Sorenson, 1996). The court decreed that even though parents may not have legal custody, they do not relinquish their rights to be a psychological guardian (Stone & Dahir, 2006).

Wilcoxon and Magnuson (1999) give definitions and considerations for working with these parents. They encourage school counselors to work with schools to create guidelines promoting family involvement rather than focusing only on custodial parents. They also suggest that counselors need to anticipate problems caused by marital decree and work to design policies and procedures sensitive to all family structures. Those guidelines should help prevent difficult school situations.

In the absence of a federal or state law otherwise, school counselors do not have to obtain parental permission before counseling students. Nonetheless, parents may have a legal right to object to their children participating in counseling (Remley & Herlihy, 2005). Welfel (2002) suggests that parents are reassured when they know counselors will not work beyond the limits of their competence, will make reasonable efforts to honor parents' requests, and will be respectful of family values. She recommends handbooks or brochures to disseminate information. In fact the ASCA (2004e) position statement on parental consent for services stipulates that such information must be provided for parents. Written information about the counseling program in brochures and consent forms helps build a climate of cooperation and open communication that can help prevent misunderstandings of counseling in schools.

Furthermore, parents can be valuable allies in work with children (Huey, 1996), and counselors should use their professional judgment for deciding whether and when to involve parents or guardians in the counseling process. For example, withholding some types of information about children, such as the use of drugs, risky sexual activity, illegal activity, and other dangerous behaviors, may lead to injuries. The Ethics Committee of ASCA (1999–2001) advises counselors to "encourage family involvement, where possible, when working with minors in sensitive areas which might be controversial" (p. 1). A general guideline for counselors is that parents are entitled to general information from the counselor about a child's progress and a short update will satisfy that request (Stromberg and colleagues, 1993). In every case counselors must be cautious in the kind and extent of information revealed (Corey, Corey, & Callanan, 1998).

Kaplan (1997) recommends focusing on academic issues and assuring parents that program activities support high expectations for all students. Her other advice includes providing effective communications with parents, forming a parent advisory group, safeguarding access to all educational programs, and involving parents in decision making. Finally, she advocates for school counselors to monitor the impact of their program on student learning. Zingaro (1983) has another proposal. He says that when it is in the best interests of the minor for an adult to have information, the counselor could tell the significant adult ways to help the child rather than revealing specific information. Strein and Hershenson (1991) suggest a "need-to-know" basis as a guideline to confidentiality when counselors have situations that are not one-to-one counseling sessions, a common situation in schools.

If parents demand to know the contents of counseling and the child does not want the parent or guardian to be told, Remley and Herlihy (2005) recommend these steps:

1. Talk to the child about the request for information and see if the minor is willing to disclose the content. Sometimes counselors are more concerned about privacy than a child. If that doesn't work, go to step 2.
2. Try to persuade the adult that the best interests of the child would not be served by revealing the information. Talk to the adult about the nature of the counseling relationship and reassure the parent or guardian that if the child were in danger, the information would be disclosed. If that doesn't work, go to step 3.
3. Hold a joint session with the adult and the minor. Mediate the session. Hope that the adult will have a change of heart or that the minor will be willing to reveal enough information to satisfy the adult. If that doesn't work, try step 4 or step 5.
4. Tell the child ahead of time and then disclose the content to the parent or guardian.
5. Refuse to disclose the information. Ask for approval from your direct supervisor before doing this and remember the adult may have a legal right to the information.

Based on the discussion on rights of parents, list the things in Jack's case that would support informing the parents of the child's actions. Also if the decision to disclose were made, describe the steps you would take in providing that information to the parents.

Mitchell, Disque, and Robertson (2002) also provide ideas for working with parents who want confidential information. They recommend using empathic skills to let the parent express concerns and to convey respect for those fears. Counselors can then explain their dilemma, ethical guidelines, and the role confidentiality plays in the counseling relationship. Children should be told about their parents' inquiry. Those authors suggest that counselors have prepared procedures and alternatives for responding to difficult situations.

Summary of Ethics and the Law

Some authors (Tompkins & Mehring, 1993; Davis & Ritchie, 1993) recommend the following critical steps when school counselors struggle with ethical dilemmas. Counselors should stay informed about the law and about state and school district policies that relate to their practice. They should operate within the ethical codes. They should review employer expectations and policies before they accept a position. School counselors should operate within the limits of their competence. Most important, they should keep the best interest of the child as their predominant concern.

The Questers study group has been reminded that school counselors meet their primary ethical obligation when they focus on students and their educational, career, emotional, and behavioral needs. Beginning the school year with careful explanations helps other people recognize that goal; therefore, the Questers look at ways to publicize their purposes and to help people understand counseling.

INFORMED CONSENT

Mary Jane tells the Questers of a situation she has encountered recently. A second-grade boy, Manny, has come to her for the past 6 weeks. Their discussions have now evolved into his retelling about a trauma that occurred when he was in kindergarten in another state. Mary Jane wants Manny to begin seeing a play therapist and the family to participate in family therapy. When she suggests this in a parent conference, the father insists the school counselor should continue working with Manny and should also begin seeing the family rather than involving other mental health professionals. Mary Jane pulls out the letter that was distributed at the beginning of the school year that describes the counseling program and talks with this family about the parameters that were outlined in that communication.

Letting people know who you are, what you do, and how you do it has many benefits. The information prevents confusion about what counseling encompasses and allows everyone to have an understanding of expectations. The Ethics Committee of ASCA (1999–2001) reminds counselors that they should be able to explain the reasons they do what they do. Colleagues will need to understand confidentiality, public and private information, and the process of consultation. Students and parents need to understand those concepts as well as the purposes, goals, techniques, and procedures of counseling so they can give counselors permission to work with them. Informed consent refers to a process that protects a person's right to understand what he or she is getting into before participating in counseling.

Written statements make the informed consent more concrete (Muro & Kottman, 1995). Therefore, school counselors are advised to begin a counseling relationship with written statements about confidentiality, privileged communication, any restraints that result from counseling in a school setting, and the chance of counselors conferring with others. The language should be simple and appropriate for the age of the student. Glosoff and Pate (2002) recommend that counselors realize that informed consent is an ongoing, clarifying part of the counseling process. Therefore, counselors are advised to begin the relationship discussing the written statement and reminding students of the contents throughout their work together. Counselors may have a simple disclosure statement to use with students and another that contains more details available for adults such as parents and teachers.

Kaplan (2001) suggests some sections to include in a disclosure statement or a counseling brochure for students. A short description of the counselor's educational background, training, degrees, and work experiences should be a part of this statement. The document should also include the theory and treatment approach most often used. Informed consent forms should have a definition of confidentiality and its limits such as a clear and present danger to others or to self; reporting child abuse, maltreatment, or neglect; and school or district policies that conflict with confidentiality. The statement should also include guidelines about appointments, how to contact the counselor, how many times the students may see the counselor, how to get teacher's permission for getting out of class, opportunities for before- or after-school sessions, and other procedural arrangements. The student can acknowledge reading and understanding the document by signing the form.

Counselors need to provide some general information for parents, teachers, and other people interested in the school counseling program. Glosoff and Pate (2002) suggest that parents have information about the counselor's role, the possible benefits of a counseling program, and the nature of program activities. A description of the program, its components, and activities will help the adults understand the scope of counseling services in the school. Counselors will also want to include the way questions or concerns about the school counseling program can be addressed. O'Connor, Plante, and Refvem (1998) offer ideas for a consent form for parents. That document should be clearly titled and include identifying information about the school and district. The informed consent should contain an explanation about counseling services; directions as to how a parent can withhold consent; details for returning the forms; and a notice that if the form is not returned by the due date, a parental permission is assumed. Counselors may also provide options (for example, group counseling, more than two sessions of individual counseling, referrals) to be checked if desired. A place to sign and date the form should be available. School counselors may find it helpful to have the informed consent posted on the school Web site and have a

What if in the discussion Mary Jane hears that the parents never received the letter? Would that change her goal of making a referral?

way that parents can submit it electronically. Local or state laws or policies may dictate that school counselors obtain parental permission.

CASE NOTES

As they conduct counseling relationships, counselors will keep records about their sessions. Those personal notes should include facts and should be written in concrete and behaviorally oriented language (James & DeVaney, 1995). One way to outline the case log is the SOAP format. The four parts of this design include sections that reflect subjective, objective, assessment, and planning information. Cameron and turtle-song (2002) provide specific instructions for using that process. Case notes that stay in the sole possession of the counselor have some protection that shared or accessible records do not. Counselors can maintain the designation of "sole possession records" by adhering to these requirements: (1) the information must be a private note created only by the person who has it, (2) the information is a personal memory aid, (3) the information is not shared or accessible to any other person, and (4) case notes only qualify if those notes include personal observations about the behavior of students or conclusions based on the counselors' interactions with a student or others (Stone & Dahir, 2006). These notes should be stored in a secure location where privacy is ensured. Case notes should be destroyed after a reasonable amount of time. In cases of child abuse, suicide, sexual harassment, violence, or other potentially legal situations, the notes may be needed by the courts and should therefore be kept for a longer period. If school counselors are asked by the court to submit the notes, they should consult with an attorney. Remley (1990) talks about counseling records and describes ways to maintain, transfer, and discard them.

RECORDS

Counselors must safeguard all information about students. They take appropriate and reasonable measures to protect students' written and electronic records. Sampson and Pyle (1988), Childers (1988), and Sampson, Kolodinski, and Greeno (1997) note ways to safeguard data. They discuss security procedures, the restriction of content and access, ways to preserve anonymity, and limited storage time. Hammond and Gantt (1998) suggest that student art should also be protected as any other form of communication would be.

School counselors use those ideas as they comply with local policies, state laws, and federal mandates. A federal act that mandates upholding the privacy of student information is known as the Family Educational Rights and Privacy Act (FERPA) (1974). Additionally, the Drug Abuse Office and Treatment Act (1976) provides stipulations about the drug and alcohol treatment records of students who are in an institution that gets federal money. Coll (1995) and

Sealander, Schwiebert, Oren, and Weekley (1999) provide guidelines for legal and ethical concerns related to confidentiality of records for students in sub-stance abuse prevention programs. Exceptions include medical emergencies, child abuse or neglect reporting, or endangering someone when the benefits produced or harms prevented override confidentiality. Linde (2003) says that under this federal guideline students may go from the stages of referral through treatment without a parent or guardian knowing. Finally, the Individuals with Disability Education Act (1997) includes regulations about safeguarding records for students who receive special education.

FERPA, or the Buckley Amendment, gives parents and eligible students (older than 18) the right to inspect school records and to control the dissemi-nation of educational records. School districts may lose federal funds if the schools do not establish and maintain procedures to allow parents access to records and to deny access without parental permission. School districts have a records policy statement and procedures that explain how those regulations are executed. Some federal agencies have guides for formulating those policies and procedures. The National Center for Education Statistics (2004) has a guide for protecting student information. A model policy, Student Records Policies and Procedures for the Alpha School District, can be obtained from the U.S. Department of Education at 600 Independence, SW, Washington, DC 20202. The department's Web site, www.ed.gov/offices/OII/fpeo/ferpa/, also has model documents and detailed descriptions of this law.

However, those documents fail to give counselors specific guidelines. Some authors (Walker & Larrabee, 1985; Fischer & Sorenson, 1996) have provided information for counselors applying FERPA standards.

- Parents and eligible students are informed of their rights under this act. Access to records is a right extended to both custodial and noncustodial parents unless a court order restricts access.
- Parents and eligible students know about the types of records that exist and the procedures for getting those records. The records may include academic progress, test scores, identification data, home background, health informa-tion, educational history, anecdotal remarks, case summaries, and recom-mendations.
- Parents and eligible students may review records. They may ask for records to be changed if they believe the contents are inaccurate or misleading. They may request a hearing if the change does not happen, and they may add personal statements if necessary.
- Parents or eligible students give written consent before any personally iden-tifiable information is released.
- Parents or eligible students may see the school's record of disclosures.
- Records made by educators that are kept in the sole possession of the person making the records and are not accessible to or shared with any other per-son are not subject to disclosure under FERPA. The discussion above out-lines the guidelines for determining whether notes can be considered "sole possession records."

MULTIPLE RELATIONSHIPS

Fisher and Hennessy (1994) explain that when counselors interact with a client in more than one capacity, potentially damaging relationships may occur. Corey, Corey, and Callanan (1998) point out that in that type of situation, incompatible roles may decrease the effectiveness of the counseling relationship. Examples of potentially damaging relationships to avoid are counseling relatives, close friends, or your associates. A common example in a school setting is that friendships with school personnel may create conflicts with a counselor–student relationship. Ethical standards clearly state that multiple relationships with students are to be avoided, but school settings complicate that principle. Those potentially detrimental relationships, also known as dual relationships, range from those that are extremely harmful such as exploitation to those with little potential for harm such as being a faculty advisor. Sexual relationships with students are prohibited by ethical standards and are illegal in many states (Kitchener & Harding, 1990).

Herlihy and Corey (1992) explain that in dual relationships, the harm to the clients comes from the practitioner who takes advantage of the situation rather than from the duality itself. Therefore, if a school counselor cannot avoid multiple relationships with student clients, particular care must be given to eliminating or reducing the potential for harm. Some practices that help protect students from the risk inherent in multiple relationships include informed consent, consultation, supervision, and documentation (Muro & Kottman, 1995). School counselors should monitor the relationship and gauge the benefits against the risks of impaired judgment or exploitation of the child. These steps may be useful when facing an ethical dilemma that results from potentially damaging relationships: (1) identity the primary client, which in most cases in schools will be the student; (2) isolate the ethical issues or dilemma; (3) consult the necessary codes and experts; and (4) think carefully before acting. Those simplified steps may be augmented by the ethical decision-making model presented earlier.

> Kevin, a high school counselor, now has increased concerns because he is also the volleyball coach. He has always referred any volleyball team members to someone else on the counseling staff, but more and more he wonders if that is enough protection for those students. How would you advise him?

CONFIDENTIALITY AND RIGHT TO PRIVACY

Confidentiality refers to the ethical obligation of counselors to ensure that whatever is said in a counseling relationship will not be revealed. Remley and Herlihy (2005) list some considerations about children and confidentiality.

- Younger children do not understand the concepts of confidentiality or privacy and are probably not as concerned about confidentiality as the counselor.
- Preadolescents and adolescents may have a higher desire for privacy because of their confusion about identity and other developmental changes.

- Some children at all ages may not be at all concerned about privacy. Counselors should not assume that young people do not want their parents or guardians to know what they are discussion in counseling.
- Sometimes children may confide in an adult with the hope that the adult will act as an intermediary in resolving their concern.
- Children's limitations in reasoning may interfere with making decisions that are in their best interests.

According to the ASCA position statement on the school counselor and confidentiality (ASCA, 2002c), the counselors are obligated to establish and maintain confidentiality in schools. That responsibility protects the privacy of information received from students, parents, and teachers. The statement places no age limitation on who is entitled to a confidential relationship. Emphasized in the position statement is that confidentiality cannot be breached unless there is a clear and present danger to the student or another person.

Stone and Isaacs (2003) asked over 900 school counselors about situations in which they might breach confidentiality. Those respondents reported that their responsibility was to protect their relationship with students. Another survey by Isaacs and Stone (1999) indicated that school counselors would disclose confidential information for these reasons: impending suicide or suicide pact, violent retaliation for mistreatment, use of crack cocaine, sexual intercourse with several partners when HIV positive, armed robbery, and indications of serious depression. The age of the minor was the most significant factor in the counselors' decision making. They considered younger children as needing more protection than high school students who were considered more able to make mature decisions.

Remley (1985) says that counselors cover their responsibilities regarding confidentiality when they talk to the child before consulting with anyone else about the child's problem, when they involve the child in the decision-making process, and when they keep the child informed about what is happening.

Student–counselor privacy may also be complicated by the policies and expectations in a school setting. Counselors must respect and probably follow directions from school principals and superintendents (Remley, 1993) who may request confidential information. Teachers, other school administrations, and staff may also ask about students. Huey (1996) clarifies by recommending that counselors adhere to local school policies to the extent possible without compromising their primary responsibility to the client. In cases of conflict between loyalty to the student and to the employer, Huey recommends a resolution that protects the rights of the student in the particular case and also working to change policies that create such conflicts. Obviously school counselors should ask about employer policies and expectations before competing demands complicate the counselor's responsibilities toward keeping a child's communications confidential.

Another dilemma may emerge over confidentiality when the counselor's personal beliefs, experiences, and values conflict with the situation. Varhely and

How could you accomplish those things in the following situation? You have been seeing Lorraine, a ninth grader, for several weeks. She has an intense home situation with her parents' crumbling marriage and multiple affairs. Her grades have dropped significantly, and she is often sullen and withdrawn in the classroom. Twice she has been disrespectful to the teacher. In the hallway Lorraine's math teacher finds you to talk about his frustration with her grades and behavior. The teacher wonders aloud why her sessions with you have not translated to better academic performance. He is asking you for information to help understand Lorraine's classroom and school problems.

Cowles (1991) admonish counselors to be aware of their own beliefs about the rights and responsibilities of children, their own needs for belonging and feeling adequate, and their personal value system. Unless counselors participate in an ongoing process of self-awareness, they may complicate already difficult situations.

The legal status relevant to a discussion of confidentiality is privileged communication, the protection clients have from their communications being disclosed in a legal proceeding. According to Glosoff, Herlihy, and Spence (2000), 45 jurisdictions have given privileged communication rights to the counselor–client relationship and in some states that includes school counselors. School counselors must investigate whether privilege applies in their state and must examine the limits to that in the law. The level of privilege involves a complicated legal determination (Waldo & Malley, 1992).

ETHICS IN GROUP WORK

Hessian works in a middle school. He is leading a group for newcomers to the school. As in most years the group conversations have evolved into the stress of being a new person in a different environment. One member of the current group, Geneva, has many home problems. She has talked about the relocation and how the mother's unemployment and distance from the extended family have made home life strained. A day after the last group meeting Hessian receives a phone call from the father of another group member who was extremely concerned about Geneva. The father thinks his child is being subjected to an unnecessary burden of another group member's problems and wants his daughter out of the group. Hessian is caught between the daughter's wanting to stay in the group and the father believing it best to remove her from this worry. Group issues of confidentiality, the rights of the minor, and the principles of group work will all be involved in the resolution of this problem.

School counselors who work with small groups will find the Ethical Guidelines for Group Counselors (Association for Specialists in Group Work, 1989) and Rapin and Keel's (1998) Best Practice Guidelines, as well as the ASCA ethical standards, valuable resources. All these standards refer to screening potential group members, protecting the safety and attending to the growth of each group member, and building a norm of confidentiality.

The planning and implementation of groups in schools may present ethical dilemmas (Terres & Larrabee, 1985; Corey, Corey, Callanan, & Russell, 1988). Before they begin, school counselors must assess their competence as a group leader for the specific type of group being planned. They must also consider the appropriateness of the particular group topic in the school setting. Counselors must gauge the suitability of the specific student to the group and to the group experience. Ritchie and Huss (2000) attend to other considerations in recruiting and screening students for groups in schools. For example, counselors must consider student and parent rights and the internal and external constraints of the school setting when planning groups. ASCA ethical standards propose notification of parents about group participation if counselors deem that appropriate and if that practice fits school district policies.

Pregroup screening concerns include age, gender, diversity, group fit, and group contribution. Hines and Fields (2002) also discuss the issues of parent permission, confidentiality, and inappropriate referrals. They provide suggestions for a protocol for screening group members in schools. Counselors will need to consider the developmental age of the participants as they make provisions for space, privacy, session length, and group duration. Counselors will also want to follow up with members after the group ends.

Counselors should give participating students and their parents information about the purpose of the group, the leader's qualifications, and other details about the group process. Counselors who begin the group with a discussion of the importance of confidentiality and remind group members of that each meeting may alleviate some problems (Corey & Corey, 2001). School counselors can only provide their personal guarantee for maintaining the standard of confidentiality but should stress to group members the importance of keeping private anything shared in the group.

EXCEPTIONS TO CONFIDENTIALITY

As mentioned earlier in order to protect children from harm some situations require counselors to breach confidentiality. Three of those circumstances are the duty to protect, the duty to warn, and the requirement to report child abuse. Counselors decide on their actions—trying to balance confidentiality and those duties to warn and protect—on a case-by-case basis (Sheeley & Herlihy, 1989). The following sections include discussions of those difficult conditions.

Danger to Self

In an all-female career exploration group one student, Sasha, answered the question "where will you be in 5 years?" by saying "I will probably be dead." The other group members asked what she meant, and she responded "I may do something stupid" and refused to give any further explanation. The group responded by avoiding further comment and moving to their own hopes. The leader of the group asked Sasha to stay for a minute after the bell rang. After being assured that she would have a ride home, Sasha sat with the group leader and another counselor in the school who asked her questions about what she meant and the details of any plan she had to kill herself. After they listened to her answers and communicated to her their concerns, the counselors called her mother to come in immediately and discuss their fears for Sasha's safety.

Some authors have the following suggestions for working with students who may be at risk of hurting themselves (Sheeley & Herlihy, 1989; Remley & Sparkman, 1993):

- Know the warning signs of students who have the potential for suicide.
- Establish a plan for dealing with the crisis.

- Have referral sources for crisis situations.
- Build the skills to work with students and families in the case of a threat of suicide.
- Take action if you determine a student is at risk.
- Consider actions that are the least intrusive but will ensure the safety of the suicidal person.
- Consult with trusted colleagues to determine risk and appropriate action.
- Inform school administrators and parents if a student is at risk of attempting suicide.
- If those adults are reluctant to become involved, do all that is possible to protect the client.

Capuzzi (2002) provides ideas for working with suicidal children in three different ways. He describes efforts aimed at suicide prevention such as talking with administrators, delivering faculty and staff in-service programs, preparing crisis teams, giving individual and group counseling options, making parent education available, and doing classroom presentations. In a crisis management stage, Capuzzi recommends assessing, directing, monitoring, and guiding a person in order to avert an act of self-destruction. He says that parents must be notified if a person is determined to be a potential suicidal by at least two professionals. He also outlines ways to work after a suicide in postvention efforts. More specifics can be found in his article.

Discuss with your classmates a situation from your school days that involved suicide or a suicide attempt. What did the adults do? How aware were you of ways to support a person who was contemplating suicide? Did students seek help for self-harming issues from mental health professionals in school? Were you aware of any prevention efforts to help depressed young people?

Stone and Dahir (2006) discuss a critical case related to suicide. They explain that negligence is a tort law that involves injury or damage to another person through a breach of duty owed to that person. In the *Eisel v. Board of Education of Montgomery County* (1991) the courts found that school counselors had a duty to notify parents when a 13-year-old student made suicidal statements to her fellow students even though Nicole Eisel denied making the comments. The counselors did not notify the parents or school administrators after questioning the girl. Shortly after Nicole and another student died as they carried out a suicide pact. The Maryland court ruling established that school counselors have a duty to take reasonable means to prevent suicide. Results in other states vary. Three rulings have found school employees legally liable for failing to prevent students' suicides and five others have not imposed liability in those cases. Stone and Dahir recommend never ignoring a suicidal threat but considering it as a cry for help of someone who is volatile and fragile. The school counselor's legal liability has been met when school officials or parents have been notified and appropriate actions have been recommended.

As you can see school counselors have some guidance when working with students at risk for suicide. Fewer resources are available to help when working with other dangerous behaviors that may be viewed as harm to self such as eating disorders, substance abuse, reckless sexual activity, cult membership, criminal behavior, and self-mutilation. School counselors must consider the degree these behaviors constitute a clear and immediate potential for harm that might necessitate breaking confidentiality. Froeschle and Moyer (2004) recommend maintaining confidentiality if at all possible. They suggest that counselors work to encourage students to share their problems with parents and for counselors to reveal information if the risk for greater self-harm increases. Josephina, one of the Questers, is relieved to hear what Froeschle and Moyer recommend. She has been working for the past 6 weeks with a ninth-grade girl who cuts herself about once a week. Josephina has been weighing the risks of revealing the girl's secret against the progress that seems to be occurring in the counseling relationship. Finally, the ninth grader has agreed to meet with Josephina and a parent to discuss her risky habit. Josephina and the other counselors have decided they are going to ask the school board attorney to clarify their legal duties in cases of dangerous behavior and then see if they can create some districtwide protocols for guidance on when to disclose those risky actions.

Duty to Warn

Another situation that may require a counselor to disclose the contents of counseling may arise when a student reveals potential danger to another person. Waldo and Malley (1992) point out that counselors must take reasonable action to protect an identifiable third party. They propose four criteria to use when counselors have to decide about the duty to warn an intended victim. First, consider if there is a special relationship to the dangerous person or to the potential victim. Then, determine if there is a clear threat and an imminence of danger. Third, consider whether the potential victim can be identified. Finally, they advise counselors to show reasonable care in making their decisions. According to Waldo and Malley the judicial system has defined some obligations of school counselors in cases that involve the duty to warn: (1) assembling necessary background information, (2) conferring with a psychiatrist when consultation is necessary, and (3) keeping careful records. They suggest seeking professional legal advice. Counselors may choose several actions to protect someone at risk. They may make a referral by notifying the parents of the student client. They may notify a probation officer or the police. They may designate someone to inform the intended victim. They can warn the potential victim. Other possibilities include detaining the client or seeking a voluntary or involuntary commitment to a mental facility.

Many times the threat may not be explicit. Hermann and Finn (2002) examine the ethical and legal duties of counselors in protecting students from violence in schools. School violence includes behaviors such as assaults, fights, threats, other destructive acts, robbery, harassment, rape, bullying, and gang violence. Hermann and Finn suggest that counselors provide violence prevention activities, risk assessment techniques, and interventions for potential risks. Their recommendations also include taking every threat seriously, attending to the context of the threat, consulting, and documenting actions. The assessment of potential violence is difficult. Herman (2002) surveyed practicing counselors who say they feel prepared to report suspected child abuse and to determine suicidal risk but need more training on determining the risk of violence. Additionally many school policies require that any threat of violence be reported thus complicating the counselors' responsibility to the child and to the school.

Ricardo had been in such a bind. An English teacher in his middle school brought him a notebook that had been left in a desk in the classroom. The book contained a detailed plan of the school building, paragraphs detailing mistreatment by a school bully, and an outline of a plan for revenge that involved knives and explosives. It did not take much investigating to determine who owned the notebook, Jerome, a small sixth grader who was having a hard time adjusting to the middle school. Ricardo and the English teacher talked to Jerome, telling him about their concerns. He was contrite and persistent in assuring them that his notebook contained only fantasies, a game he was playing with some classmates. Nevertheless the adults called in the assistant principal and the school safety officer. The school district had a zero tolerance policy and when a large knife was discovered in Jerome's locker, he was suspended for the rest of the school year. Even though Ricardo was unconvinced Jerome posed a significant risk, the precautions seemed necessary.

Reporting Child Abuse

Each state has a law that mandates some type of reporting for suspected cases of child abuse although the specifics of the laws vary by state. School counselors should know the requirements in their states and the procedures in their school district. These laws, as many others, can be revised and should be monitored for changes. Sandberg, Crabbs, and Crabbs (1988) compiled a helpful resource for understanding legal issues in child abuse in a frequently asked questions format. Some pertinent definitions can be found at the Childhelp USA Web site (www.childhelpusa.org/abuseinfo_signs.htm) as well as the information provided below.

Abuse means inflicting physical harm on the body of a child, continual psychological damage, or denial of emotional needs. Some signs and examples of child abuse are the following: extensive bruises or patterns of bruises; burns or burn patterns; lacerations, welts, or abrasions; injuries inconsistent with information offered; sexual abuse; emotional disturbances caused by continuous friction in the home, marital discord, or mentally ill parents; cruel treatment.

Neglect means the failure to provide necessities such as food, care, clothing, shelter, supervision, or medical attention for a child. Children who suffer from neglect are those who are malnourished, ill-clad, dirty, without proper sleeping arrangements, or lacking in appropriate health care. Other indications are children who are unattended and lacking adequate supervision, who are ill and lacking essential medical attention, who are irregularly and illegally absent from school, who are exploited and overworked, who lack essential psychological or emotional nurturing, or who are abandoned.

Remley and Fry (1993) recognize multiple roles school counselors play in reporting child abuse: informant, counselor to the victim or perpetrator, employee, liaison, court witness, and counselor to the family. The ASCA (2003c) position statement on the professional school counselor and child abuse and neglect includes counselor responsibilities beyond the reporting of child abuse. Counselors are encouraged to provide programs to educate and support other school personnel so they can help protect children from abuse and neglect. Minard (1993) recommends holding child abuse/neglect prevention programs. Counselors are also asked to work with the children and/or the families in crisis or to refer them to someone who can. The role of reporting child abuse, carrying out these multiple roles, and serving as a resource for many people make situations related to reporting a large responsibility for school counselors. Howell-Nigrelli (1988) suggests that counselors hone their qualities of awareness, knowledge, commitment, and effective communication skills to face this challenging process.

Bryant and Milsom (2005) have a different recommendation for school counselors. Their article refers specifically to school counselors' procedures for reporting child abuse and the decisions related to reporting or not. The authors suggest a team consultation report for each school site. The team would be charged with reviewing policies and procedures, distributing relevant research and information to school staff, serving as a support group, and mediating problems that arise. That team consultation possibility could be expanded to any of the difficult legal and ethical issues that arise in schools. Some members of the Questers will constitute that team in their schools and will report on the effectiveness of this model. Bryant and Milsom also suggest working closely with the professionals that investigate child abuse so that counselors can gain understanding about the expectations and restrictions of social service agencies.

Little information is available on rape, statutory rape, and child abuse (Mitchell & Rogers, 2003). Child sexual abuse involves someone who is in a custodial role. Rape is unlawful sexual activity with a person "without consent and usually by force or threat of injury" (p. 333). In statutory rape there is no custodial role and coercion is not included in the definition except in South Carolina. Statutory rape is unlawful sexual intercourse with someone under the age of consent (usually between 14 and 16 years). Some states include an age range between the age of consent and a specified number of years of the older partner, usually between 2 to 5 years. Mitchell and Rogers (2003) remind us that although states require the reporting of child abuse, rape and statutory rape are not included in these statutes. Counselors who are uncertain about whether sexual activity must be reported may want to present the case as a hypothetical situation and consult with others about appropriate action. Mitchell and Rogers (2003) report that California, Florida, and Tennessee have revised reporting standards for health workers in cases of rape. Counselors should investigate the laws regarding rape and statutory rape in their own states.

Special Considerations

Counselors may wrestle with situations related to youth sexuality such as counseling minors about birth control or abortion and counseling students with AIDS/HIV. Some authors (Stone & Dahir, 2006; McWhirter, McWhirter, McWhirter, & McWhirter, 2004; Gustafson & McNamara, 1987) acknowledge the stress in determining whether to tell parents about their offspring's sexual activity, particularly if the minor is seeking birth control or abortion information.

As noted previously, some states require reporting and other states prohibit reporting. In some states minors have the right to discuss sexually transmitted diseases, pregnancy prevention, or aborting a pregnancy without parents being notified (Stadler, 1986).

In an earlier review of court cases related to abortions Talbutt (1983) concluded that counselors should know school district policy, state laws, and current related court rulings. She recommends urging the young person to involve parents and asks counselors to establish procedures before the issues arise. Stone (2002) offers a more recent report. She says that 42 states have laws demanding some kind of parent involvement before a minor's abortion. She explains a case, *Arnold v. Board of Education of Escambia County* (1989), in which a young person had an abortion and decided not to inform her parents. The student had been to see a school counselor. The courts found that the school counselor had not coerced the student and was not liable for giving advice to seek the abortion. Stone notes that because school counselors have responsibility to students, parents, and schools, they must take particular care in such value-laden circumstances. Her advice is to know policies; consider the developmental level of the student and that individual's ability to make informed, sound decisions; consider parents' rights; investigate diversity issues; consult with a colleague; be aware of personal values; and avoid being involved with the student's medical care.

The ASCA (2004c) ethical standards give counselors some guidance when working with a student who is infected with a potentially fatal disease such as HIV. Unless state law dictates otherwise, those ASCA guidelines state that school counselors may reveal to a clearly identifiable third party who may be at a high risk of contracting a communicable and fatal disease (HIV/AIDS) as a result of a relationship with an infected person. The disclosure would occur only after other avenues have been tried. First, the counselor should recommend that the partner be notified by the student. The student should be admonished from persisting in such high-risk behavior. If the student refuses, the counselor should tell the student about the intent to inform the partner of the danger and then should do so. Counselors should seek legal guidance about disclosing in these cases.

Costin, Page, Pietrzak, Kerr, and Symons (2002) asked school counselors what they knew and believed about HIV/AIDS. The authors discovered a need for more education about the implications for counseling in schools, particularly one's personal beliefs about the disease and the beliefs about risks in schools. Lynch (1993) discusses counseling someone with AIDS and balancing confidentiality with the duty to protect. Her article as well as the ASCA position statement on AIDS (ASCA, 2001b) promotes positive health education, knowledge of resources, and staying in the primary role of counseling. Stone and Dahir (2006) clarify, "If there is not a state statute forbidding you to disclose a person's HIV+ status to a partner, then mental health professionals are permitted to notify partners in keeping with their ethical codes, but are not required to do so. Moreover, in most state statutes there is language that says that mental health professionals may not be held civilly or criminally liable for failure to notify their students' partner(s)" (p. 316). McWhirter and colleagues (2004) have other recommendations such as notifying state public health agencies.

What state health policies refer to the reporting of sexually transmitted diseases? What implications do those policies have for counseling someone who may have a nonfatal sexually transmitted disease?

Those authors stress that practice helps maintain the client's confidentiality while warning the identifiable third party.

Sexual Harassment

The seriousness of sexual harassment in schools cannot be overstated. Some children live in dread of walking in the hallways. The victims of harassment may blame themselves, may doubt themselves, may use techniques to avoid the harassment, and may choose to endure it rather than risking being considered a tattler (Stone & Dahir, 2006). Fortunately, school counselors have strong legal and ethical supports for addressing the unhealthy interactions sexual harassment creates. Such behavior is now understood as destructive and illegal although studies of the extent of the problem reveal an alarming pervasiveness. An average of 81% of students, boys and girls, reported being subjected to unwanted sexual attention in school (American Association of University Women, 2001).

Davis v. Monroe County Board of Education (1999) is a Supreme Court ruling that established the financial impacts of not taking action to address sexual harassment. That ruling decreed the standard that if the harassment is known to educators and is so severe, pervasive, and offensive that the victim has limited access to school's educational opportunities, schools must take corrective action. The Office of Civil Rights directs each school district to have specific policies and procedures for addressing sexual harassment in schools (Office of Civil Rights, 2001). School counselors are required to report the harassment but not the identity of the victim. "A student's request for confidentiality should be respected even if this hinders the investigation of the harassment and even if it impedes the disciplinary action against the person who is accused of the harassment" (Stone & Dahir, 2006, p. 323).

> Find a school district's sexual harassment policy and the reporting procedures. Compare what you found to the policies your classmates discovered.

Subpoenas

The Questers have reviewed many of the legal and ethical concerns they face in schools. They have looked at many policies and discussed many ways to prevent situations from becoming more difficult. They have also formed subgroups to serve as peer consultants when they need help making ethical decisions. Sydney, an elementary counselor, has a concern that has not been addressed. She has just been served with a subpoena and is not sure what to do.

Counselors may encounter the legal system in a formal way. Sometimes counselors are called to testify in cases of divorce or other legal proceedings. The formal request to comply is a legal document called a subpoena. Subpoenas are official court documents that may require counselors to supply records; to appear for a deposition, court hearing, or trial; or to both supply records and appear (Cottone & Travydas, 2006). If a subpoena is issued to a school counselor, that person should take care in responding by consulting with personal legal counsel to determine if the document is valid and whether a response is necessary. An attorney can advise about the correct manner in which to respond (Remley & Herlihy, 2005). Counselors should notify their supervisors as well. Counselors should not ignore subpoenas because they could be imprisoned or fined if the document is appropriate and they do not comply.

Remley and Herlihy (2005) explain that subpoenas are used in different ways in legal proceedings. In the discovery phase, a time when attorneys are gathering relevant information before their cases come to trial, lawyers may ask a witness to respond to written questions and/or to come to offices for depositions. Counselors should ask their own attorney to review answers or to accompany them to depositions if possible. Counselors may also be asked to appear in court and to testify in hearings or trials. In all cases the counselor will be asked to swear to tell the truth in those proceedings. Remley and Herlihy recommend sending copies of records rather than originals and to omit any information received from others, such as physicians or other mental health professionals. Both Remley and Herlihy (2005) and Cottone and Travydas (2006) have more detailed information on responding to subpoenas.

SUMMARY

The Questers have completed their study and now feel more confident in facing the difficult decisions they encounter. They have practiced a decision-making model and related it to several situations. They have compared the ethical considerations that result from their responsibilities to students, parents, the schools, and the profession. They know more now about the tension of protecting privacy and balancing safety consideration. Most important, they now have a group of colleagues with whom they can discuss their dilemmas and weigh the costs and benefits of their decisions.

PORTFOLIO COMPONENTS

1. Find your state laws related to child abuse reporting, school counselor confidentiality limitations, minor's rights to request health services, age of majority, child protective services, and juvenile justice procedures.
2. Interview two school counselors about the three most difficult ethical decisions they have faced. Summarize the similarities and differences in the situations and resulting action.
3. Discuss how you would proceed in the following situation. Barney, a sixth grader, comes to the counseling office often. He talks about playing with a BB gun and says he has shot another boy in the neighborhood but "It was fun because he wasn't hurt." Barney lives with his 80-year-old grandparents who are in failing health. The grandparents have custody. No one has information about the parents. Barney says he knows where other guns are in the house, but he's not sure about ammunition. He is a charming young man but when asked the difference between right and wrong says, "Yeah, sometimes I know and sometimes I don't and sometimes I don't care."

APPENDIX A

The Role of the Professional School Counselor

The professional school counselor is a certified/licensed educator trained in school counseling with unique qualifications and skills to address all students' academic, personal/social and career development needs. Professional school counselors implement a comprehensive school counseling program that promotes and enhances student achievement. Professional school counselors are employed in elementary, middle/junior high and high schools and in district supervisory, counselor education and post-secondary settings. Their work is differentiated by attention to developmental stages of student growth, including the needs, tasks and student interests related to those stages.

Professional school counselors serve a vital role in maximizing student achievement. Incorporating leadership, advocacy and collaboration, professional school counselors promote equity and access to opportunities and rigorous educational experiences for all students. Professional school counselors support a safe learning environment and work to safeguard the human rights of all members of the school community. Collaborating with other stakeholders to promote student achievement, professional school counselors address the needs of all students through prevention and intervention programs that are a part of a comprehensive school counseling program. To achieve maximum program effectiveness, the American School Counselor Association recommends a counselor-to-student ratio of 1:250.

Professional school counselors have a master's degree or higher in school counseling or the substantial equivalent, meet the state certification/licensure standards and abide by the laws of the states in which they are employed. They uphold the ethical and professional standards of professional counseling associations and promote the development of the school counseling program based on the following areas of the ASCA National Model: foundation, delivery, management and accountability.

FOUNDATION

Professional school counselors identify personal beliefs and philosophies as to how all students benefit from the school counseling program and act on these beliefs and philosophies to guide the development, implementation and evaluation of a comprehensive school counseling program. Professional school counselors create a mission statement supporting the school's mission and collaborate with other individuals and organizations to promote all students' academic, career and personal/social development.

DELIVERY

Professional school counselors provide services to students, parents, school staff and the community in the following areas:

- School Guidance Curriculum—This curriculum consists of structured lessons designed to help students achieve the desired competencies and to provide all students with the knowledge and skills appropriate for their developmental level. The school guidance curriculum is delivered throughout the school's overall curriculum and is systematically presented by professional school counselors in collaboration with other professional educators in K–12 classroom and group activities.
- Individual Student Planning—Professional school counselors coordinate ongoing systemic activities designed to help students establish personal goals and develop future plans.
- Responsive Services—Responsive services are preventative and/or interventive activities meeting students' immediate and future needs. These needs can be necessitated by events and conditions in students' lives and may require any of the following:
  - individual or group counseling
  - consultation with parents, teachers and other educators
  - referrals to other school support services or community resources
  - peer helping
  - information

Professional school counselors develop confidential relationships with students to help them resolve or cope with problems and developmental concerns.

- System Support—System support consists of management activities establishing, maintaining and enhancing the total school counseling program. These activities include professional development, consultation, collaboration, program management and operations. Professional school counselors are committed to continual personal and professional development and are proactively involved in professional organizations promoting school counseling at the local, state and national levels.

MANAGEMENT

Professional school counselors incorporate organizational processes and tools that are concrete, clearly delineated and reflective of the school's needs. Tools and processes include:

- Agreements developed with and approved by administrators at the beginning of the school year addressing how the school counseling program is organized and what goals will be accomplished
- Advisory councils made up of students, parents, teachers, counselors administrators and community members to review school counseling program results and to make recommendations
- Use of student data to affect systemic change within the school system so every student receives the benefit of the school counseling program
- Action plans for prevention and intervention services defining the desired student competencies and achievement results
- Allotment of 80 percent of the professional school counselor's time in direct service with students
- Use of master and weekly calendars to keep students, parents, teachers and administrators informed and to encourage active participation in the school counseling program

ACCOUNTABILITY

To demonstrate the effectiveness of the school counseling program in measurable terms, professional school counselors report on immediate, intermediate and long-range results showing how students are different as a result of the school counseling program. Professional school counselors use data to show the impact of the school counseling program on school improvement and student achievement. Professional school counselors conduct school counseling program audits to guide future action and improve future results for all students. The performance of the professional school counselor is evaluated on basic standards of practice expected of professional school counselors implementing a school counseling program.

SUMMARY

Professional school counselors are certified/licensed professionals with a masters' degree or higher in school counseling or the substantial equivalent and are uniquely qualified to address the developmental needs of all students. Professional school counselors deliver a comprehensive school counseling program encouraging all students' academic, career and personal/social development and helping all students in maximizing student achievement.

Revised June 2004

Source: From *The Role of the Professional School Counselor,* by American School
Counselor Association, 2004, Alexandria, VA: Author. Retrieved from
http://www.schoolcounselor.org/content.asp?pl=133&sl=2408&contented=240.
Reprinted by permission.

A P P E N D I X   B

ASCA National Standards

ACADEMIC DEVELOPMENT

ASCA National Standards for academic development guide school counseling programs to implement strategies and activities to support and maximize each student's ability to learn.

Standard A: Students will acquire the attitudes, knowledge and skills that contribute to effective learning in school and across the life span.

A:A1 Improve Academic Self-concept
A:A1.1   Articulate feelings of competence and confidence as learners
A:A1.2   Display a positive interest in learning
A:A1.3   Take pride in work and achievement
A:A1.4   Accept mistakes as essential to the learning process
A:A1.5   Identify attitudes and behaviors that lead to successful learning

A:A2 Acquire Skills for Improving Learning
A:A2.1   Apply time-management and task-management skills
A:A2.2   Demonstrate how effort and persistence positively affect learning
A:A2.3   Use communications skills to know when and how to ask for help when needed
A:A2.4   Apply knowledge and learning styles to positively influence school performance

A:A3 Achieve School Success
A:A3.1   Take responsibility for their actions
A:A3.2   Demonstrate the ability to work independently, as well as the ability to work cooperatively with other students
A:A3.3   Develop a broad range of interests and abilities
A:A3.4   Demonstrate dependability, productivity and initiative
A:A3.5   Share knowledge

Standard B: Students will complete school with the academic preparation essential to choose from a wide range of substantial post-secondary options, including college.

A:B1 Improve Learning

A:B1.1   Demonstrate the motivation to achieve individual potential

A:B1.2   Learn and apply critical-thinking skills

A:B1.3   Apply the study skills necessary for academic success at each level

A:B1.4   Seek information and support from faculty, staff, family and peers

A:B1.5   Organize and apply academic information from a variety of sources

A:B1.6   Use knowledge of learning styles to positively influence school performance

A:B1.7   Become a self-directed and independent learner

A:B2 Plan to Achieve Goals

A:B2.1   Establish challenging academic goals in elementary, middle/jr. high and high school

A:B2.2   Use assessment results in educational planning

A:B2.3   Develop and implement annual plan of study to maximize academic ability and achievement

A:B2.4   Apply knowledge of aptitudes and interests to goal setting

A:B2.5   Use problem-solving and decision-making skills to assess progress toward educational goals

A:B2.6   Understand the relationship between classroom performance and success in school

A:B2.7   Identify post-secondary options consistent with interests, achievement, aptitude and abilities

Standard C: Students will understand the relationship of academics to the world of work and to life at home and in the community.

A:C1 Relate School to Life Experiences

A:C1.1   Demonstrate the ability to balance school, studies, extracurricular activities, leisure time and family life

A:C1.2   Seek co-curricular and community experiences to enhance the school experience

A:C1.3   Understand the relationship between learning and work

A:C1.4   Demonstrate an understanding of the value of lifelong learning as essential to seeking, obtaining and maintaining life goals

A:C1.5   Understand that school success is the preparation to make the transition from student to community member

A:C1.6   Understand how school success and academic achievement enhance future career and vocational opportunities

CAREER DEVELOPMENT

ASCA National Standards for career development guide school counseling programs to provide the foundation for the acquisition of skills, attitudes and knowledge that enable students to make a successful transition from school to the world of work, and from job to job across the life span.

Standard A: Students will acquire the skills to investigate the world of work in relation to knowledge of self and to make informed career decisions.

C:A1 Develop Career Awareness

C:A1.1   Develop skills to locate, evaluate and interpret career information

C:A1.2   Learn about the variety of traditional and nontraditional occupations

C:A1.3   Develop an awareness of personal abilities, skills, interests and motivations

C:A1.4   Learn how to interact and work cooperatively in teams

C:A1.5   Learn to make decisions

C:A1.6   Learn how to set goals

C:A1.7   Understand the importance of planning

C:A1.8   Pursue and develop competency in areas of interest

C:A1.9   Develop hobbies and vocational interests

C:A1.10   Balance between work and leisure time

C:A2 Develop Employment Readiness

C:A2.1   Acquire employability skills such as working on a team, problem-solving and organizational skills

C:A2.2   Apply job readiness skills to seek employment opportunities

C:A2.3   Demonstrate knowledge about the changing workplace

C:A2.4   Learn about the rights and responsibilities of employers and employees

C:A2.5   Learn to respect individual uniqueness in the workplace

C:A2.6   Learn how to write a résumé

C:A2.7   Develop a positive attitude toward work and learning

C:A2.8   Understand the importance of responsibility, dependability, punctuality, integrity and effort in the workplace

C:A2.9   Utilize time- and task-management skills

Standard B: Students will employ strategies to achieve future career goals with success and satisfaction.

C:B1 Acquire Career Information

C:B1.1   Apply decision-making skills to career planning, course selection and career transition

C:B1.2   Identify personal skills, interests and abilities and relate them to current career choice

C:B1.3   Demonstrate knowledge of the career-planning process

C:B1.4   Know the various ways in which occupations can be classified

C:B1.5   Use research and information resources to obtain career information

C:B1.6   Learn to use the Internet to access career-planning information

C:B1.7   Describe traditional and nontraditional career choices and how they relate to career choice

C:B1.8   Understand how changing economic and societal needs influence employment trends and future training

C:B2 Identify Career Goals

C:B2.1   Demonstrate awareness of the education and training needed to achieve career goals

C:B2.2   Assess and modify their educational plan to support career

C:B2.3   Use employability and job readiness skills in internship, mentoring, shadowing and/or other work experience

C:B2.4   Select course work that is related to career interests

C:B2.5   Maintain a career-planning portfolio

Standard C: Students will understand the relationship between personal qualities, education, training and the world of work.

C:C1 Acquire Knowledge to Achieve Career Goals

C:C1.1   Understand the relationship between educational achievement and career success

C:C1.2   Explain how work can help to achieve personal success and satisfaction

C:C1.3   Identify personal preferences and interests influencing career choice and success

C:C1.4   Understand that the changing workplace requires lifelong learning and acquiring new skills

C:C1.5   Describe the effect of work on lifestyle

C:C1.6   Understand the importance of equity and access in career choice

C:C1.7   Understand that work is an important and satisfying means of personal expression

C:C2 Apply Skills to Achieve Career Goals

C:C2.1   Demonstrate how interests, abilities and achievement relate to achieving personal, social, educational and career goals

C:C2.2   Learn how to use conflict management skills with peers and adults

C:C2.3   Learn to work cooperatively with others as a team member

C:C2.4   Apply academic and employment readiness skills in work based learning situations such as internships, shadowing and/or mentoring experiences

PERSONAL/SOCIAL DEVELOPMENT

ASCA National Standards for personal/social development guide school counseling programs to provide the foundation for personal and social growth as students progress through school and into adulthood.

Standard A: Students will acquire the knowledge, attitudes and interpersonal skills to help them understand and respect self and others.

PS:A1 Acquire Self-knowledge

PS:A1.1   Develop positive attitudes toward self as a unique and worthy person

PS:A1.2   Identify values, attitudes and beliefs

PS:A1.3   Learn the goal-setting process
PS:A1.4   Understand change is a part of growth
PS:A1.5   Identify and express feelings
PS:A1.6   Distinguish between appropriate and inappropriate behavior
PS:A1.7   Recognize personal boundaries, rights and privacy needs
PS:A1.8   Understand the need for self-control and how to practice it
PS:A1.9   Demonstrate cooperative behavior in groups
PS:A1.10   Identify personal strengths and assets
PS:A1.11   Identify and discuss changing personal and social roles
PS:A1.12   Identify and recognize changing family roles

PS:A2 Acquire Interpersonal Skills

PS:A2.1   Recognize that everyone has rights and responsibilities
PS:A2.2   Respect alternative points of view
PS:A2.3   Recognize, accept, respect and appreciate individual differences
PS:A2.4   Recognize, accept and appreciate ethnic and cultural diversity
PS:A2.5   Recognize and respect differences in various family configurations
PS:A2.6   Use effective communications skills
PS:A2.7   Know that communication involves speaking, listening and nonverbal behavior
PS:A2.8   Learn how to make and keep friends

Standard B: Students will make decisions, set goals and take necessary action to achieve goals.

PS:B1 Self-knowledge Application

PS:B1.1   Use a decision-making and problem-solving model
PS:B1.2   Understand consequences of decisions and choices
PS:B1.3   Identify alternative solutions to a problem
PS:B1.4   Develop effective coping skills for dealing with problems
PS:B1.5   Demonstrate when, where and how to seek help for solving problems and making decisions
PS:B1.6   Know how to apply conflict resolution skills
PS:B1.7   Demonstrate a respect and appreciation for individual and cultural differences
PS:B1.8   Know when peer pressure is influencing a decision
PS:B1.9   Identify long- and short-term goals
PS:B1.10   Identify alternative ways of achieving goals
PS:B1.11   Use persistence and perseverance in acquiring knowledge and skills
PS:B1.12   Develop an action plan to set and achieve realistic goals

Standard C: Students will understand safety and survival skills.

PS:C1 Acquire Personal Safety Skills

PS:C1.1   Demonstrate knowledge of personal information (i.e., telephone number, home address, emergency contact)
PS:C1.2   Learn about the relationship between rules, laws, safety and the protection of rights of the individual

PS:C1.3 Learn about the differences between appro-
         priate and inappropriate physical contact
PS:C1.4 Demonstrate the ability to set boundaries, rights and personal
         privacy
PS:C1.5 Differentiate between situations requiring peer support and situa-
         tions requiring adult professional help
PS:C1.6 Identify resource people in the school and community, and know
         how to seek their help
PS:C1.7 Apply effective problem-solving and decision-making skills to
         make safe and healthy choices
PS:C1.8 Learn about the emotional and physical dangers of substance use
         and abuse
PS:C1.9 Learn how to cope with peer pressure
PS:C1.10 Learn techniques for managing stress and conflict
PS:C1.11 Learn coping skills for managing life events

Source: From *The ASCA National Standards,* by American School Counselor Association, Alexandria: VA: Author. Retrieved from http://www.schoolcounselor.org/rc_files/ASCA%20standards.doc. Reprinted by permissions.

Ethical Standards for School Counselors

Revised June 26, 2004

The American School Counselor Association (ASCA) is a professional organization whose members are certified/licensed in school counseling with unique qualifications and skills to address the academic, personal/social and career development needs of all students. Professional school counselors are advocates, leaders, collaborators and consultants who create opportunities for equity in access and success in educational opportunities by connecting their programs to the mission of schools and subscribing to the following tenets of professional responsibility:

- Each person has the right to be respected, be treated with dignity and have access to a comprehensive school counseling program that advocates for and affirms all students from diverse populations regardless of ethnic/racial status, age, economic status, special needs, English as a second language or other language group, immigration status, sexual orientation, gender, gender identity/expression, family type, religious/spiritual identity and appearance.
- Each person has the right to receive the information and support needed to move toward self-direction and self-development and affirmation within one's group identities, with special care being given to students who have historically not received adequate educational services: students of color, low socio-economic students, students with disabilities and students with nondominant language backgrounds.

- Each person has the right to understand the full magnitude and meaning of his/her educational choices and how those choices will affect future opportunities.
- Each person has the right to privacy and thereby the right to expect the counselor-student relationship to comply with all laws, policies and ethical standards pertaining to confidentiality in the school setting.

In this document, ASCA specifies the principles of ethical behavior necessary to maintain the high standards of integrity, leadership and professionalism among its members. The Ethical Standards for School Counselors were developed to clarify the nature of ethical responsibilities held in common by school counseling professionals. The purposes of this document are to:

- Serve as a guide for the ethical practices of all professional school counselors regardless of level, area, population served or membership in this professional association;
- Provide self-appraisal and peer evaluations regarding counselor responsibilities to students, parents/guardians, colleagues and professional associates, schools, communities and the counseling profession; and
- Inform those served by the school counselor of acceptable counselor practices and expected professional behavior.

A.1. Responsibilities to Students

The professional school counselor:

a. Has a primary obligation to the student, who is to be treated with respect as a unique individual.
b. Is concerned with the educational, academic, career, personal and social needs and encourages the maximum development of every student.
c. Respects the student's values and beliefs and does not impose the counselor's personal values.
d. Is knowledgeable of laws, regulations and policies relating to students and strives to protect and inform students regarding their rights.

A.2. Confidentiality

The professional school counselor:

a. Informs students of the purposes, goals, techniques and rules of procedure under which they may receive counseling at or before the time when the counseling relationship is entered. Disclosure notice includes the limits of confidentiality such as the possible necessity for consulting with other professionals, privileged communication, and legal or authoritative restraints. The meaning and limits of confidentiality are defined in developmentally appropriate terms to students.
b. Keeps information confidential unless disclosure is required to prevent clear and imminent danger to the student or others or when legal requirements demand that confidential information be revealed. Counselors will consult with appropriate professionals when in doubt as to the validity of an exception.

c. In absence of state legislation expressly forbidding disclosure, considers the ethical responsibility to provide information to an identified third party who, by his/her relationship with the student, is at a high risk of contracting a disease that is commonly known to be communicable and fatal. Disclosure requires satisfaction of all of the following conditions:
   - Student identifies partner or the partner is highly identifiable
   - Counselor recommends the student notify partner and refrain from further high-risk behavior
   - Student refuses
   - Counselor informs the student of the intent to notify the partner
   - Counselor seeks legal consultation as to the legalities of informing the partner

d. Requests of the court that disclosure not be required when the release of confidential information may potentially harm a student or the counseling relationship.

e. Protects the confidentiality of students' records and releases personal data in accordance with prescribed laws and school policies. Student information stored and transmitted electronically is treated with the same care as traditional student records.

f. Protects the confidentiality of information received in the counseling relationship as specified by federal and state laws, written policies and applicable ethical standards. Such information is only to be revealed to others with the informed consent of the student, consistent with the counselor's ethical obligation.

g. Recognizes his/her primary obligation for confidentiality is to the student but balances that obligation with an understanding of the legal and inherent rights of parents/guardians to be the guiding voice in their children's lives.

A.3. COUNSELING PLANS

The professional school counselor:

a. Provides students with a comprehensive school counseling program that includes a strong emphasis on working jointly with all students to develop academic and career goals.

b. Advocates for counseling plans supporting students right to choose from the wide array of options when they leave secondary education. Such plans will be regularly reviewed to update students regarding critical information they need to make informed decisions.

A.4. DUAL RELATIONSHIPS

The professional school counselor:

a. Avoids dual relationships that might impair his/her objectivity and increase the risk of harm to the student (e.g., counseling one's family members, close friends or associates). If a dual relationship is unavoidable, the counselor is responsible for taking action to eliminate or reduce the potential for harm.

Such safeguards might include informed consent, consultation, supervision and documentation.

b. Avoids dual relationships with school personnel that might infringe on the integrity of the counselor/student relationship.

A.5. APPROPRIATE REFERRALS

The professional school counselor:

a. Makes referrals when necessary or appropriate to outside resources. Appropriate referrals may necessitate informing both parents/guardians and students of applicable resources and making proper plans for transitions with minimal interruption of services. Students retain the right to discontinue the counseling relationship at any time.

A.6. GROUP WORK

The professional school counselor:

a. Screens prospective group members and maintains an awareness of participants' needs and goals in relation to the goals of the group. The counselor takes reasonable precautions to protect members from physical and psychological harm resulting from interaction within the group.
b. Notifies parents/guardians and staff of group participation if the counselor deems it appropriate and if consistent with school board policy or practice.
c. Establishes clear expectations in the group setting and clearly states that confidentiality in group counseling cannot be guaranteed. Given the developmental and chronological ages of minors in schools, the counselor recognizes the tenuous nature of confidentiality for minors renders some topics inappropriate for group work in a school setting.
d. Follows up with group members and documents proceedings as appropriate.

A.7. DANGER TO SELF OR OTHERS

The professional school counselor:
a. Informs parents/guardians or appropriate authorities when the student's condition indicates a clear and imminent danger to the student or others. This is to be done after careful deliberation and, where possible, after consultation with other counseling professionals.
b. Will attempt to minimize threat to a student and may choose to (1) inform the student of actions to be taken, (2) involve the student in a three-way communication with parents/guardians when breaching confidentiality or (3) allow the student to have input as to how and to whom the breach will be made.

A.8. STUDENT RECORDS

The professional school counselor:
a. Maintains and secures records necessary for rendering professional services to the student as required by laws, regulations, institutional procedures and confidentiality guidelines.

b. Keeps sole-possession records separate from students' educational records in keeping with state laws.

c. Recognizes the limits of sole-possession records and understands these records are a memory aid for the creator and in absence of privilege communication may be subpoenaed and may become educational records when they (1) are shared with others in verbal or written form, (2) include information other than professional opinion or personal observations and/or (3) are made accessible to others.

d. Establishes a reasonable timeline for purging sole-possession records or case notes. Suggested guidelines include shredding sole possession records when the student transitions to the next level, transfers to another school or graduates. Careful discretion and deliberation should be applied before destroying sole-possession records that may be needed by a court of law such as notes on child abuse, suicide, sexual harassment or violence.

A.9. EVALUATION, ASSESSMENT AND INTERPRETATION

The professional school counselor:

a. Adheres to all professional standards regarding selecting, administering and interpreting assessment measures and only utilizes assessment measures that are within the scope of practice for school counselors.

b. Seeks specialized training regarding the use of electronically based testing programs in administering, scoring and interpreting that may differ from that required in more traditional assessments.

c. Considers confidentiality issues when utilizing evaluative or assessment instruments and electronically based programs.

d. Provides interpretation of the nature, purposes, results and potential impact of assessment/evaluation measures in language the student(s) can understand.

e. Monitors the use of assessment results and interpretations, and takes reasonable steps to prevent others from misusing the information.

f. Uses caution when utilizing assessment techniques, making evaluations and interpreting the performance of populations not represented in the norm group on which an instrument is standardized.

g. Assesses the effectiveness of his/her program in having an impact on students' academic, career and personal/social development through accountability measures especially examining efforts to close achievement, opportunity and attainment gaps.

A.10. TECHNOLOGY

The professional school counselor:

a. Promotes the benefits of and clarifies the limitations of various appropriate technological applications. The counselor promotes technological applications (1) that are appropriate for the student's individual needs, (2) that the student understands how to use and (3) for which follow-up counseling assistance is provided.

b. Advocates for equal access to technology for all students, especially those historically underserved.

c. Takes appropriate and reasonable measures for maintaining confidentiality of student information and educational records stored or transmitted over electronic media including although not limited to fax, electronic mail and instant messaging.

d. While working with students on a computer or similar technology, takes reasonable and appropriate measures to protect students from objectionable and/or harmful online material.

e. Who is engaged in the delivery of services involving technologies such as the telephone, videoconferencing and the Internet takes responsible steps to protect students and others from harm.

A.11. STUDENT PEER SUPPORT PROGRAM

The professional school counselor:

Has unique responsibilities when working with student-assistance programs. The school counselor is responsible for the welfare of students participating in peer-to-peer programs under his/her direction.

B. Responsibilities to Parents/Guardians

B.1. PARENT RIGHTS AND RESPONSIBILITIES

The professional school counselor:

a. Respects the rights and responsibilities of parents/guardians for their children and endeavors to establish, as appropriate, a collaborative relationship with parents/guardians to facilitate the student's maximum development.

b. Adheres to laws, local guidelines and ethical standards of practice when assisting parents/guardians experiencing family difficulties that interfere with the student's effectiveness and welfare.

c. Respects the confidentiality of parents/guardians.

d. Is sensitive to diversity among families and recognizes that all parents/guardians, custodial and noncustodial, are vested with certain rights and responsibilities for the welfare of their children by virtue of their role and according to law.

B.2. PARENTS/GUARDIANS AND CONFIDENTIALITY

The professional school counselor:

a. Informs parents/guardians of the counselor's role with emphasis on the confidential nature of the counseling relationship between the counselor and student.

b. Recognizes that working with minors in a school setting may require counselors to collaborate with students' parents/guardians.

c. Provides parents/guardians with accurate, comprehensive and relevant information in an objective and caring manner, as is appropriate and consistent with ethical responsibilities to the student.
d. Makes reasonable efforts to honor the wishes of parents/guardians concerning information regarding the student, and in cases of divorce or separation exercises a good-faith effort to keep both parents informed with regard to critical information with the exception of a court order.

C. Responsibilities to Colleagues and Professional Associates

C.1. PROFESSIONAL RELATIONSHIPS

The professional school counselor:

a. Establishes and maintains professional relationships with faculty, staff and administration to facilitate an optimum counseling program.
b. Treats colleagues with professional respect, courtesy and fairness. The qualifications, views and findings of colleagues are represented to accurately reflect the image of competent professionals.
c. Is aware of and utilizes related professionals, organizations and other resources to whom the student may be referred.

C.2. SHARING INFORMATION WITH OTHER PROFESSIONALS

The professional school counselor:

a. Promotes awareness and adherence to appropriate guidelines regarding confidentiality, the distinction between public and private information and staff consultation.
b. Provides professional personnel with accurate, objective, concise and meaningful data necessary to adequately evaluate, counsel and assist the student.
c. If a student is receiving services from another counselor or other mental health professional, the counselor, with student and/or parent/guardian consent, will inform the other professional and develop clear agreements to avoid confusion and conflict for the student.
d. Is knowledgeable about release of information and parental rights in sharing information.

D. Responsibilities to the School and Community

D.1. RESPONSIBILITIES TO THE SCHOOL

The professional school counselor:

a. Supports and protects the educational program against any infringement not in students' best interest.

b. Informs appropriate officials in accordance with school policy of conditions that may be potentially disruptive or damaging to the school's mission, personnel and property while honoring the confidentiality between the student and counselor.

c. Is knowledgeable and supportive of the school's mission and connects his/her program to the school's mission.

d. Delineates and promotes the counselor's role and function in meeting the needs of those served. Counselors will notify appropriate officials of conditions that may limit or curtail their effectiveness in providing programs and services.

e. Accepts employment only for positions for which he/she is qualified by education, training, supervised experience, state and national professional credentials and appropriate professional experience.

f. Advocates that administrators hire only qualified and competent individuals for professional counseling positions.

g. Assists in developing: (1) curricular and environmental conditions appropriate for the school and community, (2) educational procedures and programs to meet students' developmental needs and (3) a systematic evaluation process for comprehensive, developmental, standards-based school counseling programs, services and personnel. The counselor is guided by the findings of the evaluation data in planning programs and services.

D.2. Responsibility to the Community

The professional school counselor:

a. Collaborates with agencies, organizations and individuals in the community in the best interest of students and without regard to personal reward or remuneration.

b. Extends his/her influence and opportunity to deliver a comprehensive school counseling program to all students by collaborating with community resources for student success.

E. Responsibilities to Self

E.1. Professional Competence

The professional school counselor:

a. Functions within the boundaries of individual professional competence and accepts responsibility for the consequences of his/her actions.

b. Monitors personal well-being and effectiveness and does not participate in any activity that may lead to inadequate professional services or harm to a student.

c. Strives through personal initiative to maintain professional competence including technological literacy and to keep abreast of professional information. Professional and personal growth are ongoing throughout the counselor's career.

E.2. DIVERSITY

The professional school counselor:

a. Affirms the diversity of students, staff and families.
b. Expands and develops awareness of his/her own attitudes and beliefs affecting cultural values and biases and strives to attain cultural competence.
c. Possesses knowledge and understanding about how oppression, racism, discrimination and stereotyping affects her/him personally and professionally.
d. Acquires educational, consultation and training experiences to improve awareness, knowledge, skills and effectiveness in working with diverse populations: ethnic/racial status, age, economic status, special needs, ESL or ELL, immigration status, sexual orientation, gender, gender identity/expression, family type, religious/spiritual identity and appearance.

F. Responsibilities to the Profession

F.1. PROFESSIONALISM

The professional school counselor:

a. Accepts the policies and procedures for handling ethical violations as a result of maintaining membership in the American School Counselor Association.
b. Conducts herself/himself in such a manner as to advance individual ethical practice and the profession.
c. Conducts appropriate research and report findings in a manner consistent with acceptable educational and psychological research practices. The counselor advocates for the protection of the individual student's identity when using data for research or program planning.
d. Adheres to ethical standards of the profession, other official policy statements, such as ASCA's position statements, role statement and the ASCA National Model, and relevant statutes established by federal, state and local governments, and when these are in conflict works responsibly for change.
e. Clearly distinguishes between statements and actions made as a private individual and those made as a representative of the school counseling profession.
f. Does not use his/her professional position to recruit or gain clients, consultees for his/her private practice or to seek and receive unjustified personal gains, unfair advantage, inappropriate relationships or unearned goods or services.

F.2. Contribution to the Profession

The professional school counselor:

a. Actively participates in local, state and national associations fostering the development and improvement of school counseling.

b. Contributes to the development of the profession through the sharing of skills, ideas and expertise with colleagues.

c. Provides support and mentoring to novice professionals.

G. Maintenance of Standards

Ethical behavior among professional school counselors, association members and nonmembers, is expected at all times. When there exists serious doubt as to the ethical behavior of colleagues or if counselors are forced to work in situations or abide by policies that do not reflect the standards as outlined in these Ethical Standards for School Counselors, the counselor is obligated to take appropriate action to rectify the condition. The following procedure may serve as a guide:

1. The counselor should consult confidentially with a professional colleague to discuss the nature of a complaint to see if the professional colleague views the situation as an ethical violation.
2. When feasible, the counselor should directly approach the colleague whose behavior is in question to discuss the complaint and seek resolution.
3. If resolution is not forthcoming at the personal level, the counselor shall utilize the channels established within the school, school district, the state school counseling association and ASCA's Ethics Committee.
4. If the matter still remains unresolved, referral for review and appropriate action should be made to the Ethics Committees in the following sequence:
    state school counselor association
    American School Counselor Association
5. The ASCA Ethics Committee is responsible for:
    - educating and consulting with the membership regarding ethical standards
    - periodically reviewing and recommending changes in code
    - receiving and processing questions to clarify the application of such standards; Questions must be submitted in writing to the ASCA Ethics chair.
    - handling complaints of alleged violations of the ethical standards. At the national level, complaints should be submitted in writing to the ASCA Ethics Committee, c/o the Executive Director, American School Counselor Association, 1101 King St., Suite 625, Alexandria, VA 22314.

Source: From *Ethical Standards for School Counselors, Revised, June 26, 2004*, by American School Counselor Association, 2004, Alexandria, VA: Author. Reprinted by permission.

APPENDIX D

Guidance Curriculum
Scope and Sequence Chart

Academic Development Domain

Standard A: Students will acquire the attitudes, knowledge and skills that contribute to effective learning in school and across the life span.

	Competency A:A1 Improve Academic Self-Concept	K-2	3-5	6-8	9-12
A:A1.1	articulate feelings of competence and confidence as learners		x		
A:A1.2	display a positive interest in learning	x			
A:A1.3	take pride in work and achievement	x			
A:A1.4	accept mistakes as essential to the learning process		x		
A:A1.5	identify attitudes and behaviors leading to successful learning			x	
	Competency A:A2 Acquire Skills for Improving Learning				
A:A2.1	apply time-management and task-management skills			x	
A:A2.2	demonstrate how effort and persistence positively affect learning		x		
A:A2.3	use communications skills to know when and how to ask for help when needed	x			
A:A2.4	apply knowledge and learning styles to positively influence school performance			x	
	Competency A:A3 Achieve School Success				
A:A3.1	take responsibility for their actions	x			
A:A3.2	demonstrate the ability to work independently, as well as the ability to work cooperatively with other students		x		
A:A3.3	develop a broad range of interests and abilities			x	
A:A3.4	demonstrate dependability, productivity and initiative		x		
A:A3.5	share knowledge		x		

Standard B: Students will complete school with the academic preparation essential to choose from a wide range of substantial postsecondary options, including college.

	Competency A:B1 Improve Learning	K-2	3-5	6-8	9-12
A:B1.1	demonstrate the motivation to achieve individual potential		x		
A:B1.2	learn and apply critical-thinking skills		x		
A:B1.3	apply the study skills necessary for academic success at each level	x			
A:B1.4	seek information and support from faculty, staff, family and peers			x	
A:B1.5	organize and apply academic information from a variety of sources			x	
A:B1.6	use knowledge of learning styles to positively influence school performance			x	
A:B1.7	become a self-directed and independent learner		x		
	Competency A:B2 Plan to Achieve Goals				
A:B2.1	establish challenging academic goals in elementary, middle/junior high and high school		x	x	x
A:B2.2	use assessment results in educational planning			x	
A:B2.3	develop and implement annual plan of study to maximize academic ability and achievement			x	x
A:B2.4	apply knowledge of aptitudes and interests to goal setting			x	
A:B2.5	use problem-solving and decision-making skills to assess progress toward educational goals			x	
A:B2.6	understand the relationship between classroom performance and success in school	x			
A:B2.7	identify postsecondary options consistent with interests, achievement, aptitude and abilities			x	

Standard C: Students will understand the relationship of academics to the world of work and to life at home and in the community.

	Competency A:C1 Relate School to Life Experience	K-2	3-5	6-8	9-12
A:C1.1	demonstrate the ability to balance school, studies, extracurricular activities, leisure time and family life		x		
A:C1.2	seek co curricular and community experiences to enhance the school experience			x	
A:C1.3	understand the relationship between learning and work	x			
A:C1.4	demonstrate an understanding of the value of lifelong learning as essential to seeking, obtaining and maintaining life goals			x	

| A:C1.5 | understand that school success is the preparation to make the transition from student to community member | | | x | |
| A:C1.6 | understand how school success and academic achievement enhance future career and vocational opportunities | | x | | |

Career Development Domain

Standard A: Students will acquire the skills to investigate the world of work in relation to knowledge of self and to make informed career decisions.

	Competency C:A1 Develop Career Awareness	K-2	3-5	6-8	9-12
C:A1.1	develop skills to locate, evaluate and interpret career information			X	
C:A1.2	learn about the variety of traditional and nontraditional occupations	X			
C:A1.3	develop an awareness of personal abilities, skills, interests and motivations	x			
C:A1.4	learn how to interact and work cooperatively in teams		X		
C:A1.5	learn to make decisions		X		
C:A1.6	learn how to set goals		x		
C:A1.7	understand the importance of planning			X	
C:A1.8	pursue and develop competency in areas of interest			x	
C:A1.9	develop hobbies and vocational interests	x			
C:A1.10	balance between work and leisure time		x		
	Competency C:A2 Develop Employment Readiness				
C:A2.1	acquire employability skills such as working on a team and problem-solving and organizational skills			x	
C:A2.2	apply job readiness skills to seek employment opportunities				x
C:A2.3	demonstrate knowledge about the changing workplace				x
C:A2.4	learn about the rights and responsibilities of employers and employees				x
C:A2.5	learn to respect individual uniqueness in the workplace				x
C:A2.6	learn how to write a resume				x
C:A2.7	develop a positive attitude toward work and learning	x			
C:A2.8	understand the importance of responsibility, dependability, punctuality, integrity and effort in the workplace			x	
C:A2.9	utilize time- and task-management skills	x			

Standard B: Students will employ strategies to achieve future career goals with success and satisfaction.

	Competency C:B1 Acquire Career Information	K-2	3-5	6-8	9-12
C:B1.1	apply decision-making skills to career planning, course selection and career transition			x	
C:B1.2	identify personal skills, interests and abilities and relate them to current career choice	x			
C:B1.3	demonstrate knowledge of the career-planning process			x	
C:B1.4	know the various ways in which occupations can be classified		x		
C:B1.5	use research and information resources to obtain career information			x	
C:B1.6	learn to use the Internet to access career-planning information			x	
C:B1.7	describe traditional and nontraditional career choices and how they relate to career choice		x		
C:B1.8	understand how changing economic and societal needs influence employment trends and future training			x	
	Competency C:B2 Identify Career Goals				
C:B2.1	demonstrate awareness of the education and training needed to achieve career goals	x			
C:B2.2	assess and modify their educational plan to support career				x
C:B2.3	use employability and job readiness skills in internship, mentoring, shadowing and/or other work experience			x	
C:B2.4	select course work that is related to career interests			x	
C:B2.5	maintain a career-planning portfolio			x	

Standard C: Students will understand the relationship between personal qualities, education, training and the world of work.

	Competency C:C1 Acquire Knowledge to Achieve Career Goals	K-2	3-5	6-8	9-12
C:C1.1	understand the relationship between educational achievement and career success	x			
C:C1.2	explain how work can help to achieve personal success and satisfaction		x		
C:C1.3	identify personal preferences and interests influencing career choice and success			x	
C:C1.4	understand that the changing workplace requires lifelong learning and acquiring new skills			x	

C:C1.5	describe the effect of work on lifestyle			x	
C:C1.6	understand the importance of equity and access in career choice		x		
C:C1.7	understand that work is an important and satisfying means of personal expression	x			
	Competency C:C2 Apply Skills to Achieve Career Goals				
C:C2.1	demonstrate how interests, abilities and achievement relate to achieving personal, social, educational and career goals		x		
C:C2.2	learn how to use conflict management skills with peers and adults	x			
C:C2.3	learn to work cooperatively with others as a team member		x		
C:C2.4	apply academic and employment readiness skills in work-based learning situations such as internships, shadowing and/or mentoring experiences				x

Personal/Social Development Domain

Standard A: Students will acquire the knowledge, attitudes and interpersonal skills to help them understand and respect self and others.

	Competency PS:A1 Acquire Self-Knowledge	K-2	3-5	6-8	9-12
PS:A1.1	develop positive attitudes toward self as a unique and worthy person				
PS:A1.2	identify values, attitudes and beliefs				
PS:A1.3	learn the goal-setting process				
PS:A1.4	understand change is a part of growth				
PS:A1.5	identify and express feelings				
PS:A1.6	distinguish between appropriate and inappropriate behavior				
PS:A1.7	recognize personal boundaries, rights and privacy needs				
PS:A1.8	understand the need for self-control and how to practice it				
PS:A1.9	demonstrate cooperative behavior in groups				
PS:A1.10	identify personal strengths and assets				
PS:A1.11	identify and discuss changing personal and social roles				
PS:A1.12	identify and recognize changing family roles				
	Competency PS:A2 Acquire Interpersonal Skills				
PS:A2.1	recognize that everyone has rights and responsibilities				
PS:A2.2	respect alternative points of view				

	Competency PS:A2 Acquire Interpersonal Skills				
PS:A2.3	recognize, accept, respect and appreciate individual differences				
PS:A2.4	recognize, accept and appreciate ethnic and cultural diversity				
PS:A2.5	recognize and respect differences in various family configurations				
PS:A2.6	use effective communications skills				
PS:A2.7	know that communication involves speaking, listening and nonverbal behavior				
PS:A2.8	learn how to make and keep friends				

Standard B: Students will make decisions, set goals and take necessary action to achieve goals.

	Competency PS:B1 Self-Knowledge Application	**K-2**	**3-5**	**6-8**	**9-12**
PS:B1.1	use a decision-making and problem-solving model				
PS:B1.2	understand consequences of decisions and choices				
PS:B1.3	identify alternative solutions to a problem				
PS:B1.4	develop effective coping skills for dealing with problems				
PS:B1.5	demonstrate when, where and how to seek help for solving problems and making decisions				
PS:B1.6	know how to apply conflict-resolution skills				
PS:B1.7	demonstrate a respect and appreciation for individual and cultural differences				
PS:B1.8	know when peer pressure is influencing a decision				
PS:B1.9	identify long- and short-term goals				
PS:B1.10	identify alternative ways of achieving goals				
PS:B1.11	use persistence and perseverance in acquiring knowledge and skills				
PS:B1.12	develop an action plan to set and achieve realistic goals				

Standard C: Students will understand safety and survival skills.

	Competency PS:C1 Acquire Personal Safety Skills	**K-2**	**3-5**	**6-8**	**9-12**
PS:C1.1	demonstrate knowledge of personal information (telephone number, home address, emergency contact)				
PS:C1.2	learn about the relationship between rules, laws, safety and the protection of rights of the individual				

	Competency PS:C1 Acquire Personal Safety Skills	K-2	3-5	6-8	9-12
PS:C1.3	learn about the differences between appropriate and inappropriate physical contact				
PS:C1.4	demonstrate the ability to set boundaries, rights and personal privacy				
PS:C1.5	differentiate between situations requiring peer support and situations requiring adult professional help				
PS:C1.6	identify resource people in the school and community, and know how to seek their help				
PS:C1.7	apply effective problem-solving and decision-making skills to make safe and healthy choices				
PS:C1.8	learn about the emotional and physical dangers of substance use and abuse				
PS:C1.9	learn how to cope with peer pressure				
PS:C1.10	learn techniques for managing stress and conflict				
PS:C1.11	learn coping skills for managing life events				

Source: Adapted from *The ASCA Model: A Framework for School Counseling Programs,* by the American School Counselor Association, Alexandria: VA: Author. Reprinted by permission.

REFERENCES

Abramson, J., & Rosenthal, B. (1995). Interdisciplinary and interorganizational collaboration. In R. Edwards (Ed.), *The encyclopedia of social work* (19th ed., pp. 1479–1480). Washington, DC: NASW Press.

Adelman, H., & Taylor, L. (1998). *Restructuring boards of education to enhance schools' effectiveness in addressing barriers to student learning.* Los Angeles, CA: Center for Mental Health in Schools, University of California at Los Angeles.

Adelman, H. S., & Taylor, L. (2006). *The school leader's guide to student learning supports.* Thousand Oaks, CA: Corwin Press.

Aiken, L. R., Jr. (2000). *Psychological testing and assessment* (10th ed.). Boston: Allyn & Bacon.

Akos, P. (2002). Student perceptions of the transition from elementary to middle school. *Professional School Counseling, 5,* 339–345.

Akos, P. (2004). Transition programming for professional school counselors. In B. T. Erford (Ed.), *Professional school counseling: A handbook of theories, programs & practices* (pp. 881–888). Austin, TX: ProEd.

Akos, P., & Galassi, J. P. (2004). Middle and high school transitions as viewed by students, parents, and teachers. *Professional School Counseling, 7,* 212–221.

Alabama State Department of Education. (2002). *Alabama professional education personnel evaluation program (PEPE) for counselors.* Retrieved October 12, 2005, from http://www.alabamapepe.com/specialty.htm#Counselors

Alabama State Department of Education. (2003). Comprehensive counseling and guidance model for Alabama Public schools. Bulletin 2003, No. 89. Montgomery, AL: Author.

Alabama State Department of Education (1996). *The revised comprehensive counseling and guidance model for Alabama's public schools.* Bulletin 1966, No. 27. Montgomery, AL: Author.

Alspaugh, J. W. (1998). Achievement loss associated with the transition to middle school and high school. *The Journal of Educational Research, 92,* 20–25.

American Association of University Women (AAUW). (1992). *How schools shortchange girls: A study of major findings on girls and education.* Washington, DC: Author.

American Association of University Women. (2001). *Hostile hallways: Bullying, teasing and sexual harassment in school.* Washington, DC: Author.

American Association for Marriage and Family Therapy. (2001). *AAMFT code of ethics.* Retrieved October 15, 2005, from http://www.aamft.org/resources/lrmplan/ethics/ethicscode2001.htm

American Bar Association. (2005). Facts about children and the law. Retrieved October 15, 2005, from www.abanet.org/media/factbooks/chl.html

American College Testing (ACT), Inc. (2000). *DISCOVER* [Computer software]. Iowa City, IA: Author.

American Counseling Association. (1993). *Counseling minor clients.* Alexandria, VA: Author.

American Counseling Association. (1999). Ethical standards for Internet on-line counseling. Retrieved September 18, 2001, from http://www.counseling.org

American Counseling Association. (2000). The truth about school counseling. Advocacy Kit: School counseling legislation, p. 5. Alexandria, VA: Author.

American Counseling Association. (2005). *Code of ethics.* Alexandria, VA: Author.

America's Career Resource Network. (2005). *National Career Development Guidelines.* Retrieved July 25, 2005, from http://www.acrnetwork.org/ncdg.htm

American School Counselor Association. (2000). *The professional school counselor and educational planning.* Retrieved July 18, 2005, from www.schoolcounselor.org

American School Counselors Association. (2001a). *ASCA national standards.* Retrieved August 22, 2005, from www.schoolcounselor.org/rc_files/ASCA%20standards.doc

American School Counselor Association (ASCA). (2001b). *ASCA position statement: The professional school counselor and HIV/AIDS* (rev. ed.). Alexandria, VA: Author.

American School Counselor Association. (2002a). *The professional school counselor and high-stakes testing.* Retrieved July 18, 2005, from www. schoolcounselor.org

American School Counselor Association. (2002b). *ASCA Position statement peer helping.* Retrieved October 13, 2005, from http://www.schoolcounselor.org/content.asp?contentid=214

American School Counselor Association (ASCA). (2002c). *ASCA position statement: The professional school counselor and confidentiality* (rev. ed.). Alexandria, VA: Author.

American School Counselor Association. (2003a). *The national model: A framework for school counseling programs.* Alexandria, VA: Author.

American School Counselor Association (ASCA). (2003b). Taking your school's temperature: How school climate affects students and staff. Retrieved November 25, 2003, from www.schoolcounselor.org

American School Counselor Association (ASCA). (2003c). *ASCA position statement: The professional school counselor and child abuse and neglect prevention* (rev. ed.). Alexandria, VA: Author.

American School Counselors Association. (2004a). *The role of the professional school counselor.* Retrieved November 19, 2004, from http://www.schoolcounselor.org/content.asp?contentid=240

American School Counselors Association. (2004b). *The ASCA national model: A framework for school counseling programs executive summary.* Retrieved November 19, 2004, from http://schoolcounselor.org/files/ExecSumm.pdf

American School Counselors Association. (2004c). Ethical standards for school counselors. December 7, 2004, from http://schoolcounselor.org/files/ethicalstandards.pdf

American School Counselors Association. (2004d). *The ASCA national model workbook.* Alexandria, VA: Author.

American School Counselor Association (ASCA). (2004e). *ASCA position statement: The professional school counselor and parent consent* (rev. ed.). Alexandria, VA: Author.

American School Counselor Association. (2005). *Survey shows too many parents lack contact with school counselors.* Retrieved September 4, 2005, from http://www.fhidc.com/asca/082205.html

Amundson, N. E., & Penner, K. (1998). Parent involved career exploration. *The Career Development Quarterly, 47,* 135–144.

Anderman, E. M., & Midgley, C. (1997). Changes in achievement goal orientations, perceived academic competence, and grades across the transition to middle-level schools. *Contemporary Educational Psychology, 22,* 269–298.

Anderson, R. S., & Reiter, D. (1995). The indispensable counselor. *The School Counselor, 42,* 268–276.

Annie E. Casey Foundation. (2005). *Kids count data book.* Retrieved on July 30, 2005, from www.aecf.org/kidscount/sld/databook.jsp

Anyon, J. (1995). Social class and the hidden curriculum. In E. Stevens & G. Woods (Eds.), *Justice, ideology,*

and education (pp. 162–178). New York: McGraw-Hill.

Apling, R. N., & Jones, N. L. (January 5, 2005). Individuals with disabilities education act (IDEA): Analysis of changes made by P.L. 108-446. *Congressional Research Service* (Order Code RL32716). Washington, DC: The Library of Congress.

Apple, M. W. (1980). Analyzing determinations: Understanding and evaluating production of social outcomes in schools. *Curriculum Inquiry, 11,* 3–42.

Apple, M. W. (1988). *Teachers and texts.* New York: Routledge.

Arnold v. Board of Education, 880 U.S. F.2d 305 (1989).

Aronson, J. (2004). The threat of stereotype. *Educational Leadership, 62,* 14–19.

Aronson, J., & Steele, C. M. (2005). Stereotypes and the fragility of human competence, motivation, and self-concept. In C. Dweck & E. Elliot (Eds.), *Handbook of competence and motivation* (pp. 436–456). New York: Guilford.

Association for Assessment in Counseling. (1998). Competencies in assessment and evaluation for school counselors. Retrieved September 18, 2001, from http://aac.ncat.edu/documents/atsc_cmptncy.htm

Association of Computer-Based Systems for Career Information. (2005). Career information delivery system (CIDS). Retrieved on October 28, 2005, from www.acsci.org/acsci_states.asp

Association for Specialists in Group Work. (1989). *Ethical guidelines for group counselors.* Alexandria, VA: Author.

Au, K. (1980). Participation structures in a reading lesson with Hawaiian children. *Anthropology and Education Quarterly, 11,* 91–115.

Aubrey, R. F. (1982). A house divided: Guidance and counseling in 20th century America. *Personnel and Guidance Journal, 61,* 198–204.

Augur, R. W., Blackhurst, A. E., & Wahl, K. H. (2005). The development of elementary-aged children's career aspirations and expectations. *Professional School Counseling, 8,* 322–329.

Aviles, R. M., Guerrero, M. P., Howarth, H. B., & Thomas, G. (1999). Perceptions of Chicano/Latino students who have dropped out of school. *Journal of Counseling & Development, 77,* 465–473.

Bae, Y., Choy, S., Geddes, C., Sable, J., Snyder, T. (2005). Trends in educational equity of girls and women. Retrieved June 23, 2005, from http://nces.ed.gov/pubs2005/equity/

Baird, B. N. (2002). *The internship, practicum, and field placement handbook: A guide for the helping professions* (3rd ed.). Upper Saddle River, NJ: Prentice Hall.

Bailey, D. F., Getch, Y. Q., & Chen-Hayes, S. (2003). Professional school counselors as social and academic advocates. In Bradley T. Erford (Ed.), *Transforming the school counseling profession* (pp. 411–434). Upper Saddle River, NJ: Merrill/Prentice Hall.

Baker, S. B. (2000). *School counseling for the twenty-first century* (3rd ed.). Upper Saddle River, NJ: Prentice Hall.

Baker, S. B., & Gerler, E. R. (2004). *School counseling for the twenty-first century* (4th ed). Upper Saddle River, NJ: Prentice Hall.

Ballantine, J. H. (2001). *The sociology of education: A systematic analysis* (5th ed.). Upper Saddle River, NJ: Prentice Hall.

Barton, P. E. (2004). Why does the gap persist? *Educational Leadership, 62*, 9–13.

Basham, A., Appleton, V. E., & Dykeman, C. (2000). *Team building in education: A how-to guidebook.* Denver, CO: Love Publishing.

Basham, A., Appleton, V., & Lambarth, C. (1998). The school counselor's role in organizational team building. In C. Dykeman (Ed.), *Maximizing school guidance program effectiveness: A guide for school administrators and program directors* (pp. 51–58). Greensboro, NC: ERIC/CASS Publications.

Bemak, F. (2000). Transforming the role of the counselor to provide leadership in educational reform through collaboration. *Professional School Counseling, 3*, 323–331.

Bennis, W. (1995). The artform of leadership. In J. T. Wren (Ed.), *The leader's companion: Insights on leadership through the ages* (pp. 377–378). New York: Free Press.

Benard, B. (1991). *Fostering resiliency in kids: Protective factors in the family, school, and community.* Portland, OR: Northwest Regional Educational Laboratory.

Benard, B. (2004). *Resilience: What we have learned.* San Francisco, CA: WestEd.

Bergmann, B. (1991). Guidance on the middle school level: The compassion component. In J. Capelluti & D. Stokes (Eds.), *Middle level education: Policies, practices and programs* (pp. 30–35). Reston, VA: NSSA.

Berk, L. E. (2004). *Development through the lifespan* (3rd ed). Boston: Allyn & Bacon.

Berliner, D. C., & Biddle, B. J. (1995). *The manufactured crisis: Myths, fraud, and the attacks on America's public schools.* Reading, MA: Addison-Wesley.

Berns, R. M. (2004). *Child family-select community: Socialization and support* (6th ed.). Belmont, CA: Wadsworth/Thomson Learning.

Berns, R. G., & Erickson, P. M. (2001). *Contextual teaching and learning: Preparing students for the new economy.* Columbus, OH: CTE National Dissemination Center.

Berry, E. H., Shillington, A. M., Peak, T., & Hohman, M. M. (2000). Multi-ethnic comparison of risk and protective factors for adolescent pregnancy. *Child and Adolescent Social Work, 17*, 79–96.

Bingman, G., & Campbell, C. (2003). Helping students improve academic achievement and school success behavior. *Professional School Counseling, 7*, 91–99.

Blanchard, K., & Johnson, S. (1983). *The one-minute manager.* New York: Berkley Books.

Bloom, B. S., Engelhart, M. D., Frost, E., Hill, W. H., & Krathwohl, D. R. (1956). Taxonomy of educational objectives. *Handbook I: Cognitive domain.* New York: David McKay.

Blum, D. J. (1998). *The school counselors book of lists.* West Nyack, NY: Center for Applied Research in Education.

Borders, L. D., & Drury, S. M. (1992). Comprehensive school counseling programs: A review for policymakers and practitioners. *Journal of Counseling and Development, 70*, 487–498.

Bowen, M. L., & Glenn, E. E. (1998). Counseling interventions for students who have mild disabilities. *Professional School Counseling, 2*, 16–25.

Bowers, C. A. (1984). *The promise of theory: Education and the politics of cultural change.* New York: Longman.

Bowlby, J. (1988). *A secure base.* New York: Basic Books.

Bracey, G. W. (2000). The 10th Bracey report on the condition of public education. *Phi Delta Kappan, 82*(2), 133–144.

Brazelton, T. B., & Greenspan, S. I. (2000). *The irreducible needs of children.* Cambridge, MA: Perseus Publishing.

Brigman, G. & Goodman, B. E. (2001). Group counseling for school counselors: A practical guide (2nd ed.). Portland, ME: J. Weston Walch.

Brigman, G., Mullis, F., Webb, L., & White, J. (2005). *School counselor consultation: Developing skills for working effectively with parents, teachers, and other school personnel.* Hoboken, NJ: Wiley & Sons.

Broderick, P. C., & Blewitt, P. (2003). *The live span: Human development for helping professionals.* Upper Saddle River, NJ: Merrill/Prentice Hall.

Bronfenbrenner, U. (1979). *The ecology of human development.* Cambridge, MA: Harvard University Press.

Bronfenbrenner, U. (1993). The ecology of cognitive developmental processes. In R. M. Lerner (Ed.), *Handbook of child psychology: Vol. I. Theoretical models of human development* (5th ed., pp. 535–584). New York: Wiley.

Brookfield, S. D. (1990). *The skillful teacher*. San Francisco: Jossey-Bass.

Brott, P. (2005). Making it count: Accountability for school counselors. In T. Davis (Ed.), *Exploring school counseling: Professional practices and perspectives* (pp. 279–297). Boston: Lahaska.

Brown, D., Pryzwansky, W. B., & Schulte, A. C. (1998). *Psychological consultation: Introduction to therapy and practice* (4th ed.). Boston: Allyn & Bacon.

Brown, D., Pryzwansky, W. B., & Schulte, A. C. (2001). *Psychological consultation: Introduction to theory and practice* (5th ed.). Boston: Allyn & Bacon.

Brown, D., & Srebalus, D. J. (1988). *An introduction to the counseling profession*. Upper Saddle River, NJ: Prentice Hall.

Brown, D., & Trusty, J. (2005). *Designing and leading comprehensive school counseling programs: Promoting student competence and meeting student needs*. Belmont, CA: Thomson.

Bruce, M. A., Shade, R. A., & Cossairt, A. (1996). Classroom-tested guidance activities for promoting inclusion. *The School Counselor, 43*, 224–231.

Brusselmans-Dehairs, C., Hencry, G. F., Beller, M., & Gafni, N. (1997). *Gender differences in learning achievement: Evidence from cross-national surveys*. Paris, France: UNESCO.

Bryant, J., & Milsom, A. (2005). Child abuse reporting by school counselors. *Professional School Counseling, 9*, 63–71.

Bulach, C., & Lunenberg, F. C. (1995). The influence of the principal's leadership style on school climate and student achievement. *People & Education, 3*, 333–351.

Bushweller, K. (1995). The high-tech portfolio. *Executive Educator, 17*, 19–22.

Cameron, S., & turtle-song, i. (2002). Learning to write case notes using the SOAP format. *Journal of Counseling and Development, 80*, 286–292.

Campbell, C. (2000). K–12 peer helper programs. In J. Wittmer (Ed.), *Managing your school counseling program: K–12 developmental strategies*. Minneapolis, MN: Educational Media.

Campbell, C., & Bowman, R. (1993). The "Fresh Start" support club: Small-group counseling for academically retained children. *Elementary School Guidance and Counseling, 27*, 172–185.

Campbell, C., & Myrick, R. (1990). Motivational group counseling for low-performing students. *Journal for Specialists in Group Work, 15*, 43–50.

Campbell, C. A., & Dahir, C. A. (1997). *Sharing the vision: National standards for school counseling programs*. Alexandria, VA: American School Counselor Association.

Canino, I. A., & Spurlock, J. (1994). *Culturally diverse children and adolescents: Assessment, diagnosis, and treatment*. New York: Guilford.

Caplan, G. C. (1970). *The theory and practice of mental health consultation*. New York: Basic Books.

Capuzzi, D. (2002). Legal and ethical challenges in counseling suicidal students. *Professional School Counseling, 6*, 36–45.

Carey, J., Harrity, J., & Dimmitt, C. (2005). The development of a self-assessment instrument to measure a school district's readiness to implement the ASCA national model. *Professional School Counselor, 8*, 305–312.

Carns, A. W., & Carns, M. R. (1991). Teaching study skills, cognitive strategies, and metacognitive skills through self-diagnosed learning styles. *The School Counselor, 38*, 341–346.

Cavaiola, A. A., & Colford, J. E. (2006). *A practical guide to crisis intervention*. Boston, MA: Lahaska/Houghton Mifflin.

Cecil, J. H., & Cobia, D. C. (1990). Educational challenge and change. In H. Hackney (Ed.), *Changing contexts for counselor preparation in the 1990s* (pp. 21–36). Alexandria, VA: Association for Counselor Education and Supervision.

Center for Research on Education, Diversity and Excellence. (2002). The five standards for effective pedagogy. Retrieved on June 23, 2005, from www.crede.org

Center for School Counseling Outcome Research at the University of Massachusetts, Amherst (2005). Research monographs. Retrieved on January 6, 2005, from http://www.umass.edu/schoolcounseling/summer.htm

Cheek, J. R., Bradley, L. J., Reynolds, J., & Coy, D. (2002). An intervention for helping elementary students reduce test anxiety. *Professional School Counseling, 6*, 162–165.

Child Trends. (2003). Child trends databank. Retrieved on July 28, 2005, from www.childtrendsdatabank.org

Childers, J. H., Jr. (1988). The counselor's use of microcomputers: Problems and ethical issues. In W. C. Huey & T. P. Remley, Jr. (Eds.), *Ethical and legal issues in school counseling* (pp. 262–270). Alexandria, VA: American School Counselor Association.

Children's Defense Fund. (2005a). The road to dropping out: Minority students and factors correlated with failure to complete high school. Retrieved on June 23, 2005, from http://www.childrensdefense.org/education/dropping_out.pdf

Children's Defense Fund. (2005b). Misidentification of minority youth in special education. Retrieved on June 23, 2005, from http://www.childrensdefense.org/education/special_ed_misidentification.pdf

Christenson, S. L., & Thurlow, M. L. (2004). School dropouts: Prevention considerations, interventions, and challenges. *Current Directions in Psychological Science, 13*, 36–39.

Chung, H., Elias, M., & Schneider, K. (1998). Patterns of individual adjustment changes during middle school transition. *Journal of School Psychology, 36*, 83–101.

Ciechalski, J. C., & Schmidt, M. W. (1995). The effects of social skills training on students with exceptionalities. *Elementary School Guidance and Counseling, 29*, 217–223.

Clark, M. A., & Loesch, L. C. (2004). Parents' questions about testing in schools and some answers. In B. T. Erford's (Ed.), *Professional school counseling: A handbook of theories, programs, & practices* (pp. 415–421). Austin, TX: ProEd.

Clark, M. A., & Stone, C. (2000). Evolving our image: School counselors as educational leaders. *Counseling Today*, 21–46.

Cochran, L. (1985). *Parent career guidance manual.* Richmond, VA: Buchanan-Kells.

Colangelo, N. (1997). Counseling gifted students: Issues and practices. In N. Colangelo & G. A. Davis (Eds.), *Handbook of gifted education* (2nd ed., pp. 353–365). Boston: Allyn & Bacon.

Cole, M., & Cole, S. R. (1996). *The development of children* (3rd ed.). New York: W. H. Freeman.

Coll, K. M. (1995). Legal challenges in secondary prevention programming for students with substance abuse problems. *The School Counselor, 43*, 35–41.

Conger, R. D., Conger, K. J., & Elder, G. (1997). Family economic hardship and adolescent academic performance: Mediating and moderating processes. In G. Duncan & J. Brooks-Gunn (Eds.), *Consequences of growing up poor* (pp. 288–310). New York: Russell Sage Foundation.

Conlin, M. (2003, May 26). The new gender gap. *Business Week Online.* Retrieved on October 29, 2005, from http://www.businessweek.com/magazine/content/03_21/b3834001_mz001.htm

Conroy, E., & Meyer, S. (1994). Strategies for consulting with parents. *Elementary School Guidance & Counseling, 29*, 60–67.

Corey, G., Corey, M. S., & Callanan, P. (1993). *Issues and ethics in the helping professions* (4th ed.). Pacific Grove: Brooks/Cole.

Corey, G., Corey, M. S., & Callanan, P. (1998). *Issues and ethics in the helping professions* (5th ed.). Pacific Grove, CA: Brooks/Cole.

Corey, G., Corey, M. S., Callanan, P., & Russell, J. M. (1988). Ethical considerations in using group techniques. In W. C. Huey & T. P. Remley, Jr. (Eds.), *Ethical and legal issues in school counseling* (pp. 211–222). Alexandria, VA: American School Counselor Association.

Corey, M., & Corey, G. (2001). *Theory and practice of group counseling* (5th ed.). Pacific Grove, CA: Brooks/Cole.

Correa, V. I., Jones, H. A., Thomas, C. C., & Morsink, C. V. (2005). *Interactive teaming: Enhancing programs for students with special needs.* Upper Saddle River, NJ: Pearson.

Costin, A. C., Page, B. J., Pietrzak, D. R., Kerr, D. L., & Symons, C. W. (2002). HIV/AIDS knowledge and beliefs among pre-service and in-service school counselors. *Professional School Counseling, 6*, 79–85.

Cotton, K. (n.d.) *Research you can use to improve results.* Alexandria, VA: Association for Supervision and Curriculum Development.

Cottone, R. R. (2001). A social constructivism model of ethical decision making in counseling. *Journal of Counseling and Development, 79*, 39–45.

Cottone, R. R., & Travydas, V. (2006). *Ethical and professional issues in counseling* (3rd ed.). Upper Saddle River, NJ: Merrill/Prentice Hall.

Council for Accreditation of Counseling and Related Educational Programs (CACREP). (2001). Specialty standards for school counseling. Retrieved November 20, 2004; June 2, 2005, from http://www.cacrep.org/2001Standards.html

Crites, J. O., & Savickas, M. L. (1996). Revision of career maturity inventory. *Journal of Career Assessment, 4*, 131–138.

D'Andrea, M., & Daniels, J. (1995). Helping students learn to get along: Assessing the effectiveness of a multicultural development guidance project. *Elementary School Guidance and Counseling, 30*, 143–154.

D'Andrea, M., & Daniels, J. (1999). Youth advocacy. Retrieved October 10, 1999, from http://www.counseling.org/conference/advocacy5.htm

Dahir, C. A., Sheldon, C. B., & Valiga, M. J. (1998). *Vision into action: Implementing the national standards for school counseling programs*. Alexandria, VA: American School Counselor Association.

Danielson, C. (2002). *Enhancing student achievement: A framework for school improvement*. Alexandria, VA: Association for Supervision and Curriculum Development.

Davis, J. L., & Mickelson, D. J. (1994). School counselors: Are you aware of ethical and legal aspects of counseling? *The School Counselor, 42*, 5–13.

Davis v. Monroe County Board of Education et al. 120 F.3d 1390. (Supreme Court, May 24, 1999).

Davis, T. (2005). *Exploring school counseling: Professional practices and perspectives*. Boston: Lahaska.

Davis, T., & Ritchie, M. (1993). Confidentiality and the school counselor: A challenge for the 1990s. *The School Counselor, 41*, 23–30.

DeBlois, R. (2000). The everyday work of leadership. *Phi Delta Kappan, 82*, 25–27.

DeRosier, M. E. (2004). Building relationships and combating bullying: Effectiveness of a school-based social skills group intervention. *Journal of Clinical Child and Adolescent Psychology, 33*, 196–201.

Dettmer, P. A., Dyck, N. T., & Thurston, L. P. (1996). *Consultation, collaboration, and teamwork for students with special needs* (2nd ed.). Boston: Allyn & Bacon.

DeVoss, J. (2004). Organization development in schools. In B. T. Erford (Ed.), *Professional school counseling: A handbook of theories, programs, & practices* (pp. 379–385). Upper Saddle River, NJ: Merrill/Prentice Hall.

Dimmitt, C. (2003). Transforming school counseling practice through collaboration and the use of data: A study of academic failure in high school. *Professional School Counseling, 6*, 340–349.

Dinkmeyer, D., Pew, W., & Dinkmeyer, D., Jr. (1979). *Adlerian counseling and psychotherapy*. Monterey, CA: Brooks/Cole.

Dollarhide, C. T., & Saginak, K. A. (2003). *School counseling in the secondary school: A comprehensive process and program*. Boston: Pearson Education.

Dorsey, J. (2000). Institute to End School Violence (Online). In *End School Violence*. Retrieved March 25, 2005, from http://www.endschoolviolence.com/strategy/

Dougherty, A. M. (2000). *Psychological consultation and collaboration in school and community settings* (3rd ed.). Pacific Grove, CA: Brooks/Cole.

Drug Abuse Office and Treatment Act. (1976). 42 U.S.C. 290 §3 & 42 C.F.R. Part 2.

Drummond, R. J., & Ryan, C. W. (1995). *Career counseling: A developmental approach*. Englewood Cliffs, NJ: Merrill/Prentice Hall.

DuFour, R. (2004). What is a "professional learning community?" *Educational Leadership, 61*, 6–11.

Durodoye, B. A., Combes, B. H., & Bryant, R. M. (2004). Counselor intervention in the post-secondary planning of African American students with learning disabilities. *Professional School Counseling, 7*, 133–140.

Dykeman, C., Wood, C., Ingram, M. A., Pehrsson, D., Mandsager, N., & Herr, E. L. (2003). The structure of school career development interventions: Implications for school counselors. *Professional School Counseling, 6*, 272–278.

Echterling, L. G., Presbury, J. H., & McKee, J. E. (2005). *Crisis intervention: Promoting resilience and resolution in troubled times*. Upper Saddle River, NJ: Merrill/Prentice Hall.

Education Trust. (2003a). Transforming school counselor preparation. Retrieved November 18, 2004, from http://www2.edtrust.org/EdTrust/Transforming+School+Counseling/rationale.htm

Education Trust. (2003b). Transforming school counselor preparation. Retrieved November 18, 2004, from http://www2.edtrust.org/EdTrust/Transforming+School+Counseling/main

Education Trust. (2003c). Transforming school counselor preparation. Retrieved November 19, 2004, from http://www2.edtrust.org/edtrust/Transforming+School+Counseling/counseling+background

Education Trust. (2003d). Transforming school counseling. Retrieved April 15, 2005 from http://www2.edtrust.org/EdTrust/Transforming+School+Counseling/scope+work.htm

Education Trust. (1999). *Dispelling the myth: High poverty schools exceeding expectations*. Washington, DC: Author.

Education Trust. (n.d.). *Education watch: Education Trust community data guide*. Washington, DC: Author.

Educational Testing Service. (1997). *SIGI Plus*. Princeton, NJ: Author.

Ehly, S., & Dustin, R. (1989). *Individual and group counseling in schools*. New York: Guilford Press.

Eisel v. Board of Education of Montgomery County, 324 MD. 376, 597 A. 2d 447 (Md. Ct. App. 1991).

Elias, M. J., Gara, M. A., Schuyler, T. F., Brandon-Muller, L. R., & Sayette, M. A. (1991). The promotion of social competence: Longitudinal study of a preventative school-based program. *American Journal of Orthopsychiatry, 61*, 409–417.

Elliott, J. (2004). Assessment of and accountability for students with disabilities: Putting theory into practice. In J. E. Wall & G. R. Walz (Eds.), *Measuring up: Assessment issues for teacher, counselors, and administrators* (pp. 177–196). Greensboro, NC: CAPS.

Ellis, A. (1996). *Better, deeper, and more enduring brief therapy*. New York: Brunner/Mazel.

Ellis, B. B., & Raju, N. S. (2004). Test and item bias: What they are, what they aren't, and how to detect them. In J. E. Wall & G. R. Walz (Eds.), *Measuring up: Assessment issues for teacher, counselors, and administrators* (pp. 89–98). Greensboro, NC: CAPS.

Ellis, C. M. (2004). Conducting a structured observation. In B. T. Erford (Ed.), *Professional school counseling: A handbook of theories, programs, & practices* (pp. 467–474). Austin, TX: ProEd.

English, A., & Kenney, K. E. (2003). *State minor consent laws: A summary*. Chapel Hill, NC: Center for Adolescent Health & the Law.

ERIC/CAPPS. (1990). *Building comprehensive school counseling programs*. Greensboro, NC: Author.

Erickson, F. (2001). Culture in society and in educational practices. In J. A. Banks & C. A. McGee Banks (Eds.), *Multicultural education: Issues and perspectives* (pp. 31–58). New York: Wiley.

Erikson, E. (1963). *Childhood and society*. New York: W. W. Norton.

Erikson, E. (1980). *Identity and the life cycle* (2nd ed.). New York: Norton.

Esposito, C. (1999). Learning in urban blight: School climate and its effect on the school performance of urban, minority, low-income children. *School Psychology Review, 28,* 365–378.

Ethics Committee of the American School Counselor Association. (1999–2001). Ethical issues: Tips for school counselors. Retrieved on September 4, 2005, from http://www.schoolcounselor.org/ethics/ethicaltips.htm

Evans, H. H., & Burck, H. D. (1992). The effects of career education interventions on academic achievement. A meta-analysis. *Journal of Counseling and Development, 71,* 63–68.

Fairchild, T. N. (1997). School-based helpers' role in crisis intervention. In T. Fairchild (Ed.), *Crisis intervention strategies for school-based helpers* (2nd ed., pp. 3–19). Springfield, IL: Charles C. Thomas.

Fall, M. (1994). Developing curriculum expertise: A helpful tool for school counselors. *The School Counselor, 42,* 92–99.

Family Educational Rights and Privacy Act. (1974). 20 U.S.C.A. §1232g. [Buckley Amendment.] (1991).

Implementing regulations 34 C.F.R. 99.3. Fed. Reg. 56, §117, 28012.

Feller, R. W. (2003). Aligning school counseling, the changing workplace, and career development assumptions. *Professional School Counseling, 6,* 262–271.

Felner, R., Brand, S., Adan, A., Mulhall, P., Flowers, N., Sartain, B., & Dubois, D. (1993). Restructuring the ecology of the school as an approach to prevention during school transitions: Longitudinal follow-ups and extensions of the School Transition Environment Project (STEP). *Prevention in Human Services, 10,* 103–136.

Ferguson, R. E. (December 2002). *Addressing racial disparities in high-achieving suburban schools*. Retrieved February 17, 2005, from www.ncrel.org/policy/pubs/html/pivol13/dec2002b.htm

Fischer, L., & Sorenson, G. P. (1996). *School law for counselors, psychologists, and social workers* (3rd ed.). White Plains, NY: Longman.

Fisher, C. B., & Hennessy, J. (1994). Ethical issues. In J. L. Ronch, W. Van Ornum, & N. C. Stilwel (Eds.), *The counseling sourcebook: A practical reference on contemporary issues* (pp. 175–185). New York: Crossroad.

Flannery, D. J., Vazsonyi, A. T., Liau, A. K., Guo, S., Powell, K. E., Atha, H., Vesterday, W., & Embry, D. (2003). Initial behavior outcomes for the Peace-Builders universal school-based violence prevention program. *Developmental Psychology, 39,* 292–308.

Forester-Miller, H., & Davis, T. E. (1995). *A practitioner's guide to ethical decision-making*. Alexandria, VA: American Counseling Association.

Forester-Miller, H., & Rubenstein, R. L. (1992). Group counseling: Ethics and professional issues. In D. Capuzzi & D. R. Gross (Eds.), *Introduction to group counseling* (pp. 307–323). Denver, CO: Love Publishing.

Fowler, J. W. (1981). *Stages of faith*. New York: Harper Collins Publisher.

Fox, R. W., Wandry, D., Pruitte, P., & Anderson, G. (1998). School to adult life transitions for students with disabilities: Forging a new alliance. *Professional School Counseling, 1,* 48–52.

Freiberg, H. J. (1998). Measuring school climate: Let me count the ways. *Educational Leadership, 56,* 22–27.

Friend, M., & Cook, L. (1992). *Interactions: Collaboration skills for school professionals*. White Plains, NY: Longman.

Friend, M., & Cook, L. (2000). *Interactions: Collaboration skills for school professionals* (3rd ed.). New York: Longman.

Froeschle, J., & Moyer, M. (2004). Just cut it out: Legal and ethical challenges in counseling students who self-mutilate. *Professional School Counseling, 7,* 231–235.

Gallessich, J. (1982). *The profession and practice of consultation.* San Francisco: Jossey-Bass.

Garcia, J. G., Cartwright, B., Winston, S. M., & Borzuchowska, B. (2003). A transcultural integrative model for ethical decision making in counseling. *Journal of Counseling and Development, 81,* 268–277.

Gardner, H. (1993). *Multiple intelligences: The theory in practice.* New York: Basic Books.

Gardner, H. (1999). *The disciplined mind.* New York: Simon & Schuster.

Garrett, M., & Crutchfield, L. (1997). Moving full circle: A unity model of group work with children. *Journal for Specialists in Group Work, 22,* 715–188.

Gauvain, M. (2001). *The social context of cognitive development.* New York: Guilford Press.

Geisinger, K. F. (2004). Testing students with limited English proficiency. In J. E. Wall & G. R. Walz (Eds.), *Measuring up: Assessment issues for teacher, counselors, and administrators* (pp. 147–160). Greensboro, NC: CAPS.

Gerler, E. R., & Herndon, E. Y. (1993). Learning how to succeed academically in middle school. *Elementary School Guidance and Counseling, 27,* 186–197.

Gerler, E. R., Kinney, J., & Anderson, R. F. (1985). The effects of counseling on classroom performance. *Journal of Humanistic Education and Development, 23,* 155–165.

Gibson, R. L., & Mitchell, M. H. (1995). *Introduction to counseling and guidance* (4th ed.). Englewood Cliffs, NJ: Prentice Hall.

Gibson, R. L., & Mitchell, M. H. (1999). *Introduction to counseling and guidance* (5th Ed.). Upper Saddle River, NJ: Merrill/Prentice Hall.

Gilligan, C. (1982). *In a different voice: Psychological theory and women's development.* Cambridge, MA: Harvard University Press.

Ginzberg, E. (1972). Toward a theory of occupational choice: A restatement. *Vocational Guidance Quarterly, 20,* 169–176.

Gladding, S. T. (2004). *Counseling: A comprehensive profession* (5th ed). Upper Saddle River, NJ: Merrill/Prentice Hall.

Gladding, S. T. (2005). *Counseling as an art: Creative arts in counseling* (3rd ed.). Alexandria, VA: American Counseling Association.

Glasser, W. (1998). *Choice theory: A new psychology of personal freedom.* New York: Harper Collins.

Glosoff, H. L., Herlihy, B., & Spence, E. B. (2000). Privileged communication in the counselor-client relationship. *Journal of Counseling and Development, 78,* 454–462.

Glosoff, H. L., & Pate, R. H., Jr. (2002). Privacy and confidentiality in school counseling. *Professional School Counseling, 6,* 20–27.

Goldberg, M. (2000). Town Meeting—the National Alliance of Business and School Counselors. Speech presented at Symposium on the Role of School Counseling in Preparing Students for the 21st Century. Washington, DC.

Goldman, L. (1994). The marriage between tests and counseling redux: Summary of the 1972 article. *Measurement and Evaluation in Counseling and Development, 26,* 214–216.

Goldsmith, S. M. (2004). Lost in translation: Issues in translating tests for non-English speaking, limited English proficient, and bilingual students. In J. E. Wall & G. R. Walz (Eds.), *Measuring up: Assessment issues for teacher, counselors, and administrators* (pp. 127–146). Greensboro, NC: CAPS.

Goleman, D. (1995). *Emotional intelligence. Why it can matter more than I.Q.* New York: Bantam Books.

Gonzalez, G. M., & Myrick, R. D. (2000). The teacher as student advisors program (TAP): An effective approach for drug education and other developmental guidance activities. In J. Wittmer (Ed.), *Managing your school counseling program: K–12 developmental strategies* (2nd ed., pp. 243–252). Minneapolis, MN: Educational Media Corporation.

Goodnough, G., Perusse, R., & Erford, B. T. (2003). Developmental classroom guidance. In B. T. Erford (Ed.), *Transforming the school counseling profession* (pp. 121–152). Upper Saddle River, NJ: Merrill/Prentice Hall.

Gottfredson, G. D. (1988). An evaluation of an organizational development approach to reducing school disorder. *Evaluation Review, 11,* 739–763.

Gottfredson, L. S. (1996). Gottfredson's theory of circumspection and compromise. In D. Brown, L. Brooks, & Associates (Eds.), *Career choice and development* (3rd ed., pp. 179–228). San Francisco: Jossey-Bass.

Graham, B. C., & Pulvino, C. (2000). Multicultural conflict resolution: Development, implementation, and assessment of a program for third graders. *Professional School Counseling, 3,* 172–182.

Graham, P. A. (1993). What America has expected of its schools for the past century. *American Journal of Education, 101,* 83–98.

Grant, C. A., & Sleeter, C. E. (2001). Race, class, gender and disability in the classroom. In J. A. Banks & C. A. M. Banks (Eds.), *Multicultural education: Issues and perspectives* (4th ed., pp. 59–82). New York: Wiley.

Grassley Amendment. (1994). Sec. 1017 of GOALS 2000: The Educate America Act under the heading "Protection of Pupils." 20 U.S.C. §1232h.

Greenberg, K. R. (2003). *Group counseling in K–12 schools: A handbook for school counselors.* Boston: Allyn & Bacon.

Greenberg, J. M., & Shaffer, S. (1991). Elements of equity: Criteria for equitable schools. Mid-Atlantic Equity Consortium. Retrieved on October 18, 2001, from http://www.maec.org

Gronlund, N. E. (1995). *How to write and use instructional objectives* (5th ed.). Englewood Cliffs, NJ: Merrill.

Gronlund, N. E. (2004). *How to write and use instructional objectives* (7th ed.). Upper Saddle River, NJ: Merrill/Prentice Hall.

Grossman, D. C., Neckerman, H. J., Koepsell, T. D., Liu, P., Asher, K. N., Beland, K., Frey, K., & Rivara, F. P. (1997). Effectiveness of a violence prevention curriculum among children in elementary school. *Journal of the American Medical Association, 227,* 1605–1611.

Guillot-Miller, L., & Partin, P. W. (2003). Web-based resources for legal and ethical issues in school counseling. *Professional School Counseling, 7,* 52–57.

Guindon, M. H. (2003). Assessment. In B. T. Erford (Ed.), *Transforming the school counseling profession* (pp. 331–355). Upper Saddle River, NJ: Pearson.

Gunter, M. A., Estes, T. H., & Schwab, J. (1999). *Instruction: A models approach* (3rd ed.). Boston: Allyn & Bacon.

Gunter, M. A., Estes, T. H., & Schwab, J. (2003). *Instruction: A models approach* (4th ed.). Needham Heights, MA: Allyn & Bacon.

Gurian, M., & Stevens, K. (2004). With boys and girls in mind. *Educational Leadership, 62,* 21–26.

Gustafson, K. E., & McNamara, J. R. (1987). Confidentiality with minor clients: Issues and guidelines for therapists. *Professional Psychology: Research and Practice, 18,* 503–508.

Gysbers, N. C. (1995). Evaluating school guidance programs ERIC Digest (On-line). Retrieved on November 15, 2001, from http:www.ed.gov/databases/ERIC_Digests/ed388887.html

Gysbers, N. C. (2004). Comprehensive guidance and counseling programs: The evolution of accountability. *Professional School Counseling, 8,* 1–14.

Gysbers, N. C., & Henderson, P. (2000). *Developing & managing your school guidance program* (3rd ed.). Alexandria, VA: American Counseling Association.

Gysbers, N. C., Lapan, R. T., & Jones, B. A. (2000). School board policies for guidance and counseling: A call to action. *Professional School Counseling, 3,* 349–355.

Hammond, L. C., & Gantt, L. (1998). Using art in counseling: Ethical considerations. *Journal of Counseling and Development, 76,* 271–276.

Harkins, M. A. (2001). Developmentally appropriate career guidance: Building concepts to last a lifetime. *Early Childhood Education Journal, 28,* 169–174.

Harris-Bowlsbey, J., Dikel, M. R., & Sampson, J. P. (1998). *The Internet: A tool for career planning.* Columbus, OH: National Career Development Association.

Harter, S. (1996). *The construction of the self: A developmental perspective.* New York: Guilford.

Hartman, N. S., McDaniel, M. A., & Whetzel, D. L. (2004). Racial and ethnic difference in performance. In J. E. Wall & G. R. Walz (Eds.), *Measuring up: Assessment issues for teacher, counselors, and administrators* (pp. 99–116). Greensboro, NC: CAPS.

Havighurst, R. J. (1972). *Developmental tasks and education* (3rd ed.). New York: David McKay.

Heath, S. V. (1983). *Ways with words: Language, life, and work in communities and classrooms.* New York: Cambridge University Press.

Helms, J. E. (1994). The conceptualization of racial identity and other racial constructs. In E. J. Trickett, R. J. Watts, & D. Birman (Eds.), *Human diversity: Perspectives on people in context* (pp. 185–311). San Francisco: Jossey-Bass.

Helms, J. E. (2004). Fair and valid use of educational tests in grades K–12. In J. E. Wall & G. R. Walz (Eds.), *Measuring up: Assessment issues for teacher, counselors, and administrators* (pp. 81–88). Greensboro, NC: CAPS.

Helms, J. E., & Cook, D. A. (1999). *Using race and culture in counseling and psychotherapy: Theory and process.* Needham Heights, MA: Allyn & Bacon.

Henderson, D. A., & Fall, M. (1998). School counseling. In R. R. Cottone & V. M. Tarvydas (Eds.), *Ethical and professional issues in counseling* (pp. 263–293). Upper Saddle River, NJ: Merrill/Prentice Hall.

Henderson, P., & Gysbers, N.C. (1998). *Leading & managing your school guidance program staff: A manual for school administrators and directors of guidance.* Alexandria, VA: American Counseling Association.

Henderson, P. A., Kelby, T. J., & Engebretson, K. M. (1992). Effects of a stress-control program on children's locus of control, self-concept, and coping behavior. *The School Counselor, 40,* 125–130.

Herbert, D. (1986). Career guidance, families and school counselors. Retrieved on August 15, 2001, from http://www.ed.gov/databases/ERIC_Digests/ed279991.html

Herlihy, B., & Corey, G. (1992). *Dual relationships in counseling.* Alexandria, VA: American Association for Counseling and Development.

Hermann, M. A. (2002). A study of legal issues encountered by school counselors and perceptions of their preparedness to respond to legal challenges. *Professional School Counseling, 6,* 12–20.

Hermann, M. A., & Finn, A. (2002). An ethical and legal perspective on the role of school counselors in preventing violence in schools. *Professional School Counseling, 6,* 46–55.

Hernandez, T. J., & Seem, S. R. (2004). A safe school climate: A systemic approach and the school counselor. *Professional School Counseling, 7,* 256–262.

Herr, E. L. (1995). *Counseling employment bound youth.* Greensboro, NC: ERIC.

Herr, E. L., Cramer, S. H., & Niles, S. G. (2004). *Career guidance and counseling through the lifespan: Systematic approaches* (6th ed.). Boston: Allyn & Bacon.

Herring, R. D. (1997). *Multicultural counseling in schools: A synergetic approach.* Alexandria, VA: American Counseling Association.

Herring, R. D. (1998). *Career counseling in schools: Multicultural and developmental perspectives.* Alexandria, VA: American Counseling Association.

Herting-Wahl, K. L., & Blackhurst, A. (2000). Factors affecting the occupational and educational aspirations of children and adolescents. *Professional School Counseling, 3,* 367–374.

Hibert, K. M. (2000). Mentoring leadership. *Phi Delta Kappan, 82*(1), 16–18.

Hill, M., Glaser, K., & Harden, J. (1995). A feminist model for ethical decision making. In E. J. Rave & C. C. Larsen (Eds.), *Ethical decision making in therapy: Feminist perspectives* (pp. 18–37). New York: Guilford Press.

Hines, P. L., & Fields, T. H. (2002). Pregroup screening issues for school counselors. *Journal for Specialists in Group Work, 27,* 358–376.

Ho, B. S. (2001). Family-centered, integrated services: Opportunities for school counselors. *Professional School Counseling, 4,* 357–361.

Holcomb-McCoy, C. (2004). Assessing the multicultural competence of school counselors: A checklist. *Professional School Counseling, 7,* 178–186.

Holcomb-McCoy, C., & Rahill, S. (2002). Importance of the CACREP school counseling standards: School counselors' perceptions. *Professional School Counseling, 6,* 112–118.

Hollins, E. R. (1999). Relating ethnic and racial identity development to teaching. In R. H. Sheets & E. R. Hollins (Eds.), *Racial and ethnic identity in school practices: Aspects of human development* (pp. 183–193). Mahwah, NJ: Lawrence Erlbaum.

Holmgren, S. V. (1996). *Elementary school counseling: An expanding role.* Boston: Allyn & Bacon.

House, R. M., & Martin, P. J. (1998). Advocating for better futures for all students: A new vision for school counselors. *Education, 119,* 284–291.

Howell-Nigrelli, J. (1988). Shared responsibility for reporting child abuse cases: A reaction to Spiegel. *Elementary School Guidance and Counseling, 22,* 289–290.

Huey, W. C. (1996). Counseling minor clients. In B. Herlihy & G. Corey (Eds.), *ACA ethical standards casebook* (5th ed., pp. 241–245). Alexandria, VA: American Counseling Association.

Hughes, K. I. L., & Karp, M. M. (2004). *School-based career development: A synthesis of the literature.* Teachers College, Columbia University: Institute of Education and the Economy.

Hughes, R. L., Ginnett, R. C., & Curphy, G. R. (1995). What is leadership? In J. T. Wren (Ed.), *The leader's companion: Insights on leadership through the ages* (pp. 39–48). New York: Free Press.

Individuals with Disabilities Education Act of 1997. (1997). Publ. L. No. 105-17, 34 CFR 300.574.

Isaacs, M. L. (1997). The duty to warn and protect: Tarasoff and the elementary school counselor. *Elementary School Guidance and Counseling, 31,* 326–342.

Isaacs, M. L., & Stone, C. (1999). School counselors and confidentiality: Factors affecting professional choices. *Professional School Counseling, 2,* 258–266.

Jackson, C. M. (2005). The school counselor and advocacy: Taking a stand. In Tamara Davis (Ed.), *Exploring school counseling: Professional practices and perspectives* (pp. 260–271). Boston: Lahaska Press.

Jackson, D. S. (2000). The school improvement journey: Perspectives on leadership. *School Leadership & Management, 20*(1), 61–79.

James, S. H., & DeVaney, S. B. (1995). Preparing to testify: The school counselor as court witness. *School Counselor, 43*(2), 97–103.

Janosz, M., LeBlanc, M., Boulerice, B., & Tremblay, R. E. (2000). Predicting different types of school dropouts:

A typological approach with two longitudinal samples. *Journal of Educational Psychology, 92,* 171–190.

Jencks, C., Bartlett, S., Corcoran, M., Crouse, J., Eaglesfield, D., Jackson, G., McClelland, K., Mueser, P., Olneck, M., Schwartz, J., Ward, S., & Williams, J. (1979). *Who gets ahead? The determinants of economic success in America.* New York: Basic Books.

Jencks, C., & Phillips, M. (1998). *America's next achievement test: Closing the black-white test score gap.* Retrieved October 28, 2005, from www.prospect.org/print/V9/40/jencks-c.html

Jimerson, S. R., Egeland, B., Stoufe, L. A., & Carlson, B. (2000). A perspective longitudinal study of high school dropouts: Examining multiple predictors across development. *Journal of School Psychology, 38,* 525–549.

Johnson, D. W., & Johnson, F. P. (1997). *Joining together: Group theory and group skills* (6th ed.). Needham Heights, MA: Allyn & Bacon.

Johnson, D. W., & Johnson, F. P. (2000). *Joining together: Group theory and group skills.* Boston: Allyn & Bacon.

Johnson, D. W., & Johnson, R. T. (1999). *Learning together and alone: Cooperative, competitive, and individualistic learning.* Boston: Allyn & Bacon.

Johnson, L. S. (2000). Promoting professional identity in an era of educational reform. *Professional School Counseling, 4,* 31–40.

Johnson, R. S. (2002). *Using data to close the achievement gap: How to measure equity in our schools.* Thousand Oaks, CA: Corwin Press.

Junhke, G. A. (1997). After school violence: An adapted critical incident stress debriefing model for student survivors and their parents. *Elementary School Guidance & Counseling, 31,* 163–171.

Kagan, S., & Neuman, M. (1998). Lessons from three decades of transition research. *Elementary School Journal, 98,* 365–379.

Kahn, B. B. (2000). A model of solution-focused consultation for school counselors. *Professional School Counseling, 3,* 248–255.

Kail, R. V., & Cavanaugh, J. C. (2004). *Human development* (3rd ed.). Belmont, CA: Wadsworth.

Kameen, M. C., Robinson, E. H., & Rotter, J. C. (1985). Coordination activities: A study of perceptions of elementary and middle school counselors. *Elementary School Guidance & Counseling, 20,* 97–104.

Kampwirth, T. J. (2006). *Collaborative consultation in the schools: Effective practices for students with learning and behavior problems.* Upper Saddle River, NJ: Merrill.

Kaplan, D. M. (2001). Developing an informed consent brochure for secondary students. Retrieved on October 5, 2005, from http://www.schoolcounselor.org/ethics/

Kaplan, L. S. (1997). Parents' rights: Are school counselors at risk? *The School Counselor, 44,* 334–343.

Kaplan, L. S., & Geoffroy, K. E. (1990). Enhancing the school climate: New opportunities for the counselor. *School Counselor, 38,* 7–13.

Kaplan, P. S. (2000). *A child's odyssey* (3rd ed.). Belmont, CA: Wadsworth.

Katzenbach, J., Beckett, F., Dichter, S., Feigen, M., Gagnon, C., Hope, Q., & Ling, T. (1995). *Real change leaders.* New York: Random House.

Kelly, F. R., Jr. (1996). "That's not fair!"—Using RET to address the issue of fairness in classroom guidance. *Elementary School Guidance & Counseling, 30,* 235–238.

Kenyon, P. (1999). *What would you do? An ethical case workbook for human service professionals.* Pacific Grove, CA: Brooks/Cole.

Kerpelman, J. L., Shoffner, M. F., & Ross-Griffin, S. (2002). African American mothers' and daughters' beliefs about possible selves and their strategies for reaching the adolescents' future academic and career goals. *Journal of Youth & Adolescence, 31,* 289–302.

Keys, S. G., Bemak, F., & Lockhart, E. J. (1998). Transforming school counseling to serve the mental health needs of at-risk youth. *Journal of Counseling and Development, 76,* 381–388.

Kiselica, M. S., Baker, S. B., Thomas, R. N., & Reedy, S. (1994). Effects of stress inoculation training on anxiety, stress, and academic performance of adolescents. *Journal of Counseling Psychology, 41,* 335–342.

Kitchener, K. S. (1984). Intuition, critical evaluation, and ethical principles: The foundation for ethical decision in counseling psychology. *Counseling Psychologist, 12,* 43–55.

Kitchener, K. S. (1986). Teaching applied ethics in counselor education: An integration of psychological processes and philosophical analysis. *Journal of Counseling and Development, 64,* 306–310.

Kitchener, K. S., & Harding, S. S. (1990). Dual role relationships. In B. Herlihy & L. Golden (Eds.), *Ethical standards casebook* (4th ed., pp. 145–148). Alexandria, VA: American Association for Counseling and Development.

Knapp, S. E., & Jongsma, A. E. (2002). *The school counseling and school social work treatment planner.* Hoboken, NJ: Wiley.

Kohlberg, L. (1969). Stage and sequence: the cognitive developmental approach to socialization. In D. Goslin (Ed.), *Handbook of socialization theory and research* (pp. 347–480). Chicago: Rand-McNally.

Kormanski, C. (1999). *The team: Explorations in group process.* Denver, CO: Love Publishing.

Kormanski, C. L., & Mozenter, A. (1987). A new model of team building: A technology for today and tomorrow. In J. W. Pfeiffer (Ed.), *The 1987 annual: Developing human resources* (pp. 255–268). San Diego, CA: University Associates.

Kosciulek, J. F. (2003). An empowerment approach to career counseling with people with disabilities. In N. C. Gysbers, M. J. Heppner, & J. A. Johnston (Eds.), *Career counseling: Process, issues, and techniques* (2nd ed., pp. 139–153). Boston: Allyn & Bacon.

Kottman, T., Ashby, J., & DeGraaf, D. (2001). *Adventures in guidance: How to put fun into your guidance program.* Alexandria, VA: American Counseling Association.

Krathwohl, D. R., Bloom, B. S., & Masia, B. B. (1964). Taxonomy of educational objectives. *Handbook II: Affective domain.* New York: David McKay.

Kretzmann, J., & McKnight, J. (1993). *Building communities from the inside out: A path toward finding and mobilizing a community's assets.* Chicago: ACTA Publications.

Kurpius, D. J., & Fuqua, D. R. (1993). Fundamental issues in defining consultation. *Journal of Counseling and Development, 71,* 598–600.

Kurpius, D. J., & Rozecki, T. (1992). Outreach, advocacy, and consultation: A framework for prevention and intervention. *Elementary School Guidance and Counseling, 26,* 176–190.

Kush, K., & Cochran, L. (1993). Enhancing a sense of agency through career planning. *Journal of Counseling Psychology, 40,* 434–439.

Ladany, N., Melincoff, D. S., Constantine, M. G., & Love, R. (1997). At-risk urban high school students' commitment to career choices. *Journal of Counseling and Development, 76,* 45–52.

Ladson-Billings, G. (1994). *The dreamkeepers: Successful teachers of African American children.* San Francisco: Jossey-Bass.

Lambert, L. (1998). *Building leadership capacity in schools.* Alexandria, VA: Association for Supervision and Curriculum Development.

Lambert, L. (2003). *Leadership capacity for lasting school improvement.* Alexandria, VA: Association for Supervision and Curriculum Development.

Lapan, R. T. (2001). Results-based comprehensive guidance and counseling programs: A framework for planning and evaluation. *Professional School Counselor, 4,* 289–299.

Lapan, R. T. (2004). *Career development across the K–16 years: Bridging the present to satisfying and successful futures.* Alexandria, VA: American Counseling Association.

Lapan, R. T., Gysbers, N., Hughey, K., & Arni, T. J. (1993). Evaluating a guidance and language arts unit for high school juniors. *Journal of Counseling and Development, 71,* 444–451.

Lapan, R. T., Gysbers, N. C., & Sun, Y. (1997). The impact of more fully implemented guidance programs on the school experiences of high school students: A statewide evaluation study. *Journal of Counseling & Development, 75,* 292–302.

Lawrence, G. & Robinson Kurpius, S. E. (2000). Legal and ethical issues involved when counseling minors in nonschool settings. *Journal of Counseling and Development, 78,* 130–136.

Lazarus, A. A. (1976). *Multimodal behavior therapy.* New York: Springer.

Lee, C. E. (1993). *Signifying as a scaffold for literary interpretation: The pedagogical implications of an African American discourse.* Urbana, IL: National Council of Teachers of English.

Lee, R. S. (1993). Effects of classroom guidance on student achievement. *Elementary School Guidance and Counseling, 27,* 163–171.

Lee, V. E., & Burkam, D. T. (2002). *Inequality at the gate: Social background differences in achievement as children begin school.* Retrieved February 17, 2005, from www.epinet.org/books/starting_gate.html

Lee, V. E., & Burkam, D. T. (2003). Dropping out of high school: The role of school organization and structure. *American Educational Research Journal, 40,* 353–393.

Legum, H. L., Hoare, C. H. (2004). Impact of a career intervention on at-risk middle school students' career maturity levels, academic achievement, and self-esteem. *Professional School Counseling, 8,* 148–155.

Leinbaugh, T. (2004). Understanding special education policies and procedures. In B. T. Erford (Ed.), *Professional school counseling: A handbook of theories, programs, & practices* (pp. 647–654). Austin, TX: ProEd.

Lewis, J., Lewis, M., Packard, T., & Souflee, F. (2001). *Management of human service programs.* Belmont, CA: Wadsworth/Thomson.

Lippitt, G., & Lippitt, R. (1986). *The consulting process in action* (2nd ed.). La Jolla, CA: University Associates.

Linde, L. (2003). Ethical, legal, and professional issues in school counseling. In B. T. Erford (Ed.), *Transforming the school counseling profession* (pp. 39–62). Upper Saddle River, NJ: Merrill/Prentice Hall.

Littrell, J. M., & Peterson, J. S. (2001). Facilitating systemic change using the MRI problem-solving approach: One school's experience. *Professional School Counseling, 5,* 27–33.

Locke, D. C. (1993). *Multicultural counseling.* Ann Arbor, MI: Clearinghouse on Counseling and Personnel Services. (ERIC Document No. EDO-CG-93-1).

Lockhart, E. J. (2003). Students with disabilities. In B. T. Erford (Ed.), *Transforming the school counseling profession* (pp. 357–410). Upper Saddle River, NJ: Pearson.

Lockhart, E. J., & Keys, S. G. (1998). The mental health counseling role of school counselors. *Professional School Counseling, 1,* 3–6.

Loesch, L. C., & Ritchie, M. H. (2005). *The accountable school counselor.* Austin, TX: ProEd.

Loesch, L. C., & Vacc, N. A. (2001). Counseling uses of test. In D. Capuzzi & D. R. Gross (Eds.), *Introduction to the counseling profession* (3rd ed., pp. 249–269). Boston: Allyn & Bacon.

Luongo, P. E. (2000). Partnering child welfare, juvenile justice, and behavioral health with schools. *Professional School Counseling, 3,* 308–314.

Lundberg, D., & Kirk, W. (2004). A test user's guide to serving a multicultural community. In J. E. Wall & G. R. Walz (Eds.), *Measuring up: Assessment issues for teacher, counselors, and administrators* (pp. 117–126). Greensboro, NC: CAPS.

Lusky, M. B., & Hayes, R. L. (2001). Collaborative consultation and program evaluation. *Journal of Counseling and Development, 79,* 26–38.

Lutzker, J. R., & Martin, J. A. (1981). *Behavior change.* Pacific Grove, CA: Brooks/Cole.

Lynch, S. K. (1993). AIDS: Balancing confidentiality and the duty to protect. *Journal of College Student Development, 34,* 148–153.

MacIver, D. J., & Epstein, J. L. (1991). Responsive practices in the middle grades: Teacher teams, advisory groups, remedial instruction, and school transition programs. *American Journal of Education, 99,* 587–622.

Mager, R. (1975). *Preparing instructional objectives* (2nd ed.). Palo Alto, CA: Fearon.

Magnuson, S. (1997). Guidance portfolios: Documenting components of children's personal and career development. *The School Counselor, 44,* 309–311.

Marzano, R. J., Pickering, D. J., & Pollock, J. E. (2001). *Classroom instruction that works: Research-based strategies for increasing student achievement.* Alexandria, VA: Association for Supervision and Curriculum Development.

Maslow, A. (1954). *Motivation and personality.* New York: Harper and Row.

Masten, A. (2001). Ordinary magic: Resilience processes in development. *American Psychologist, 56,* 227–238.

Masten, A. S., & Coatsworth, J. D. (1998). The development of competence in favorable and unfavorable environments: Lessons from research on successful children. *American Psychologist, 53,* 205–220.

Mau, W., & Bikos, L. H. (2000). Educational and vocational aspirations of minority and female students: A longitudinal study. *Journal of Counseling & Development, 78,* 186–194.

McEvoy, A., & Welker, R. (2000). Antisocial behavior, academic failure, and school climate: A critical review. *Journal of Emotional and Behavioral Disorders, 8,* 130–141.

McDaniels, C. (1982). Comprehensive career information systems for the 1980s. *Vocational Guidance Quarterly, 30,* 344–350.

McDivitt, P. J. (2004). High-stakes testing: What counselors need to know. In J. E. Wall & G. R. Walz (Eds.), *Measuring up: Assessment issues for teacher, counselors, and administrators* (pp. 407–413). Greensboro, NC: CAPS.

McElroy, C. M. (2000). Middle school programs that work. *Phi Delta Kappan, 82,* 277–279.

McFarland, L. J., Senn, L. E., & Childress, J. R. (1995). Redefining leadership for the next century. In J. T. Wren (Ed.), *The leader's companion: Insights on leadership through the ages* (pp. 456–463). New York: Free Press.

McGannon, W., Carey, J., & Dimmitt, C. (May 2005). *Research Monograph, Number 2: The current status of school counseling outcome research.* Amherst, MA: Center for School Counseling Outcome Research.

McWhirter, E. H., Crothers, M., & Rasheed, S. (2000). The effects of high school career education on social-cognitive variables. *Journal of Counseling Psychology, 47,* 330–341.

McWhirter, J. J., McWhirter, B. T., McWhirter, E. H., & McWhirter, R. J. (2004). *At-risk youth: A comprehensive response* (3rd ed.). Belmont, CA: Brooks-Cole.

Meara, N. M., Schmidt, L. D., & Day, J. D. (1996). Principles and virtues: A foundation for ethical decisions, policies and character. *The Counseling Psychologist, 24,* 4–77.

Meisels, S. (1999). Assessing readiness. In R. Pianta & M. Cox (Eds.), *The transition to kindergarten: Research, policy, training, and practice* (pp. 39–66). Baltimore: Paul Brooks Publishers.

Metcalf, L. (1995). *Counseling toward solutions: A practical solution-focused program for working with students, teachers, and parents*. West Nyack, NJ: Center for Applied Research in Education.

Meyers, J., Brent, D., Faherty, E., & Modafferi, C. (1993). Caplan's contributions to the practice of psychology in schools. In W. P. Erchul (Ed.), *Consultation in community, school, and organizational practice: Gerald Caplan's contribution in professional psychology* (pp. 99–122). Washington, DC: Taylor & Francis.

Milone, M. N. (1995). Electronic portfolios: Who's doing them and how? *Technology and Learning, 16,* 28–36.

Milsom, A., Akos, P., & Thompson, M. (2004). A psychoeducational group approach to postsecondary transition planning for students with learning disabilities. *Journal of Specialists in Group Work, 29,* 395–411.

Minard, S. M. (1993). The school counselor's role in confronting child sexual abuse. *The School Counselor, 41,* 9–15.

Mitchell, C. W., Disque, J. G., & Robertson, P. (2002). When parents want to know: Responding to parental demands for confidential information. *Professional School Counseling, 6,* 156–162.

Mitchell, C. W., & Rogers, R. E. (2003). Rape, statutory rape, and child abuse: Legal distinctions and counselor duties. *Professional School Counseling, 6,* 332–338.

Mortenson, T. (2000). *Postsecondary education opportunity*. The Mortenson research seminar on public policy analysis of opportunity for postsecondary education. Iowa City, Iowa: Author.

Munson, H. L., & Rubenstein, B. J. (1992). School IS work: Work task learning in the classroom. *Journal of Career Development, 18,* 289–297.

Muro, J. J., & Kottman, T. (1995). *Guidance and counseling in the elementary and middle schools: A practical approach*. Dubuque: Benchmark & Brown.

Murphy, J. J. (1997). *Solution-focused counseling in middle and high schools*. Upper Saddle River, NJ: Merrill Education.

Myrick, R. D. (1997). *Developmental guidance and counseling: A practical approach* (3rd ed.). Minneapolis: Educational Media.

National Association for College Admission Counseling, American Counseling Association, The Education Trust, American School Counselor Association, Sallie Mae Foundation. (2000). *The role of school counseling in preparing students for the 21st century: policies that foster effective school counseling programs*. Washington, DC: Author.

National Association for the Education of Young Children. (2002). NAEYC Position Statement on School Readiness. Retrieved June 27, 2005, from http://naeyconline.org

National Assessment of Educational Progress. (2004). *NAEP data tool*. National Center for Education Statistics. Retrieved June 23, 2005, from http://nces.ed.gov/nationsreportcard/naepdata/

National Association of Peer Programs. (n.d.). *Programmatic standards and ethics*. Retrieved on October 14, 2005, from http://www.peerprograms.org/publications/publications/standards/

National Association of Social Workers. (1999). *Code of ethics of the National Association of Social Workers*. Washington, DC: Author.

National Board of Certified Counselors. (2005). *Code of ethics*. Retrieved on September 30, 2005, from www.nbcc.org/extras/pdfs/NBCC-CodeofEthics.pdf

National Center for Children Living in Poverty. (2005). Basic facts about low income children: Birth to 18 years. Retrieved on July 25, 2005, from http://nccp.org/pub_lic05.html

National Center for Education Statistics. (2003). *Digest of Education Statistics, 2003*. Retrieved on November 18, 2004, from http://nces.ed.gov/programs/digest.asp

National Center for Education Statistics. (2004). *Forum guide to protecting the privacy of student information: State and local education agencies*. NCES 2003-330. Washington, DC: Author.

National Center for Education Statistics. (2005a). Long-term trends. Retrieved on July 14, 2005, from www.nces.ed.gov/nationsreportcard/ltt/results2004

National Center for Education Statistics. (2005b). *Children with selected disabilities in schools*. Retrieved on July 25, 2005, from http://nces.ed.gov/programs/coe/2005/section1/indicator06.asp

National Commission on Excellence in Education. (1983). *A nation at risk*. Washington, DC: U.S. Department of Education.

National Council on Education Standards and Testing. (1992). *Raising standards for American education*. Washington, DC: Author.

National Education Association. (2002). *Rankings & Estimates: Rankings of the States 2001 and Estimates of School Statistics 2002*. Washington, DC: Author.

National Education Association. (2005). *C.A.R.E.: Strategies for closing the achievement gaps*. Retrieved on June 14, 2005, from http://www.nea.org/teachexperience/careguide.html

National Occupational Information Coordinating Committee (NOICC). (1988). *The National Career Counseling and Development Guidelines-Postsecondary Institutions*. Washington, DC: Author.

National Occupational Information Coordinating Committee (NOICC). U.S. Department of Labor. (1992). *The national career development guidelines project*. Washington, DC: U.S. Department of Labor.

National School Boards Association. (1986). *Resolution on guidance and counseling*. Alexandria, VA: Author.

Nauta, M. M., Saucier, A. M., & Woodard, L. E. (2001). Interpersonal influences on students' achievement and career decisions: The impact of sexual orientation. *The Career Development Quarterly, 49*, 352–362.

Nelson, D. E., & Gardner, J. L. (1998). *An evaluation of the comprehensive guidance program in Utah public schools*. Salt Lake City, UT: The Utah State Office of Education.

Neuman, M., & Simmons, W. (2000). Leadership for student learning. *Phi Delta Kappan, 82*(1), 9–12.

Newman, B. M., & Newman, P. R. (2003). *Development through life: A psychosocial approach* (8th ed.). Belmont, CA: Wadsworth.

Newmann, F. M., & Wehlage, G. G. (1995). *Successful school restructuring: A report to the public and educators by the Center on Organization and Restructuring of Schools*. Madison, WI: Center on Organization and Restructuring of Schools.

Newmeyer, A. J., & Newmeyer, M. (2004). Understanding section 504 policies and procedures. In B. T. Erford (Ed.), *Professional school counseling: A handbook of theories, programs, & practices* (pp. 655–658). Austin, TX: ProEd.

Niles, S. G., & Akos, P. (2003). Fostering educational and career planning in students. In B. T. Erford (Ed.), *Professional school counseling: A handbook of theories, programs, & practices* (pp. 153–170). Austin, TX: ProEd.

Norwood, P. M., & Atkinson, S. E. (1997). Contextualizing parent education programs in urban schools. The impact on minority parents and students. *Urban Education, 32*, 411–433.

Nystul, M. S. (2003). *Introduction to counseling: An art and science perspective* (2nd ed.). Boston, MA: Allyn & Bacon.

O'Brien, K. M., Bikos, L. H., Epstein, K. L., Flores, L. Y., Dukstein, R. D., & Kamatuka, N. A. (2000). Enhancing the career decision-making self-efficacy of upward bound students. *Journal of Career Development, 28*, 277–293.

O'Brien, K. M., Dukstein, R. D., Jackson, S. L., Tomlinson, M. J., & Kamatuka, N. A. (1999). Broadening career horizons for students in at-risk environment. *The Career Development Quarterly, 47*, 215–229.

O'Connor, K., Plante, J., & Refvem, J. (1998, March). *Parental consent and the school counselor*. Poster session presented at the annual conference of the North Carolina Counseling Association, Chapel Hill, NC as cited in S. B. Baker & E. R. Gerler, Jr., *School counseling for the 21st century* (4th ed.). Upper Saddle River, NJ: Merrill/Prentice Hall.

Office of Civil Rights. (2001). *Revised sexual harassment policy guidance: Harassment of students by school employees, other students or third parties*. Retrieved on October 20, 2005, from www.ed.gov/offices/list/ocr/index.html

Office of Special Education Programs. (2004). The individuals with disabilities education improvement act of 2004. Retrieved on August 13, 2005, from http://www.ed.gov/about/offices/list/osers/osep/index.html

Oliver, L. W., & Spokane, A. R. (1988). Career-intervention outcome: What contributes to client gain? *Journal of Counseling Psychology, 35*, 447–462.

O'Looney, J. (1996). *Redesigning the work of human services*. Westport, CT: Quorum.

Omizo, M. M., Omizo, A. A., & D'Andrea. (1992). Promoting wellness among elementary school children. *Journal of Counseling and Development, 71*, 194–198.

Orange County Public Schools. (1999). OCPS Core Curriculum: Student Development. Retrieved on May 23, 2002, from http://www.ocps.K12.fl.us/framework

Ormrod, J. E. (1999). *Human learning* (3rd ed.). Upper Saddle River, NJ: Merrill/Prentice Hall.

Ormrod, J. E. (2000). *Educational psychology: Developing learners*. Upper Saddle River, NJ: Merrill/Prentice Hall.

Osterman, K. F. (2000). Students' needs for belonging in the school community. *Review of Educational Research, 70*, 323–367.

Pai, Y., & Adler, S. A. (1997). *Cultural foundations of education* (2nd ed.). Upper Saddle River, NJ: Merrill/Prentice Hall.

Paisley, P. O. (2001). Maintaining and enhancing the developmental focus in school counseling programs. *Professional School Counseling, 4*, 271–277.

Paisley, P. O., & Hubbard, G. T. (1994). *Developmental school counseling programs: From theory to practice*. Alexandria, VA: American Counseling Association.

Palmer, S., & Cochran, L. (1988). Parents as agents of career development. *Journal of Counseling Psychology, 35*, 71–76.

Perelman, J. L., Shaffer, M. F., & Ross-Griffin, S. (2002). African American mothers' and daughters' beliefs about possible selves and their strategies for reaching the adolescents' future academic and career goals. *Journal of Youth & Adolescence, 31*, 289–302.

Perrone, P. A. (1997). Gifted individuals' career development. In N. Colangelo & G. A. Davis (Eds.), *Handbook of gifted education* (2nd ed., pp. 398–407). Boston: Allyn & Bacon.

Peterson, G. W., Long, K. L., & Billups, A. (1999). The effect of three career interventions on educational choices of eight grad students. *Professional School Counseling, 3*, 34–42.

Philips, S. (1983). *The invisible culture: Communication in classroom and community on the Warm Springs Indian Reservation.* New York: Longman.

Phillips, P., Sears, S., Snow, B., & Jackson, C. M. (2005). The professional school counselor as a leader. In Tamara Davis (Ed.), *Exploring school counseling: Professional practices and perspectives* (pp. 215–234). Boston: Lahaska Press.

Piaget, J. (1954). *The construction of reality in the child.* New York: Basic Books.

Pianta, R., & Cox, M. (1999). *The transition to kindergarten: Research, policy, training, and practice.* Baltimore: Paul Brooks Publishers.

Pipho, C. (2000a). Stateline: Saving public education for the new century. *Phi Delta Kappan, 81*, 341–342.

Pipho, C. (2000b). Governing the American dream of universal public education. In R. S. Brandt (Ed.), *Education in a new era* (pp. 5–19). Alexandria, VA: Association for Supervision and Curriculum Development.

Porter, L. (1999). *Young children's behavior: Practical approaches for caregivers and teachers.* Sydney, Australia: Brooks.

Pounder, D. G., & Ogawa, R. T. (1995). Leadership as an organization-wide phenomena: Its impact on school performance. *Educational Administration Quarterly, 31*(4), 564–589.

Pryor, D. B., & Tollerud, T. R. (1999). Applications of Adlerian principles in school settings. *Professional School Counseling, 2*, 299–305.

Public Schools of North Carolina. (2005a). *NC standard course of study: Guidance.* Retrieved on September 2, 2005, from www.ncpublicschools.org/curriculum/guidance

Public Schools of North Carolina. (2005b). *Elementary blueprints.* Retrieved on September 2, 2005, from http://www.ncpublicschools.org/doc/curriculum/guidance/scos/02ebprints.pdf

Purkey, W. W., & Novak, J. (1996). *Inviting school success* (3rd ed.). Belmont, CA: Wadsworth.

Purkey, W. W., & Schmidt, J. J. (1990). *Invitational learning for counseling and development.* Ann Arbor, MI: ERIC/CAPS.

Purkey, W. W., & Schmidt, J. J. (1996). *Invitational counseling: A self-concept approach to professional practice.* Pacific Grove, CA: Brooks/Cole.

Purkey, W. W., & Strahan, D. B. (2002). *Inviting positive classroom discipline.* Westerville, OH: National Middle School Association.

Quintana, S. M. (1998). Children's developmental understanding of ethnicity and race. *Applied and Preventive Psychology, 7*, 27–45.

Rabasca, L. (2000). Pre-empting racism. *Monitor on Psychology, 31*(11), 60.

Rak, C., & Patterson, L. E. (1996). Resiliency in children. *Journal of Counseling and Development, 74*, 268–373.

Ramey, C., & Ramey, S. (1999). Beginning school for children at risk. In R. Pianta & M. Cox (Eds.), *The transition to kindergarten: Research, policy, training, and practice* (2nd ed., pp. 271–252). Baltimore: Paul Brooks.

Rapin, L., & Keel, L. (1998). *Association for specialists in group work best practice guidelines.* Retrieved on September 22, 2005, from http://asgw.educ.kent.edu/best.htm

Rathus, S. A. (2006). *Childhood and adolescence: Voyages in development* (2nd ed.). Belmont, CA: Thompson.

Rathvon, N. (1999). *Effective school interventions: Strategies for enhancing academic achievement and social competence.* New York: Guilford Press.

Rauch, C. F., & Behling, O. (1984). Functionalism: Basis for an alternate approach to the study of leadership. In J. G. Hunt, D. M. Hosking, C. A. Schriescheim, & R. Steward (Eds.), *Leaders and managers: International perspectives on managerial behavior and leadership* (pp. 45–62). Elmsford, NY: Pergamon.

Rave, E. J., & Larsen, C. C. (Eds.). (1995). *Ethical decision making in therapy: Feminist perspectives.* New York: Guilford Press.

Reeder, J., Douzenis, C., & Bergin, J. (1997). The effects of small group counseling on the racial attitudes of second grade students. *Professional School Counseling 1*, 15–18.

Reis, S. M., & Colbert, R. (2004). Counseling needs of academically talented students with learning disabilities. *Professional School Counseling, 8*, 156–167.

Remley, T. P., Jr. (1985). The law and ethical practices in elementary and middle schools. *Elementary School Guidance and Counseling, 19,* 181–189.

Remley, T. P., Jr. (1990). Counseling records: Legal and ethical issues. In B. Herlihy & L. Golden (Eds.), *AACD ethical standards casebook* (4th ed., pp. 162–169). Alexandria, VA: American Association for Counseling and Development.

Remley, T. P., Jr. (1993). What responsibilities do I have for student counseling records? *The American Counselor, 2*(4), 32–33.

Remley, T. P., Jr., & Fry, L. J. (1993). Reporting suspected child abuse: Conflicting roles for the counselor. *The School Counselor, 40,* 253–259.

Remley, T. P., Jr., & Herlihy, B. (2001). *Ethical, legal, and professional issues in counseling.* Upper Saddle River, NJ: Merrill/Prentice Hall.

Remley, T. P., Jr., & Herlihy, B. (2005). *Ethical, legal, and professional issues in counseling* (2nd ed.). Upper Saddle River, NJ: Merrill/Prentice Hall.

Remley, T. P., Jr., & Sparkman, L. B. (1993). Student suicides: The counselor's limited legal liability. *The School Counselor, 40,* 164–169.

Reskin, B. F. (1993). Sex segregation in the workplace. *Annual Review of Sociology, 19,* 241–270.

Riedinger, S. (1997). *Even start: Facilitating the transitions in to kindergarten.* Washington, DC: U.S. Department of Education.

Ripley, V., Erford, B. T., Dahir, C., & Eschbach, L. (2003). Planning and implementing a 21st-century comprehensive developmental school counseling program. In B. Erford (Ed.), *Transforming the school counseling profession* (pp. 63–119). Upper Saddle River, NJ: Merrill/Prentice Hall.

Ritchie, M. H., & Huss, S. N. (2000). Recruitment and screening of minors for group counseling. *Journal for Specialists in Group Work, 25*(2), 146–156.

Robinson, T. L., & Howard-Hamilton, M. (2000). *The convergence of race, ethnicity, and gender: Multiple identities in counseling.* Upper Saddle River, NJ: Prentice Hall.

Roeber, E. (2004). Steps in the right direction: Reporting assessment results to students, parents, school board members, and the media. In B. T. Erford (Ed.), *Professional school counseling: A handbook of theories, programs, & practices* (pp. 557–580). Austin, TX: ProEd.

Rogers, C. R. (1977). *Carl Rogers on personal power: Inner strength and its revolutionary impact.* New York: Delacorte Press.

Rogers, C. R. (1992). The necessary and sufficient conditions of therapeutic personality change. *Journal of Consulting and Clinical Psychology, 60,* 827–832.

Rooney, J. (2005). School culture: An invisible essential. *Educational Leadership, 62,* 86.

Rosenbaum, M. (1982). Ethical problems of group psychotherapy. In M. Rosenbaum (Ed.), *Ethics and values in psychotherapy: A guidebook* (pp. 237–257). New York: Free Press.

Rosener, J. B. (1995). Ways women lead. In J. T. Wren (Ed.), *The leader's companion: Insights on leadership through the ages* (pp. 149–160). New York: Free Press.

Rosenfield, S., & Gravois, T. A. (1993). Educating consultants for applied clinical and educational settings. In J. E. Zins, T. R. Kratochwill, & S. N. Elliott (Eds.), *Handbook of consultation services for children.* (pp. 373–393). San Francisco: Jossey-Bass.

Roth, A., & Fonagy, P. (1996). *What works for whom?* New York: Guilford Press.

Rothstein, R. (2004). *Class and schools: Using social, economic and educational reform to close the black-white achievement gap.* New York: The Economic Policy Institute & Teachers College Press.

Rudolph, D. K., Lambert, S. F., Clark, A. G., & Kurlakowsky, K. D. (2001). Negotiating the transition to middle school: The role of self-regulatory processes. *Child Development, 72,* 929–946.

Rysiew, K. J., Shore, B. M., & Leeb, R. T. (1999). Multipotentiality, giftedness, and career choice: A review. *Journal of Counseling & Development, 77,* 423–430.

Sabella, R. A. (1996). School counselors and computers: Specific time-saving tips. *Elementary School Guidance & Counseling, 31,* 83–96.

Sabella, R. A. (2000). School counseling and technology. In J. Wittmer (Ed.), *Managing your school counseling program: K–12 developmental strategies* (pp. 337–357). Minneapolis: Educational Media Corporation.

Sampson, J. P., Jr., Kolodinski, R. W., & Greeno, B. P. (1997). Counseling on the information highway: Future possibilities and potential problems. *Journal of Counseling and Development, 75,* 203–212.

Sampson, J. P., Jr., Peterson, G. W., Lenz, J. G., & Reardon, R. C. (1992). A cognitive approach to career services: Translating concepts into practice. *Career Development Quarterly, 41,* 67–73.

Sampson, J. P., Jr., & Pyle, K. R. (1988). Ethical issues involved with the use of computer-assisted counseling, testing, and guidance systems. In W. C. Huey & T. P. Remley, Jr. (Eds.), *Ethical and legal issues in school counseling* (pp. 249–261). Alexandria, VA: American School Counselor Association.

Sandberg, D. N., Crabbs, S. K., & Crabbs, M. A. (1988). Legal issues in child abuse: Questions and answers for counselors. *Elementary School Guidance and Counseling, 22,* 268–274.

Saphier, J., & Gower, R. (1997). *The skillful teacher.* Carlisle, MA: Research for Better Teaching, Inc.

Saunders, L. (1995). Relative earnings of black and white men by region, industry. *Monthly Labor Review, 118*(4), 68–73.

Savickas, M. L. (2005). The theory and practice of career construction. In S. D. Brown & R. W. Lent (Eds.), *Career development and counseling: Putting theory and research to work* (pp. 42–70). Hoboken, NJ: Wiley.

Schaefer-Schiumo, K., & Ginsberg, A. P. (2003). The effectiveness of the warning signs program in education youth about violence prevention: A study with urban high school students. *Professional School Counseling, 7,* 1–9.

Schein, E. H. (1990). Organizational culture. *American Psychologist, 45,* 109–119.

Schlossberg, S. M., Morris, J. D., & Lieberman, M. G. (2001). The effects of a counselor-led guidance intervention on students' behaviors and attitudes. *Professional School Counseling, 4,* 156–164.

Schmidt, J. J. (1999). *Counseling in schools: Essential services and comprehensive programs* (3rd ed.). Boston: Allyn & Bacon

Schmidt, J. J. (2003). *Counseling in schools: Essential services and comprehensive programs* (4th ed.). Boston: Allyn & Bacon.

Schneider, M., & McCurdy-Myers, J. (1999). Academic and career choices for lesbian and gay young adults. *National Consultation on Career Development Papers 1999,* 7–16.

Scholtes, P. R. (1998). *The leader's handbook: A guide to inspiring your people and managing the daily workflow.* New York: McGraw-Hill.

Schwallie-Giddis, P., & Kobylarz, L. (2000). Career development: The counselor's role in preparing K–12 students for the 21st century. In J. Wittmer (Ed.), *Managing your school counseling program: K–12 developmental strategies* (2nd ed., pp. 211–218). Minneapolis, MN: Educational Media Corporation.

Schwiebert, V. L., Sealander, K. A., & Bradshaw, M. (1998). Preparing students with attention deficit disorders for entry into the workplace and postsecondary education. *Professional School Counseling, 2,* 26–32.

Sciarra, D. T. (2004). *School counseling: Foundations and contemporary issues.* Belmont, CA: Thomson.

Sealander, K. A., Schwiebert, V. L., Oren, T. A., & Weekley, J. L. (1999). Confidentiality and the law. *Professional School Counseling, 3*(2), 122–127.

Search Institute. (1999). *Search institute profiles of student life: Attitudes and behaviors.* Minneapolis, MN: Author.

Sears, S. (1999, January). Transforming school counseling: Making a difference for all students. *NASSP Bulletin 83,* 47–53.

Sears, S. J. (2005). Large group guidance: Curriculum development and instruction. In C. A. Sink (Ed.), *Contemporary school counseling: Theory, research and practice* (pp. 189–213). New York: Lahaska Press.

Sears-Jones, S. (1995). Career and educational planning in the middle school level. *NASSP Bulletin, 79,* 36–42.

Selman, R. L. (1980). *The growth of interpersonal understanding: Developmental and clinical analysis.* New York: Academic Press.

Seligman, L. (1994). *Developmental career counseling and assessment* (2nd ed.). Thousand Oaks, CA: Sage Publications.

Sellers, N., Satcher, J., & Comas, R. (1999). Children's occupational aspirations: Comparisons by gender, gender role identity, and socioeconomic status. *Professional School Counseling, 2,* 314–317.

Senge, P. M. (1999). *The fifth discipline: The art & practice of the learning organization.* New York: Doubleday.

Senge, P., Cambron-McCabe, N., Lucas, T., Smith, R., Dutton, J., & Kleiner, A. (2000). *Schools that learn: A fifth discipline fieldbook for educators, parents, and everyone who cares about education.* New York: Doubleday.

Sexton, T. L., Whiston, S. C., Bleuer, J. C., & Walz, G. R. (1997). *Integrating outcome research into counseling practice and training.* Alexandria, VA: American Counseling Association.

Sheeley, V. L., & Herlihy, B. (1989). Counseling suicidal teens: A duty to warn and protect. *The School Counselor, 37,* 89–97.

Shelton, C. F. & James, E. L. (2005). Best practices for effective secondary school counselors. Thousand Oaks, CA: Corwin Press and American School Counselor Association.

Shepard-Tew, D., & Creamer, D. A. (1998). Elementary school integrated services teams: Applying case-management techniques. *Professional School Counseling, 2,* 141–145.

Sheridan, S. M., & Welch, M. (1996). Is consultation effective? *Remedial & Special Education, 17,* 341–355.

Shoffner, M. F., & Williamson, R. D. (2000). Engaging preservice school counselors and principals in dialogue and collaboration. *Counselor Education and Supervision, 40,* 128–140.

Silver, H., Strong, R., & Perini, M. (1997). Integrating learning styles and multiple intelligences. *Educational Leadership, 55,* 22–27.

Silver, S. (1995). *Organized to be the best: New timesaving ways to simplify and improve how you work* (3rd ed.). Los Angeles: Adams-Hall.

Sink, C. A., & MacDonald, G. (1998). The status of comprehensive guidance and counseling in the United States. *Professional School Counseling 2,* 88–94.

Sink, C. A., & Stroh, H. R. (2003). Raising achievement test scores of early elementary school students through comprehensive school counseling programs. *Professional School Counseling, 6,* 350–365.

Sklare, G. B. (2005). *Brief counseling that works: A solution-focused approach for school counselors and administrators* (2nd ed.). Thousand Oaks, CA: Corwin.

Snow, B. M., & Jackson, M. (2004). Professional credentials in school counseling. In Bradly T. Erford (Ed.), *Professional school counseling: A handbook of theories, programs, and practice* (pp. 65–70). Austin, TX: ProEd.

Sori, C. F. & Hecker, L. L. (eds.). *The therapist's notebook for children and adolescents: Homework, handouts, and activities for use in psychotherapy.* Binghampton, NY: Hayworth Clinical Practice Press.

Spokane, A. R., & Oliver, L. W. (1983). The outcomes of vocational interventions. In S. H. Osipow & W. B. Walsh (Eds.), *Handbook of vocational psychology* (Vol. 2, pp. 99–136). Hillsdale, NJ: Erlbaum.

Stadler, H. A. (1986). Making hard choices: Clarifying controversial ethical issues. *Counseling and Human Development, 19,* 1–10.

Steinberg, L. (1996). *Adolescence* (4th ed.). New York: McGraw-Hill.

Steinberg, L., Brown, B. B., & Dornbusch, S. M. (1996). Ethnicity and adolescent achievement. *American Educator, 20,* 28–35.

Steinberg, L. D. (1996). *Beyond the classroom: Why school reform has failed and what parents need to do.* New York: Simon & Schuster.

Stone, C. B. (2002). Negligence in academic advising and abortion counseling: Courts rulings and implications. *Professional School Counseling, 6,* 28–35.

Stone, C. (2004). Ethical and legal considerations for students, parents, and professional school counselors. In B. T. Erford (Ed.), *Professional school counseling: A handbook of theories, programs & practices* (pp. 57–64). Austin, TX: ProEd.

Stone, C. B., & Dahir, C. A. (2004). *The transformed school counselor.* Boston: Lahaska.

Stone, C. B., & Dahir, C. A. (2006). *The transformed school counselor.* Boston: Lahaska Press.

Stone, C., & Isaacs, M. (2003). Confidentiality with minors: The need for policy to promote and protect. *The Journal of Educational Research, 96,* 140–150.

Strein, W., & Hershenson, D. B. (1991). Confidentiality in nondyadic counseling situations. *Journal of Counseling and Development, 69,* 312–316.

Stringer, E. (2004). *Action research in education.* Upper Saddle River, NJ: Prentice Hall.

Stromberg, C., and his colleagues in the law firm of Hogan & Harson of Washington, D.C. (1993, April). Privacy, confidentiality and privilege. The Psychologist's Legal Update. Washington, DC: National Register of Health Service Providers in Psychology. As Cited in G. Corey, M. S. Corey, & P. Callanan. (1998). *Issues and ethics in the helping professions* (5th ed.). Pacific Grove, CA: Brooks/Cole.

Struder, J. R. (2005). *The professional school counselor: An advocate for students.* Pacific Grove, CA: Brooks/Cole.

Sue D. W., Arrendondo, P., & McDavis, R. J. (1992). Multicultural competencies and standards: A call to the profession. *Journal of Multicultural Counseling and Development, 20,* 64–90.

Sutton, J. M., & Fall, M. (1995). The relationship of school climate factors to counselor self-efficacy. *Journal of Counseling & Development, 73,* 331–336.

Super, D. E. (1990). A life-span, life-space approach to career development. In D. Brown, L. Brooks, & Associates (Eds.), *Career choice and development: Applying contemporary theories to practice* (2nd ed., pp. 197–261). San Francisco: Jossey-Bass.

Super, D. E. (1994). A life-span, life-space approach to career development. In M. L. Savickas & R. W. Lent (Eds.), *Convergence in career development theories* (pp. 63–74). Palo Alto, CA: Consulting Psychologists Press.

Super, D. E., Savickas, M. L., & Super, C. M. (1996). The life span, life-space approach to careers. In D. Brown & L. Brooks (Eds.), *Career choice and development: Applying contemporary theories to practice* (3rd ed., pp. 121–178). San Francisco: Jossey-Bass.

Talbert, J. E., & McLaughlin, M. W. (1999). Assessing the school environment: Embedded context and bottom-up research strategies, In S. L. Friedman & T. D. Wachs (Eds.), *Measuring environment across lifespan: Emerging methods and concepts* (pp. 197–227). Washington, DC: American Psychological Association.

Talbutt, L. C. (1983). Current legal trends regarding abortions for minors: A dilemma for counselors. *The School Counselor, 31*, 120–124.

Tang, M. (2004). Assessing and changing school culture. In B. Erford (Ed.), *Transforming the school counseling profession* (pp. 387–395). Upper Saddle River, NJ: Merrill/Prentice Hall.

Taylor, D. L., & Tashakkori, A. (1995). Decision participation and school climate as predictors of job satisfaction and teachers' sense of efficacy. *Journal of Experimental Education, 63*, 217–231.

Taylor, L. M., & Adelman, H. S. (2000). Connecting schools, families, and communities. *Journal of Counseling and Development, 3*, 298–307.

Terres, C. K., & Larrabee, M. J. (1985). Ethical issues and group work with children. *Elementary School Guidance and Counseling, 19*, 190–197.

Tharinger, D. J., & Lambert, N. M. (1999). The application of developmental psychology to school psychology practice: Informing assessment, intervention, and prevention efforts. In C. R. Reynolds & T. B. Gutkin, (Eds.), *The handbook of school psychology* (3rd ed., pp. 137–166). New York: Wiley.

Thompson, C. L., Rudolph, L. B., & Henderson, D. A. (2004). *Counseling children* (6th ed.). Pacific Grove, CA: Brooks/Cole.

Thompson, C. L., & O'Quinn, S. D. III (2001, June). *Eliminating the black-white achievement gap: A summary of research*. Raleigh, NC: North Carolina Research Council. Retrieved on February 17, 2005, from http://21stcenturyschools.northcarolina.edu/reports.xml

Thurlow, M. L., & Thompson, S. J. (2004). Inclusion of students with disabilities in state and district assessments. In J. E. Wall & G. R. Walz (Eds.), *Measuring up: Assessment issues for teacher, counselors, and administrators* (pp. 161–176). Greensboro, NC: CAPS.

Tobbell, J. (2003). Students' experiences of the transition from primary to secondary school. *Educational and child Psychology, 20*, 4–14.

Tolerance. org. (2005). Dig deeper: Test yourself for hidden bias. Retrieved on August 13, 2005, from http://www.tolerance.org/hidden_bias/index.html

Tollerud, T. R., & Nejedlo, R. J. (2004). Designing a developmental counseling curriculum. In A. Vernon (Ed.), *Counseling children and adolescents* (3rd ed., pp. 391–423). Denver, CO: Love Publishing.

Tomlinson, C. A. (1999). *The differentiated classroom: Responding to the needs of all learners*. Alexandria, VA: Association for Supervision and Curriculum Development.

Tompkins, L., & Mehring, T. (1993). Client privacy and the school counselor: Privilege, ethics, and employer policies. *The School Counselor, 40*, 335–342.

Travydas, V. M. (1987). Decision-making models in ethics: Models for increasing clarity and wisdom. *Journal of Applied Rehabilitation Counseling, 22*, 11–18.

Trusty, J. (1999). Effects of eighth-grade parental involvement on late adolescents' educational expectations. *Journal of Research and Development in Education, 32*, 224–233.

Trusty, J. (2001). Family influences on educational expectations of late adolescents. *The Journal of Educational Research, 91*, 260–270.

Trusty, J., & Niles, S. G. (2004). A practical approach to career assessment in schools. In B. T. Erford (Ed.), *Professional school counseling: A handbook of theories, programs, & practices* (pp. 431–441). Austin, TX: ProEd.

Trusty, J., Robinson, C. R., Plata, M., & Ng, K. (2000). Effects of gender, socioeconomic status, and early academic performance on postsecondary educational choice. *Journal of Counseling and Development, 78*, 463–472.

Trusty, J., Watts, R. E., & Crawford, R. (1996). Career information resources for parents of public school seniors: findings from a national study. *Journal of Career Development, 22*, 227–238.

Trusty, J., Watts, R. E., & Erdman, P. (1997). Predictors of parents' involvement in their teens' career development. *Journal of Career Development, 23*, 189–201.

Turner, S. L., & Lapan, R. T. (2005). Promoting career development and aspirations in school-age youth. In S. D. Brown & R. W. Lent (Eds.), *Career development and counseling: Putting theory and research to work* (pp. 417–440). San Francisco: Jossey-Bass.

Ubben, G. C., Hughes, L. W., & Norris, C. J. (2004). *The principalship: Creative leadership for effective schools* (4th ed.). Boston, MA: Allyn & Bacon.

U.S. Bureau of Labor Statistics (BLS). (2005). *Occupational outlook handbook*. Online at www.bls.gov/oco/. Retrieved on January 15, 2001, from http://www.ed.gov/pubs/schoolpoverty/index.html

U.S. Census Bureau. (2004). *Current population survey, 2004 annual social and economic supplement*. Retrieved on June 23, 2005, from http://pubdb3.census.gov/macro/032004/perinc/new04_001.htm

U.S. Department of Education. (2001). No child left behind. Retrieved on November 18, 2004, from http://www.ed.gov/nclb/overview/intro/guide/guide.pdf

U.S. Department of Education. (2002). The State of U.S. Education: 2001. Retrieved on November 20, 2004, from http://www.policyalmanac.org/education/archive/doe_state_of_education.shtml

U.S. Department of Education, National Center for Education Statistics (2000). *The condition of education 2000*, NCES 2000-062. Washington, DC: U.S. Government Printing Office.

U.S. Department of Education, National Center for Education Statistics. (2001). *Entering kindergarten: A portrait of American children when they enter school*. Washington, DC: U.S. Government Printing Office.

U.S. Department of Education, National Center for Education Statistics (2004). *Digest of Education Statistics, 2003* (NCES 2005-025), *Chapter 2*. Retrieved on July 25, 2005, from http://nees.ed.gov/fastfacts/display.asp?id=64

U.S. Department of Education. (2005a). Comprehensive school reform. Retrieved on November 20, 2004, from www.ed.gov/programs/compreform.html

U.S. Department of Education. (2005b). Individuals with Disabilities Act (IDEA) Retrieved on July 23, 2005, from http://www.ed.gov/about/offices/list/osers/osep/index.html

U.S. Department of Labor. (1991). *The dictionary of occupational titles* (4th ed.). Washington DC: U.S. Government Printing Office.

U.S. Department of Labor. (2000). Secretary's Commission on Achieving Necessary Skills (SCAN) Report: *Learning a living: A blueprint for high performance*. Baltimore: The Johns Hopkins University Institute for Policy Studies.

Vacc, N., & Juhnke, G. (1997). The use of structural clinical interviews for assessment in counseling. *Journal of Counseling and Development, 75,* 470–480.

Van Hoose, W. H., & Kottler, J. A. (1985). *Ethical and legal issues in counseling and psychotherapy*. San Francisco: Jossey-Bass.

VanZandt, C. E. (1990). Professionalism: A matter of personal initiatives. *Journal of Counseling and Development, 68,* 243–245.

VanZandt, C. E., & Hayslip, J. B. (1994). *Your comprehensive school guidance and counseling program*. New York: Longman.

VanZandt, C. E., & Hayslip, J. B. (2001). *Developing your school counseling program: A handbook for systemic planning*. Pacific Grove, CA: Brooks/Cole.

Varenhorst, B. B. (2003). *Asset builder's guide to training peer helpers*. Minneapolis: Search Institute.

Varhely, S. C., & Cowles, J. (1991). Counselor self-awareness and client confidentiality: A relationship revisited. *Elementary School Guidance and Counseling, 25,* 269–276.

Vernon, A. (1999). Counseling children and adolescents: Developmental considerations. In A. Vernon (Ed.), *Counseling children and adolescents* (2nd ed., pp. 1–30). Denver, CO: Love Publishing.

Vernon, A. (2002). *What works when with children and adolescents: A handbook of individual counseling techniques*. Champaign, IL: Research Press.

Vernon, A. (2004). Working with children, adolescents, and their parents: Practical application of developmental theory. In A. Vernon (Ed.), *Counseling children and adolescents* (3rd ed., pp. 1–34). Denver, CO: Love Publishing.

Vernon, A., & Al-Mabuk, R. (1995). *What growing up is all about: A parent's guide to child and adolescent development*. Champaign, IL: Research Press.

Vernon, A., & Clemente, R. (2005). *Assessment and intervention with children and adolescents: Developmental and multicultural approaches* (2nd ed.). Alexandria, VA: American Counseling Association.

Vygotsky, L. (1978). *Mind in society: The development of higher psychological processes*. Cambridge, MA: Harvard University Press.

Wadsworth, J., Milsom, A., & Cocco, K. (2004). Career development for adolescents and young adults with mental retardation. *Professional School Counseling, 8,* 141–147.

Wahl, K. H., & Blackhurst, A. (2000). Factors affecting the occupational and educational aspirations of children and adolescents. *Professional School Counseling, 3,* 367–374.

Waldo, S. L., & Malley, P. (1992). Tarasoff and its progeny: Implications for the school counselor. *The School Counselor, 40,* 46–54.

Walker, M. M., & Larrabee, M. J. (1985). Ethics and school records. *Elementary School Guidance and Counseling, 19,* 210–216.

Walter, J., & Pellar, J. (1992). *Becoming solution-focused in brief therapy*. New York: Brunner/Mazel.

Webb, L. D., Metha, A., & Jordan, K. F. (2003). *Foundations of American education* (4th ed.). Englewood Cliffs, NJ: Merrill/Prentice Hall.

Welfel, E. R. (1998). *Ethics in counseling and psychotherapy: Standards, research, and emerging issues*. Pacific Grove, CA: Brooks/Cole.

Welfel, E. R. (2002). *Ethics in counseling and psychotherapy: Standards, research, and emerging issues* (2nd ed.). Pacific Grove, CA: Brooks/Cole.

Welfel, E. R., & Lipsitz, N. E. (1983). Wanted: A comprehensive approach to ethics research and education. *Counselor Education and Supervision, 22,* 320–332.

Welsh, W. N. (2000). The effects of school climate on school disorder. *Annals of the American Academy of Political & Social Science, 567,* 88–108.

Werner, E., & Smith, R. (2001). *Journeys from childhood to the midlife: Risk, resilience, and recovery.* New York: Cornell University Press.

Whiston, S. C., & Bouwkamp, J. C. (2005). Peer programs and family counseling. In Christopher Sink (Ed.), *Contemporary school counseling: Theory, research and practice.* Boston: Lahaska Press.

Whiston, S. C., Brecheisen, B. K., & Stephens, J. (2003). Does treatment modality effect career counseling effectiveness? *Journal of Vocational Behavior, 62,* 390–410.

Whiston, S. C., & Sexton, T. L. (1998). A review of school counseling outcome research: Implications for practice. *Journal of Counseling and Development, 76,* 412–426.

Whiston, S. C., Sexton, T. L., & Lasoff, D. L. (1998). Career-intervention outcome: A replication and extension of Oliver and Spokane (1988). *Journal of Counseling Psychology, 45,* 150–165.

Wigfield, A., & Eccles, J. A. (1994). Children's competence beliefs, achievement values, and general self-esteem change across elementary and middle school. *Journal of Early Adolescence, 14,* 107–138.

Wiggins, G., & McTighe, J. (1998). *Understanding by design.* Alexandria, VA: Association for Supervision and Curriculum Development.

Wilcoxon, S. A., & Magnuson, S. (1999). Considerations for school counselors serving non-custodial parents: Premises and suggestions. *Professional School Counseling, 2,* 275–280.

Williamson, E. G. (1950). *Counseling adolescents.* New York: McGraw-Hill.

Wilson, C. (1993). Providing support for high school transfer students. *School Counselor, 40,* 234–237.

Wittmer, J. (2000). Promoting a K–12 developmental guidance program. In J. Wittmer (Ed.), *Managing your school counseling program: K–12 developmental strategies* (2nd ed., pp. 306–313). Minneapolis: Educational Media.

Wittmer, J., Thompson, D. W., & Loesch, L. C. (1997). *Classroom guidance activities: A sourcebook for elementary school counselors.* Minneapolis, MN: Educational Media.

Woolfolk, A. E. (1998). *Educational psychology* (7th ed.). Boston: Allyn & Bacon.

Wren, D. J. (1999). School culture: Exploring the hidden curriculum. *Adolescence, 34* (135), 593–597.

Wrenn, G. (1962). *The counselor in a changing world.* Washington, DC: APGA Press.

Yang, J. (1991). Career counseling of Chinese American women: Are they in limbo? *The Career Development Quarterly, 39,* 350–359.

Young, M. E. (2001). *Learning the art of helping: Building blocks and techniques* (2nd ed.). Upper Saddle River, NJ: Merrill/Prentice Hall.

Zambelli, G., & DeRosa, A. (1992). Bereavement support groups for school-age children: Theory, intervention, and case example. *American Journal of Orthopsychiatry, 62,* 484–493.

Ziebarth, T. (2004, April). *Models of state education governance.* Retrieved on November 18, 2004, from www.ecs.org

Zingaro, J. C. (1983). Confidentiality: To tell or not to tell. *Elementary School Guidance and Counseling, 17,* 261–267.

Zunker, V. G. (1998). *Career counseling: Applied concepts of life planning.* Pacific Grove, CA: Brooks/Cole Publishing.

Zunker, V. G. (2002). *Career counseling: Applied concepts of life planning* (6th ed.). Pacific Grove, CA: Brooks/Cole Publishing.

Zunker, V. G. (2006). *Career counseling: A holistic approach* (7th ed.). Belmont, CA: Thomson.

Zunker, V. G., & Norris, D. (1998). *Using assessment results for career development* (5th ed.). Pacific Grove, CA: Brooks/Cole.

AUTHOR INDEX

SUBJECT INDEX

DEVELOPING AN EFFECTIVE AND ACCOUNTABLE SCHOOL COUNSELING PROGRAM

SECOND EDITION

Debra C. Cobia
Auburn University

Donna A. Henderson
Wake Forest University

PEARSON

Merrill
Prentice Hall

Upper Saddle River, New Jersey
Columbus, Ohio

Library of Congress Cataloging in Publication Data

Cobia, Debra C.
  Developing an effective and accountable school counseling program / Debra C. Cobia,
Donna A. Henderson.—2nd ed.
    p. cm.
  Previous ed. published under title: Handbook of school counseling. c2003.
  Includes bibliographical references and index.
  ISBN 0-13-170632-2
    1. Educational counseling—Handbooks, manuals, etc.   I. Henderson, Donna A.   II. Cobia, Debra C. Handbook of school
counseling.   III. Title.

LBI027.5.C57 2007
371.4—dc22
                                                                   2006046045

Vice President and Executive Publisher: Jeffery W. Johnston
Publisher: Kevin M. Davis
Associate Editor: Meredith Sarver
Editorial Assistant: Sarah N. Kenoyer
Production Editor: Mary Harlan
Production Coordinator: Rebecca K. Giusti, GGS Book Services
Design Coordinator: Diane C. Lorenzo
Photo Coordinator: Maria B. Vonada
Text Design and Illustrations: GGS Book Services
Cover Design: Candace Rowley
Cover Image: Corbis
Production Manager: Laura Messerly
Director of Marketing: David Gesell
Marketing Manager: Autumn Purdy
Marketing Coordinator: Brian Mounts

This book was set in Goudy by GGS Book Services. It was printed and bound by R. R. Donnelley & Sons Company. The cover was
printed by R. R. Donnelley & Sons Company.

First edition entitled *Handbook of School Counseling*.

Photo Credits: Laura Bolesta/Merrill: pp. 2, 40; Scott Cunningham/Merrill: p. 20; George Dodson/PH College: p. 178; Kathy
Kirtland/Merrill: p. 88; Anthony Magnacca/Merrill: pp. 58, 112, 218; Liz Moore/Merrill: p. 72; Robert Pham/PH College: p. 144;
Barbara Schwartz/Merrill: p. 238; Teri Leigh Stratford/PH College: p. 200.

Pearson Education Ltd.
Pearson Education Singapore Pte. Ltd.
Pearson Education Canada, Ltd.
Pearson Education–Japan

Pearson Education Australia Pty. Limited
Pearson Education North Asia Ltd.
Pearson Educación de Mexico, S.A. de C.V.
Pearson Education Malaysia Pte. Ltd.

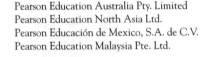
10 9 8 7 6 5 4 3 2 1
ISBN: 0-13-170632-2